WHO AM I THIS TIME?

Female Portraits in British
and American Literature

WOMEN'S STUDIES PROGRAM
UNIVERSITY OF DAYTON
ST. JOSEPH

"Who are you?" said the Caterpillar.

. . . Alice replied, rather shyly, "I—I hardly know, sir, just at present—at least I know who I was when I got up this morning, but I think I must have been changed several times since then."

—*Lewis Carroll*, Alice in Wonderland

WHO AM I THIS TIME?

Female Portraits in British and American Literature

Carol Pearson

Katherine Pope

University of Colorado, Boulder

McGRAW-HILL BOOK COMPANY

New York   St. Louis   San Francisco   Auckland   Düsseldorf
Johannesburg   Kuala Lumpur   London   Mexico   Montreal   New Delhi
Panama   Paris   São Paulo   Singapore   Sydney   Tokyo   Toronto

This book was set in Palatino by Black Dot, Inc.
The editors were Ellen B. Fuchs and Laura D. Warner;
the designer was J. E. O'Connor;
the production supervisor was Dennis J. Conroy.
R. R. Donnelley & Sons Company was printer and binder.

WHO AM I THIS TIME?
Female Portraits in British
and American Literature

1 2 3 4 5 6 7 8 9 0 D O D O 7 8 3 2 1 0 9 8 7 6

Library of Congress Cataloging in Publication Data
Main entry under title:

Who am I this time?

    Bibliography: p.
    1. English literature. 2. American literature.
3. Women in literature. I. Pearson, Carol,
date II. Pope, Katherine, date
PR1111.W6W5   820'.8'0352   75-29130
ISBN 0-07-049032-5

See Acknowledgments on pages 304–306. Copyrights
included on this page by reference.

To Our Mothers

CONTENTS

THE HELPMATE   97

THE HERO

THE SAGE   145

THE ARTIST   193

THE WARRIOR   242

IN ACKNOWLEDGMENT

We would like to thank Gene Black for his able and gracious assistance in researching and writing the headnotes, in gaining permissions, in proofing, and generally in aiding us in the completion of the anthology.

We are indebted to Helen Barchilon and to Fran Metzger, who enthusiastically researched the world of art so that we might include the most appropriate illustrations to accompany the text.

Special thanks also to Florence Howe, whose generous suggestions for improvement of the anthology were very helpful to us; to David Merkowitz for editing and criticizing the introductory comments; and to Aladeen Smith for her patience and skill in the typing of the manuscript. Thanks also to the following people who aided this project in a variety of ways: Barbara Ellington, Hardy Long Frank, Doris Havice, Sheryll Herdt, Elizabeth Jameson, Siegfried Mandel, Judith Nelson, Mary Beth Nelson, Elihu Pearlman, William Piper, Carolyn Porter, Jeffrey Robinson, J. D. Schuchter, Ruth Schrock, Monroe Spears, Janet Weinger, and Constance Wright.

Carol Pearson also thanks David, Jeffrey, and Stephen Merkowitz for supporting her in this project and for teaching her that people who are warriors can also be helpmates to each other.

We are grateful also to our sisters in the feminist movement.

Finally, we would like to thank each other for the experience of a true collaboration. Editing this anthology was an enjoyable sharing experience in which we learned from each other about literature and about being free and fulfilled women.

Carol Pearson
Katherine Pope

WHO AM I THIS TIME?

Female Portraits in British
and American Literature

WHO AM I THIS TIME ?

Female Portraits in British and American Literature

Willem de Kooning: *Woman, I* (1961). [*Private collection. Photography by Eric Pollitzer.*]

Feminist criticism is new and has not yet formulated a comprehensive typology of female portraits equivalent to Northrup Frye's model for myth criticism in *Anatomy of Criticism* or Joseph Campbell's definition of the hero in *The Hero with a Thousand Faces. Who Am I This Time?* is a collection of literary works and critical commentary which provides the basis for such a typology. A typology of literary portraits of women, like other critical approaches, should expand and enrich traditional literary analysis. It should also encourage the reader to relate literary portraits to women's actual experience. We hope that the selections included in this anthology will stimulate the reader to use the tools of feminist criticism in order to achieve a clearer understanding of literature and of the images which influence women's lives.

Portraits of female characters fall into two general categories: the woman as heroine and the woman as hero. The section on the heroine has three subdivisions—"The Virgin," "The Mistress," and "The Helpmate." These parallel Joseph Campbell's three categories of women—the goddess, the temptress, and the earth mother—whom the male hero encounters on his mythical journey. The subdivisions of the section on the hero are "The Sage," "The Artist," and "The Warrior"—the three traditional heroes. The portraits in the six sections represent the major literary achievements of female and male authors in Britain and America. They therefore reflect the myths and literary conventions that have affected women in Western culture from the Anglo-Saxon period in Britain and the colonial period in America to the present. The balance of female and male voices and the chronological arrangement of each section provide an opportunity for comparison and contrast of female and male and of traditional and contemporary viewpoints and literary techniques.

Women can allow others to define them, or they can choose to define themselves. As modern therapy has taught us, we become our own best jailers when we internalize societal and parental messages. For women, freedom from definition by others depends on an understanding of the psychological elements and cultural assumptions which cause them to be self-destructive and which cause men and other women to treat them in a destructive manner. This anthology, as the title suggests, was designed to clarify the interaction between cultural myth and social reality and thus to promote the understanding that leads to freedom for both women and men. This freedom through personal redefinition is a necessary part of the struggle for psychological, theological, moral, economic, and political change.

The selections included in this anthology were published and have survived because they were considered to be valuable by publishers, editors, and critics, who, with a few exceptions, were male. Writings by members of a subculture, as women are in a patriarchy, are often not valued enough to be published, and the themes of their literary works are not seen as universal. The literary portraits therefore generally reflect, like most classic literary works, the upper- and middle-class male point of view. The problem is further complicated because some members of society (such as racial minorities, working-class people, and women) may not benefit from the dominant culture's myths, but may nevertheless internalize the dominant values. Accordingly, works by women authors which have managed to appear and to

Portions of this introduction appeared as an article entitled "A Typology of Female Portraits in Literature" in *The CEA Critic*, May 1975.

survive provide less of a dual perspective than might be expected because they often reflect upper-class male ideologies.

People with power always have defined correct behavior—lords establish what is virtuous behavior for vassals; racial majorities, for racial minorities; and men, for women—and myth and literature are powerful propaganda vehicles. Literature teaches women "appropriate" female behavior. Little girls read about Cinderella, Rapunzel, and Sleeping Beauty; women read D. H. Lawrence's *Lady Chatterley's Lover*. The message of all these works is that women must wait for a prince to come and fulfill them. Although the selections in this anthology reflect a patriarchal viewpoint, a closer reading of even the most traditional works often demonstrates that literature is more interesting and complicated than cultural myths or stereotypes. Good realistic literature, like Gustave Flaubert's *Madame Bovary* and Kate Chopin's *The Awakening*, often explores the negative effects of cultural myths about women. Furthermore, characters such as Geoffrey Chaucer's Wife of Bath or Henry James's May Bartram, in "The Beast in the Jungle," have more insight and courage than can be explained with reference to the stereotype. In fact, authors—such as Nathaniel Hawthorne in *The Scarlet Letter* and Edward Albee in *Tiny Alice*—often initially portray women stereotypically or archetypally and then lead the reader to admire them as heroic women. In some literary works, by both female and male authors, we find explicit criticism of the role limitations placed on women. Ann Finch, in "The Unequal Fetters," exposes marriage as oppressive to women. In Robert Browning's *The Ring and the Book*, Pompelia, the thirteen-year-old wife, recognizes that she is a victim being led to the altar, and she plays the role of the ideal, selfless, obedient helpmate. Her husband, Guido, responds bitterly to her compliance:

> I resent my wrong,
> . . . .
> Resent the very obedience? . . .
>
> . . . .
> There has been compensation in revolt—
> Revolt's to quell; but martyrdom rehearsed,
> But predetermined saintship. . . .

The heroine section of this anthology includes literary portraits of women which are predominantly stereotypical or archetypal. When realistic, they explore the effect of cultural myths on women who do not challenge those myths and who therefore are defined primarily in relationship to a man. The hero section traces an alternative tradition of female characterization. Female heroes refuse the supporting, dependent role and are seen by themselves and/or by others as the primary character in their own stories. We have tried to avoid simplistic examples of female stereotypes in misogynistic literature and have selected works which are interesting as literature and which add some element of complexity or paradox to the traditional assumptions about women. Introductory comments before each section analyze each category and provide a theoretical context for the selections. The comments which follow in this general introduction suggest uses for the text, provide a theoretical discussion of the relationship of myth and literature to life, and sketch the historical development of images of women in literature.

USES OF THIS ANTHOLOGY

This anthology can be used in a variety of English courses, including freshman English, critical writing, a survey of English and/or American literature, and a survey of images of women in literature. The study of portraits of women in literature is valuable to teachers and literary critics because it raises critical questions about the relationship of literature to life and because it stimulates a reconsideration of the adequacy of traditional critical methodology. The reader may employ the methods of formalism and structuralism in order to compare the aesthetic details—characterization, form, imagery, point of view, and diction—used to convey one theme, that of the deserted wife, for example, in different periods. By employing techniques of myth and psychological, Marxist, and historical criticism, the reader can relate the literature to human experience and thereby discover the limitations of each critical approach. Distortions in each of these critical methods are partially the result of an inadequate understanding of sex roles in our society. Therefore, feminist critics are needed to correct the theory and practice of each of the traditional critical schools.

Students and teachers of psychology, sociology, history, and interdisciplinary women studies courses also can employ this anthology to examine the interaction of archetype, cultural myth, and stereotype with human life. History classes might relate literary portraits to historical reality. This text could be taught along with social histories about women and women's diaries and journals. The anthology could be used in psychology classes in conjunction with actual case histories of women. (As Phyllis Chesler explains in *Women and Madness,* cultural myths about women contribute to their mental illnesses.) In sociology courses, literary portraits might be compared with students' observations about the lives of real women of different ages, classes, races, and cultural backgrounds. Philosophy and religious studies courses might use this anthology in the study of archetypes. In both sociology and literature classes, images of women in literature can be compared with images of women in popular culture. An interdisciplinary women studies course might combine all these approaches.

THE STUDY OF FEMALE PORTRAITS

The following comments suggest some of the ways that the study of female portraits helps us to understand literature, myth, and social roles. As our attitudes about male and female roles affect and limit our critical methodology and terminology, the archetypes and mythic patterns, which are the basis of literature, influence our society's sex role patterns.

Patriarchal society views women essentially as supporting characters in the drama of life: Men change the world, and women help them. This assumption has led to inaccurate literary terminology and criticism. For some time critics have called male protagonists "heroes" or "villains," and female protagonists "heroines." However, in classifying female protagonists, we discovered a conceptual difficulty. It is misleading to speak of Antigone, Hester Prynne, and Alice as heroines, and of Creon, Dimmesdale, and the Cheshire Cat as heroes. Like the traditional hero, the three women venture out on the path to self-discovery, while the male characters function in supporting roles. In fact, male and female protagonists encounter surprisingly similar supporting characters. Male heroes meet virgins, whores, wives, and mothers; female heroes encounter saints, rakes, husbands, and fathers. Male heroes meet light and dark heroines, who represent virtue and sexuality, respectively (for example, Alice and Cora Munro, in James Fenimore Cooper's *The Last of the Mohicans*), and female heroes encounter light and dark men (St. John Rivers and Mr. Rochester, in Charlotte Brontë's *Jane Eyre*). On the basis of characters like Penelope, in Homer's *Odyssey,* and Mrs. Ramsay, in Virginia Woolf's *To the Lighthouse,* critics have defined women as preserving order while men explore the unknown. As early as the fifth century B.C., however, Antigone is the aggressive, adventuresome hero, and Creon is devoted to order; more recently, Henrik Ibsen's Nora slams the door on her dollhouse existence, while her husband, Torvald, appeals to her in the name of convention and duty.

Traits assumed to be inherently male or female may simply correspond—in literature—to major and minor roles or to contrasting roles: adventuresomeness is contrasted with conservatism, aggression with passivity, and reason with emotion. A complex counterbalancing occurs in Nathaniel Hawthorne's *Blithedale Romance.* The active Hollingsworth is paired with the passive Priscilla, but he is also contrasted with the equally inactive Coverdale. Hollingsworth's reformist spirit provokes conservatism in Coverdale, but when Zenobia demands feminist reform, Hollingsworth responds in a reactionary way.

Any discussion of supporting roles in literature leads to a consideration of stereotypes and archetypes. Since heroines are most often supporting characters in a man's story, they may not be fully developed as characters, but portrayed only as the "star" sees them. According to Joseph Campbell, in *The Hero with a Thousand Faces:*

> The hegemony wrested from the enemy, the freedom won from the malice of the monster, the life energy released from the toils of the tyrant Holdfast—is symbolized as a woman. She is the maiden of the innumerable dragon slayings, the bride abducted from the jealous father, the virgin rescued from the unholy lover. She is the "other portion of the hero himself—for each is both": if his stature is that of the world monarch, she is the world, and if he is the warrior, she is fame. She is the image of his destiny which he is to release from the pressure of enveloping circumstances.[1]

If the work focuses on the psychological "inner" truth of the protagonist, supporting female characters are usually portrayed as archetypes; for example, Edgar Allen Poe's Ligeia personifies the protagonist's encounter with a metaphysical or psychological truth. If the work focuses on the interaction of the hero with society, heroines are likely to be portrayed as stereotypes; like Nancy, in Charles Dickens's *Oliver Twist,* they may be characterized according to their social role. The character may of course be both stereotype and archetype, but there is a need, particularly in feminist criticism, which is concerned with sexual bias, to distinguish between the two. Cordelia, in *King Lear,* may represent the good woman as passive and long-suffering, but she may also be interpreted as an embodiment of *caritas,* or charity.

Each of the three subdivisions in the section on the heroine—"The Virgin," "The Mistress," and "The Helpmate"—includes archetypal, stereotypical, and realistic portraits. To distinguish women characters in this way leads naturally to the study of genre. In a novel of manners, for example, we are likely to encounter a realistic young woman who begins as a virgin and becomes a wife. We are equally likely to find stereotyped female portraits in naturalistic novels and archetypal female portraits in romances. The progression within the typology from virgin goddess to old maid, sex goddess to whore, and idealized wife to shrew parallels Northrup Frye's generic progression, discussed in *Anatomy of Criticism,* from myth to realism to irony and suggests interesting literary correlations between an artist's conception of human potential and literary form.

The consideration of archetypal, stereotypical, and realistic portraits of women also clarifies the relationship of myth to reality in our culture. The similarity between male and female main and supporting characters shows that on the deepest psychological level—the level of archetypal patterns—there is little if any difference between the experience of the sexes. When the central character is male, the principle of the world or of the spiritual goal is often personified as a woman. When a woman is the protagonist, the goal is male. In literature, it is appropriate for both female and male protagonists to encounter characters who essentially are projections of aspects of their psyches. Both Henry Fielding's Tom Jones and Thomas Hardy's Tess, in *Tess of the D'Urbervilles,* meet characters of the opposite sex who represent their own Apollonian and Dionysian qualities. Many works of literature, then, include a collection of characters who represent various aspects of a single human soul which is too complex and too self-contradictory to be presented in one character. According to this view of literature as a form of psychomachia, any character may be considered a representation of a human individual and a symbol of a single value or characteristic.

Female portraits in literature often are explorations of the anima—the female principle within a man—and therefore may have little relationship to real women. One seldom runs into Poe's Ligeia or Keats's Belle Dame sans Merci in the grocery store. Men often project onto women qualities they hate or deny in themselves or qualities they desire but feel they lack. In doing so, a man does not deal with these positive or negative qualities within him because the focal point of his response is not the female within but a real woman. In Robert Browning's *The Ring and the Book,* Guido sees Pompelia as a projection of part of himself. He ultimately kills her for having those virtues he wishes to get rid of in himself. Guido understands this process and explains:

> . . . I'm my wife outright
> In this unmanly appetite for truth,
> This careless courage as to consequence,
> This instantaneous sight through things and through,
> This voluble rhetoric, if you please,—'t is she!
> Here you have the Pompelia whom I slew,
> Also the folly for which I slew her!

This process of projection enables men to evade responsibility for their actions. Although men have wielded political control for thousands of years, they often present themselves as having little effect on human history, while women, who have not even had control over their own bodies or the right to own property, often are credited with causing all human events. Recall Helen of Troy and Delilah. Piers

Plowman, in Robert Langland's medieval poem, speaks of the closing and reopening of the gates of heaven to humankind: "Through Eve was it closed to all, / And through the Virgin Mary was it opened again." It is common in the twentieth century to blame "Mom" for all the evils of society, as Ken Kesey does with his portrait of Big Nurse in *One Flew over the Cuckoo's Nest.* Kesey's Big Nurse; Edward Albee's Tiny Alice; Iris Murdoch's Hannah, in *The Unicorn;* and Lawrence Durrell's Justine, in *The Alexandria Quartet,* are presented as overwhelming mythical figures before whom men are reduced to humiliated little boys. In *Love and Death in the American Novel,* Leslie Fiedler shows that the absence of realistic female characters from many American works is a result of male fear of women. Similarly, in such contemporary films as *Deliverance, The Longest Yard,* and *The Long Goodbye* women either are totally absent or are treated sadistically.

The tendency in literature to portray women as projections of the male mind becomes destructive to women when translated into life. Myth and literature often provide us with two half-women—one all good, and the other completely evil. Since female evil is associated with sexuality, these women are best known to us as the archetypes of the virgin and the whore. These archetypal personages, unfortunately, are often confused with real women. In the Victorian period in England, for example, this confusion affected social and religious assumptions about individual women. Since purity and goodness were associated with light, and evil with darkness, the "good woman" was envisioned as the fair-skinned upper-class female, while the "bad woman" was visualized as a dark-skinned Mediterranean or African or as a working-class woman. The upper- or middle-class fragile woman, furthermore, was destined for heaven, and the working-class woman for hell. The modesty of the upper-class woman was supposedly protected by men, but after the passage of the Contagious Diseases Act in the 1860s, the lower-class woman from the age of twelve was subject to arrest and examination for venereal disease.[2]

Evidence of different sexual expectations about women according to class exists throughout literature. In the sixteenth century William Shakespeare's Othello kills his faithful wife, Desdemona, for the mere appearance of unfaithfulness. Her maid, Emilia (Iago's wife), on the other hand, is openly adulterous and goes unpunished. Even earlier, Geoffrey Chaucer's faithful Griselda is an appropriate wife for an aristocrat, while the lecherous Wife of Bath is not. In Samuel Richardson's eighteenth-century novel *Pamela,* the servant-girl protagonist is chided at the beginning of the novel for refusing her master's sexual overtures. She is told it is presumptuous to assume that as a servant she should be chaste. The upwardly mobile Pamela therefore adopts chastity along with gloves and fine manners as a value in order to move into the aristocracy. When Thomas Hardy's Tess gives birth out of wedlock, her peasant mother says, "'Tis natar, after all, and what do please God"; but when, after their marriage, Tess's middle-class husband, Angel Clare, learns of the event, he deserts her. In such works as "Cinderella" and *Pamela* the purity of a poor girl qualifies her for a higher social class. Both Cinderella and Pamela are rewarded with wealthy husbands.

Kate Millett's *Sexual Politics* traces the way the chivalric ideal historically has masked sexual and economic exploitation of women in the patriarchal system. The myth that all women are pampered and rich "ladies" kept the society as a whole from recognizing the plight of women who worked fourteen-hour days for little pay in sweatshops, factories, mines, and fields. Caroline Bird's *Born Female* demonstrates the continuing effect of such myths on women.[3] The widespread belief that all women are middle-class housewives who work for pin money, if they work at all, has kept women's wages very low. In 1968, according to U.S. Department of Labor statistics, women high school graduates earned less than men who had not completed the eighth grade. Furthermore, many women internalize these myths and do not demand equal pay because they believe themselves to be temporary workers waiting for prosperous men to marry them or for their husbands to make enough money to support them and their families.[4]

The portraits that follow show how men define appropriate male and female behavior and the effect of these definitions on a woman's self-concept. The values the culture admires are generally seen as male; women therefore are defined as embodiments of the opposite, negative qualities. In contrast to "manly," for example, "womanly" is often used as a negative term. Shakespeare frequently refers to his male characters as "womanly" when they are not being strong. In the eighteenth century, when reason was celebrated, women repeatedly were portrayed as irrational. Furthermore, initiative, assertiveness, strength, aggressiveness, and physical or intellectual superiority, which are positive traits for men, are considered to be negative and unnatural traits for women. Thus arose the misogynist portraits of Eve, the witch, and the shrew.

Literary portraits of women reveal that men are ambivalent about them even when they fulfill the definition of the ideal woman. When women are defined as passive, their passivity may be interpreted as frailty and moral weakness. Like slaves and children, women are portrayed as needing care and control because they are physically and/or morally weak. The ideal then becomes a justification for subjection. Both the negative and the positive definitions of women therefore have damaging effects on women's lives because they justify negative treatment of women. Not only do stereotypes and archetypes influence the social and economic treatment of women, but stereotypical and archetypal characters also affect women's psychology and behavior if they are seen as models to emulate or as villains whose characteristics must be avoided. The idealization of upper-class women in Victorian England as sexless angels may have led them to become frigid or to feel guilty about experiencing passion unless they could ignore their society's expectations. In the twentieth century, Freudians have taught that women have two kinds of orgasms. Many women either felt inadequate for having only one kind, possibly the wrong kind, or actually believed they experienced two until Masters and Johnson proved differently. The female ideal of selflessness affects women negatively if they repress the self to the point of mental illness.

The female qualities that are praised and condemned in literature in each historical period to some extent influence women's behavior and self-concept. Although some eras tend to focus on one aspect of womanhood—praising the virgin, extolling motherhood, or exalting the heroic female spirit—female heroines and heroes are generally found in all periods of literature, and each role is subjected variously to positive, negative, and mixed or ambiguous treatments. Each subdivision in the section on the heroine contains examples of praise for the virgin, mistress, or wife. Other portraits, however, illustrate that no heroine type escapes some form of condemnation or rejection. The attractive, childlike woman, often depicted as the ideal, beautiful heroine, also may be presented as trivial or inadequate in comparison to the more serious, active, and adult male; the noble, resistant virgin may come to be seen as the arrested, unemerging woman; the sexual woman, who is initially praised for her physical charms and pleasure-giving talents, is likely to be derided, betrayed, and punished for being a whore. If a woman marries, she is often presented not as the "angel of the house" but as a shrew. Furthermore, virgins, mistresses, and wives are consistently portrayed negatively as they get older or if they are not beautiful. The effect of this rejection is complicated by women's economic powerlessness. The old maid and cast-off mistress or wife are likely to be poor.

The section on the heroine ultimately reveals, therefore, that it is virtually impossible for a woman to be fulfilled and successful in any one of the three heroine roles. One reason is that the roles of passive virgin, active sexual partner, and selfless helpmate are mutually exclusive because the major qualities praised in one role are condemned in another. Not only is the virgin or the mistress an inherently partial being, but she also often finds it impossible to fulfill the partial role adequately. For example, women are encouraged to become housewives and then are denigrated as unproductive and shallow if they do. Another example is the dilemma of the sexual woman, who must provide a man with both satisfaction and continuing anticipation. A character in William Congreve's *The Double Dealer* exclaims: "Pox on't! that a man can't drink without quenching his thirst." The impossibility of fulfilling the requirements of one role—virgin, mistress, or helpmate—is apparent even to those who have imposed the categories: In John Dryden's *Marriage à la Mode*, Palamede responds to Rhodophil's complaints about Doralice: "O, now I have found it! you dislike her for no other reason but because she's your wife." Rhodophil replies, "And is not that enough? All that I know of her perfections now, is only by memory. . . . At last we arrived at that point, that there is nothing left in us to make us new to one another. . . ." Palamede's advice is, "You must get you a mistress, Rhodophil. That, indeed, is living upon cordials; but, as fast as one fails, you must supply it with another."

The ideal wife is rejected because she is not also the ideal maiden or mistress. It is common for women's magazines to enjoin wives to play the parts of virgin and mistress in order to keep their husbands interested in them. "Wives should always be lovers too," advised one popular song of the 1960s. This pressure to play mutually exclusive roles causes some women to forgo selfhood in favor of multiple role playing. In Jean Genet's *The Balcony* a prostitute is required by her clients to dress up as Sister Theresa and the Virgin Mary. The demand for women to be all things to all men is reduced to its patent absurdity in Tomasso Landolfi's Russian short story "Gogol's Wife," in which Gogol invents a balloon that he takes for a wife so that he can redesign her fresh for his pleasure every day.

The section on the hero focuses on female characters who have by choice, accident, or circumstance escaped definition exclusively in terms of sex roles. The aging woman, for example, may find herself no longer defined in relation to a man, and she therefore becomes heroic by necessity. Female heroes may be virgins like St. Joan, sexual women like Cleopatra, or wives and mothers like Millamant or Mother Courage, but they all have found an individual identity apart from the myths that the culture provides for their emulation.

The hero categories of the sage and the artist are tributes to the heroism of traditional women. Both appear to the outside observer to be defined by heroine roles. The sage is heroic because she is wise, but she cannot translate her understanding into productive action. The artist transforms her world, but does so by consciously playing the role of virgin, mistress, or wife. Only the warrior openly refuses to be seen as a supporting character in a man's drama and attempts to change her world through direct action. All three heroic categories conform in some way to the pattern of heroic action defined by Lord Raglan in *The Hero* and Joseph Campbell in *The Hero with a Thousand Faces,* and thus they provide informative parallels to male heroes. The recognition of the female hero should end the tendency to analyze heroes in intrinsically male terms, while increasing our awareness that male heroism and female heroism in a patriarchal society often have taken different forms, corresponding to the restrictions and opportunities afforded each sex.

Women authors are more likely to portray women as heroes, and male authors to portray them as heroines. This can be explained by the tendency of authors to write about protagonists of their own sex. Men are also likely to portray women as heroines because they do not know about women's real beliefs or about women's actions when men are not around. As suggested by the selections in the sections on the artist and the sage, women purposefully may keep this knowledge from men in order to gain some power. William Faulkner, for example, implies frequently that his female characters are wise. Except in the case of Judith Sutpen, however, he seldom ventures to explain what they know. In some instances—for example, Lena Grove, in *Light in August,* or Dilsey, in *The Sound and the Fury*—women's wisdom is nonverbal, but in others one might conjecture that just as Freud admittedly did not know what women want, Faulkner did not know what they know.

The increase in heroic portraits of women in twentieth-century literature may result in part from the increasing opportunity afforded women to write honestly about their lives. Greek, Roman, and Judeo-Christian culture for the last 2500 years has created images of women in literature and in life which have been either glorified or denigrating and which have had little relation to real women. As Katharine Rogers recounts, "Roman ambivalence toward the love object, Greek patriarchal disparagement of women's character and importance, and early Christian hostility to her as a sexual temptation laid the foundations for the mass of misogynistic writing which has appeared in every period of English literature."[5] Although portraits of virgins, mistresses, helpmates, sages, artists, and warriors appear in every period of English and American literature, certain female traits are emphasized more than others in any given period. Rogers lists, among the negative stereotypes, "the whore in Jewish and classical antiquity and again in the Renaissance, the shrewish wife in the Middle Ages, the 'unfeminine' woman in the nineteenth century, and the devouring mother in the twentieth."[6]

The dualistic, unrealistic, and destructive myths about women are still with us. However, we are presently witnessing a countertendency. The integrated and constructive myths about women we see today bear a strong resemblance to the images of women in the totemic cults of Western Europe and of early Hebrew, Greek, and Roman civilizations. In these early societies, women were perceived positively as embodiments of sexuality, fertility, and the regenerative powers of nature. In addition, they were the supervisors not only of the home but also of the entire community. They were the spiritual and practical force at the center of all human life. For example, women generally were respected as having magic powers related to their intimate knowledge of the forces of nature, which made them, among other things, the originators of medicine. Anglo-Saxon portraits of strong women warriors such as Judith reflect a past in which women were seen as physically, morally, and intellectually strong and effective. Kate Millett, in *Sexual*

Politics, and Elizabeth Gould Davis, in *The First Sex,* posit similar matriarchal cultures in Greek history.

In the twentieth century, female sexuality is again seen as positive and regenerative. James Joyce's Molly Bloom, in *Ulysses,* and Lawrence Durrell's Justine, in *The Alexandria Quartet,* for example, are positive embodiments of female sexuality and female mystic power. While women are still identified with sex in such portraits and often are portrayed as limited human beings, their sexuality is once again a positive force. Such portraits free women to be proud of their bodies and to increase their self-esteem. Furthermore, instead of being portrayed as static "sex symbols" who inspire male sexuality, women in many literary works are now portrayed freely choosing and actively seeking and enjoying sexual encounters without becoming subservient to, or dependent on, men. The positive image of women as sexually powerful and active is accompanied by a growing awareness of their ability to act forcefully in other contexts. Thus the reemergence of images of the female as independent, whole, and strong implies the fusing of previously dualistic definitions of womanhood. The image of women has also improved as a result of the renewed respect for other values that are associated in our culture with women. Such writers as Robert Bly, in *Sleepers Joining Hands,* and Ken Kesey, in *Garage Sale,* call for the acceptance of the female principle in both men and women. In doing so, they identify the faults of American culture—the individuality that leads to alienation, the rationality that becomes sterile and machinelike, the desire to dominate nature and other people by violence if necessary—as male qualities. The values seen by the counterculture as the antidote to the dehumanization of modern American life are the female qualities of relatedness, nurturance, emotion, joyous fecundity, and mystic oneness with the natural and the spiritual worlds.

Female writers have gone further, redefining women as both mythically powerful and capable of active heroism in the world. Such collections of contemporary women's poetry as *No More Masks* and *Rising Tides* and such novelists as Virginia Woolf and Doris Lessing have begun to provide us with these new images. In terms of traditional sex role definitions, the new women they envision are androgynous. The celebration of values traditionally associated with women, combined with the assertion of the androgynous potential open to both women and men, is giving rise to new definitions of womanhood and manhood which will encourage rather than repress the development of full human capabilities in all of us. Women are now portrayed as intellectual and sexual, aggressive and nurturing, independent and loving, effective in both the public arena and the home. And in these portraits they are both mythically and practically positive and powerful.

Such postdualistic images affect women's expectations and aspirations and accordingly encourage them to live fuller, richer, and more independent lives than their foremothers did. These new myths also affect social and political institutions. As the concept of the divine right of kings gave way to more egalitarian ideas about political governance, the concept that one sex must dominate the other is losing ground to the realization that women and men will benefit from equal personal, social, political, and economic relationships. Whether the positive myths about women will prevail over patriarchal stereotypes and whether the institutions of our society will be restructured on nonsexist lines will depend in good measure on the continued perseverance of liberated men and women. An understanding of the old myths and stereotypes that shape our assumptions about women is essential to effect this change.

NOTES

[1](Cleveland: The World Publishing Company, 1949), p. 342.

[2]See Kate Millett, *Sexual Politics* (New York: Avon Book Division, The Hearst Corporation, 1969, 1970), pp. 23–234.

[3](New York: David McKay Company, Inc., 1968), passim.

[4]Millett, loc. cit.

[5]*The Troublesome Helpmate: A History of Misogyny in Literature* (Seattle: University of Washington Press, 1966), p. 54.

[6]Ibid., p. 265.

THE HEROINE

THE VIRGIN

Gerard Davis: *The Virgin of the Annunciation* (Flemish, late fourteenth or early fifteenth century).
[*The Metropolitan Museum of Art. Bequest of Mary Stillman Harkness, 1950.*]

The concept of the virgin originally referred to the woman who was "one-in-herself." She engaged in sexual experience and had children, but she did not belong to a man. The "holy virgins" at the Temple of Ishtar, for example, were sacred prostitutes; Aphrodite was worshiped as a virgin and as the goddess of sexual love and fertility; and although the Virgin Mary is chaste, she is a mother. When the Romans invaded and Christianized Europe, the Europeans renamed to Mary statues and shrines sacred to pagan fertility goddesses and continued worshiping them as before. To this day, the Virgin Mary is often the primary deity worshiped in many Christian countries.[1] Henry Adams speaks of the virgin as "the greatest force the Western world ever felt." She "had drawn man's activities to herself more strongly than any other power, natural or supernatural, had ever done." She inspired "four-fifths of his [humanity's] noblest art." She had the power of a physical force, and that force was sexuality. Relating the virgin to classic goddesses, Adams writes: "Every one, even among Puritans, knew that neither Diana of the Ephesians nor any of the Oriental goddesses was worshipped for her beauty. She was goddess because of her force; she was the animated dynamo; she was reproduction—the greatest and most mysterious of all energies; all she needed was to be fecund."[2]

When her chastity is emphasized, the virgin is the embodiment of mother love. Her love, like that of a mother, is unconditional and nonjudgmental; she intercedes with a harsh, patriarchal god to save the sinful. In Judeo-Christian culture, the identification of sex with sin explains the Western redefinition of the virgin as the chaste, nonsexual woman. Henry Adams points out that "an American Virgin would never dare command; an American Venus would never dare exist" because American "society regarded this victory over sex as its greatest triumph."[3] Not only did puritanism banish the virgin from America, but, as Leslie Fiedler points out in *Love and Death in the American Novel,* it also almost completely banished women from the American novel. In both England and America, the ideal woman is divested of the power of her fertility and sexuality. The ideal love, as Denis de Rougemont explains in *Love in the Western World,* is a love which is not consummated. The greatest lovers are Tristan and Isolde, who sleep with a sword between them, or Eloise and Abelard after Abelard is castrated and he has become a monk, and she a nun. Catherine and Heathcliff, the star-crossed lovers in Emily Brontë's *Wuthering Heights,* can be together only in death: their bodies embrace in the coffin while their spirits haunt the moors. This love is ideal because it escapes existence in the everyday world of time and death. Thus it is an attempt to bring about the union of passion and permanence. John Keats addresses the young man on the Grecian urn captured in art before the consecration of a kiss:

> Bold lover, never, never canst thou kiss,
> Though winning near the goal—yet, do not grieve;
>   She cannot fade, though thou hast not thy bliss,
>   Forever wilt thou love, and she be fair!

Because nothing can be perfect in the world of experience, the virgin exists in the prelapsarian, timeless world of pure being. Archetypally, she is associated with the Apollonian and Platonic ideas of pure spiritual form. In this world of pure form, the virgin can avoid participation in the fertility cycle of birth, growth, sexuality, and death, or—in Christian terms—creation, sin, and death. The ironic result of this attempt to escape death may be a lifeless existence. The virgin ideal becomes the purity of nonaction and nonsexuality, the purity of emptiness. In literary works about mortal women, the virgin is the embodiment of potential which will become realized only through relationship with a man. Like Mary, she awaits the coming of the male spirit to give her meaning and purpose. In literature she is the "light woman" (Miss Sophia Western, in Henry Fielding's *Tom Jones*), who waits to be awakened into sexuality and marriage. Virgins (except for nuns, who are the virgin wives of Christ) are portrayed positively only when they are young girls.

Poems about virgin heroines generally divide into the praised virgin, the waiting woman, and the unemerging woman. Works praising the virgin emphasize the beauty of youth and of presexual innocence. In myth, the praised virgins are Mary, Saints Theresa and Cecelia, the Muses, the inert statue Pygmalion, and the Greek goddess Diana. Dickens's Little Nell and Little Dorrit are examples of the woman-child as redeemer, a predominant theme in the nineteenth century. The ideal virgin is also the more human Sarah Pierrepont of Jonathan Edwards and John Skelton's Mistress Margaret Hussey. Mistress Hussey is typically imbued "With solace and gladness, / Much mirth and no madness, / All good and no badness. . . ." In their most demythologized form, they are young women of common sense who are neither coquettes nor prudes. These sensible women predominate in the eighteenth century and include Matthew Prior's Jinny the Just; Alexander Pope's Clarissa, in *The Rape of the Lock;* and Sir Thomas Overbury's Fair and Happy Milkmaid, whose "excellencies stand in her so silently as if they had stolen upon her without her knowledge." In the eighteenth and nineteenth centuries, a young woman proves her moral worth by protecting her chastity against the onslaughts of lustful—and therefore evil—men. The goodness of Samuel Richardson's Pamela, sexually pursued by her master, Mr. B——, is equated with the retention of her hymen. The emphasis on chastity in women is related to laws of primogeniture. It has been considered important that young women be chaste and wives faithful to ensure the legitimacy of the heirs.

The ideal of female chastity has been a primary force in circumscribing the lives of women. Eighteenth- and nineteenth-century novels contain numerous instances in which even the appearance of unchastity renders the woman undesirable as a potential wife. In Fanny Burney's *Evelina,* male admirers take Evelina's walking with immoral people as evidence of unchastity. The combined fears of being thought unchaste and of becoming an "old maid" dictate female obedience to rigid role definitions and prevent self-fulfillment. In *A Room of One's Own,* Virginia Woolf shows that the limitations imposed on a woman to protect her from immorality have made it difficult for women to become great writers. Discussing Shakespeare's probable fate had he been a woman, Woolf writes:

> No girl could have walked to London and stood in the stage door and forced her way into the presence of actor-managers without doing herself a violence and suffering an anguish which may have been irrational—for chastity may be a fetish invented by certain societies for unknown reasons—but were nonetheless inevitable. Chastity had then, it has even now, a religious importance in a woman's life, and has so wrapped itself round with nerves and instincts that to cut it free and bring it to light of day demands courage of the rarest.[4]

The value placed on chastity has also invested sexuality with overtones of guilt, which is a primary cause of frigidity in women.

Because the virgin is an embodiment of potentiality and not of experience, she often appears as the waiting woman. The medieval damsel in distress must wait patiently while the knight slays the dragon. According to the poet Robert Graves, "Man does, woman is." The waiting woman, then, is the reward for male action. John Dryden insists that "none but the brave deserve the fair," and Robert Burns proclaims:

> How blythely wad I bide the stoure,
> A weary slave frae sun to sun,
> Could I the rich reward secure—
> The lovely Mary Morison!

In a world dominated by active male values, the woman may be condemned for her passivity and labeled trivial and irrelevant. Ben Jonson sees women as "men's shadows"; John Donne wonders whether they should be afforded souls along with men; and Alexander Pope claims that "most women have no characters at all." Such condemnations of the virgin result from the fact that her definition is couched in negative terms: She is not active, not sexual, etc. Pericles, as quoted in Joseph Addison's *Spectator,* No. 81, admonishes women: "Think it your greatest commendation not to be talked of one way or other."

The concept of woman as potential, waiting to be awakened by a man, discourages the unmarried woman from developing definite qualities, interests, and abilities because these might interfere with her marriageability. Like Rapunzel and Sleeping Beauty, she may be pictured as imprisoned or sleeping. Until the prince comes, her only attributes are her beauty and passive goodness. If she develops a personality that "he" does not like, he may not choose her. Only in and through the relationship with the male and under his supervision is she permitted to develop a self. When men choose women younger than themselves to marry, the discrepancy in age allows them to play the father figure to the woman, who is the unformed and therefore unthreatening child. In Fanny Burney's *Evelina,* for example, Evelina's fiancé, Lord Orville, replaces her absent foster father, the Reverend Villars, as her moral and social adviser. The father, however, may ultimately be unwilling to relinquish that protective role. Thus in realistic literature, the oppressive father is often presented as responsible for his daughter's sexual repression. In William Faulkner's "A Rose for Emily," Emily's father drives away the potential suitors who come to the house. After she dies, the townspeople discover in her bed the corpse of the man who courted her after her father's death. Faulkner implies that she killed her suitor and slept with his corpse. The daughter in Eugene O'Neill's *Mourning Becomes Electra* hates her tyrannical father while he is alive, but at his death she dresses in black and never again leaves their home. Katherine Anne Porter's "Daughters of the Late Colonel" portrays a similar situation in which the father prevents his daughters from developing their own lives. Sigmund Freud explored the tendency of a parent to repress a child of the opposite sex, preventing him or her from developing adult sexual relationships because of the parent's unrecognized sexual attraction to the child. This attraction is naturally reciprocated at a certain age of development, but may be prolonged unhealthily into adulthood.

Because of the Western association of sexuality and sin as well as the preference for the unformed female mate, a father may prefer his daughter to his wife because the wife embodies both sexuality and the aggressive implications of a developed self. In fairy tales, the virgin is usually entrapped by an evil older woman—the wicked stepmother or wicked witch. The biological mother tends not only to be passive and good but also to die at the birth of the girl child. Thus the fairy-tale virgin has no biological connection (and hence no spiritual affinity) with the adult material embodiment of sexuality and evil who becomes her mother-captor. The negative portrayal of the older woman is also explained by the competition of the older woman and the younger one for men in patriarchal culture. The older woman's increasing disadvantage due to age may make her ambivalent or even hostile toward her younger competitors.

The story of Cinderella links the imprisonment-rescue myth of the virgin with the spinster's economic reality. The society relegates women to low-paying, unrewarding clerical and domestic jobs on the assumption that a woman will soon be saved by a wealthy prince charming and will no longer need to work. However, as in Alfred, Lord Tennyson's "Mariana," Prince Charming may never come. Katherine Anne Porter's "The Jilting of Granny Weatherall" portrays a woman deserted at the altar in her youth. The disappointment and humiliation of that experience remain with her to the end of her life; and, even though she marries another man and has children and grandchildren, she stays the waiting woman for whom neither the earthly nor the heavenly bridegroom ever comes to give her life meaning. Dying, she cries, " 'God, give a sign!' For the second time there was no sign. Again no bridegroom and the priest in the house. She could not remember any other sorrow because this grief wiped them all away."

If the bridegroom does appear, wedding poems, such as Edmund Spenser's "Epithalamion," John Suckling's "Ballad upon a Wedding," and Percy Bysshe Shelley's "Epipsychidion," celebrate a positive future, using beautiful, verdant imagery to describe the moment of emergence from the virgin state and awakening into fertility. William Congreve's play *Love for Love* presents innocence on the brink of seduction: in the famous scene from the Restoration comedy, Tatter teaches Prue the etiquette of sexual emergence. In novels, the happy ending, for example, includes marriage to a wealthy man. Marriage solves all the virgin's problems, from loneliness to poverty.

The postvirgin state has its dangers, however, of which both fictional and real-life virgins are aware. In awakening to sexuality, the virgin symbolically enters the world of time and death. Her emergence is associated with the sin of Eve's fall. Edmund Spenser admonishes in Sonnet 84: "Let not one sparke of filthy lustfull fyre / breake out, that may her sacred peace molest. . . ." Henry Purcell, in a song from *Orpheus Britannicus,* describes the no-win situation of women, who may be abandoned for either refusing or accepting sexual overtones:

Fate affords no other way,
But Denying or Complying;
What can we poor Females do?
And Resenting, or Consenting,
Does alike our Loves betray.

Marriage is an equally questionable alternative. Tennyson's St. Agnes rejects earthly marriage for a spiritual marriage; she is drawn up to heaven, where "the Heavenly Bridegroom waits, / To make me pure of sin." In John Keats's "The Eve of St. Agnes," however, when Prospero elopes with his bride and they go out into a storm, their departure is described in ominous images of sorrow and death. James Joyce's Eveline senses that the man who would marry her "would drown her." One specific danger in marriage is that the unattainable virgin, who is the reward of the romantic quest, may become boring and/or bored as the attainable wife. Aphra Behn warns, in *The Emperor of the Moon,* "When maidens are young / They should take pleasure because / When they age it is all hum-drum." And John Dryden suggests in *Marriage à la Mode:* "The only way to keep us new / To one another, is never to enjoy. . . ." In the most idyllic Western love stories such as those of Tristan and Isolde or Eloise and Abelard, domesticity is rendered impossible by separation or by death.

Because of the negative aspects of the postvirginal state, virgins may elect not to move into the realm of sexuality, whether it is proposed in the form of seduction, rape, or marriage. Some women writers, such as Mary Wilkins Freeman, in "A New England Nun," portray positively the woman who lives a chaste life in order to remain one-in-herself. After Freeman's protagonist breaks her engagement, the narrator tells us:

> If Louisa Ellis had sold her birthright she did not know it, the taste of the pottage was so delicious, and had been her sole satisfaction for so long. Serenity and placid narrowness had become to her as the birthright itself. She gazed ahead through a long reach of future days strung together like pearls in a rosary, every one like the others, and all smooth and flawless and innocent, and her heart went up in thankfulness.

In Sir Walter Ralegh's "The Nymph's Reply," the speaker argues that the virgin cannot afford to love because love will fade. Virgin heroes in the saints' lives, such as Joan of Arc and Cynewulf's Juliana, remain celibate out of loyalty to spiritual values, forgoing transient sexual love for the immortal love of God. In numerous saints' lives and in Samuel Richardson's *Clarissa,* the virgin must choose between sex, in the form of rape, and death.

The life of the resistant virgin, however much it may be admired by some, is often presented as sterile and deathlike. The *carpe diem* poems of Andrew Marvell, Christopher Marlowe, Sir Walter Ralegh, Ben Jonson, and John Donne rest on the assumption that a woman's life will be empty without sexuality and the love of a man. The poets threaten and cajole women with reminders that youthful beauty, which supposedly attracts men, is fleeting. According to William Butler Yeats, in "In Memory of Eva Gore-Booth and Con Markeiwicz," "The innocent and the beautiful / Have no enemy but time." The women who refuses to become a sexual partner or a wife frequently is described as a repressed, arrested creature. Her mythological embodiment is the Cumaean Sibyl, who was punished for her refusal of Apollo's love by being granted immortal life without eternal youth. As a result, she wasted away into nothingness. In William Blake's "The Book of Thel," the unemerging woman becomes emblematic of all those who resist the call of experience.

In twentieth-century literature, sexual freedom necessitates a virgin substitute. In Norman Mailer's "The Time of Her Time," a man's efforts to force a young woman to experience her first orgasm and thereby to dominate her replace the nineteenth-century emphasis on deflowering as a means by which a man dominates a woman. The unemerging woman is thus joined by the equally condemned frigid girl friend or wife who tolerates sex but cannot or will not enjoy it. If a woman chooses chastity, she may be seen as exhibiting a willfulness and power deserving of punishment. Even though the resistant virgin in the saint's life may be seen as acting out of love for God, female virginity more often represents the refusal to idolize the human male, whose dominant role is closely associated with that of the patriarchal God. In the Bible and in medieval and Victorian thought, disobedience of the husband and/or father was equated with disobeying God. Mailer's story suggests that forced sex is considered just punishment for virgin pride.

More typically, authors assume that all women desire marriage. Therefore, a spinster is portrayed as a reject who is so unattractive that no man could love her. As John Updike states in "The Bulgarian Poetess," "in America, only the uncharming fail to marry." The spinster is ridiculed in W. H. Auden's "Miss Gee: A Ballad" and pitied in Sherwood Anderson's "The Teacher." In *The Bostonians,* Henry James describes the first meeting between Basil Ransom and Olive Chancellor:

> What Basil Ransom actually perceived was that Miss Chancellor was a signal old maid. That was her quality, her destiny; nothing could be more distinctly written. There are women who are unmarried by accident, and others who are unmarried by option; but Olive Chancellor was unmarried by every implication of her being. She was a spinster as Shelley was a lyric poet, or as the month of August is sultry.

The spinster's life is portrayed as joyless, lifeless, and rigid. James likened Olive's smile to a "thin ray of moonlight resting upon the wall of a prison." The drab, untouched, and aging secretary in Randall Jarrell's "The Woman at the Washington Zoo" compares herself to the caged animals, whom she sees as better off than she because they are in "themselves, the trap," because they do not have knowledge of death, and because the world comes to them and sees them. Wildly she cries out: "Oh, bars of my own body, / Open, open!" She appeals to the wild vulture to come to her "as man": "You know what I was, / You see what I am: change me, change me!"

To remain a pure virgin forever is the ideal of womanhood as symbolized by the Virgin Mary. And yet in more realistic portrayals of the virgin heroine, time eventually takes away the joy of the virgin state. The solution to this paradox appears in the category of writings in praise of the dead girl, in which death keeps her pure and young forever. Spenser speaks of Dido in *The Shepheardes Calendar IX:*

> She reigns a goddess now emong the saintes,
> That whilome was a saynt of shepheardes light;
> And is enstalled nowe in heavens hight.

The selections which follow explore the relationship of the ideal of the perfect virgin, who lives in the world of timeless beauty, to the situation of the virgin who lives in the real world. Because of cultural ambivalence toward sexuality and toward aging, the ideal woman of Western society is often young and chaste. However, even the positive definition implies condemnation because the virginal embodiment of Apollonian beauty and perfection is outside the realm of experience. The virgin state is seen, therefore, as deathlike as well as pure. Such portraits imply that in order to participate in life, a woman must become a mistress or a wife.

THE VIRGIN: NOTES

[1]Esther Harding, *Women's Mysteries: Ancient and Modern* (New York: Bantam Books, Inc., 1971, 1973), pp. 115–121.

[2]*The Education of Henry Adams* (Boston: Houghton Mifflin Company, 1918), pp. 384–385, 388.

[3]Ibid., p. 385.

[4](New York: Harcourt, Brace & World, Inc., 1957), p. 51.

I SYNG OF A MAYDEN

This anonymous fifteenth-century lyric appears in the Sloane manuscript, now in the British Museum, and has been frequently printed. Its simplicity and depth have established its preeminence in the body of medieval religious poetry in honor of the Virgin Mary.

I syng of a mayden
   that is makeles,[1]
Kyng of alle kynges
   To here sone che ches.[2]

He cam also stylle
   ther his moder was,
As dew in Aprylle
   that fallyt on the gras.

He cam also stylle
   to his moderes bowr,
As dew in Aprille
   that fallyt on the flour.

He cam also stylle
   ther his moder lay,
As dew in Aprille
   that fallyt on the spray.

Moder & maydyn
   was neuer non but che.
Wel may swych a lady
   Godés moder be.

10

20

QUEENE VERTUE'S COURT, WHICH
SOME CALL STELLA'S FACE

Sir Philip Sidney   (1554–1586)

Sidney, who was born into the highest circles of English nobility and was the godson of Philip II of Spain, was universally loved and admired, even to the point of

[1]*makeles:* matchless.
[2]*ches:* chose.

being offered the vacant throne of Poland. He spent three years at Oxford, without taking a degree, and became one of Queen Elizabeth's most important courtiers. His literary fame rests upon three works: the pastoral romance *Arcadia* (1590), which he wrote for his sister, the Countess of Pembroke; his critical *Defense of Poetry* (1594); and his sonnet cycle *Astrophel and Stella* (1591). Appointed governor of Flushing, he was killed in the Battle of Zutphen.

"Queene Vertue's court" is the ninth of the 108 sonnets which, with eleven songs, make up *Astrophel and Stella.* It is likely that the poem was written during the summer of 1582.

Queene *Vertue's* court, which some call *Stella's* face,
  Prepar'd by Nature's chiefest furniture,
  Hath his front built of Alablaster pure;
Gold is the covering of that stately place.
The doore by which sometimes comes forth her Grace,
  Red Porphir is, which locke of pearle makes sure:
  Whose porches rich (which name of cheekes endure)
Marble mixt red and white do enterlace.
  The windowes now through which this heav'nly guest
Looks over the world, and can find nothing such,
Which dare claime from those lights the name of best,
Of touch they are that without touch doth touch,
  Which *Cupid's* selfe from Beautie's myne did draw:
  Of touch they are, and poore I am their straw.

LET NOT ONE SPARKE OF FILTHY LUSTFULL FYRE

Edmund Spenser   (1552?–1599)

Born in London, Spenser entered Cambridge in 1569, where he began writing poetry. After receiving his M.A. degree in 1576, he entered the Earl of Leicester's circle, making the acquaintance there of Sir Philip Sidney. Spenser became secretary to Lord Grey, the Lord Deputy of Ireland, and thereafter spent much of his life on that island. At about the same time, Spenser began work on his epic *The Faerie Queene,* which was to engage him until his death. In 1594 Spenser married Elizabeth Boyle and wrote for her his *Epithalamion* and a series of sonnets called the *Amoretti.*

"Let not one sparke" is one of the *Amoretti* sonnets, which were published, together with *Epithalamion,* in 1595.

Let not one sparke of filthy lustfull fyre
  breake out, that may her sacred peace molest:

ne one light glance of sensuall desyre
　Attempt to work her gentle mindes vnrest.
But pure affections bred in spotlesse brest,
　and modest thoughts breathd from wel tempred sprites,
　goe visit her in her chast bowre of rest,
　accompanyde with angelick delightes.
There fill your selfe with those most ioyous sights,
　the which my selfe could neuer yet attayne:
　but speake no word to her of these sad plights,
　which her too constant stiffnesse doth constrayn.
Onely behold her rare perfection,
　and blesse your fortunes fayre election.

TO HIS COY MISTRESS

Andrew Marvell　　(1621–1678)

The son of a Yorkshire vicar, Marvell attended Cambridge from 1633 to 1641, and
he traveled on the Continent from 1642 to 1646. A friend of Milton, Marvell held
various posts during the Commonwealth period and served in Parliament from 1659
until his death, except for a three-year period as secretary to the Earl of Carlisle in
his embassy to Russia and Scandinavia. During his lifetime, Marvell was known
principally for his satires and broadsides against the restored Stuart monarchs.

"To His Coy Mistress" was published in 1681 in the posthumous volume *Poems.*

Had we but World enough, and Time,
This coyness Lady were no crime.
We would sit down, and think which way
To walk, and pass our long Loves Day.
Thou by the *Indian Ganges* side
Should'st Rubies find: I by the Tide
Of *Humber* would complain. I would
Love you ten years before the Flood:
And you should if you please refuse
Till the Conversion of the *Jews.*　　　　　　　10
My vegetable Love should grow
Vaster then Empires, and more slow.
An hundred years should go to praise
Thine Eyes, and on thy Forehead Gaze.
Two hundred to adore each Breast:
But thirty thousand to the rest.
An Age at least to every part,
And the last Age should show your Heart.

For Lady you deserve this State;
Nor would I love at lower rate.   20
   But at my back I alwaies hear
Times winged Charriot hurrying near:
And yonder all before us lye
Desarts of vast Eternity.
Thy Beauty shall no more be found;
Nor, in thy marble Vault, shall sound
My ecchoing song: then Worms shall try
That long preserv'd Virginity:
And your quaint Honour turn to dust;
And into ashes all my Lust.   30
The Grave's a fine and private place,
But none I think do there embrace.
   Now therefore, while the youthful hew
Sits on thy skin like morning dew,
And while thy willing Soul transpires
At every pore with instant Fires,
Now let us sport us while we may:
And now, like am'rous birds of prey,
Rather at once our Time devour,
Than languish in his slow-chapt pow'r.   40
Let us roll all our Strength, and all
Our sweetness, up into one Ball:
And tear our Pleasures with rough strife,
Thorough the Iron gates of Life.
Thus, though we cannot make our Sun
Stand still, yet we will make him run.

SONG from THE CONVENT OF PLEASURE

Margaret Lucas Cavendish, Duchess of Newcastle   (1624?–1674)

Born into the nobility, Margaret Lucas became a lady-in-waiting at the court. She
married William Cavendish, Duke of Newcastle, one of the Royalist commanders
during the civil wars. They lived in exile during the Commonwealth period, but
returned to England at the Restoration and joined the court of Charles II. The
Duchess was a prolific writer of plays, poems, and essays, and her biography of her
husband has become a classic of English biographical literature. She was buried in
Westminster Abbey on January 7, 1674.

"Song" from *The Convent of Pleasure* describes the pleasures of the virgin state. The
play was never performed, but was printed in 1668.

My cabinets are oyster-shells,
In which I keep my orient pearls:
To open them I use the tide,
As keys to locks, which opens wide
The oyster-shells; then out I take
Those orient pearls and crowns do make;
And modest coral I do wear,
Which blushes when it touches air.
On silver waves I sit and sing,
And then the fish lie listening: 10
Then sitting on a rocky stone
I comb my hair with fishes' bone:
The whilest Apollo with his beams
Doth dry my hair from watery streams.
His light doth glaze the water's face,
Make the large sea my looking-glass:
So when I swim on waters high,
I see myself as I glide by:
But when the sun begins to burn,
I back into my waters turn,   20
And dive into the bottom low:
Then on my head the waters flow
In curled waves and circles round,
And thus with waters am I crowned.

TO THE PIOUS MEMORY OF THE ACCOMPLISHT YOUNG LADY MRS ANNE KILLIGREW

John Dryden   (1631–1700)

Born into a country family of Northamptonshire, Dryden received his B.A. at Cambridge in 1654; although he inherited his father's estate, his income was so small that he began writing for the stage in order to supplement it. In 1663 he married Lady Elizabeth Howard, but the marriage was unhappy. The actress Ann Reeves remained his mistress. In 1668 Dryden became poet laureate, extending that office to include writing satires against the King's opponents. In 1685, at the ascension of the Catholic James II, Dryden himself turned Catholic, but he refused to recant when the Protestant William and Mary came to power in 1688. Consequently, he was deprived of the laureateship, and he returned to writing for the stage. His translation of the *Aeneid* was published in 1697.

"To the Pious Memory" first appeared at the front of the volume *Anne Killigrew's Poems* (1685). The selection that follows is the first of a ten-part tribute to Mrs. Killigrew.

To the Pious Memory of the Accomplisht Young Lady Mrs Anne Killigrew, Excellent in the two Sister-Arts of Poësie, and Painting. An Ode

I

Thou Youngest Virgin-Daughter of the Skies,
Made in the last Promotion of the Blest;
Whose Palmes, new pluckt from Paradise,
In spreading Branches more sublimely rise,
Rich with Immortal Green above the rest:
Whether, adopted to some Neighbouring Star,
Thou rol'st above us, in thy wand'ring Race,
   Or, in Procession fixt and regular,
   Mov'd with the Heavens Majestick Pace;
   Or, call'd to more Superiour Bliss,   10
Thou tread'st, with Seraphims, the vast Abyss:
What ever happy Region is thy place,
Cease thy Celestial Song a little space;
(Thou wilt have Time enough for Hymns Divine,
   Since Heav'ns Eternal Year is thine.)
Hear then a Mortal Muse thy Praise rehearse,
    In no ignoble Verse:
But such as thy own voice did practise here,
When thy first Fruits of Poesie were giv'n;
To make thy self a welcome Inmate there: 20
    While yet a young Probationer,
     And Candidate of Heav'n.

SARAH PIERREPONT

Jonathan Edwards   (1703–1758)

This famous Congregational clergyman, theologian, and philosopher was born at East Windsor, Connecticut, into a family of ministers. He was admitted to Yale at the age of twelve, and he entered the ministry in New York in 1722, beginning a career marked by controversy. He married Sarah Pierrepont in 1727, and they were the parents of eleven children.

Edwards wrote "Sarah Pierrepont" on a blank page in one of his books in 1723, when Sarah was thirteen and he was twenty. They were married four years later.

They say there is a young lady in [New Haven] who is beloved of that Great Being, who made and rules the world, and that there are certain seasons in which this Great Being, in some way or other invisible, comes to her and fills her mind with exceeding sweet delight, and that she hardly cares for anything, except to meditate on him—that she expects after a while to be received up where he is, to be raised up out of the world and caught up into heaven; being assured that he loves her too well to let her remain at a distance from him always. There she is to dwell with him and to be ravished with his love and delight forever. Therefore, if you present all the world before her, with the richest of its treasures, she disregards it and cares not for it, and is unmindful of any pain or affliction. She has a strange sweetness in her mind, and singular purity in her affections; is most just and conscientious in all her conduct; and you could not persuade her to do any thing wrong or sinful, if you give her all the world, lest she should offend this Great Being. She is of a wonderful sweetness, calmness and universal benevolence of mind; especially after this Great God has manifested himself to her mind. She will sometimes go about from place to place, singing sweetly; and seems to be always full of joy and pleasure; and no one knows for what. She loves to be alone, walking in the fields and groves, and seems to have some one invisible always conversing with her.

ON THE DEATH OF A YOUNG LADY OF FIVE YEARS OF AGE

Phillis Wheatley   (1753–1784)

Brought from Africa in 1761, Wheatley was bought by the Boston tailor John Wheatley as an attendant for his wife, Susannah, who encouraged her poetic gifts and gave her a good education, which included Latin and astronomy. Her first published poem (1770) was addressed to the Countess of Huntingdon, who introduced Wheatley to many notables during her visit to England in 1773. Wheatley returned to Boston, and after the deaths of Susannah and John Wheatley she married John Peters. They lived with their three children in poverty. She took up work in a cheap lodging house and died in 1784. Her last surviving child died so soon after as to be buried in the same grave with her.

"On the death of a young lady" first appeared in *Poems on Various Subjects, Religious and Moral* (1773).

From dark abodes to fair etherial light
Th' enraptur'd innocent has wing'd her flight;
On the kind bosom of eternal love
She finds unknown beatitude above.
This known, ye parents, nor her loss deplore,
She feels the iron hand of pain no more;

The dispensations of unerring grace,
Should turn your sorrows into grateful praise;
Let then no tears for her henceforward flow,
No more distress'd in our dark vale below.   10

    Her morning sun, which rose divinely bright,
Was quickly mantled with the gloom of night;
But hear in heav'n's blest bow'rs your *Nancy* fair,
And learn to imitate her language there.
"Thou, Lord, whom I behold with glory crown'd,
"By what sweet name, and in what tuneful sound
"Wilt thou be prais'd? Seraphic pow'rs are faint
"Infinite love and majesty to paint.
"To thee let all their grateful voices raise,
"And saints and angels join their songs of praise."   20

    Perfect in bliss she from her heav'nly home
Looks down, and smiling beckons you to come;
Why then, fond parents, why these fruitless groans?
Restrain your tears, and cease your plaintive moans.
Freed from a world of sin, and snares, and pain,
Why would you wish your daughter back again?
No—bow resign'd. Let hope your grief control,
And check the rising tumult of the soul.
Calm in the prosperous, and adverse day.
Adore the God who gives and takes away;   30
Eye him in all, his holy name revere,
Upright your actions, and your hearts sincere,
Till having sail'd through life's tempestuous sea,
And from its rocks, and boist'rous billows free,
Yourselves, safe landed on the blissful shore,
Shall join your happy babe to part no more.

THE BOOK OF THEL

William Blake   (1757–1827)

Born in London and encouraged to pursue his artistic talents, Blake was apprenticed
to an engraver and in 1781 entered the Royal Academy, which he found too
restrictive and soon left. In 1782 he fell in love with a girl who laughed at his
proposal of marriage. Catherine Boucher said that she pitied him, and Blake replied,
"Then I love you for it." They were married soon thereafter. Blake taught Catherine
to read and write and to help him color engravings. According to Stanley Kunitz,
"they were inseparable companions, and she echoed his every thought and opinion,

but it is doubtful if their marriage was ever consummated; certainly it was childless, in a prolific age." Despite his initial success as an engraver and illustrator, Blake's increasing radicalism and growing absorption in mysticism soon led him to outdistance his audience, and he died in poverty.

"The Book of Thel" was printed in 1789.

THEL'S MOTTO

> *Does the Eagle know what is in the pit,*
> *Or wilt thou go ask the Mole?*
> *Can Wisdom be put in a silver rod?*
> *Or Love in a golden bowl?*

THEL

I

The daughters of Mne Seraphim led round their sunny flocks,
All but the youngest: she in paleness sought the secret air,
To fade away like morning beauty from her mortal day.
Down by the river of Adona her soft voice is heard,
And thus her gentle lamentation falls like morning dew:

'O life of this our spring! why fades the lotus of the water?
Why fade these children of the spring, born but to smile & fall?
Ah! Thel is like a wat'ry bow, and like a parting cloud,
Like a reflection in a glass, like shadows in the water,
Like dreams of infants, like a smile upon an infant's face,   10
Like the dove's voice, like transient day, like music in the air.
Ah! gentle may I lay me down and gentle rest my head,
And gentle sleep the sleep of death, and gentle hear the voice
Of him that walketh in the garden in the evening time.'

The Lilly of the valley breathing in the humble grass
Answer'd the lovely maid and said: 'I am a wat'ry weed,
And I am very small, and love to dwell in lowly vales;
So weak, the gilded butterfly scarce perches on my head.
Yet I am visited from heaven, and he that smiles on all
Walks in the valley, and each morn over me spreads his hand,   20
Saying: "Rejoice, thou humble grass, thou new-born lilly flower,
Thou gentle maid of silent valleys and of modest brooks;
For thou shalt be clothed in light, and fed with morning manna,
Till summer's heat melts thee beside the fountains and the springs
To flourish in eternal vales:" then why should Thel complain?
Why should the mistress of the vales of Har utter a sight?'

She ceas'd & smil'd in tears, then sat down in her silver shrine.

Thel answer'd: 'O thou little virgin of the peaceful valley,
Giving to those that cannot crave, the voiceless, the o'ertired.
Thy breath doth nourish the innocent lamb; he smells thy milky
   garments;   30
He crops thy flowers while thou sittest smiling in his face,
Wiping his mild and meekin mouth from all contagious taints.
Thy wine doth purify the golden honey; thy perfume,
Which thou dost scatter on every little blade of grass that springs,
Revives the milked cow & tames the fire-breathing steed.
But Thel is like a faint cloud kindled at the rising sun:
I vanish from my pearly throne, and who shall find my place?'

'Queen of the vales,' the Lilly answer'd, 'ask the tender cloud,
And it shall tell thee why it glitters in the morning sky,
And why it scatters its bright beauty thro' the humid air.   40
Descend, O little cloud, & hover before the eyes of Thel.'

The Cloud descended, and the Lilly bow'd her modest head,
And went to mind her numerous charge among the verdant grass.

II

'O little Cloud,' the virgin said, 'I charge thee tell to me
Why thou complainest not when in one hour thou fade away.
Then we shall seek thee, but not find. Ah, Thel is like to thee.
I pass away; yet I complain, and no one hears my voice.'

The Cloud then shew'd his golden head & his bright form emerg'd,
Hovering and glittering on the air before the face of Thel.

'O virgin, know'st thou not our steeds drink of the golden springs   50
Where Luvah doth renew his horses? look'st thou on my youth,
And fearest thou because I vanish and am seen no more?
Nothing remains? O maid, I tell thee, when I pass away,
It is to tenfold life, to love, to peace and raptures holy.
Unseen descending weigh my light wings upon balmy flowers,
And court the fair eyed dew to take me to her shining tent.
The weeping virgin trembling kneels before the risen sun,
Till we arise link'd in a golden band and never part,
But walk united, bearing food to all our tender flowers.'

'Dost thou, O little Cloud? I fear that I am not like thee,   60
For I walk thro' the vales of Har, and smell the sweetest flowers.
But I feed not the little flowers; I hear the warbling birds,
But I feed not the warbling birds; they fly and seek their food.
But Thel delights in these no more, because I fade away,
And all shall say: "without a use this shining woman liv'd;
Or did she only live to be at death the food of worms?"'

The Cloud reclin'd upon his airy throne, and answer'd thus,

'Then if thou art the food of worms, O virgin of the skies,
How great thy use, how great thy blessing! every thing that lives
Lives not alone nor for itself: fear not, and I will call   70
The weak worm from its lowly bed, and thou shalt hear its voice.
Come forth, worm of the silent valley, to thy pensive queen.'

The helpless worm arose, and sat upon the Lilly's leaf:
And the bright Cloud sail'd on, to find his partner in the vale.

III

Then Thel astonish'd view'd the Worm upon its dewy bed.

'Art thou a Worm, image of weakness, art thou but a Worm?
I see thee like an infant wrapped in the Lilly's leaf.
Ah, weep not, little voice! thou canst not speak, but thou canst weep.
Is this a Worm? I see thee lay helpless & naked, weeping,
And none to answer, none to cherish thee with mother's smiles.'   80

The Clod of Clay heard the Worm's voice & rais'd her pitying head;
She bow'd over the weeping infant, and her life exhal'd
In milky fondness: then on Thel she fix'd her humble eyes.
'O beauty of the vales of Har, we live not for ourselves.
Thou seest me the meanest thing, and so I am indeed,
My bosom of itself is cold, and of itself is dark;
But he that loves the lowly pours his oil upon my head
And kisses me, and binds his nuptial bands around my breast,
And says: "Thou mother of children, I have loved thee,
And I have given thee a crown that none can take away."   90
But how this is, sweet maid, I know not, and I cannot know.
I ponder, and I cannot ponder; yet I live and love.'

The daughter of beauty wip'd her pitying tears with her white veil,
And said: 'Alas! I knew not this, and therefore did I weep.
That God would love a Worm I knew, and punish the evil foot
That wilful bruis'd its helpless form; but that he cherish'd it
With milk and oil I never knew: and therefore did I weep;
And I complain'd in the mild air, because I fade away,
And lay me down in thy cold bed, and leave my shining lot.'

'Queen of the vales,' the matron Clay answer'd, 'I heard thy sighs,   100
And all thy moans flew o'er my roof, but I have call'd them down.
Wilt thou, O Queen, enter my house? 'tis given thee to enter
And to return: fear nothing, enter with thy virgin feet.'

IV

The eternal gates' terrific porter lifted the northern bar.
Thel enter'd in & saw the secrets of the land unknown.

She saw the couches of the dead, & where the fibrous roots
Of every heart on earth infixes deep its restless twists,
A land of sorrows & of tears where never smile was seen.

She wander'd in the land of clouds thro' valleys dark, list'ning
Dolours & lamentations; waiting oft beside a dewy grave   110
She stood in silence, list'ning to the voices of the ground,
Till to her own grave plot she came, & there she sat down,
And heard the voice of sorrow breathed from the hollow pit.

'Why cannot the Ear be closed to its own destruction,
Or the glist'ning Eye to the poison of a smile?
Why are Eyelids stor'd with arrows ready drawn,
Where a thousand fighting men in ambush lie;
Or an Eye of gifts & graces show'ring fruits & coined gold?
Why a Tongue impress'd with honey from every wind?
Why an Ear, a whirlpool fierce to draw creations in?   120
Why a Nostril wide inhaling terror, trembling & affright?
Why a tender curb upon the youthful, burning boy?
Why a little curtain of flesh on the bed of our desire?'

The Virgin started from her seat, & with á shriek
Fled back unhinder'd till she came into the vales of Har.

THE END

THE EVE OF ST. AGNES

John Keats   (1795–1821)

Born in London, Keats lost his father in 1804 and his mother in 1810. Following her death, he was removed from school and apprenticed to a surgeon at Edmundton, but in 1814 he went to London to study. There Keats was introduced to Leigh Hunt and his circle of artistic and literary acquaintances. Following the publication of *Poems* (1817), Keats gave up surgery for writing, and he soon encountered financial difficulties. Early in 1820 he began to cough blood and realized that it was his "death warrant." He sailed for Italy in September and died in Rome the following spring.

"The Eve of St. Agnes" was published in 1819.

I
  St. Agnes' Eve—Ah, bitter chill it was!
  The owl, for all his feathers, was a-cold;
  The hare limp'd trembling through the frozen grass,

And silent was the flock in woolly fold:
Numb were the Beadsman's fingers, while he told
His rosary, and while his frosted breath,
Like pious incense from a censer old,
Seem'd taking flight for heaven, without a death,
Past the sweet Virgin's picture, while his prayer he saith.

II

His prayer he saith, this patient, holy man;   10
Then takes his lamp, and riseth from his knees,
And back returneth, meagre, barefoot, wan,
Along the chapel aisle by slow degrees:
The sculptur'd dead, on each side, seem to freeze,
Emprison'd in black, purgatorial rails:
Knights, ladies, praying in dumb orat'ries,
He passeth by; and his weak spirit fails
To think how they may ache in icy hoods and mails.

III

Northward he turneth through a little door,
And scarce three steps, ere Music's golden tongue   20
Flatter'd to tears this aged man and poor:
But no—already had his deathbell rung;
The joys of all his life were said and sung:
His was harsh penance on St. Agnes' Eve:
Another way he went, and soon among
Rough ashes sat he for his soul's reprieve,
And all night kept awake, for sinners' sake to grieve.

IV

That ancient Beadsman heard the prelude soft;
And so it chanc'd, for many a door was wide,
From hurry to and fro. Soon, up aloft,   30
The silver, snarling trumpets 'gan to chide:
The level chambers, ready with their pride,
Were glowing to receive a thousand guests:
The carved angels, ever eager-eyed,
Star'd, where upon their heads the cornice rests,
With hair blown back, and wings put cross-wise on their breasts.

V

At length burst in the argent revelry,
With plume, tiara, and all rich array,
Numerous as shadows haunting fairily
The brain, new stuff'd, in youth, with triumphs gay   40
Of old romance. These let us wish away,
And turn, sole-thoughted, to one Lady there,
Whose heart had brooded, all that wintry day,
On love, and wing'd St. Agnes' saintly care,

As she had heard old dames full many times declare.

VI

    They told her how, upon St. Agnes' Eve,
    Young virgins might have visions of delight,
    And soft adorings from their loves receive
    Upon the honey'd middle of the night,
    If ceremonies due they did aright;   50
    As, supperless to bed they must retire,
    And couch supine their beauties, lily white:
    Nor look behind, nor sideways, but require
Of Heaven with upward eyes for all that they desire.

VII

    Full of this whim was thoughtful Madeline:
    The music, yearning like a God in pain,
    She scarcely heard: her maiden eyes divine,
    Fix'd on the floor, saw many a sweeping train
    Pass by—she heeded not at all: in vain
    Came many a tiptoe, amorous cavalier,   60
    And back retir'd; not cool'd by high disdain,
    But she saw not: her heart was otherwhere:
She sigh'd for Agnes' dreams, the sweetest of the year.

VIII

    She danc'd along with vague, regardless eyes,
    Anxious her lips, her breathing quick and short:
    The hallow'd hour was near at hand: she sighs
    Amid the timbrels, and the throng'd resort
    Of whisperers in anger, or in sport;
    'Mid looks of love, defiance, hate, and scorn,
    Hoodwink'd with faery fancy; all amort,   70
    Save to St. Agnes and her lambs unshorn,
And all the bliss to be before to-morrow morn.

IX

    So, purposing each moment to retire,
    She linger'd still. Meantime, across the moors,
    Had come young Porphyro, with heart on fire
    For Madeline. Beside the portal doors,
    Buttress'd from moonlight, stands he, and implores
    All saints to give him sight of Madeline,
    But for one moment in the tedious hours,
    That he might gaze and worship all unseen;   80
Perchance speak, kneel, touch, kiss—in sooth such things have been.

X

    He ventures in: let not buzz'd whisper tell:
    All eyes be muffled, or a hundred swords

Will storm his heart, Love's fev'rous citadel:
For him, those chambers held barbarian hordes,
Hyena foemen, and blooded lords,
Whose very dogs would execrations howl
Against his lineage: not one breast affords
Him any mercy, in that mansion foul,
Save one old beldame, weak in body and in soul.   90

XI

Ah, happy chance! the aged creature came,
Shuffling along with ivory-headed wand,
To where he stood, hid from the torch's flame,
Behind a broad hall-pillar, far beyond
The sound of merriment and chorus bland:
He startled her; but soon she knew his face,
And grasp'd his fingers in her palsied hand,
Saying, 'Mercy, Porphyro! hie thee from this place:
'They are all here to-night, the whole blood-thirsty race!

XII

'Get hence! get hence! there's dwarfish Hildebrand;   100
'He had a fever late, and in the fit
'He cursed thee and thine, both house and land:
'Then there's that old Lord Maurice, not a whit
'More tame for his gray hairs—Alas me! flit!
'Flit like a ghost away.'—'Ah, Gossip dear,
'We're safe enough; here in this arm-chair sit,
'And tell me how'—'Good Saints' not here, not here;
'Follow me, child, or else these stones will be thy bier.'

XII

He follow'd through a lowly arched way,
Brushing the cobwebs with his lofty plume,   110
And as she mutter'd 'Well-a—well-a-day!'
He found him in a little moonlight room,
Pale, lattic'd, chill, and silent as a tomb.
'Now tell me where is Madeline,' said he,
'O tell me, Angela, by the holy loom
'Which none but secret sisterhood may see,
'When they St. Agnes' wool are weaving piously.'

XIV

'St. Agnes! Ah! it is St. Agnes' Eve—
'Yet men will murder upon holy days:
'Thou must hold water in a witch's sieve,   120
'And be liege-lord of all the Elves and Fays,
'To venture so: it fills me with amaze
'To see thee, Porphyro!—St. Agnes' Eve!
'God's help! my lady fair the conjuror plays
'This very night: good angels her deceive!

'But let me laugh awhile, I've mickle time to grieve.'

XV

Feebly she laugheth in the languid moon,
While Porphyro upon her face doth look.
Like puzzled urchin on an aged crone
Who keepeth clos'd a wond'rous riddle-book,   130
As spectacled she sits in chimney nook.
But soon his eyes grew brilliant, when she told
His lady's purpose; and he scarce could brook
Tears, at the thought of those enchantments cold
And Madeline asleep in lap of legends old.

XVI

Sudden a thought came like a full-blown rose,
Flushing his brow, and in his pained heart
Made purple riot: then doth he propose
A stratagem, that makes the beldame start:
'A cruel man and impious thou art: 140
'Sweet lady, let her pray, and sleep, and dream
'Alone with her good angels, far apart
'From wicked men like thee. Go, go!—I deem
'Thou canst not surely be the same that thou didst seem.'

XVII

I will not harm her, by all saints I swear,'
Quoth Porphyro: "O may I ne'er find grace
'When my weak voice shall whisper its last prayer,
'If one of her soft ringlets I displace,
'Or look with ruffian passion in her face:
'Good Angela, believe me by these tears;   150
'Or I will, even in a moment's space,
'Awake, with horrid shout, my foemen's ears,
'And beard them, though they be more fang'd than wolves and bears.'

XVIII

'Ah! why wilt thou affright a feeble soul?
'A poor, weak, palsy-stricken, churchyard thing,
'Whose passing-bell may ere the midnight toll;
'Whose prayers for thee, each morn and evening,
'Were never miss'd.'—Thus plaining, doth she bring
A gentler speech from burning Porphyro;
So woful, and of such deep sorrowing,   160
That Angela gives promise she will do
Whatever he shall wish, betide her weal or woe.

XIX

Which was, to lead him, in close secrecy,
Even to Madeline's chamber, and there hide

Him in a closet, of such privacy
That he might see her beauty unespied,
And win perhaps that night a peerless bride,
While legion'd fairies pac'd the coverlet,
And pale enchantment held her sleepy-eyed.
Never on such a night have lovers met,   170
Since Merlin paid his Demon all the monstrous debt.

XX

'It shall be as thou wishest,' said the Dame:
'All cates and dainties shall be stored there
'Quickly on this feast-night: by the tambour frame
'Her own lute thou wilt see: no time to spare,
'For I am slow and feeble, and scarce dare
'On such a catering trust my dizzy head.
'Wait here, my child, with patience; kneel in prayer
'The while: Ah! thou must needs the lady wed,
'Or may I never leave my grave among the dead.'   180

XXI

So saying, she hobbled off with busy fear.
The lover's endless minutes slowly pass'd;
The dame return'd, and whisper'd in his ear
To follow her; with aged eyes aghast
From fright of dim espial. Safe at last,
Through many a dusky gallery, they gain
The maiden's chamber, silken, hush'd, and chaste;
Where Porphyro took covert, pleas'd amain.
His poor guide hurried back with agues in her brain.

XXII

Her falt'ring hand upon the balustrade,   190
Old Angela was feeling for the stair,
When Madeline, St. Agnes' charmed maid,
Rose, like a mission'd spirit, unaware:
With silver taper's light, and pious care,
She turn'd, and down the aged gossip led
To a safe level matting. Now prepare,
Young Porphyro, for gazing on that bed;
She comes, she comes again, like ring-dove fray'd and fled.

XXIII

Out went the taper as she hurried in;
Its little smoke, in pallid moonshine, died: 200
She clos'd the door, she panted, all akin
To spirits of the air, and visions wide:
No uttered syllable, or woe betide!
But to her heart, her heart was voluble,
Paining with eloquence her balmy side;

As though a tongueless nightingale should swell
Her throat in vain, and die, heart-stifled, in her dell.

XXIV
A casement high and triple-arch'd there was,
All garlanded with carven imag'ries
Of fruits, and flowers, and bunches of knot-grass,   210
And diamonded with panes of quaint device,
Innumerable of stains and splendid dyes,
As are the tiger-moth's deep-damask'd wings;
And in the midst, 'mong thousand heraldries,
And twilight saints, and dim emblazonings,
A shielded scutcheon blush'd with blood of queens and kings.

XXV
Full on this casement shone the wintry moon,
And threw warm gules on Madeline's fair breast,
As down she knelt for heaven's grace and boon;
Rose-bloom fell on her hands, together prest,   220
And on her silver cross soft amethyst,
And on her hair a glory, like a saint:
She seem'd a splendid angel, newly drest,
Save wings, for heaven:—Porphyro grew faint:
She knelt, so pure a thing, so free from mortal taint.

XXVI
Anon his heart revives: her vespers done,
Of all its wreathed pearls her hair she frees;
Unclasps her warmed jewels one by one;
Loosens her fragrant boddice; by degrees
Her rich attire creeps rustling to her knees: 230
Half-hidden, like a mermaid in sea-weed,
Pensive awhile she dreams awake, and sees,
In fancy, fair St. Agnes in her bed,
But dares not look behind, or all the charm is fled.

XXVII
Soon, trembling in her soft and chilly nest,
In sort of wakeful swoon, perplex'd she lay,
Until the poppied warmth of sleep oppress'd
Her soothed limbs, and soul fatigued away;
Flown, like a thought, until the morrow-day;
Blissfully haven'd both from joy and pain;   240
Clasp'd like a missal where swart Paynims pray;
Blinded alike from sunshine and from rain,
As though a rose should shut, and be a bud again.

XXVIII
Stol'n to this paradise, and so entranced,

Porphyro gazed upon her empty dress,
And listen'd to her breathing, if it chanced
To wake into a slumberous tenderness;
Which when he heard, that minute did he bless,
And breath'd himself: then from the closet crept,
Noiseless as fear in a wide wilderness,   250
And over the hush'd carpet, silent, stept,
And 'tween the curtains peep'd, where, lo!—how fast she slept.

XXIX

Then by the bed-side, where the faded moon
Made a dim, silver twilight, soft he set
A table, and, half anguish'd, threw thereon
A cloth of woven crimson, gold, and jet:—
O for some drowsy Morphean amulet!
The boisterous, midnight, festive clarion,
The kettle-drum, and far-heard clarionet,
Affray his ears, though but in dying tone:—   260
And hall door shuts again, and all the noise is gone.

XXX

And still she slept an azure-lidded sleep,
In blanched linen, smooth, and lavender'd,
While he from forth the closet brought a heap
Of candied apple, quince, and plum, and gourd
With jellies soother than the creamy curd,
And lucent syrops, tinct with cinnamon;
Manna and dates, in argosy transferr'd
From Fez; and spiced dainties, every one,
From silken Samarcand to cedar'd Lebanon.   270

XXXI

These delicates he heap'd with glowing hand
On golden dishes and in baskets bright
Of wreathed silver: sumptuous they stand
In the retired quiet of the night;
Filling the chilly room with perfume light.—
'And now, my love, my seraph fair, awake!
'Thou art my heaven, and I thine eremite:
'Open thine eyes, for meek St. Agnes' sake,
'Or I shall drowse beside thee, so my soul doth ache.'

XXXII

Thus whispering, his warm, unnerved arm   280
Sank in her pillow. Shaded was her dream
By the dusk curtains:—'twas a midnight charm
Impossible to melt as iced stream:
The lustrous salvers in the moonlight gleam;
Broad golden fringe upon the carpet lies:

It seem'd he never, never could redeem
From such a stedfast spell his lady's eyes;
So mus'd awhile, entoil'd in woofed phantasies.

XXXIII
Awakening up, he took her hollow lute,—
Tumultuous,—and, in chords that tenderest be,   290
He play'd an ancient ditty, long since mute,
In Provence call'd, 'La belle dame sans mercy:'
Close to her ear touching the melody;—
Wherewith disturb'd, she utter'd a soft moan:
He ceased—she panted quick—and suddenly
Her blue affrayed eyes wide open shone:
Upon his knees he sank, pale as smooth-sculptured stone.

XXXIV
Her eyes were open, but she still beheld,
Now wide awake, the vision of her sleep:
There was a painful change, that nigh expell'd   300
The blisses of her dream so pure and deep
At which fair Madeline began to weep,
And moan forth witless words with many a sigh;
While still her gaze on Porphyro would keep;
Who knelt, with joined hands and piteous eye,
Fearing to move or speak, she look'd so dreamingly.

XXXV
'Ah, Porphyro!' said she, 'but even now
'Thy voice was at sweet tremble in mine ear,
'Made tuneable with every sweetest vow;
'And those sad eyes were spiritual and clear: 310
'How chang'd thou art! how pallid, chill, and drear!
'Give me that voice again, my Porphyro,
'Those looks immortal, those complainings dear!
'Oh leave me not in this eternal woe,
'For if thou diest, my Love, I know not where to go.'

XXXVI
Beyond a mortal man impassion'd far
At these voluptuous accents, he arose,
Ethereal, flush'd, and like a throbbing star
Seen mid the sapphire heaven's deep repose
Into her dream he melted, as the rose   320
Blendeth its odour with the violet,—
Solution sweet: meantime the frost-wind blows
Like Love's alarum pattering the sharp sleet
Against the window-panes; St. Agnes' moon hath set.

XXXVII

    'Tis dark: quick pattereth the flaw-blown sleet:
    'This is not dream, my bride, my Madeline!'
    'Tis dark: the iced gusts still rave and beat:
    'No dream, alas! alas! and woe is mine!
    'Porphyro will leave me here to fade and pine.—
    'Cruel! what traitor could thee hither bring?   330
    'I curse not, for my heart is lost in thine
    'Though thou forsakest a deceived thing;—
'A dove forlorn and lost with sick unpruned wing.'

XXXVIII

    'My Madeline! sweet dreamer! lovely bride!
    'Say, may I be for aye thy vassal blest?
    'Thy beauty's shield, heart-shap'd and vermeil dyed?
    'Ah, silver shrine, here will I take my rest
    'After so many hours of toil and quest,
    'A famish'd pilgrim,—saved by miracle.
    'Though I have found, I will not rob thy nest   340
    'Saving of thy sweet self; if thou think'st well
'To trust, fair Madeline, to no rude infidel.'

XXXIX

    'Hark! 'tis an elfin-storm from faery land,
    'Of haggard seeming, but a boon indeed:
    'Arise—arise! the morning is at hand;—
    'The bloated wassaillers will never heed:—
    'Let us away, my love, with happy speed;
    'There are no ears to hear, or eyes to see,—
    'Drown'd all in Rhenish and the sleepy mead:
    'Awake! arise! my love, and fearless be,   350
'For o'er the southern moors I have a home for thee.'

XL

    She hurried at his words, beset with fears,
    For there were sleeping dragons all around,
    At glaring watch, perhaps, with ready spears—
    Down the wide stairs a darkling way they found.—
    In all the house was heard no human sound.
    A chain-droop'd lamp was flickering by each door;
    The arras, rich with horseman, hawk, and hound,
    Flutter'd in the besieging wind's uproar;
And the long carpets rose along the gusty floor.   360

XLI

    They glide, like phantoms, into the wide hall;
    Like phantoms, to the iron porch, they glide;

Where lay the Porter, in uneasy sprawl,
With a huge empty flaggon by his side:
The wakeful bloodhound rose, and shook his hide,
But his sagacious eye an inmate owns:
By one, and one, the bolts full easy slide:—
The chains lie silent on the footworn stones:—
The key turns, and the door upon its hinges groans.

XLII

And they are gone: ay, ages long ago   370
These lovers fled away into the storm.
That night the Baron dreamt of many a woe,
And all his warrior-guests, with shade and form
Of witch, and demon, and large coffin-worm,
Were long be-nightmar'd. Angela the old
Died palsy-twitch'd, with meagre face deform;
The Beadsman, after thousand aves told,
For aye unsought for slept among his ashes cold.

THE CAPTIVE DOVE

Ann Brontë   (1820–1849)

The youngest of five sisters, Brontë had little formal schooling, but held positions as governess between 1839 and 1845. These experiences formed the basis of her novel *Agnes Grey,* which was published under the pseudonym "Acton Bell" in 1847, along with Emily Brontë's *Wuthering Heights.* Her second novel, *The Tenant of Wildfell Hall,* was published the year before her death from tuberculosis.

"The Captive Dove" was begun in the spring of 1842 and is dated October 31, 1843.

Poor restless dove, I pity thee;
   And when I hear thy plaintive moan,
I mourn for thy captivity,
   And in thy woes forget mine own.

To see thee stand prepared to fly,
   And flap those useless wings of thine,
And gaze into the distant sky,
   Would melt a harder heart than mine.

In vain—in vain! Thou canst not rise;

Thy prison roof confines thee there;   10
Its slender wires delude thine eyes,
  And quench thy longings with despair.

Oh, thou wert made to wander free
  In sunny mead and shady grove,
And far beyond the rolling sea,
  In distant climes, at will to rove!

Yet, hadst thou but one gentle mate
  Thy little drooping heart to cheer,
And share with thee thy captive state,
  Thou couldst be happy even there.   20

Yes, even there, if, listening by,
  One faithful dear companion stood;
While gazing on her full bright eye,
  Thou mightst forget thy native wood.

But thou, poor solitary dove,
  Must make, unheard, thy joyless moan;
The heart that Nature formed to love
  Must pine, neglected, and alone.

THE WITCH

Mary Elizabeth Coleridge   (1861–1907)

Born in London, and at first more inclined toward painting than writing, Coleridge began to contribute to periodicals at the age of twenty. Her first novel was published in 1893, and her first book of poems in 1896. From 1895 until her death, Coleridge taught English literature at the Working Women's College of London. Her entire life was spent with her family; she died suddenly and unexpectedly following a brief illness.

"The Witch" is dated 1892.

I have walked a great while over the snow,
And I am not tall nor strong.
My clothes are wet, and my teeth are set,
And the way was hard and long.
I have wandered over the fruitful earth,
But I never came here before.
Oh, lift me over the threshold, and let me in at the door!

The cutting wind is a cruel foe.
I dare not stand in the blast.
My hands are stone, and my voice a groan,   10
And the worst of death is past.
I am but a little maiden still,
My little white feet are sore.
Oh, lift me over the threshold, and let me in at the door.

Her voice was the voice that women have,
Who plead for their heart's desire.
She came—she came—and the quivering flame
Sank and died in the fire.
It never was lit again on my hearth
Since I hurried across the floor,   20
To lift her over the threshold, and let her in at the door.

A ROSE FOR EMILY

William Harrison Faulkner   (1897–1962)

Faulkner grew up in Oxford, Mississippi. He joined the British Air Force in Canada after being rejected by the United States forces, but never saw action in the First World War. He attended the University of Mississippi but did not take a degree. In 1924 Faulkner published his first work, a book of pastoral poetry. He became a journalist in New Orleans, but after a short stay in Europe and the publication of his first novel, *Soldiers' Pay* (1926), he settled in Oxford to work on his novels of Yoknapatawpha County. In 1929, after the failure of his first marriage, he married Estelle Oldham, his high school sweetheart. He received the Nobel Prize in 1950 and Pulitzer Prizes in 1955 and 1962.

"A Rose for Emily" first appeared in *The Forum* for April 1930 and was reprinted in Faulkner's collection *These Thirteen* the following year.

I

When Miss Emily Grierson died, our whole town went to her funeral: the men through a sort of respectful affection for a fallen monument, the women mostly out of curiosity to see the inside of her house, which no one save an old manservant—a combined gardener and cook—had seen in at least ten years.

It was a big, squarish frame house that had once been white, decorated with cupolas and spires and scrolled balconies in the heavily lightsome style of the seventies, set on what had once been our most select street. But garages and cotton gins had encroached and obliterated even the august names of that neighborhood; only Miss Emily's house was left, lifting its stubborn and coquettish decay above the cotton wagons and the gasoline pumps—an eyesore among eyesores. And now Miss Emily had gone to join the representatives of those august names where they lay in the cedar-bemused cemetery among the ranked and anonymous graves of Union and Confederate soldiers who fell at the battle of Jefferson.

Alive, Miss Emily had been a tradition, a duty, and a care; a sort of hereditary obligation upon the town, dating from that day in 1894 when Colonel Sartoris, the mayor—he who fathered the edict that no Negro woman should appear on the streets without an apron—remitted her taxes, the dispensation dating from the death of her father on into perpetuity. Not that Miss Emily would have accepted charity. Colonel Sartoris invented an involved tale to the effect that Miss Emily's father had loaned money to the town, which the town, as a matter of business, preferred this way of repaying. Only a man of Colonel Sartoris' generation and thought could have invented it, and only a woman could have believed it.

When the next generation, with its more modern ideas, became mayors and aldermen, this arrangement created some little dissatisfaction. On the first of the year they mailed her a tax notice. February came, and there was no reply. They wrote her a formal letter, asking her to call at the sheriff's office at her convenience. A week later the mayor wrote her himself, offering to call or to send his car for her, and received in reply a note on paper of an archaic shape, in a thin, flowing calligraphy in faded ink, to the effect that she no longer went out at all. The tax notice was also enclosed, without comment.

They called a special meeting of the Board of Aldermen. A deputation waited upon her, knocked at the door through which no visitor had passed since she ceased giving china-painting lessons eight or ten years earlier. They were admitted by the old Negro into a dim hall from which a stairway mounted into still more shadow. It smelled of dust and disuse—a close, dank smell. The Negro led them into the parlor. It was furnished in heavy, leather-covered furniture. When the Negro opened the blinds of one window, they could see that the leather was cracked; and when they sat down, a faint dust rose sluggishly about their thighs, spinning with slow motes in the single sun-ray. On a tarnished gilt easel before the fireplace stood a crayon portrait of Miss Emily's father.

They rose when she entered—a small, fat woman in black, with a thin gold chain descending to her waist and vanishing into her belt, leaning on an ebony cane with a tarnished gold head. Her skeleton was small and spare; perhaps that was why what would have been merely plumpness in another was obesity in her. She looked bloated, like a body long submerged in motionless water, and of that pallid hue. Her eyes, lost in the fatty ridges of her face, looked like two small pieces of coal pressed into a lump of dough as they moved from face to another while the visitors stated their errand.

She did not ask them to sit. She just stood in the door and listened quietly until the spokesman came to a stumbling halt. Then they could hear the invisible watch ticking at the end of the gold chain.

Her voice was dry and cold. "I have no taxes in Jefferson. Colonel Sartoris explained it to me. Perhaps one of you can gain access to the city records and satisfy yourselves."

"But we have. We are the city authorities, Miss Emily. Didn't you get a notice from the sheriff, signed by him?"

"I received a paper, yes," Miss Emily said. "Perhaps he considers himself the sheriff . . . I have no taxes in Jefferson."

"But there is nothing on the books to show that, you see. We must go by the—"

"See Colonel Sartoris. I have no taxes in Jefferson."

"But, Miss Emily—"

"See Colonel Sartoris." (Colonel Sartoris had been dead almost ten years.) "I have no taxes in Jefferson. Tobe!" The Negro appeared. "Show these gentlemen out."

II

So she vanquished them, horse and foot, just as she had vanquished their fathers thirty years before about the smell. That was two years after her father's death and a short time after her sweetheart—the one we believed would marry her—had deserted her. After her father's death she went out very little; after her sweetheart went away, people hardly saw her at all. A few of the ladies had the temerity to call, but were not received, and the only sign of life about the place was the Negro man—a young man then—going in and out with a market basket.

"Just as if a man—any man—could keep a kitchen properly," the ladies said; so they were not surprised when the smell developed. It was another link between the gross, teeming world and the high and mighty Griersons.

A neighbor, a woman, complained to the mayor, Judge Stevens, eighty years old.

"But what will you have me do about it, madam?" he said.

"Why, send her word to stop it," the woman said. "Isn't there a law?"

"I'm sure that won't be necessary," Judge Stevens said, "It's probably just a snake or a rat that nigger of hers killed in the yard. I'll speak to him about it."

The next day he received two more complaints, one from a man who came in diffident deprecation. "We really must do something about it, Judge. I'd be the last one in the world to bother Miss Emily, but we've got to do something." That night the Board of Aldermen met—three graybeards and one younger man, a member of the rising generation.

"It's simple enough," he said. "Send her word to have her place cleaned up. Give her a certain time to do it in, and if she don't . . ."

"Dammit, sir," Judge Stevens said, "will you accuse a lady to her face of smelling bad?"

So the next night, after midnight, four men crossed Miss Emily's lawn and slunk about the house like burglars, sniffing along the base of the brickwork and at the cellar openings while one of them performed a regular sowing motion with his hand out of a sack slung from his shoulder. They broke open the cellar door and sprinkled lime there, and in all the outbuildings. As they recrossed the lawn, a window that had been dark was lighted and Miss Emily sat in it, the light behind her, and her upright torso motionless as that of an idol. They crept quietly across the lawn and into the shadow of the locusts that lined the street. After a week or two the smell went away.

That was when people had begun to feel really sorry for her. People in our town, remembering how old lady Wyatt, her great-aunt, had gone completely crazy at last, believed that the Griersons held themselves a little too high for what they really were. None of the young men were quite good enough for Miss Emily and such. We had long thought of them as a tableau, Miss Emily a slender figure in white in the background, her father a spraddled silhouette in the foreground, his back to her and clutching a horsewhip, the two of them framed by the back-flung front door. So when she got to be thirty and was still single, we were not pleased exactly, but vindicated; even with insanity in the family she wouldn't have turned down all of her chances if they had really materialized.

When her father died, it got about that the house was all that was left to her; and in a way, people were glad. At last they could pity Miss Emily. Being left alone, and a pauper, she had become humanized. Now she too would know the old thrill and the old despair of a penny more or less.

The day after his death all the ladies prepared to call at the house and offer condolence and aid, as is our custom. Miss Emily met them at the door, dressed as usual and with no trace of grief on her face. She told them that her father was not dead. She did that for three days, with the ministers calling on her, and the doctors, trying to persuade her to let them dispose of the body. Just as they were about to resort to law and force, she broke down, and they buried her father quickly.

We did not say she was crazy then. We believed she had to do that. We remembered all the young men her father had driven away, and we knew that with nothing left, she would have to cling to that which had robbed her, as people will.

III

She was sick for a long time. When we saw her again, her hair was cut short, making her look like a girl, with a vague resemblance to those angels in colored church windows—sort of tragic and serene.

The town had just let the contracts for paving the sidewalks, and in the summer after her father's death they began the work. The construction company came with niggers and mules and machinery, and a foreman named Homer Barron, a Yankee—a big, dark, ready man, with a big voice and eyes lighter than his face. The little boys would follow in groups to hear him cuss the niggers, and the niggers singing in time to the rise and fall of picks. Pretty soon he knew everybody in town. Whenever you heard a lot of laughing anywhere about the square, Homer Barron would be in the center of the group. Presently we began to see him and Miss Emily on Sunday afternoons driving in the yellow-wheeled buggy and the matched team of bays from the livery stable.

At first we were glad that Miss Emily would have an interest, because the ladies all said, "Of course a Grierson would not think seriously of a Northerner, a day laborer." But there were still others, older people, who said that even grief could not cause a real lady to forget *noblesse oblige*—without calling it *noblesse oblige*. They just said, "Poor Emily. Her kinsfolk should come to her." She had some kin in Alabama; but years ago her father had fallen out with them over the estate of old lady Wyatt, the crazy woman, and there was no communication between the two families. They had not even been represented at the funeral.

And as soon as the old people said, "Poor Emily," the whispering began. "Do you suppose it's really so?" they said to one another. "Of course it is. What else could . . ." This behind their hands; rustling of craned silk and satin behind jalousies closed upon the sun of Sunday afternoon as the thin, swift clop-clop-clop of the matched team passed: "Poor Emily."

She carried her head high enough—even when we believed that she was fallen. It was as if she demanded more than ever the recognition of her dignity as the last Grierson; as if it had wanted that touch of earthiness to reaffirm her imperviousness. Like when she bought the rat poison, the arsenic. That was over a year after they had begun to say "Poor Emily," and while the two female cousins were visiting her.

"I want some poison," she said to the druggist. She was over thirty then, still a slight woman, though thinner than usual, with cold, haughty black eyes in a face the flesh of which was strained across the temples and about the eye-sockets as you imagine a lighthouse-keeper's face ought to look. "I want some poison," she said.

"Yes, Miss Emily. What kind? For rats and such? I'd recom—"

"I want the best you have. I don't care what kind."

The druggist named several. "They'll kill anything up to an elephant. But what you want is—"

"Arsenic," Miss Emily said. "Is that a good one?"

"Is . . . arsenic? Yes ma'am. But what you want—"

"I want arsenic."

The druggist looked down at her. She looked back at him, erect, her face like a strained flag. "Why, of course," the druggist said. "If that's what you want. But the law requires you to tell what you are going to use it for."

Miss Emily just stared at him, her head tilted back in order to look him eye for eye, until he looked away and went and got the arsenic and wrapped it up. The Negro delivery boy brought her the package; the druggist didn't come back. When she opened the package at home there was written on the box, under the skull and bones: "For rats."

IV

So the next day we all said, "She will kill herself"; and we said it would be the best thing. When she had first begun to be seen with Homer Barron, we had said, "She will marry him." Then we said, "She will persuade him yet," because Homer himself had remarked—he liked men, and it was known that he drank with the younger men in the Elks' Club—that he was not a marrying man. Later we said, "Poor Emily" behind the jalousies as they passed on Sunday afternoon in the glittering buggy, Miss Emily with her head high and Homer Barron with his hat cocked and a cigar in his teeth, reins and whip in a yellow glove.

Then some of the ladies began to say that it was a disgrace to the town and a bad example to the young people. The men did not want to interfere, but at last the ladies forced the Baptist minister—Miss Emily's people were Episcopal—to call upon her. He would never divulge what happened during that interview, but he refused to go back again. The next Sunday they again drove about the streets, and the following day the minister's wife wrote to Miss Emily's relations in Alabama.

So she had blood-kin under her roof again and we sat back to watch developments. At first nothing happened. Then we were sure that they were to be married. We learned that Miss Emily had been to the jeweler's and ordered a man's set in silver, and with letters H. B. on each piece. Two days later we learned that she had bought a complete outfit of men's clothing, including a nightshirt, and we said, "They are married." We were really glad. We were glad because the two female cousins were even more Grierson than Miss Emily had ever been.

So we were not surprised when Homer Barron—the streets had been finished some time since—was gone. We were a little disappointed that there was not a public blowing-off, but we believed that he had gone on to prepare for Miss Emily's coming, or to give her a chance to get rid of the cousins. (By that time it was a cabal, and we were all Miss Emily's allies to help circumvent the cousins.) Sure enough, after another week they departed. And, as we had expected all along, within three days Homer Barron was back in town. A neighbor saw the Negro man admit him at the kitchen door at dusk one evening.

And that was the last we saw of Homer Barron. And of Miss Emily for some time. The Negro man went in and out with the market basket, but the front door remained closed. Now and then we would see her at a window for a moment, as the men did that night when they sprinkled the lime, but for almost six months she did not appear on the streets. Then we knew that this was to be expected too; as if that quality of her father which had thwarted her woman's life so many times had been too virulent and too furious to die.

When we next saw Miss Emily, she had grown fat and her hair was turning gray. During the next few years it grew grayer and grayer until it attained an even pepper-and-salt iron-gray, when it ceased turning. Up to the day of her death at seventy-four it was still that vigorous iron-gray, like the hair of an active man.

From that time on her front door remained closed, save for a period of six or seven years, when she was about forty, during which she gave lessons in china-painting. She fitted up a studio in one of the downstairs rooms, where the daughters and granddaughters of Colonel Sartoris' contemporaries were sent to her with the same regularity and in the same spirit that they were sent to church on Sundays with a twenty-five piece for the collection plate. Meanwhile her taxes had been remitted.

Then the newer generation became the backbone and the spirit of the town, and the painting pupils grew up and fell away and did not send their children to her with boxes of color and tedious brushes and pictures cut from the ladies' magazines. The front door closed upon the last one and remained closed for good. When the town got free postal delivery, Miss Emily alone refused to let them fasten the metal numbers above her door and attach a mailbox to it. She would not listen to them.

Daily, monthly, yearly we watched the Negro grow grayer and more stooped, going in and out with the market basket. Each December we sent her a tax notice, which would be returned by the post office a week later, unclaimed. Now and then we would see her in one of the downstairs windows—she had evidently shut up the top floor of the house—like the carven torso of an idol in a niche, looking or not looking at us, we could never tell which. Thus she passed from generation to generation—dear, inescapable, impervious, tranquil, and perverse.

And so she died. Fell ill in the house filled with dust and shadows, with only a doddering Negro man to wait on her. We did not even know she was sick; we had long since given up trying to get any information from the Negro. He talked to no one, probably not even to her, for his voice had grown harsh and rusty, as if from disuse.

She died in one of the downstairs rooms, in a heavy walnut bed with a curtain, her gray head propped on a pillow yellow and moldy with age and lack of sunlight.

V

The Negro met the first of the ladies at the front door and let them in, with their hushed, sibilant voices and their quick, curious glances, and then he disappeared. He walked right through the house and out the back and was not seen again.

The two female cousins came at once. They held the funeral on the second day, with the town coming to look at Miss Emily beneath a mass of bought flowers, with the crayon face of her father musing profoundly above the bier and the ladies sibilant and macabre; and the very old men—some in their brushed Confederate uniforms—on the porch and the lawn, talking of Miss Emily as if she had been a contemporary of theirs, believing that they had danced with her and courted her perhaps, confusing time with its mathematical progression, as the old do, to whom all the past is not a diminishing road but, instead, a huge meadow which no winter ever quite touches, divided from them now by the narrow bottle-neck of the most recent decade of years.

Already we knew that there was one room in the region above stairs which no one had seen in forty years, and which would have to be forced. They waited until Miss Emily was decently in the ground before they opened it.

The violence of breaking down the door seemed to fill this room with pervading dust. A thin, acrid pall as of the tomb seemed to lie everywhere upon this room decked and furnished as for a bridal: upon the valance curtains of faded rose color, upon the rose-shaded lights, upon the dressing table, upon the delicate array of crystal and the man's toilet things backed with tarnished silver, silver so tarnished that the monogram was obscured. Among them lay a collar and tie, as if they had just been removed, which, lifted, left upon the surface a pale crescent in the dust. Upon a chair hung the suit, carefully folded; beneath it the two mute shoes and the discarded socks.

The man himself lay in the bed.

For a long while we just stood there, looking down at the profound and fleshless grin. The body had apparently once lain in the attitude of an embrace, but now the long sleep that outlasts love, that conquers even the grimace of love, had cuckolded him. What was left of him, rotted beneath what was left of the nightshirt, had become inextricable from the bed in which he lay; and upon him and upon the pillow beside him lay that even coating of the patient and biding dust.

Then we noticed that in the second pillow was the indentation of a head. One of us lifted something from it, and leaning forward, that faint and invisible dust dry and acrid in the nostrils, we saw a long strand of iron-gray hair.

THE VIRGIN: SUPPLEMENTARY READING

Sherwood Anderson: "The Teacher," from *Winesburg, Ohio*
Anonymous: "King Horn"
Anonymous: "The Matchless Maid"
W. H. Auden: "Miss Gee: A Ballad"
Sally Benson: "Little Woman"

Cynewulf: *Juliana*
Charles Dickens: *Little Dorrit*
Theodore Dreiser: "The Second Choice"
George Eliot: *The Mill on the Floss*
T. S. Eliot: "Mariana" and "Portrait of a Lady"
James Joyce: "Evelene"
D. H. Lawrence: "The Horse Dealer's Daughter"
Katherine Mansfield: "The Daughters of the Late Colonel"
Carson McCullers: "Wunderkind"
William Morris: "The Haystack in the Floods"
Eugene O'Neill: *Mourning Becomes Electra*
Samuel Richardson: *Pamela*
Dante Gabriel Rossetti: "The Blessed Damozel"
Edmund Spenser: "Epithalamion"
Tennessee Williams: *The Glass Menagerie*

THE MISTRESS

François Boucher: *The Toilet of Venus* (French, 1751). [*The Metropolitan Museum of Art. Bequest of William K. Vanderbilt, 1920.*]

The change from virgin to sexual woman is one from innocence to experience and from timelessness to existence in time. The virgin represents the purity of Apollonian form; the sexual heroine embodies the Dionysian principle of energy. Portrayed in vibrating lines in the drawing of Loïe Fuller by Thomas Theodor Heine (1899), the female figure is the emblem of experience. The archetypal sexual woman is associated with the earth and its fertility. She is Venus rising from the sea and Demeter, the earth mother. In this guise she is celebrated for her naturalness by poets such as Sir Walter Ralegh in "Nature that washt her hands in milke," Robert Herrick in "Cherry Ripe," and George Peele in a song from *The Old Wives' Tale:*

When as the rye reach to the chin,
And chopcherry, chopcherry ripe within,
Strawberries swimming in the cream,
And schoolboys playing in the stream;
Then oh, then oh, then oh, my true love said,
Till that time come again
She could not live a maid!

The sexual woman who is defined in terms of a man is the mistress. Portraits of the mistress in literature divide generally into those of the praised sexual woman, the temptress, and the fallen woman. Female authors who associate sexuality with wisdom and creativity, like Denise Levertov, in "Our Bodies," exalt their sexuality and the beauty of their bodies. Male writers typically praise the sexual woman for physical rather than spiritual beauty. W. B. Yeats writes, in "For Anne Gregory," that "only God, my dear, / Could love you for yourself alone / And not your yellow hair." They may celebrate sexuality itself by praising the love object, as in Edmund Waller's "On a Girdle," Robert Herrick's "To Her Hair," and E. E. Cummings's "i like my body when it is with your body." Writers also exalt the sexual woman who symbolizes fertility. Earth mothers—such as Molly Bloom, in James Joyce's *Ulysses,* and Olga, in Tennessee Williams's "The Mattress by the Tomato Patch"—seem wise and powerful both because they exist totally within the natural world and hence understand life and because their actions have the power of a force of nature.

The sexual woman also may be admired for her vitality and attractiveness and for her freedom from restraint, her unconventionality, and her control over men. Lena Grove, in William Faulkner's *Light in August,* for example, refuses to play the role of the "ruined woman" and manages to make Byron Bunch take care of her without relinquishing control over her own destiny. In "Portrait d'une Femme," Ezra Pound admires his subject for her freedom because there is "nothing that's quite your own." Robert Burns's maid in "Sodger Laddie" says, "Full soon I grew sick of my sanctified sot; / The regiment at large for a husband I got. . . ." George Bernard Shaw's Mrs. Warren, who is a prosperous professional mistress, and Jean Genet's Irma, who runs a brothel in *The Balcony,* are admired for their strength, for their mastery of the circumstances in which they have found themselves, and for their professional and business talents. Such sexual women are portrayed as heroes because they control their own lives.

Male praise of the mistress frequently appears in the form of a comparison between the nurturing, unthreatening selflessness of the "whore with the heart of gold" and the emotional independence of the frigid wife or the aggressiveness of the intellectual or professional woman. Like all heroines, the sexual woman may be viewed sympathetically when she is powerless and suffering. If she controls a man, however, or if she benefits from her sexuality, she is likely to be condemned as a deliberately seductive temptress who leads men to destruction. In Christian terms, all women are suspect because Eve brought sin, chaos, and death into the world. Similarly, in Greek mythology Pandora is made responsible for the unleashing of evil. Likewise, Helen causes the Trojan War, and Guinevere instigates the fall of Camelot.

Although Thomas Campion prefers "kind Amaryllis, / The wanton country maid" to her more sophisticated urban counterpart, even the innocent sexual woman is seen as potentially destructive. When she is associated with the physical world of nature, she may be seen as a lesser being to be left for the finer world of the spirit. Sir Phillip Sidney writes: "Leave me, o Love, which reachest but to dust; / And thou, my mind, aspire to higher things." Poets describe their romantic attraction to her in metaphors of illness and entrapment. Edmund Spenser refers, in "What guile is this?," to the golden snare of her hairnet and to the folly of coveting fetters even though they are golden. Because the sexual woman's beauty is considered a snare and a danger to man's soul, she comes to represent mystery and the spiritual power of evil. In the medieval romance *Sir Gawain and the Green Knight,* the two types of sexual women—the well-meaning Guinevere, who commits adultery with Launcelot, and the intentionally destructive Morgan le Fey—both appear. The idea of the sexual woman as morally corrupt leads Jonathan Swift to describe a woman's body as disgusting. The sexual woman may even be portrayed in literature as an animal, as she is in Edward Field's "She." Germaine Greer, in *The Female Eunuch,* points out that the association of a woman with sexuality and evil may explain why many women view their bodies as objects of fear or disgust.

When negatively portrayed, sexuality is an uncontrollable force which entraps men, as Homer's Sirens entrap Ulysses. In John Keats's "La Belle Dame sans Merci," the woman who wreaks destruction and death on her helpless male victim is a symbol of the overpowering nature of both sexuality and poetic inspiration. In the Christian medieval tradition, where the association of woman with sex and sin was strong, it was fashionable to make lists of famous men who had been destroyed by such women: the list that appears in *Sir Gawain and the Green Knight* includes Adam, Solomon, Samson, and David. Thomas Otway, in *The Orphan,* sums up this misogynous viewpoint:

> What mighty Ills have not been done by Woman?
> Who was it betray'd the Capitol? A Woman.
> Who lost *Mark Antony* the world? A Woman.
> Who was the cause of a long ten years War,
> And laid at last Old-Troy in Ashes? Woman.
> Destructive, damnable, deceitful Woman.

In Jungian terms, the denigration of the sexual woman is explained by the principle of projection. People project into others qualities that they cannot accept in themselves. This theory may explain why the Puritans persecuted witches, who they believed had sexual intercourse with the devil. Men associate sexuality with women; the Anglo-Saxon identifies sexuality with dark-skinned people; and the upper and middle classes associate it with the working class. Thus the sexual woman in

American literature, like Mark Twain's Roxana, in *Pudd'nhead Wilson,* may be black and poor. In European literature she is often Jewish. If linked with evil, the sexual woman usually has dark characteristics, such as black hair. In literary criticism, therefore (for example, Leslie Fiedler's *Love and Death in the American Novel*), she is known as the "dark woman." At the conclusion of Herman Melville's *Pierre,* the "dark" heroine envelops the destroyed hero in her long black tresses. In Nathaniel Hawthorne's "Rappaccini's Daughter," the evil which is equated with sexuality is a force within the dark-haired heroine of which she is an innocent victim. Traditionally, the dark woman appears together with the virginal light woman—for example, Molly Seagrim and Sophia Western, in Henry Fielding's *Tom Jones.* However, if both the light and the dark heroines are virginal, as in James Fenimore Cooper's *The Last of the Mohicans,* William Shakespeare's *Much Ado about Nothing,* and the Grimm brothers' fairy tale of "Snow White and Rose Red," the dark woman is active and strong, and the light woman is passive and conventional.

The virginal light woman provides the male hero with spiritual inspiration; the dark woman initiates him into the world of knowledge and experience. According to Carl Jung, a man must confront his anima, his female part, to achieve psychic and spiritual integration. In positive guise, the anima may appear as the virginal and beautiful Beatrice, who makes possible Dante's vision of paradise, or she may appear as Poe's sexual Ligeia, who opens the door to the mysteries of the unconscious mind. If a man represses his female qualities, his anima may appear as the temptress who can destroy him. However, although the anima figure threatens him with psychic or spiritual damnation that is identified with death, his initiation has come to be called the "fortunate fall" when symbolic death is followed by the possibility of rebirth.

Because portraits of the temptress are archetypal projections of the male fear of sexuality or of the compelling, threatening mystery of the unconscious, they do not realistically portray individualized women. The characterizations combine sexuality, violence, and indifference. T. S. Eliot's Rachel *née* Rabinovitch "yawns and draws a stocking up"; she "tears at the grapes with murderous paws"; and "she and the lady in the cape / are suspect, thought to be in league. . . ."

The woman in Edward Arlington Robinson's "Another Dark Lady" has cloven feet like the devil. Female destructiveness is the result of beauty coupled with deception, but the appearance of the temptress is frightening as well as compelling in Samuel Daniel's "Ulysses and the Siren," Robert Herrick's "The Hag," Dante Gabriel Rossetti's "Card Dealer," the anonymous "Thomas the Rhymer," and John Keats's "La Belle Dame sans Merci" and "Lamia." Samuel Taylor Coleridge, in "The Rime of the Ancient Mariner," envisions such a fearsome temptress:

> Her lips were red, her looks were free,
> Her locks were yellow as gold:
> Her skin was as white as leprosy,
> The nightmare Life-in-Death was she,
> Who thicks man's blood with cold.

In the debate over who is responsible for unchastity, Eve or Don Juan, William Habington writes "against those who lay unchastity to the sex of women." William Congreve's song in *Love for Love* concludes, however, that "the Nymph may be chaste, that has never been Try'd"; and John Donne, speaking "In Defense of Woman's Inconstancy," explains it as part of her charm. Many literary works represent love as a crime, and a number of classical couples have shared the blame and punishment: Tristan and Isolde, Eloise and Abelard, Hero and Leander, Pyramus and Thisbe, and Launcelot and Guinevere. The sins of Launcelot and Guinevere, which are described in famous works by Sir Thomas Mallory; Alfred, Lord Tennyson; and William Morris, result in the fall of Camelot. The evils of lust frequently also lead to tragic personal consequences. Death by poison is a favorite. Most often, however, because of the identification of woman, sex, and sin, it is only the woman who is punished, and often both author and reader see this as justified. Oliver Goldsmith portrays the woman who stoops to folly as guilty though betrayed. Furthermore, it is her duty to save her lover by bringing about his repentance. In the Victorian period, sexual repression resulted in a veritable obsession with the "fallen woman." The ambivalence with which she is treated suggests she is a scapegoat. Here men project fear and contempt not only for their own sexuality but also for their own vulnerability because, as in Hardy's *Tess of the D'Urbervilles,* it is often her openness, sensitivity, and trust, as much as her sexuality, that cause her downfall.

The sufferings of the mistress often result from her dependence on a man. The archetypal sexual woman is "in time" because of her association with nature; the realistic sexual heroine lives in the moment because she cannot afford to think about the future, in which her beauty will fade and her lover may leave her. Praise for the aging or dead mistress is the theme of F. R. Higgins's "Song for the Clatter-Bones" and John Kinsella's "Lament for Mrs. Mary Moore," which ends, "What shall I do for pretty girls / Now my old bawd is dead?" However, portraits of the aging sexual woman, such as those in Samuel Daniel's "When Winter Snows," John Crowe Ransom's "Blue Girls," and William Butler Yeats's "When You Are Old," assume that the old woman will be unattractive to men and, as a result, will be lonely. The aging Hollywood star is the subject of Robert Frost's poem "Provide, Provide":

> The witch that came (the withered hag)
> To wash the steps with pail and rag,
> Was once the beauty Abishag,
> The picture pride of Hollywood.

The stereotype of the foolish old woman who is still pursuing love is a staple of Restoration comedy. A delightful example is Lady Wishfort, in William Congreve's *The Way of the World.* In more realistic portraits the sexual woman sees time, aging, and disease as her enemies. The woman in Matthew Prior's "Lady Who Offers Her Looking Glass to Venus" prays:

> Venus, take my votive glass,
> Since I am not what I was;
> What from this day I shall be,
> Venus, let me never see.

A more immediate threat to the young woman is stated in a song from Thomas Southern's "Sir Anthony Love": "For Love is but Discovery, / When that is made, the Pleasure's done." Often love and marriage are promised in return for sex, but are not forthcoming. In Oliver Goldsmith's *The Vicar of Wakefield,* the rake may even arrange a phony wedding to seduce the unsuspecting woman into immorality. In this connection, men are portrayed as betrayers and deceivers, and women as "fallen" victims who forfeit their sexual attractiveness and social respectability. The classic male seducers include Don Juan; Rochester, in *Jane Eyre;* Heathcliff, in *Wuthering Heights;* and Alec D'Urberville, in Thomas Hardy's *Tess of the D'Urbervilles.* Even though the female fall is not "fortunate," the literally portrayed fallen woman may be presented sympathetically because she is a victim. Samuel Richardson's Pamela realizes that the options for fallen women are few in the eighteenth century. She writes to Mrs. Jarvis:

> Let me ask you, if he can stoop to like such a poor girl as me, as perhaps he may (for I have read of things almost as strange, from great men to poor damsels), What can it be *for*—He may condescend, perhaps to think I may be good enough for his harlot; and those things don't disgrace men that ruin poor women, as the world goes. And so if I was wicked enough, he would keep me till I was undone, and till his mind changed; for even wicked men, I have read, soon grow weary of wickedness with the same person, and love variety. Well, then, poor Pamela must be turned off, and looked upon as a vile abandoned creature, and every body would despise her; ay, and *justly* too, Mrs. Jarvis; for she that can't keep her virtue, ought to live in disgrace.

Even when she is blameless, like Richardson's Clarissa, the fallen woman pays the price for sin, while her seducer goes unpunished in this world if not in the next. Rossetti's Victorian painting *Found* portrays a cowering fallen woman hiding from her country lover, Andrew, who has brought his vegetables to town. In William Wordsworth's "The Thorn" and the Mexican folktale "La Llorona," the fallen woman and raped woman, respectively, have been forced by shame and poverty to kill their illegitimate children and to go insane from grief and guilt. Portraits of the fallen and aging woman reveal that the mistress's plight is analogous to the spinster's. She is praised and rewarded when she is desirable to men, but if she becomes morally or physically unattractive to men— if she loses her beauty or her hymen—she may be reviled, ridiculed, or pitied. In a society in which a woman's economic and social position is determined by a man, the cast-off mistress may find herself suffering from poverty and social ostracism.

On the symbolic level the situation of the raped or fallen woman who is totally in the power of her ravisher may be used as the vehicle for exploration of positive transcendental experience. In W. B. Yeats's "Leda and the Swan," Muriel Rukeyser's "Mortal Girl," and Emily Dickinson's "I started Early—Took my Dog," the rape or seduction is likened to a religious visitation, and the relationship of rapist to victim is symbolic of humankind's relationship to God. "Leda" assumes that the power relationship between God and humanity is analogous to that between men and women. In each case the powerless victim reveres the powerful victimizer and sees "good" as man's will or God's will. John Donne uses a similar sexual metaphor for his own relationship to the deity in "Batter my heart, three person'd God."

The selections that follow reflect our culture's ambivalence about sexuality and the mysteries of Dionysian energy, and they dramatize the ways in which this ambivalence affects the life of the unmarried sexual woman. Like the virgin, the mistress learns that she must marry to be socially respectable. A consideration of the plights of the virgin and the mistress, therefore, leads us to the subject of the helpmate.

KEMP OWYNE

This anonymous ballad recounts an adventure of Sir Gawain which is not recorded elsewhere in the body of literature concerning King Arthur and his knights. In *English and Scottish Popular Ballads* (1883–1896), Francis James Child traces the fundamental elements of this ballad back beyond its northern Scottish form to a Danish ballad found in a sixteenth-century manuscript and back beyond that to an Icelandic saga. The idea that a kiss can undo a spell is common in folklore, as is the idea that the love of a man can either awaken or tame a young woman.

1
Her mother died when she was young,
    Which gave her cause to make great moan;
Her father married the warst woman
    That ever lived in Christendom.

2
She served her with foot and hand,
    In every thing that she could dee,
Till once, in an unlucky time,
    She threw her in ower Craigy's sea.

3
Says, 'Lie you there, dove Isabel,
    And all my sorrows lie with thee;
Till Kemp Owyne come ower the sea,   10
    And borrow you with kisses three,
Let all the warld do what they will,
    Oh borrowed shall you never be!'

4
Her breath grew strang, her hair grew lang,
    And twisted thrice about the tree,
And all the people, far and near,
    Thought that a savage beast was she.

5
These news did come to Kemp Owyne,
    Where he lived, far beyond the sea;
He hasted him to Craigy's sea,   20
    And on the savage beast lookd he.

6
Her breath was strang, her hair was lang,
    And twisted was about the tree,

And with a swing she came about:
  'Come to Craigy's sea, and kiss with me.

7
'Here is a royal belt,' she cried,
  'That I have found in the green sea;
And while your body it is on,
  Drawn shall your blood never be;   30
But if you touch me, tail or fin,
  I vow my belt your death shall be.'

8
He stepped in, gave her a kiss,
  The royal belt he brought him wi;
Her breath was strang, her hair was lang,
  And twisted twice about the tree,
And with a swing she came about:
  'Come to Craigy's sea, and kiss with me.

9
'Here is a royal ring,' she said,
  'That I have found in the green sea;   40
And while your finger it is on,
  Drawn shall your blood never be;
But if you touch me, tail or fin,
  I swear my ring your death shall be.'

10
He stepped in, gave her a kiss,
  The royal ring he brought him wi;
Her breath was strang, her hair was lang,
  And twisted ance about the tree,
And with a swing she came about:
  'Come to Craigy's sea, and kiss with me.   50

11
'Here is a royal brand,' she said,
  'That I have found in the green sea;
And while your body it is on,
  Drawn shall your blood never be;
But if you touch me, tail or fin,
  I swear my brand your death shall be.'

12
He stepped in, gave her a kiss,
  The royal brand he brought him wi;
Her breath was sweet, her hair grew short,
  And twisted nane about the tree,   60
And smilingly she came about,
  As fair a woman as fair could be.

DEFILED IS MY NAME FULL SORE

Anne Boleyn   (1507?–1536)

Boleyn's father and grandfather were both influential ministers under Henry VIII, and her sister Mary, was, for a brief time, Henry's mistress. Her planned marriage to Henry Percy was broken off at the King's insistence. He took an interest in her, and she accompanied him to France in 1531; they were secretly married in January 1533. The marriage was announced when Henry's marriage to his first wife, Catherine of Aragon, was declared void. Boleyn was crowned in June, and in September gave birth to the future Queen Elizabeth. Boleyn suffered a miscarriage in 1534 and had a stillborn son in 1536, after which Henry felt she could not provide him with a male heir and had her committed to the Tower on charges of adultery. Four of her reputed lovers were executed for treason. She and her brother, who was also charged with being her lover, were condemned at a trial presided over by their uncle. Protesting her innocence to the last, she was beheaded.

"Defiled is my name full sore" is attributed to Anne Boleyn. If the poem is actually from her hand, it was most likely written in the Tower.

Defiled is my name full sore
  Through cruel spite and false report,
That I may say for evermore,
  Farewell, my joy! adieu comfort!
For wrongfully ye judge of me
  Unto my fame a mortal wound,
Say what ye list, it will not be,
  Ye seek for that can not be found.

NATURE THAT WASHT HER HANDS IN MILKE

Sir Walter Ralegh   (1552?–1618)

Born in Devonshire, Ralegh was an adventurer *par excellence.* He fought with the Huguenot army in France in 1569 and served in subduing rebellion in Ireland in 1580. He led numerous expeditions against the Spaniards and the Portuguese, and he headed two gold-hunting expeditions to South America. He also served with Essex in the Azores. A favorite of Queen Elizabeth, Ralegh lost her favor by marrying Elizabeth Throgmorton, her maid of honor. Accused of atheism and conspiracy, he was beheaded by James I.

"Nature that washt her hands in milke," though difficult to date, was probably written between 1589 and 1593.

Nature that washt her hands in milke
   And had forgott to dry them,
In stead of earth tooke snow and silke
   At Loves request to trye them,
If she a mistresse could compose
To please Loves fancy out of those.

Her eyes he would should be of light,
   A Violett breath, and Lipps of Jelly,
Her haire not blacke, nor over bright,
   And of the softest downe her Belly,   10
And for her inside hee'ld have it
Only of wantonnesse and witt.

At Loves entreaty, such a one
   Nature made, but with her beauty
She hath framed a heart of stone,
   So as Love by ill destinie
Must dye for her whom nature gave him
Because her darling would not save him.

But Time which nature doth despise,
   and rudely gives her love the lye,   20
Makes hope a foole, and sorrow wise,
   His hands doth neither wash, nor dry,
But being made of steele and rust,
Turnes snow, and silke, and milke to dust.

The Light, the Belly, lipps and breath,
   He dimms, discolours, and destroyes,
With those he feedes, but fills not death,
   Which sometimes were the foode of Joyes;
Yea Time doth dull each lively witt,
And dryes all wantonnes with it.   30

Oh cruell Time which takes in trust
   Our youth, our Joyes and all we have,
And payes us but with age and dust,
   Who in the darke and silent grave
When we have wandred all our wayes
Shutts up the story of our dayes.

MY MISTRESS' EYES ARE NOTHING LIKE THE SUN

William Shakespeare (1564–1616)

Shakespeare was born at Stratford-on-Avon. His father, a wool dealer, apparently ran into financial difficulties that kept Shakespeare from attending either Cambridge or Oxford. In 1582 he married Anne Hathaway, some eight years his senior, but he left her to go to London. By 1592 Shakespeare was established as an actor. In 1593 he published *Venus and Adonis; The Rape of Lucrece* was published in 1594. Thereafter, Shakespeare's writing talents were turned to the stage. Although the sonnets were presumably written in the early 1590s, they were not published until 1609. In 1611 Shakespeare retired to Stratford. He was survived by his wife and two married daughters.

"My mistress' eyes" is Sonnet 130 of his 154 sonnets. It begins as a satire on the courtly love sonnet, in which the woman is praised for her various perfect physical attributes, which are equated with their perfect equivalents in nature.

My mistress' eyes are nothing like the sun;
Coral is far more red than her lips' red;
If snow be white, why then her breasts are dun;
If hairs be wires, black wires grow on her head.
I have seen roses damask'd, red and white,
But no such roses see I in her cheeks;
And in some perfumes is there more delight
Than in the breath that from my mistress reeks.
I love to hear her speak, yet well I know
That music hath a far more pleasing sound;
I grant I never saw a goddess go;
My mistress, when she walks, treads on the ground:
　　And yet, by heaven, I think my love as rare
　　As any she beli'd with false compare.

BEAUTY IS BUT A PAINTED HELL

Thomas Campion (1567–1619)

Born in London, Campion lost both his parents by the age of thirteen. Although he spent four years at Peterhouse College, he did not take a degree. He entered Grey's

Inn in 1586 to read law, but was never admitted to the bar. In 1591 Campion's first poems appeared, in Latin, and he went to the Continent and participated in the siege of Rouen. He later studied, but did not practice, medicine. Campion's real and greatest interest was in music, and his fame rests upon the airs for which he wrote both text and music. He never married.

"Beauty is but a painted hell" is from Campion's *Fourth Book of Aryes,* originally published in an undated edition around 1617.

Beauty is but a painted hell:
      Ay me, ay me!
She wounds them that admire it,
She kills them that desire it.
      Give her pride but fuel,
      No fire is more cruel.

Pity from every heart is fled:
      Ay me, ay me!
Since false desire could borrow
Tears of dissembled sorrow,
      Constant vows turn truthless,
      Love cruel, Beauty ruthless.

Sorrow can laugh, and Fury sing:
      Ay me, ay me!
My raving griefs discover
I lived too true a lover.
      The first step to madness
      Is the excess of sadness.

ON A GIRDLE

Edmund Waller   (1606–1687)

Born into the gentry, Waller attended Cambridge and left without taking a degree. In 1631 he married Anne Banke, an orphan heiress. The aldermen of London, who acted as Banke's guardians, objected to the marriage; however, Charles I intervened on Waller's behalf. A Royalist, Waller was involved in a plot in 1643 to hand London over to the King; however, the plot failed, and Waller was first imprisoned and then exiled by Cromwell. Cromwell recalled him in 1651 and appointed him commissioner of trade. At the Restoration of Charles II, Waller wrote a poem in praise of the King, which won him royal favor, and he sat in every Parliament from 1661 until his death.

"On a Girdle" first appeared in *Poems* (1645).

That which her slender waist confined,
Shall now my joyful temples bind;
No monarch but would give his crown,
His arms might do what this has done.
   It was my heaven's extremest sphere,
The pale which held that lovely deer.
My joy, my grief, my hope, my love,
Did all within this circle move!
   A narrow compass! and yet there
Dwelt all that's good, and all that's fair;
Give me but what this ribband bound,
Take all the rest the sun goes round.

THE DISAPPOINTMENT

Aphra Amis Behn   (1640–1689)

Although the details of her early life are unknown, it appears she spent some time in Surinam, South America (the setting of her novel *Oroonoko*), where her father may have been lieutenant governor. Returning to London after her father's death, she married a Dutch merchant named Behn. He died in 1665, leaving her impoverished, and it is likely that she spent some time in debtor's prison. She was employed by Charles II as a secret agent in the Low Countries but was never paid for her services. Turning to writing, she became the first woman in England to earn her own living by her pen. Although she considered herself primarily a poet, she also wrote plays and prose fiction. She was buried in the Poets' Corner of Westminster Abbey.

"The Disappointment" appeared in *Poems on Several Occasions* (1684).

One day the amorous Lysander,
By an impatient passion swayed,
Surprised fair Cloris, that loved maid,
Who could defend herself no longer.
All things did with his love conspire;
The gilded planet of the day,
In his gay chariot drawn by fire,
Was now descending to the sea,
And left no light to guide the world
But what from Cloris' brighter eyes was hurled.

In a lone thicket made for love,
Silent as yielding maid's consent,
She with a charming languishment,
Permits his force, yet gently strove;
Her hands his bosom softly meet,
But not to put him back designed,
Rather to draw 'em on inclined:
Whilst he lay trembling at her feet,
Resistance 'tis in vain to show;
She wants to pow'r to say—*Ah! what d'ye do?*   20

Her bright eyes sweet and yet severe,
Where love and shame confus'dly strive,
Fresh vigor to Lysander give;
And breathing faintly in his ear,
She cried—*Cease, cease—your vain desire,*
Or I'll call out—what would you do?
My dearer honor ev'n to you
I cannot, must not give—Retire,
or take this life, whose chiefest part
I gave you with the conquest of my heart.   30

But he as much unused to fear,
As he was capable of love,
The blessed minutes to improve
Kisses her mouth, her neck, her hair;
Each touch her new desire alarms;
His burning, trembling hand he prest
Upon her swelling snowy breast,
While she lay panting in his arms.
All her unguarded beauties lie
The spoils and trophies of the enemy.   40

And now without respect or fear
He seeks the object of his vows,
(His love no modesty allows)
By swift degrees advancing—where
His daring hand that altar seized,
Where gods of love do sacrifice:
That awful throne, that paradise
Where rage is calmed, and anger pleased;
That fountain where delight still flows,
And gives the universal world respose.   50

Her balmy lips encount'ring his,
Their bodies, as their souls, are joined;
Where both in transports unconfined
Extend themselves upon the moss.

Cloris half dead and breathless lay;
Her soft eyes cast a humid light
Such as divides the day and night;
Or falling stars, whose fires decay:
And now no signs of life she shows,
But what in short-breathed sighs returns and goes.   60

He saw how at her length she lay;
He saw her rising bosom bare;
Her loose thin robes, through which appear
A shape designed for love and play;
Abandoned by her pride and shame
She does her softest joys dispense,
Off'ring her virgin-innocence
A victim to love's sacred flame;
While the o'er-ravished shepherd lies
Unable to perform the sacrifice.   70

Ready to taste a thousand joys,
The too transported hapless swain
Found the vast pleasure turned to pain;
Pleasure which too much love destroys:
The willing garments by he laid,
And heaven all opened to his view.
Mad to possess, himself he threw
On the defenceless lovely maid.
But oh what envying god conspires
To snatch his power, yet leave him the desire!   80

Nature's support, (without whose aid
She can no human being give)
Itself now wants the art to live;
Faintness its slackened nerves invade:
In vain th'enraged youth essayed
To call its fleeting vigor back;
No motion 'twill from motion take;
Excess of love his love betrayed:
In vain he toils, in vain commands:
The insensible fell weeping in his hand.   90

In this so amorous cruel strife,
Where love and fate were too severe,
The poor Lysander in despair
Renounced his reason with his life:
Now all the brisk and active fire
That should the nobler part inflame
Served to increase his rage and shame,
And left no spark for new desire:

Not all her naked charms could move
Or calm that rage that had debauched his love.   100

Cloris returning from the trance
Which love and soft desire had bred,
Her timorous hand she gently laid
(Or guided by design or chance)
Upon that fabulous Priapus,
That potent god, as poets feign:
But never did young shepherdess,
Gath'ring the fern upon the plain,
More nimbly draw her fingers back,
Finding beneath the verdant leaves a snake: 110

Than Cloris her fair hand withdrew,
Finding that god of her desires
Disarmed of all his awful fires,
And cold as flow'rs bathed in the morning dew.
Who can the nymph's confusion guess?
The blood forsook the hinder place,
And strewed with blushes all her face,
Which both disdain and shame exprest:
And from Lysander's arms she fled,
Leaving him fainting on the gloomy bed.   120

Like lightning through the grove she hies,
Or Daphne from the Delphic God,
No print upon the grassy road
She leaves, t'instruct pursuing eyes.
The wind that wantoned in her hair
And with her ruffled garments played,
Discovered in the flying maid
All that the gods e'er made, if fair.
So Venus, when her Love was slain,
With fear and haste flew o'er the fatal plain.   130

The nymph's resentments none but I
Can well imagine or condole:
But none can guess Lysander's soul,
But those who swayed his destiny.
His silent griefs swell up to storms,
And not on god his fury spares;
He cursed his birth, his fate, his stars;
But more the shepherdess's charms,
Whose soft bewitching influence
Had damned him to the hell of impotence.   140

SATURDAY: THE SMALL POX

Lady Mary Wortley Montagu   (1689–1762)

Born into the nobility, Mary Wortley formed a close friendship with Anne Montagu. After her death in 1709, Edward Montagu continued his sister's correspondence with Mary Wortley, and they eloped in 1712. She accompanied him to Turkey, where he was ambassador from 1716 to 1718. Her letters concerning that then-unfamiliar country were well received in England because of their wit and accuracy. After her own beauty was marred by smallpox, she brought back to England the practice of inoculation, which she fervently advocated. In 1739 she left her husband and lived alone in Italy until 1761, returning to England only after his death. She died of cancer.

"Saturday: The Small Pox" appeared as one of the *Town Eclogues* in 1715.

The wretched Flavia on her couch reclined,
Thus breathed the anguish of a wounded mind,
A glass reversed in her right hand she bore,
For now she shunned the face she sought before.
    "How am I changed! alas! how am I grown
A frightful spectre, to myself unknown!
Where's my complexion, where my radiant bloom,
That promised happiness for years to come?
Then with what pleasure I this face surveyed!
To look once more, my visits oft delayed!   10
Charmed with the view, a fresher red would rise,
And a new life shot sparkling from my eyes!

    "Ah! faithless glass, my wonted bloom restore;
Alas! I rave, that bloom is now no more!
The greatest good the gods on men bestow,
Ev'n youth itself to me is useless now.
There was a time (oh! that I could forget!)
When opera-tickets poured before my feet;
And at the ring, where brightest beauties shine,
The earliest cherries of the spring were mine.   20
Witness, O Lilly; and thou, Motteux, tell,
How much japan these eyes have made ye sell.
With what contempt ye saw me oft despise
The humble offer of the raffled prize!
For at the raffle still each prize I bore,
With scorn rejected, or with triumph wore!
Now beauty's fled, and presents are no more!

"For me the patriot has the House forsook,
And left debates to catch a passing look:
For me the soldier has soft verses writ: 30
For me the beau has aimed to be a wit.
For me the wit to nonsense was betrayed;
The gamester has for me his dun delayed,
And overseen the card he would have played.
The bold and haughty by success made vain,
Awed by my eyes, have trembled to complain;
The bashful squire touched by a wish unknown,
Has dared to speak with spirit not his own;
Fired by one wish, all did alike adore;
Now beauty's fled, and lovers are no more!   40

"As round the room I turn my weeping eyes,
New unaffected scenes of sorrow rise.
Far from my sight that killing picture bear,
The face disfigure, and the canvas tear;
That picture which with pride I used to show,
The lost resemblance but upbraids me now.
And thou, my toilette! where I oft have sat,
While hours unheeded passed in deep debate,
How curls should fall, or where a patch to place,
If blue or scarlet best became my face;   50
Now on some happier nymph your aid bestow;
On fairer heads, ye useless jewels, glow!
No borrowed lustre can my charms restore;
Beauty is fled, and dress is now no more!

"Ye meaner beauties I permit ye shine;
Go, triumph in the hearts that once were mine;
But 'midst your triumphs with confusion know,
'Tis to my ruin all your arms ye owe.
Would pitying heaven restore my wonted mien,
Ye still might move unthought of and unseen: 60
But oh, how vain, how wretched is the boast
Of beauty faded, and of empire lost!
What now is left but weeping, to deplore
My beauty fled, and empire now no more?

"Ye cruel chemists, what withheld your aid?
Could no pomatum save a trembling maid?
How false and trifling is that art ye boast!
No art can give me back my beauty lost.
In tears, surrounded by my friends I lay,
Masked o'er and trembling at the sight of day;   70
Mirmillio came my fortune to deplore,
(A golden-headed cane well carved he bore)

Cordials, he cried, my spirits must restore!
Beauty is fled, and spirit is no more!

"Galen, the grave, officious Squirt was there,
With fruitless grief and unavailing care;
Machaon too, the great Machaon, known
By his red cloak and his superior frown;
And why, he cried, this grief and this despair,
You shall again be well, again be fair;   80
Believe my oath; (with that an oath he swore)
False was his oath; my beauty is no more!

"Cease hapless maid, no more thy tale pursue.
Forsake mankind, and bid the world adieu!
Monarchs and beauties rule with equal sway;
All strive to serve, and glory to obey:
Alike unpitied when deposed they grow,
Men mock the idol of their former vow.

"Adieu! ye parks!—in some obscure recess,
Where gentle streams will weep at my distress,   90
Where no false friend will in my grief take part
And mourn my ruin with a joyful heart;
There let me live in some deserted place,
There hide in shades this lost inglorious face,
Plays, operas, circles, I no more must view!
My toilette, patches, all the world adieu!"

ELOÏSA TO ABELARD

Alexander Pope   (1688–1744)

The son of a Roman Catholic linen merchant who had retired with a moderate
fortune, Pope was educated privately. His first success came with his *Pastorals*
(1709). The "Essay on Criticism" appeared in 1711, and the first version of *The Rape
of the Lock* in 1712. For the next twelve years Pope engaged himself with his
translations of the *Iliad* and the *Odyssey*. In 1712 Pope had, along with Jonathan
Swift, John Gay, and others, formed the Scriblerus Club, and in 1728 he published
his most famous Scriblerus work, *The Dunciad,* to ridicule the critic Theobald, who
had attacked Pope's edition of Shakespeare (1725).

Pope composed "Eloïsa to Abelard" in 1716 and published the poem in the 1717
edition of his *Works*. He sent a copy of the edition to Lady Mary Wortley Montagu

in Constantinople. He also wrote to her: "There are few things but what you have seen, except for the Epistle of Eloïsa to Abelard, in which you will find one passage that I cannot tell whether to wish you should understand, or not." Pope may have been referring to the personal closing section. George Sherburn has speculated that perhaps the "mysterious quarrel between Pope and Lady Mary, which left them after 1727 such ardent enemies, may account for Pope's later depreciation of this poem."

ARGUMENT

> *Abelard and Eloïsa flourished in the twelfth Century; they were two of the most distinguished persons of their age in learning and beauty, but for nothing more famous than for their unfortunate passion. After a long course of calamities, they retired each to a several Convent, and consecrated the remainder of their days to religion. It was many years after this separation, that a letter of Abelard's to a Friend, which contained the history of his misfortune, fell into the hands of Eloïsa. This awakening all her tenderness, occasioned those celebrated letters (out of which the following is partly extracted) which give so lively a picture of the struggles of grace and nature, virtue and passion. P.*

. . . .

   Yet write, oh write me all, that I may join
Griefs to thy griefs, and echo sighs to thine.
Nor foes nor fortune take this power away;
And is my Abelard less kind than they?
Tears still are mine, and those I need not spare,
Love but demands what else were shed in prayer;
No happier task these faded eyes pursue;
To read and weep is all they now can do.
   Then share thy pain, allow that sad relief;
Ah, more than share it, give me all thy grief.   50
Heaven first taught letters for some wretch's aid,
Some banished lover, or some captive maid;
They live, they speak, they breathe what love inspires,
Warm from the soul, and faithful to its fires,
The virgin's wish without her fears impart,
Excuse the blush, and pour out all the heart,
Speed the soft intercourse from soul to soul,
And waft a sigh from Indus to the Pole.
   Thou knowst how guiltless first I met thy flame,
When Love approached me under Friendship's name;   60
My fancy formed thee of angelic kind,
Some emanation of th' all-beauteous Mind.
Those smiling eyes, attempering every ray,
Shone sweetly lambent with celestial day.
Guiltless I gazed; heaven listened while you sung;
And truths divine came mended from that tongue.
From lips like those what precept failed to move?

Too soon they taught me 'twas no sin to love:
Back through the paths of pleasing sense I ran,
Nor wished an Angel whom I loved a Man.
Dim and remote the joys of saints I see;   70
Nor envy them that heaven I lose for thee.
　How oft, when pressed to marriage, have I said,
Curse on all laws but those which love has made?
Love, free as air, at sight of human ties,
Spreads his light wings, and in a moment flies.
Let wealth, let honour, wait the wedded dame,
August her deed, and sacred be her fame;
Before true passion all those views remove,
Fame, wealth, and honour! what are you to Love?   80
The jealous God, when we profane his fires,
Those restless passions in revenge inspires,
And bids them make mistaken mortals groan,
Who seek in love for aught but love alone.
Should at my feet the world's great master fall,
Himself, his throne, his world, I'd scorn 'em all:
Not Caesar's empress would I deign to prove;
No, make me mistress to the man I love;
If there be yet another name more free,
More fond than mistress, make me that to thee!   90
Oh! happy state! when souls each other draw,
When love is liberty, and nature, law:
All then is full, possessing, and possessed,
No craving void left aching in the breast:
Even thought meets thought, ere from the lips it part,
And each warm wish springs mutual from the heart.
This sure is bliss (if bliss on earth there be)
And once the lot of Abelard and me.
　Alas, how chanted! what sudden horrors rise!
A naked Lover bound and bleeding lies!   100
Where, where was Eloïse? her voice, her hand,
Her poniard, had opposed the dire command.
Barbarian, stay! that bloody stroke restrain;
The crime was common, common be the pain.
I can no more; by shame, by rage suppressed,
Let tears, and burning blushes speak the rest.
　Canst thou forget that sad, that solemn day,
When victims at yon altar's foot we lay?
Canst thou forget what tears that moment fell,
When, warm in youth, I bad the world farewell?   110
As with cold lips I kissed the sacred veil,
The shrines all trembled, and the lamps grew pale:
Heaven scarce believed the Conquest it surveyed,
And Saints with wonder heard the vows I made.
Yet then, to those dread altars as I drew,
Not on the Cross my eyes were fixed, but you:

Not grace, or zeal, love only was my call,
And if I lose thy love, I lose my all.
Come! with thy looks, thy words, relieve my woe;
Those still at least are left thee to bestow. 120
Still on that breast enamoured let me lie,
Still drink delicious poison from thy eye,
Pant on thy lip, and to thy heart be pressed;
Give all thou canst—and let me dream the rest.
Ah no! instruct me other joys to prize,
With other beauties charm my partial eyes,
Full in my view set all the bright abode,
And make my soul quit Abelard for God. . . .

THE LADY'S DRESSING ROOM

Jonathan Swift   (1667–1745)

The son of an Englishman who had settled in Ireland, Swift was educated at Trinity College, Dublin. He became secretary in the household of Sir William Temple, whose essay "On Ancient and Modern Learning" (1690) fueled the controversy over whether modern writers excelled the Greeks and Romans. Swift entered the fray with *The Battle of the Books*. During this period Swift met Esther Johnson, his "Stella," also a member of Temple's household. After Temple's death, Swift went to England, where he entered public life, joining the Tory party in 1710. After the death of Queen Anne in 1714 ended hopes for Tory power, Swift returned to Ireland, where he became dean of St. Patrick's Cathedral. His penchant for misanthropic satire came to its climax between 1721 and 1725 with *Gulliver's Travels*. In 1742, troubled by deafness and disease, Swift was declared of unsound mind.

"The Lady's Dressing Room," dated 1730, was published in 1732.

Five hours (and who can do it less in?)
By haughty Celia spent in dressing;
The goddess from her chamber issues,
Array'd in lace, brocades, and tissues.
   Strephon, who found the room was void,
And Betty otherwise employ'd,
Stole in, and took a strict survey
Of all the litter as it lay:
Whereof, to make the matter clear,
An inventory follows here. 10
   And, first, a dirty smock appear'd,
Beneath the arm-pits well besmear'd;

Strephon, the rogue, display'd it wide,
And turn'd it round on every side:
On such a point, few words are best,
And Strephon bids us guess the rest;
But swears, how damnably the men lie
In calling Celia sweet and cleanly.
　　Now listen, while he next produces
The various combs for various uses;
Fill'd up with dirt so closely fixt, 　　　　　　　　　　　　20
No brush could force a way betwixt;
A paste of composition rare,
Sweat, dandriff, powder, lead, and hair:
A fore-head cloth with oil upon't,
To smooth the wrinkles on her front:
Here alum-flour, to stop the steams
Exhaled from sour unsavoury streams:
There night-gloves made of Tripsey's hide,
Bequeath'd by Tripsey when she died; 　　　　　　　　　30
With puppy-water, beauty's help,
Distill'd from Tripsey's darling whelp.
Here gallipots and vials placed,
Some fill'd with washes, some with paste;
Some with pomatums, paints, and slops,
And ointments good for scabby chops.
Hard by a filthy basin stands,
Foul'd with the scouring of her hands:
The basin takes whatever comes,
The scrapings from her teeth and gums, 　　　　　　　40
A nasty compound of all hues,
For here she spits, and here she spews.
　　But, oh! it turn'd poor Strephon's bowels,
When he beheld and smelt the towels,
Begumm'd, bematter'd, and beslimed,
With dirt, and sweat, and ear-wax grimed;
No object Strephon's eye escapes;
Her petticoats in frouzy heaps;
Nor be the handkerchiefs forgot,
All varnish'd o'er with snuff and snot. 　　　　　　　50
The stockings why should I expose,
Stain'd with the moisture of her toes,
Or greasy coifs, or pinners reeking,
Which Celia slept at least a week in?
A pair of tweezers next he found,
To pluck her brows in arches round;
Or hairs that sink the forehead low,
Or on her chin like bristles grow.
　　The virtues we must not let pass
Of Celia's magnifying glass; 　　　　　　　　　　　　　60
When frighted Strephon cast his eye on't,

It shew'd the visage of a giant:
A glass that can to sight disclose
The smallest worm in Celia's nose,
And faithfully direct her nail
To squeeze it out from head to tail;
For, catch it nicely by the head,
It must come out, alive or dead.
    Why, Strephon, will you tell the rest?
And must you needs describe the chest?   70
That careless wench! no creature warn her
To move it out from yonder corner!
But leave it standing full in sight,
For you to exercise your spite?
In vain the workman shew'd his wit,
With rings and hinges counterfeit,
To make it seem in this disguise
A cabinet to vulgar eyes:
Which Strephon ventured to look in,
Resolved to go through thick and thin.   80
He lifts the lid; there needs no more,
He smelt it all the time before.
    As, from within Pandora's box,
When Epimetheus oped the locks,
A sudden universal crew
Of human evils upward flew;
He still was comforted to find
That hope at last remain'd behind:
So Strephon, lifting up the lid,
To view what in the chest was hid,   90
The vapours flew from out the vent;
But Strephon, cautious, never meant
The bottom of the pan to grope,
And foul his hands in search of hope.
O! ne'er may such a vile machine
Be once in Celia's chamber seen!
O! may she better learn to keep
Those "secrets of the hoary deep."
    As mutton-cutlets, prime of meat,
Which, though with art you salt and beat,   100
As laws of cookery require,
And roast them at the clearest fire;
If from adown the hopeful chops
The fat upon the cinder drops,
To stinking smoke it turns the flame,
Poisoning the flesh from whence it came,
And up exhales a greasy stench,
For which you curse the careless wench:
So things which must not be exprest,
When plump'd into the reeking chest,   110

Send up an excremental smell
To taint the parts from whence they fell:
The petticoats and gown perfume,
And waft a stink round every room.
   Thus finishing his grand survey,
Disgusted Strephon stole away;
Repeating in his amorous fits,
"Oh! Celia, Celia, Celia sh—!"
But Vengeance, goddess never sleeping,
Soon punish'd Strephon for his peeping: 120
His foul imagination links
Each dame he sees with all her stinks;
And, if unsavoury odours fly,
Conceives a lady standing by.
All women his description fits,
And both ideas jump like wits;
By vicious fancy coupled fast,
And still appearing in contrast.
   I pity wretched Strephon, blind
To all the charms of woman kind.   130
Should I the Queen of Love refuse,
Because she rose from stinking ooze?
To him that looks behind the scene,
Statira's but some pocky queen.
   When Celia all her glory shews,
If Strephon would but stop his nose,
(Who now so impiously blasphemes
Her ointments, daubs, and paints, and creams,
Her washes, slops, and every clout,
With which he makes so foul a rout;)   140
He soon will learn to think like me,
And bless his ravish'd eyes to see
Such order from confusion sprung,
Such gaudy tulips raised from dung.

WHEN LOVELY WOMAN STOOPS TO FOLLY

Oliver Goldsmith   (1730–1774)

Born in Ireland, the second son of a poor curate, Goldsmith was sent to Trinity College, Dublin, as a work-study student and obtained his B.A. there in 1749. In 1754 he went to the Continent and then came back to London, where he set up as a physician. He had no success in the field of medicine and was soon reduced to hack writing. Although in 1761 Goldsmith met Samuel Johnson, who attempted to aid him, he achieved no real success until his comedy *She Stoops to Conquer* was produced in 1773. It opened March 15, was published March 25, and sold 4000 copies in three days. During his final illness, his physician asked Goldsmith, "Is your mind at rest?" Goldsmith's last words were, "No, it is not."

"When lovely woman stoops to folly" appeared in 1766 in Goldsmith's novel *The Vicar of Wakefield.*

When lovely woman stoops to folly,
　And finds too late that men betray,
What charm can sooth her melancholy,
　What art can wash her guilt away?

The only art her guilt to cover,
　To hide her shame from every eye,
To give repentance to her lover,
　And wring his bosom—is to die.

SODGER LADDIE

Robert Burns　　　(1759–1796)

The son of an Ayrshire farmer, Burns himself became a laborer and bought a farm with his brother after their father's death in 1784. Already the father of one illegitimate child, Burns married Jean Armour, who was carrying his child, but her parents forced her to repudiate the marriage. Following the death of his fiancée, Mary Campbell, Burns determined to go to Jamaica and published *Poems Chiefly in the Scottish Dialect* to raise money for that purpose. Suddenly famous, Burns began collecting some 300 Scots ballads and traditional songs. In 1789 he found employment as a customs official, though his sympathy with the French Revolution kept him from promotion.

"Sodger Laddie" is one of the songs from Burns's *The Jolly Beggars* (1785), a cantata based on Scottish folk songs.

AIR

Tune: "Sodger[1] Laddie"

I once was a maid, tho' I cannot tell when,
And still my delight is in proper young men:

[1]*sodger:* soldier.

Some one of a troop of dragoons was my daddie,
No wonder I'm fond of a sodger laddie.

                Sing, lal de lal, etc.

The first of my loves was a swaggering blade,
To rattle the thundering drum was his trade;
His leg was so tight,[2] and his cheek was so ruddy,
Transported I was with my sodger laddie.

But the godly old chaplain left him in the lurch;   10
The sword I forsook for the sake of the church:
He ventur'd the soul, and I riskèd the body,
'Twas then I proved false to my sodger laddie.

Full soon I grew sick of my sanctified sot,
The regiment at large for a husband I got;
From the gilded spontoon to the fife I was ready,
I asked no more but a sodger laddie.

But the peace it reduc'd me to beg in despair,
Till I met my old boy in a Cunningham fair;
His rags regimental, they flutter'd so gaudy,   20
My heart it rejoic'd at a sodger laddie.

And now I have liv'd—I know not how long,
But still I can join in a cup and a song;
And whilst with both hands I can hold the glass steady,
Here's to thee, my hero, my sodger laddie.

TO HELEN

Edgar Allan Poe   (1809–1849)

The son of itinerant actors, Poe was born in Boston. After his parents died, he was taken into the household of Richmond merchant John Allan. He attended school in England, where he went with the Allans. Poe attended the University of Virginia briefly, but soon quarreled with Allan over gambling debts and went to Boston, where he published *Tamarlane* (1827). Allan got Poe an appointment to West Point, but Poe was soon dismissed, going then to live with an aunt in Baltimore, where he

[2]*tight:* trim.

began to publish magazine stories. He married his aunt's daughter, thirteen-year-old Virginia, and worked briefly for the *Southern Literary Messenger*. He went to New York and, later, Philadelphia, taking jobs with various magazines and publishing his poems, stories, and critical pieces wherever he happened to be working. Virginia died in 1845; his own health ruined by depression and alcoholism, Poe died in Baltimore.

"To Helen" was first published in *Poems* (1831).

Helen, thy beauty is to me
  Like those Nicéan barks of yore,
That gently, o'er a perfumed sea,
  The weary, way-worn wanderer bore
  To his own native shore.

On desperate seas long wont to roam,
  Thy hyacinth hair, thy classic face,
Thy Naiad airs have brought me home
  To the glory that was Greece,
And the grandeur that was Rome.

Lo! in yon brilliant window-niche
  How statue-like I see thee stand,
  The agate lamp within thy hand!
Ah, Psyche, from the regions which
  Are Holy-Land!

RAPPACCINI'S DAUGHTER

Nathaniel Hawthorne   (1804–1864)

The son of a prominent puritan family, Hawthorne graduated from Bowdoin College in 1825. Thereafter, his life alternated between periods of writing and periods of public service. In 1836 he began working for a Boston publisher, writing children's books. From 1839 to 1841 he served in the Boston Customs House and then lived briefly at the experimental Brook Farm, later marrying Sophia Peabody, a follower of the Concord school of transcendentalism. He was surveyor of the port of Salem from 1846 to 1849, publishing *The Scarlet Letter* the following year. Hawthorne wrote the campaign biography of Franklin Pierce, who rewarded him by making him consul at Liverpool from 1853 to 1857. Hawthorne then spent two years in Italy before returning to Concord.

"Rappaccini's Daughter," the short story from which the following excerpts are taken, appeared in 1844 and was reprinted in Hawthorne's collection *Mosses from an Old Manse* (1846).

[A young man named Giovanni Guasconti arrives in Padua to attend the university and takes lodgings which overlook a garden "cultivated by the own hands of Signor Giacomo Rappaccini, the famous doctor," who "distils these plants into medicines that are as potent as a charm." Watching from his window, Giovanni catches sight of Rappaccini's daughter Beatrice.]

Soon there emerged from under a sculptured portal the figure of a young girl, arrayed with as much richness of taste as the most splendid of the flowers, beautiful as the day, and with a bloom so deep and vivid that one shade more would have been too much. She looked redundant with life, health, and energy; all of which attributes were bound down and compressed, as it were, and girdled tensely, in their luxuriance, by her virgin zone. Yet Giovanni's fancy must have grown morbid while he looked down into the garden; for the impression which the fair stranger made upon him was as if here were another flower, the human sister of these vegetable ones, as beautiful as they, more beautiful than the richest of them, but still to be touched only with a glove, nor to be approached without a mask. As Beatrice came down the garden path, it was observable that she handled and inhaled the odor of several of the plants which her father had most sedulously avoided. . . .

Then, with all the tenderness in her manner that was so strikingly expressed in her words, she busied herself with such attentions as the plant seemed to require; and Giovanni, at his lofty window, rubbed his eyes and almost doubted whether it were a girl tending her favorite flower, or one sister performing the duties of affection to another. The scene soon terminated. Whether Dr. Rappaccini had finished his labors in the garden, or that his watchful eye had caught the stranger's face, he now took his daughter's arm and retired. Night was already closing in; oppressive exhalations seemed to proceed from the plants and steal upward past the open window; and Giovanni, closing the lattice, went to his couch and dreamed of a rich flower and beautiful girl. Flower and maiden were different, and yet the same, and fraught with some strange peril in either shape.

[Giovanni continues to watch the garden daily.]

At first, as we have said, the garden was a solitude. Soon, however,—as Giovanni had half hoped, half feared, would be the case,—a figure appeared beneath the antique sculptured portal, and came down between the rows of plants, inhaling their various perfumes as if she were one of those beings of old classic fable that lived upon sweet odors. On again beholding Beatrice, the young man was even startled to perceive how much her beauty exceeded his recollection of it; so brilliant, so vivid, was its character, that she glowed amid the sunlight, and, as Giovanni whispered to himself, positively illuminated the more shadowy intervals of the garden path. Her face being now more revealed than on the former occasion, he was struck by its expression of simplicity and sweetness,—qualities that had not entered into his idea of her character, and which made him ask anew what manner of mortal she might be. Nor did he fail again to observe, or imagine, an analogy between the beautiful girl and the gorgeous shrub that hung its gemlike flowers over the fountain,—a resemblance which Beatrice seemed to have indulged a fantastic humor in heightening, both by the arrangement of her dress and the selection of its hues.

Approaching the shrub, she threw open her arms, as with a passionate ardor, and drew its branches into an intimate embrace—so intimate that her features were hidden in its leafy bosom and her glistening ringlets all intermingled with the flowers.

"Give me thy breath, my sister." exclaimed Beatrice; "for I am faint with common air. And give me this flower of thine, which I separate with gentlest fingers from the stem and place it close beside my heart."

With these words the beautiful daughter of Rappaccini plucked one of the richest blossoms of the shrub, and was about to fasten it in her bosom. But now, unless Giovanni's draughts of wine had bewildered his senses, a singular incident occurred. A small orange-colored reptile, of the lizard or chameleon species, chanced to be creeping along the path, just at the feet of Beatrice. It appeared to Giovanni,—but, at the distance from which he gazed, he could scarcely have seen anything so minute,—it appeared to him, however, that a drop or two of moisture from the broken stem of the flower descended upon the lizard's head. For an instant the reptile contorted itself violently, and then lay motionless in the sunshine. Beatrice observed this remarkable phenomenon, and crossed herself, sadly, but without surprise; nor did she therefore hesitate to arrange the fatal flower in her bosom. There it blushed, and almost glimmered with the dizzling effect of a precious stone, adding to her dress and aspect the one appropriate charm which nothing else in the world could have supplied. But Giovanni, out of the shadow of his window, bent forward and shrank back, and murmured and trembled.

[Later, Giovanni presents Beatrice with a bouquet, which she quickly takes into the house.]

But few as the moments were, it seemed to Giovanni, when she was on the point of vanishing beneath the sculptured portal, that his beautiful bouquet was already beginning to wither in her grasp. It was an idle thought; there could be no possibility of distinguishing a faded flower from a fresh one at so great a distance.

[Now convinced that Rappaccini is using Beatrice to test his theory "that all medicinal virtues are comprised within those substances we term vegetable poisons," Giovanni appeals to Pietro Baglioni, a professor of medicine, for an antidote, which he persuades Beatrice to drink.]

"My father," said Beatrice, feebly,—and still as she spoke she kept her hand upon her heart,—"wherefore didst thou inflict this miserable doom upon thy child?"

"Miserable!" exclaimed Rappaccini. "What mean you, foolish girl? Dost thou deem it misery to be endowed with marvellous gifts against which no power nor strength could avail an enemy—misery, to be able to quell the mightiest with a breath—misery, to be as terrible as thou art beautiful? Wouldst thou, then, have preferred the condition of a weak woman, exposed to all evil and capable of none?"

"I would fain have been loved, not feared," murmured Beatrice, sinking down upon the ground. "But now it matters not. I am going, father, where the evil which thou hast striven to mingle with my being will pass away like a dream—like the fragrance of these poisonous flowers, which will no longer taint my breath among the flowers of Eden. Farewell, Giovanni! Thy words of hatred are like lead within my heart; but they, too, will fall away as I ascend. . . ."

To Beatrice,—so radically had her earthly part been wrought upon by Rappaccini's skill,—as poison had been life, so the powerful antidote was death; and thus the poor victim of man's ingenuity and of thwarted nature, and of the fatality that attends all such efforts of perverted wisdom, perished there, at the feet of her father and Giovanni.

I STARTED EARLY—TOOK MY DOG

Emily Elizabeth Dickinson   (1830–1886)

The daughter of a prominent Amherst lawyer, Dickinson attended the Amherst Academy and spent one year at the Mount Holyoke Female Seminary. She lived quietly at home and during the last half of her life was a recluse. Although she showed her poems to a few friends, only two were published during her lifetime, neither with her consent.

I started Early–Took my Dog–
And visited the Sea–
The Mermaids in the Basement
Came out to look at me–

And Frigates–in the Upper Floor
Extended Hempen Hands–
Presuming Me to be a Mouse–
Aground–upon the Sands–

But no Man moved Me–till the Tide
Went past my simple Shoe–   10
And past my Apron–and my Belt
And past my Bodice–too–

And made as He would eat me up–
As wholly as a Dew
Upon a Dandelion's Sleeve–
And then–I started–too–

And He–He followed–close behind–
I felt His Silver Heel
Upon my Ankle–Then my Shoes   20
Would overflow with Pearl–

Until We met the Solid Town–
No One He seemed to know–
And bowing–with a Mighty look–
At me–The Sea withdrew–

BODY'S BEAUTY

Dante Gabriel Rossetti   (1828–1882)

Christened Gabriel Charles Dante in honor of his godfather, the geologist Charles
Lyell, Rossetti left school at fourteen to prepare for a career as a painter. His first
book of poems was printed privately when he was fifteen. He became one of the
leaders of the Pre-Raphaelite Brotherhood, a group of painters seeking to restore the
naturalism and attention to realistic detail they believed characteristic of painting
before Raphael (1483–1520). After a nine-year engagement, Rossetti married
Elizabeth Eleanor Siddall, the model for many of his famous paintings. She
committed suicide in 1862, and Rossetti, guilty over her death, had the manuscripts
of his poems buried with her. He had the poems exhumed seven years later and
published the following year. His moodiness aggravated by drinking, Rossetti
became the victim of a persecution mania which lasted until his death, though he
rallied to produce a final volume of poems in 1881.

"Body's Beauty" was entitled "Lilith" when it appeared in *Poems* (1870). The poem
was given its present title when it appeared as Sonnet 78 in the sonnet sequence
The House of Life in 1881.

Of Adam's first wife, Lilith, it is told
  (The witch he loved before the gift of Eve,)
  That, ere the snake's, her sweet tongue could deceive,

And her enchanted hair was the first gold.
And still she sits, young while the earth is old,
   And, subtly of herself contemplative,
   Draws men to watch the bright net she can weave.
Till heart and body and life are in its hold.

The rose and poppy are her flowers; for where
   Is he not found, O Lilith, whom shed scent
And soft-shed kisses and soft sleep shall snare?
   Lo! as that youth's eyes burned at thine, so went
   Thy spell through him and left his straight neck bent,
And round his heart one strangling golden hair.

THE HARLOT'S HOUSE

Oscar Fingal O'Flahertie Willis Wilde   (1854–1900)

Oscar Wilde was born in Dublin, where his father was a surgeon and his mother a poet of some note who published under the pseudonym "Speranza." Wilde's literary career began at Oxford, as did his promotion of the "New Aestheticism," which Gilbert and Sullivan satirized in *Patience* (1881). Following *Poems* (1881), Wilde undertook a lecture tour of the United States. His marriage in 1884 to Constance Lloyd ended Wilde's financial worries. From 1887 to 1891, Wilde devoted himself to prose writings. His success with drama began with *Lady Windermere's Fan* (1892) and ended with *The Importance of Being Earnest* (1895). In that year, the Marquess of Queensberry, objecting to Wilde's friendship with his son, Lord Alfred Douglas, left a calling card at Wilde's club on which was written the single word "Sodomite." Wilde sued for libel, but lost. He was imprisoned for homosexuality for two years following the trial. His final two years were spent on the Continent, where he lived on funds provided by friends.

"The Harlot's House," one of Wilde's uncollected poems, was published posthumously in 1904.

We caught the tread of dancing feet,
We loitered down the moonlit street,
And stopped beneath the harlot's house.

Inside, above the din and fray,
We heard the loud musicians play
The "Treues Liebes Herz"[1] of Strauss.

---

[1] *"Treues Liebes Herz"*: "True Love's Heart," a waltz.

Like strange mechanical grotesques,
Making fantastic arabesques,
The shadows raced across the blind.

We watched the ghostly dancers spin   10
To sound of horn and violin,
Like black leaves wheeling in the wind.

Like wire-pulled automatons,
Slim silhouetted skeletons
Went sidling through the slow quadrille.

They took each other by the hand,
And danced a stately saraband;
Their laughter echoed thin and shrill.

Sometimes a clockwork puppet pressed
A phantom lover to her breast,   20
Sometimes they seemed to try to sing.

Sometimes a horrible marionette
Came out, and smoked its cigarette
Upon the steps like a live thing.

Then, turning to my love, I said,
"The dead are dancing with the dead,
The dust is whirling with the dust."

But she—she heard the violin,
And left my side, and entered in:
Love passed into the house of lust.   30

Then suddenly the tune went false,
The dancers wearied of the waltz,
The shadows ceased to wheel and whirl.

And down the long and silent street,
The dawn, with silver-sandaled feet,
Crept like a frightened girl.

AND YOU AS WELL MUST DIE, BELOVÈD DUST

Edna St. Vincent Millay   (1892–1950)

Millay, whose poem "Renascence" brought her fame while she was still in her teens, was born in Maine. She graduated from Vassar in 1917 and moved to Greenwich Village. Her flippant, cynical sonnets and lyrics made her a model for the independent free spirit of the jazz age. Her mature poetry is marked by its elegiac disillusionment and by consummate craftsmanship. Millay wrecked her reputation by the publication in 1940 of *Make Bright the Arrow,* poems on war preparedness which were attacked as propagandistic doggerel. No further collection of new poems was published until the posthumous volume *Mine the Harvest* (1954).

"And you as well must die, belovèd dust" appeared in *Second April* (1921).

And you as well must die, belovèd dust,
And all your beauty stand you in no stead;
This flawless, vital hand, this perfect head,
This body of flame and steel, before the gust
Of Death, or under his autumnal frost,
Shall be as any leaf, be no less dead
Than the first leaf that fell,—this wonder fled,
Altered, estranged, disintegrated, lost.
Nor shall my love avail you in your hour.
In spite of all my love, you will arise
Upon that day and wander down the air
Obscurely as the unattended flower,
It mattering not how beautiful you were,
Or how belovèd above all else that dies.

FERN

Jean Toomer   (1894–   )

Toomer, the grandson of a Reconstruction governor of Louisiana, was born in Washington, D.C. He studied law at the University of Wisconsin and the City College of New York. Toomer was a member of writers' colonies at Carmel, California, and later at Taos, New Mexico.

"Fern" was printed in *Cane,* a collection of Toomer's prose and verse that appeared in 1923, growing in large part from his experiences as a teacher in Georgia. The book's sales were not large, and Toomer's subsequent manuscripts remain unpublished.

Face flowed into her eyes. Flowed in soft cream foam and plaintive ripples, in such a way that wherever your glance may momentarily have rested, it immediately thereafter wavered in the direction of her eyes. The soft suggestion of down slightly darkened, like the shadow of a bird's wing might, the creamy brown color of her upper lip. Why, after noticing it, you sought her eyes, I cannot tell you. Her nose was aquiline, Semitic. If you have heard a Jewish cantor sing, if he has touched you and made your own sorrow seem trivial when compared with his, you will know my feeling when I follow the curves of her profile, like mobile rivers, to their common delta. They were strange eyes. In this, that they sought nothing—that is, nothing that was obvious and tangible and that one could see, and they gave the impression that nothing was to be denied. When a woman seeks, you will have observed, her eyes deny. Fern's eyes desired nothing that you could give her; there was no reason why they should withhold. Men saw her eyes and fooled themselves. Fern's eyes said to them that she was easy. When she was young, a few men took her, but got no joy from it. And then, once done, they felt bound to her (quite unlike their hit and run with other girls), felt as though it would take them a lifetime to fulfill an obligation which they could find no name for. They became attached to her, and hungered after finding the barest trace of what she might desire. As she grew up, new men who came to town felt as almost everyone did who ever saw her: that they would not be denied. Men were everlastingly bringing her their bodies. Something inside of her got tired of them, I guess, for I am certain that for the life of her she could not tell why or how she began to turn them off. A man in fever is no trifling thing to send away. They began to leave her, baffled and ashamed, yet vowing to themselves that some day they would do some fine thing for her: send her candy every week and not let her know whom it came from, watch out for her wedding-day and give her a magnificent something with no name on it, buy a house and deed it to her, rescue her from some unworthy fellow who had tricked her into marrying him. As you know, men are apt to idolize or fear that which they cannot understand, especially if it be a woman. She did not deny them, yet the fact was that they were denied. A sort of superstition crept into their consciousness of her being somehow above them. Being above them meant that she was not to be approached by anyone. She became a virgin. Now a virgin in a small southern town is by no means the usual thing, if you will believe me. That the sexes were made to mate is the practice of the South. Particularly, black folks were made to mate. And it is black folks whom I have been talking about thus far. What white men thought of Fern I can arrive at only by analogy. They let her alone.

Anyone, of course, could see her, could see her eyes. If you walked up the Dixie Pike most any time of day, you'd be most like to see her resting listless-like on the railing of her porch, back propped against a post, head tilted a little forward because there was a nail in the porch post just where her head came which for some reason or other she never took the trouble to pull out. Her eyes, if it were sunset, rested idly where the sun, molten and glorious, was pouring down between the fringe of pines. Or maybe they gazed at the gray cabin on the knoll from which an evening folk-song was coming. Perhaps they followed a cow that had been turned loose to roam and feed on cotton-stalks and corn leaves. Like as not they'd settle on some vague spot above the horizon, though hardly a trace of wistfulness would come to them. If it were dusk, then they'd wait for the search-light of the evening train which you could see miles up the track before it flared across the Dixie Pike, close to her home. Wherever they looked, you'd follow them and then waver back. Like her face, the whole countryside seemed to flow into her eyes. Flowed to them with the soft listless cadence of Georgia's South. A young Negro, once, was looking at her, spellbound, from the road. A white man passing in a buggy had to flick him with his whip if he was to get by without running him over. I first saw her on her porch. I was passing with a fellow whose crusty numbness (I was from the North and suspected of being prejudiced and stuck-up) was melting as he found me warm. I asked him who she was. "That's Fern," was all that I could get from him. Some folks already thought that I was given to nosing around; I let it go at that, so far as questions were concerned. But at first sight of her I felt as I heard a Jewish cantor sing. As if his singing rose above the unheard chorus of a folk-song. And I felt bound to her. I too had my dreams: something I would do for her. I have knocked about from town to town too much not to know the futility of mere change of place. Besides, picture if you can, this cream-colored solitary girl sitting at a tenement window looking down on the indifferent throngs of Harlem. Better that she listen to folk-songs at dusk in Georgia, you would say, and so would I. Or, suppose she came up North and married. Even a doctor or a lawyer, say, one who would be sure to get along—that is, make money. You and I know, who have had experience in such things, that love is not a thing like prejudice which can be bettered by changes of town. Could men in Washington, Chicago, or New York, more than the men of Georgia, bring her something left vacant by the bestowal of their bodies? You and I who know men in these cities will have to say, they could not. See her out and out a prostitute along State Street in Chicago. See her move into a southern town where white men are more aggressive. See her become a white man's concubine . . . Something I must do for her. There was myself. What could I do for her? Talk, of course. Push back the fringe of pines upon new horizons. To what purpose? and what for? Her? Myself? Men in her case seem to lose their selfishness. I lost mine before I touched her. I ask you, friend (it makes no difference if you sit in the Pullman or the Jim Crow as the train crosses her road), what thought would come to you—that is, after you'd finished with the thoughts that leap into men's minds at the sight of a pretty woman who will not deny them; what thoughts would come to you, had you seen her in a quick flash, keen and intuitively, as she sat there on her porch when your train thundered by? Would you have got off at the next station and come back for her to take her where? Would you have completely forgotten her as soon as you reached Macon, Atlanta, Augusta, Pasadena, Madison, Chicago, Boston, or New Orleans? Would you tell your wife or sweetheart about a girl you saw? Your thoughts can help me, and I would like to know. Something I would do for her . . .

One evening I walked up the Pike on purpose, and stopped to say hello. Some of her family were about, but they moved away to make room for me. Damn if I knew how to begin. Would you? Mr. and Miss So-and-So, people, the weather, the crops, the new preacher, the frolic, the church benefit, rabbit and possum hunting, the new soft drink they had at old Pap's store, the schedule of the trains, what kind of town Macon was, Negro's migration north, boll-weevils, syrup, the Bible—to all these things she gave a yassur or nassur, without further comment. I began to wonder if perhaps my own emotional sensibility had played one of its tricks on me. "Lets take a walk," I at last ventured. The suggestion, coming after so long an isolation, was novel enough, I guess, to surprise. But it wasnt that. Something told me that men before me had said just that as a prelude to the offering of their bodies. I tried to tell her with my eyes. I think she understood. The thing from her that made my throat catch, vanished. Its passing left her visible in a way I'd thought, but never seen. We walked down the Pike with people on all the porches gaping at us. "Doesnt it make you mad?" She meant the row of petty gossiping people. She meant the world. Through a canebrake that was ripe for cutting, the branch was reached. Under a sweet-gum tree, and where reddish leaves had dammed the creek a little, we sat down. Dusk, suggesting the almost imperceptible procession of giant trees, settled with a purple haze about the cane. I felt strange, as I always do in Georgia, particularly at dusk. I felt that things unseen to men were tangibly immediate. It would not have surprised me had I had vision. People have them in Georgia more often than you would suppose. A black woman once saw the mother of Christ and drew her in charcoal on the courthouse wall . . . When one is on the soil of one's ancestors, most anything can come to one . . . From force of habit, I suppose, I held Fern in my arms—that is, without at first noticing it. Then my mind came back to her. Her eyes, unusually weird and open, held me. Held God. He flowed in as I've seen the countryside flow in. Seen men. I must have done something—what, I dont know, in the confusion of my emotion. She sprang up. Rushed some distance from me. Fell to her knees, and began swaying, swaying. Her body was tortured with something it could not let out. Like boiling sap it flooded arms and fingers till she shook them as if they burned her. It found her throat, and spattered inarticulately in plaintive, convulsive sounds, mingled with calls to Christ Jesus. And then she sang, brokenly. A Jewish cantor singing with a broken voice. A child's voice, uncertain, or an old man's. Dusk hid her; I could hear only her song. It seemed to me as though she were pounding her head in anguish upon the ground. I rushed to her. She fainted in my arms.

There was talk about her fainting with me in the canefield. And I got one or two ugly looks from town men who'd set themselves up to protect her. In fact, there was talk of making me leave town. But they never did. They kept a watch-out for me, though. Shortly after, I came back North. From the train window I saw her as I crossed her road. Saw her on her porch, head tilted a little forward where the nail was, eyes vaguely focused on the sunset. Saw her face flow into them, the countryside and something that I call God, flowing into them . . . Nothing ever really happened. Something I would do for her. Some fine unnamed thing . . . And, friend, you? She is still living, I have reason to know. Her name, against the chance that you might happen down that way, is Fernie May Rosen.

THE FIRE SERMON from THE WASTE LAND

Thomas Stearns Eliot   (1888–1965)

Born in St. Louis, Eliot graduated from Harvard in 1910. After study at the Sorbonne and Oxford, he returned to Harvard as an instructor of philosophy. In 1914 he returned to Europe, becoming a British citizen in 1927. Eliot's first volume of poetry was published in 1917. He conveys the sterility of modern life in *The Waste Land* (1922). Eliot's conversion to the Church of England is evident in "Ash Wednesday" (1930) and in his later work. He received the Nobel Prize in 1948. Eliot is also well known for his criticism and is credited with much of the modern interest in Donne and Dryden.

This excerpt from *The Waste Land,* "The Fire Sermon," is the modern rewriting of Oliver Goldsmith's "When lovely woman stoops to folly" and is intended to demonstrate the meaninglessness of sexuality in the modern world.

. . . .

He, the young man carbuncular, arrives,
A small house agent's clerk, with one bold stare,
One of the low on whom assurance sits
As a silk hat on a Bradford millionaire.
The time is now propitious, as he guesses,
The meal is ended, she is bored and tired,

Endeavours to engage her in caresses
Which still are unreproved, if undesired.
Flushed and decided, he assaults at once;
Exploring hands encounter no defence;
His vanity requires no response,
And makes a welcome of indifference.

. . . .

   She turns and looks a moment in the glass,
Hardly aware of her departed lover;
Her brain allows one half-formed thought to pass:
"Well now that's done: and I'm glad it's over."
When lovely woman stoops to folly and
Paces about her room again, alone,
She smoothes her hair with automatic hand,
And puts a record on the gramophone.

. . . .

LEDA AND THE SWAN

William Butler Yeats　　(1865–1939)

The son of Irish painter J. B. Yeats, Yeats studied for three years at the School of Art in Dublin, where his friendship with George Russell ("A.E.") developed his interest in mysticism and the supernatural. He abandoned art for literature, and his first writings dealt with national folktales and history. He and Lady Gregory were largely responsible for establishing an Irish national theater. In 1917 Yeats married Georgie Hyde-Lees, whose experiments with automatic writing profoundly influenced his philosophy and style. In 1923 he received the Nobel Prize in literature. Yeats died in the south of France, but in 1948 his body was brought back to Ireland for interment at Drumcliff in Sligo.

"Leda and the Swan" appeared in Yeats's 1928 collection, *The Tower*.

A sudden blow: the great wings beating still
Above the staggering girl, her thighs caressed
By the dark webs, her nape caught in his bill,
He holds her helpless breast upon his breast.

How can those terrified vague fingers push
The feathered glory from her loosening thighs?
And how can body, laid in that white rush,

But feel the strange heart beating where it lies?
A shudder in the loins engenders there
The broken wall, the burning roof and tower
And Agamemnon dead.
                    Being so caught up,
So mastered by the brute blood of the air,
Did she put on his knowledge with his power
Before the indifferent beak could let her drop?

MORTAL GIRL

Muriel Rukeyser   (1913–   )

Born in New York City, Rukeyser attended Vassar, Columbia, and the Roosevelt
Aviation School. Her first book, *Theory of Flight,* won the Yale Younger Poets
competition in 1935. In addition to poetry and criticism, Rukeyser has written
biographies of the American mathematician and physicist Willard Gibbs (1942) and
of the Elizabethan author and adventurer Thomas Hariot (1970).

"Mortal Girl" appeared in Rukeyser's 1944 collection, *Beast in View.*

The girl being chosen stood in her naked room
Singing at last alone naked and proud
Now that the god had departed and his doom
Guarded her door forever and the sky
Would flame in trophies all night and every day.

Sang : When your white sun stood still, I put away
My garments and my crafts and you came down.
When you took me as a flame, I turned to flame;
In whiteness lay on the mist-flower river-bank
When you as a swan arrived, and cloudy in my tower   10
For you as a shower of gold, the lily bright in my hand
Once, you as unthinkable light.
                          Make me more human,
Give me the consciousness
Of every natural shape, to lie here ready
For love as every power.
I wait in all my hopes,
Poet beast and woman,
Wait for the superhuman,
The god who invaded the gold lady,   20
The god who spoke to the naked princess,

The storm over the fiery wanderer.
Within me your city burning, and your desperate tree,
All that the song and the apparition gave
To seal my mouth with fire, make me mad
With song and pain and waiting, leave me free
In all my own shapes, deep in the spirit's cave
To sing again the entrance of the god.

THE MISTRESS: SUPPLEMENTARY READING

Samuel Taylor Coleridge: "Cristabel"
Stephen Crane: *Maggie: A Girl of the Streets*
Shelagh Delaney: *A Taste of Honey*
F. Scott Fitzgerald: "Winter Dreams" and "The Last of the Belles"
William Faulkner: *The Hamlet*
Elizabeth Gaskell: *Ruth*
Thomas Hardy: *Tess of the D'Urbervilles*
Robert Henryson: *The Testament of Cresseid*
William Dean Howells: "Editha"
John Keats: "Lamia" and "La Belle Dame sans Merci"
Norman Mailer: "The Time of Her Time"
Vladimir Nabokov: *Lolita*
Dorothy Parker: "Mr. Durant"
Edgar Allan Poe: "Ligeia"
Samuel Richardson: *Clarissa*
Gertrude Stein: "Melanctha"
Alfred, Lord Tennyson: "Merlin and Vivien," from *Idylls of the King*
Jean Toomer: "Blood-Burning Moon"
Tennessee Williams: "The Mattress by the Tomato Patch"
William Wordsworth: "The Thorn"

THE HELPMATE

Grant Wood: *American Gothic* (American, 1930). [*The Art Institute of Chicago.*]

Marriage in myth and literature symbolizes the reconciliation of opposites. In Chinese philosophy, these opposites are the female, yin, and the male, yang, which together constitute the universe. In Jungian psychology, they are the masculine conscious mind and the feminine unconscious. In Christian tradition, the marriage is used as a metaphor to describe the proper relationship between Christ and his church and therefore between heaven and earth and between spirit and flesh. Marriage at the end of a comedy signals the triumph of community over alienation and division.

Theoretically, marriage affords the helpmate an opportunity for psychological integration which is denied the virgin and the mistress because the helpmate can be both virtuous and sexual. However, because the metaphor of unity in marriage rests on the assumption that men and women are incomplete without each other, wives in literature rarely are portrayed as complete, androgynous beings. In Virginia Woolf's *To the Lighthouse,* the intuitive powers of Mrs. Ramsay and the ratiocinative powers of her husband are complementary. Only as a couple do the Ramsays provide a model of psychological wholeness.

Most creation myths relate the division of humanity into two sexes to the problems of alienation and isolation and see marriage as at least a partial solution to loneliness. Joseph Campbell, in *The Masks of God: Oriental Mythology,* isolates an archetypal creation myth in an Indian legend preserved in the Brihadaranyaka Upanishad:

> This universe was nothing but the Self in the form of a man. It looked around and saw that there was nothing but itself, whereupon its first thought was, "It is I:"
>
> However, he still lacked delight (therefore, we lack delight when alone) and desired a second. He was exactly as large as a man and a woman embracing. This Self then divided itself in two parts; and with that, there were a master and a mistress. The male embraced the female, and from that the human race arose.[1]

The Greeks believed that the first people were androgynous and that the gods were threatened by their power. The gods decided to split them into two parts so that the now lonely and incomplete people would spend all their time getting back together. The first biblical account of creation in Genesis 1 calls for the simultaneous creation of both man and woman. In the story of the Fall in Genesis 2, however, Eve is created out of Adam's rib because Adam was lonely and needed company. Literary works such as John Donne's "A Valediction: Forbidding Mourning," Anne Bradstreet's "A Letter to Her Husband Absent on Public Employment," and Denise Levertov's "Bedtime" praise the fulfilling, happy marriage and emphasize the unity between husband and wife, as contrasted to their feelings of incompleteness and loneliness without each other.

Eve's story provides us with many of the basic elements of the treatment of the wife in literature. She is both the blessed mother who gives life to humankind and the temptress who brings sin and death into the world. The archetype of the Great Mother combines these two roles because she presides over, and participates in, the fertility cycle of birth, growth, aging, and death. In her guise as the benevolent mother, or "nurturing womb," she is responsible for the magic of birth, of baking, of weaving, and of spiritual transformation. As the wicked "tooth mother" (or "devouring womb"), she causes pain and destruction. The menstrual cycle, connected to the waxing and waning lunar cycle, was an evidence in primitive society that all women experience the entire fertility cycle in intimate ways and thus understand the interrelatedness of creation and destruction.[2] Portraits of helpmates in literature demonstrate that the archetypal connection of women with the Great Mother is still with us. However, because of the Western tendency to think dualistically, artists generally present us with "good" wives and mothers, who embody the Great Mother's nurturing qualities, and "bad" wives and mothers, who destroy their husbands and children.

The Virgin Mary is the embodiment of the good wife and mother. As literal woman, she is a selfless helpmate to Joseph, to God, and to her son, Jesus. As goddess, she is the helpmate to all humanity, interceding for the sinful with a judgmental, patriarchal god. Her relationship as a mortal to her immortal husband also sets the pattern for the subservience expected of the ideal wife. In medieval England, the story of the obedient wife becomes an exemplum of the ideal Christian: It is assumed that humankind is subject to God as womankind is to man. In Geoffrey Chaucer's "The Clerk's Tale," Griselda obeys her husband without complaint, even when he pretends to have murdered her children.

As the ideal Christian merges the individual will with God's, the ideal wife merges her will with that of her husband. As the feudal serf swore fealty to his lord, wives promise obedience to their husbands in the wedding ceremony. Accordingly, throughout the ages men have defined the ideal wife as selfless and subservient. In "Sir Thomas Overbury His Wife . . ." (1616), Sir Thomas explains that the perfect wife is:

> . . . a man's best movable; . . . nothing pleaseth her that doth not him. She is relative in all; and he without her, but half himself. She is his absent hands, eyes, ears, and mouth: his present and absent all. She frames her nature unto his howsoever: the hyacinth follows not the sun more willingly. Stubbornness and obstinacy are herbs that grow not in her garden. She leaves tattling to the gossips of the town, and is more seen than heard.

Since it is assumed that all women should become wives, descriptions of the ideal helpmate are often identical with those of the ideal woman. In the nineteenth century, Rousseau explains (in *Émile, or A Treatise on Education*): "The whole education of women ought to be relative to men. To please them, to be useful to them . . . to make life sweet and agreeable to them."[3] In the twentieth century Freud envisions the normal woman not simply as virtuous and selfless but as passive and masochistic.

The helpmate, like the virgin and the mistress, is seen primarily as the Other, as a supporting character in a man's drama. She embodies the opposite of whatever attributes the culture defines at the time as male. She may be treated positively or negatively according to the author's individual emotional response to those values, as well as his or her feelings about women, but most authors agree that a woman's place is in the home.

When Hitler emphasizes the complementary nature of men and women, he idealizes the woman as a conservative force, but (in politically active Germany) he reserves politics for men:

> The man upholds the nation as the woman upholds the family. The equal rights of women consist in the fact that in the realm of life determined for her nature she

experiences two quite different types of being. Reason is dominant in man. He searches, analyzes and often opens new immeasurable realms. But all things that he approaches merely by reason are subject to change. Feeling in contrast is much more stable than reason and woman is the feeling and therefore the stable element.[4]

In the practical, action-oriented nineteenth century, John Ruskin associates the ideal wife with conservative Apollonian values, in contrast to the husband's Dionysian nature:

The man's power is active, progressive, defensive. He is eminently the doer, the creator, the discoverer, the defender. His intellect is for speculation and invention; his energy for adventure, for war and for conquest. . . . But the woman's power is for rule, not for battle, and her intellect is not for invention or recreation, but sweet ordering, arrangement, and decision. . . . [5]

Because the helpmate is often portrayed as the Other, or the Not-Me, she is more likely to be idealized or condemned than to be portrayed realistically. The woman who orders and arranges the moral, social, and physical life of the family may be portrayed as a hero because she is an artist. If portrayed as a heroine, the ideal Apollonian wife still appears superhuman. Like the virgin, she is so spiritually perfect that she exists outside the realm of ordinary mortal life. As William Wordsworth writes in "Perfect Woman," she is:

A perfect woman, nobly planned,
To warm, to comfort, to command;
And yet a spirit still, and bright
With something of angelic light.

The ideal wife in the nineteenth century becomes the "angel of the house" who redeems her husband by providing him with a moral example in all things, but particularly by saving him from his sexuality. The myth of the woman as savior is portrayed symbolically in the fairy tale "Beauty and the Beast," which celebrates the power of a woman's love to transform a beast into a good husband. In realistic, nineteenth-century terms, the ideal woman's distaste for sexuality saves her husband from his lustful, sinful self; she makes sex so uninviting to her husband that he finds a way to transcend his physicality.

The positive, nurturing archetype of the Great Mother is also associated with Dionysian values. Like Ma in John Steinbeck's *The Grapes of Wrath,* the sexual and fearless helpmate exhibits great life-perpetuating qualities. Thomas Hardy, in *Tess of the D'Urbervilles,* exalts Tess's naturalness and chronicles her destruction at the hands of a puritan culture. In fact, if the Dionysian woman is a mother but not a wife (Bertold Brecht's Mother Courage) or if she is a strong, independent wife (Millamant, in William Congreve's *The Way of the World*), she is most often a hero rather than a heroine.

Real women, of course, cannot be so easily restricted to either the Apollonian or the Dionysian category. Most women provide order in the home and to the family and also enjoy the sexual pleasures of marriage and allow both themselves and the other family members a healthy amount of freedom. However, in literary portraits of the heroine, oversimplification is a logical result of her supporting role; as the Other, she exists only as a projection of the hero's character which he has not yet psychologically integrated. The Apollonian helpmate, for example, is often portrayed as repressive. Like Mrs. Ormsby in Wright Morris's "The Ram in the Thicket," she may be frigid. Indeed, because Apollonian perfection can be deathlike, the women who are exalted as perfect helpmates are often literally dead, as in John Milton's "Methought I Saw My Late Espousèd Saint" and E. E. Cummings's "if there are any heavens my mother will (all by herself) have / one." Others die physically or psychologically as a result of efforts to achieve the ideal. In Nathaniel Hawthorne's "The Birthmark," Aylmer kills his wife by operating on her to remove a birthmark in an attempt to save her from imperfection. In Robert Browning's "My Last Duchess," the Duke envisions his wife as a beautiful art object which exists for his pleasure. When she shows signs of a separate human identity, he has her killed. In Eugene O'Neill's *The Iceman Cometh,* the rakish husband murders his wife, whom he describes as perfect and selfless, because her goodness is a reproach to him.

As the virgin may be portrayed negatively on the assumption that she does not exist until a man loves her, the Apollonian wife may be portrayed negatively as having no existence apart from her husband's. This assumption is present in the conclusion of the Christian myth of the Fall. As punishment for eating the apple, Adam must work hard to support his family, and Eve must experience pain in childbirth and obey her husband (see Genesis 3). The establishment of these rigid sex roles in marriage results in a sexual politics which makes a woman economically, socially, politically, and morally dependent upon her husband. In England and the United States until well into the nineteenth century, a woman who married ceased to exist legally and was "covered" by her husband. According to Blackstone's *Commentaries,* "By marriage, the husband and wife are one person in law: that is, the very being or legal existence of the woman is suspended during marriage. . . . But though our law in general considers man and wife as one person, yet there are some instances in which she is separately considered; as inferior to him, and acting by his compulsion." Accordingly, women could not vote or own property. While such laws left a wife economically powerless, tradition told a woman that her husband's will should be hers, that she should agree with everything he said and do everything he desired. In short, she should entirely renounce her own will and desires. The poet Stephen Tropp, in his poem "My Wife Is My Shirt," describes a surrealistic extension of the helpmate's selfless role:

> I put my hands through her armpits
> slide my head through her mouth
> & finally button her blood around my hands

Many negative portraits portray the helpmate as lacking a self. When seen from an unsympathetic point of view, the perfect wife becomes the vacuous housewife. E. E. Cummings describes "the Cambridge ladies with furnished souls," and John Updike, in *Rabbit, Run,* presents Rabbit's wife as a mindless alcoholic. This objectification of the woman who has given up her identity to be an adjunct to the male is satirized in Sylvia Plath's "The Applicant," in which the woman has become a service machine:

A living doll, everywhere you look.
It can sew, it can cook,
It can talk, talk, talk.

It works, there is nothing wrong with it.
You have a hole, it's a poultice,
You have an eye, it's an image.
. . . .
Will you marry it, marry it, marry it.

Woman's work in the home is not recognized as labor because it is not paid. It also is not generally understood that woman's economic role as consumer of the nation's goods is necessary to the continuation of capitalism. Thus the wife is often criticized, as in Phillip Wylie's *Generation of Vipers,* for devouring the energy of her hardworking husband, who kills himself indulging her irrational desire to spend money. Both men and women tend to blame each other for the limiting roles they are assigned in the family unit by the capitalistic system. These role definitions of provider and consumer make marriage, in the words of Ambrose Bierce, "the state or condition of community consisting of a master, a mistress, and two slaves, making in all, two."

The destructive Great Mother, when Apollonian in characteristics, is reincarnated in the stereotypes of the Jewish mother (Phillip Roth's Mrs. Portnoy, for example) and in the American "Mom." The repressive helpmate is frequently portrayed as castrating. In *The American Dream,* Edward Albee's "Mother" unsexes her husband and then enlists his aid in ridding their son of his Dionysian impulses toward sexuality and spontaneity. As Grandma explains, the parents of the "all-American boy" "cut off its you-know-what," and yet he still "put its hands under the cover, *looking* for its you-know-what. So, finally, they *had* to cut off its hands at the wrists."

While the negative helpmate in Apollonian guise may destroy her family as a result of accepting her ordering role, the negative Dionysian helpmate is destructive because she challenges the social order. According to Jewish folklore, Lilith, the first woman, was thrown out of paradise for her refusal to play the helpmate role. Her replacement, Eve, is also a temptress and destroyer who brings chaos into the ordered Garden of Eden and sin and death into the world. Grendel's mother, in the Anglo-Saxon epic poem *Beowulf,* is a holdover from a matriarchal culture, a "monstrous hag" who fights like a man. In response, Beowulf's sword fails.

While portraits of the Apollonian "Mom" describe her as imposing a deathly order on her husband and children, the Dionysian helpmate is shown causing chaos if she is not tamed or killed. Lady MacBeth violates the principle of the great chain of being by dominating her husband and pursuing inappropriate political ambitions. The result is a proliferation of senseless and brutal murders which result in political and domestic chaos. Some helpmates become destructive when scorned. The most famous is Juno, whose response to Zeus's infidelity is to destroy his mistresses. Similarly, when Jason deserts Medea for Glauce, Medea kills Glauce and her own two children in his presence.

The destructive "tooth mother" appears as a witch or wicked stepmother in folklore and fairy tales. Each of the children in "Snow White," "Hansel and

Gretel," and "Cinderella" has both an Apollonian and a Dionysian mother. The biological mother is good, pious, and passive and dies soon after giving birth, and the woman who functions as the mother in the child's development is portrayed as the witch or wicked stepmother. According to this "salmon" theory of motherhood, good mothers fulfill their biological function and then die.

The Dionysian helpmate suffers from the same dangers as the mistress. She may be consumed by the energy which defines her. To symbolize the destructive nature of her vitality, the Dionysian helpmate may be associated with uncontrolled fire. In Charlotte Brontë's *Jane Eyre,* Bertha, Rochester's passionate and willful wife, goes insane and burns the house down, killing herself and maiming her husband. On the level of psychological realism, artists tell us that strong women, like Martha, in Edward Albee's *Who's Afraid of Virginia Woolf?,* castrate weak men because of sexual frustration or barrenness. Indeed, the unfulfilled, destructive wife may be symbolic of the frustrated and bored "everyperson" imprisoned by the sterility and inflexibility of modern bourgeois society. Gustave Flaubert's Madame Bovary commits suicide because her romantic dreams cannot be realized within a bourgeois marriage. "Madame Bovary," Flaubert confesses, "c'est moi."

Because she challenges moral and social order, the Dionysian wife and mother is often killed, or else punished so that she may correct her behavior and be saved from herself. She thereby is purged of her rebelliousness and restored to the social and moral order built on the principle of male supremacy. The Dionysian wife is seen as necessarily governed by the Apollonian husband, as the body must be governed by the head. Shakespeare's Kate, in *The Taming of the Shrew,* for example, is subjected to physical and emotional cruelty until she agrees to domination by her husband. She is tamed because she learns that her husband has complete control over her; he can starve her and make her dress in rags. She ends by enjoining the other wives to obey their husbands because:

A woman mov'd is like a fountain troubled,
Muddy, ill-seeming, thick, bereft of beauty;
. . . .
Thy husband is thy lord, thy life, thy keeper,
Thy head, thy sovereign;
. . . .
And when she is forward, peevish, sullen, sour,
And not obedient to his honest will,
What is she but a foul contending rebel
And graceless traitor to her loving lord?

In twentieth-century mythology the rebellious woman may be conquered by sexual domination rather than by outright cruelty. Often, as in D. H. Lawrence's "The Woman Who Rode Away" or in Norman Mailer's "The Time of Her Time," sex is accompanied by metaphoric or literal violence. In Mailer's *An American Dream,* however, the protagonist cannot tame his wife with sex, and so he fulfills his version of the "American dream" by murdering her and goes unpunished.

Whether the wife is associated with Dionysian or Apollonian qualities, both male and female writers chronicle her unhappiness. If the prince does not come, the maiden who believes in the romantic love myth may be forced to marry one of the dwarfs. Even after the days of arranged marriages, women, such as Mrs. Gaskell's Sylvia, may marry for economic support. Henrik Ibsen's Hedda Gabler explains her betrothal to the professor, Jörgen Tesman: "I had actually waltzed myself tired, my dear Mr. Brack. My day was done—(*with a slight shiver*). . . . And then, since he was so determined, with might and main, to support me—I really don't see why I shouldn't have accepted his offer. . . . It was more than my other admiring friends were willing to do for me, my dear Mr. Brack." Another well-known example is Tennessee Williams's Mrs. Wingfield, in *The Glass Menagerie,* who married Mr. Wingfield, only to be deserted by him. Because her life is frustrating and meaningless, she finds strength from the girlhood memory of one evening's seventeen gentlemen callers, but she lives in a fantasy world and thus cannot equip her children for life. Hedda Gabler also responds to her meaningless existence by living in a romantic fantasy which ultimately requires her suicide. Charlotte Mew, in "The Farmer's Bride," and Robert Frost, in "The Hill Wife," document the suffering of the unfulfilled and unhappy wife and suggest that the unhappiness stems from the inadequacy of the husband. Anne Finch, in "The Unequal Fetters," denounces the institution of marriage as imprisoning to women. In Charlotte Perkins Gilman's "The Yellow Wall-Paper," the wife slowly goes mad because of the restraints of the helpmate role and in spite of the solicitations of a loving but insensitive husband. Eugene O'Neill's *Long Day's Journey into Night* portrays a capable, talented woman who gives up the possibility of an independent life to take on the role of the selfless helpmate. She becomes a martyr and, as a result, inadvertently destroys herself, her husband, and her children.

Portraits of the helpmate by women authors also reveal some ambivalence about motherhood. The self-renunciation required of the wife is accentuated by the demands of children. Until children are old enough to take care of their own physical needs and temper their egocentricity, the demands on the full-time mother are unending. Dilys Laing's "Private Entry into the Diary of a Female Parent" reflects concern about the effects of parental self-sacrifice on women. After bearing three children in three years, the nineteen-year-old Mary Shelley wrote *Frankenstein:* the dilemma of the scientist who is morally responsible for the creature he has created but cannot control is analogous to the experience of the mother.

If she is happy with her role as mother and wife, she may nevertheless find herself deserted, either intermittently or permanently. The faithful Penelope spent years spinning while Ulysses traveled. The husband in Ezra Pound's "River Merchant's Wife: A Letter" deserts his wife for work. In the Anglo-Saxon poem "The Wife's Lament" and in John Dryden's translation of "The Parting of Hector and Andromache," the husband leaves to fight in the war. It is cold comfort for the emotionally or physically deserted wife to know, in the words of Richard Lovelace, in "To Lucasta, Going to the Wars," "I could not love thee dear so much, / Loved I not honor more." The wife who has given her life for husband and children, moreover, often finds herself deserted by her husband just as the children leave home. As in Doris Lessing's *Summer before the Dark,* he may leave her for younger women, or, as in Eudora Welty's *A Curtain of Green,* he may die. In either case, the perfect helpmate, like Sir Albert Morton's wife in Henry Wotton's two-line poem, may be ill equipped to live her life alone: "He first deceased; she for a little tried / To live without him: liked it not, and died."

Collectively, literary portraits of the helpmate show that marriage may be beautiful and fulfilling, as Denise Levertov proposes in "Bedtime." Furthermore, the ideal of selflessness, so often associated with the helpmate (and with Mary and Christ), is of great worth. However, in a patriarchal culture which exalts aggression and self-expression, selflessness is not ultimately admired, and the selfless helpmate may develop a negative self-image which leads to the dehumanization of herself and others. Even more damaging to the helpmate are the assumptions that she should be subservient and economically, socially, morally, and mentally dependent on her husband. Such role definitions give rise to the destructive and dehumanizing portraits of the helpmate in the following selections.

THE HELPMATE: NOTES

[1](New York: The Viking Press, Inc., 1972), pp. 9–10.

[2]Erich Neumann, *The Great Mother,* translated by Ralph Manheim (Princeton, N.J.: Princeton University Press, 1974), pp. 24–48.

[3]Edited by William H. Payne (New York: D. Appleton & Company, Inc., 1893), p. 263.

[4]*Mein Kampf,* translated by John Chamberlain et al. (New York: Reynal & Hitchcock, Inc., 1939), p. 659.

[5]"Of Queen's Gardens," from *Sesame and Lilies* (London: George Allen & Unwin, Ltd., 1960), p. 107.

THE WIFE'S LAMENT

"The Wife's Lament," an anonymous poem, is contained in the *Exeter Book,* one of
the four main codices of Old English poetry. The book was given to Exeter
Cathedral by Leofric, Bishop of Devon and Cornwall, who died in 1072. This is one
of the few surviving examples of Anglo-Saxon love poetry; it dates from the period
between A.D. 780 and 830.

This modern version is by the contemporary American poet Ann Stanford.

I make this song   about me full sadly
my own warfaring.   I a woman tell
what griefs I had   since I grew up
new or old   never more than now.
Ever I know   the dark of my exile.

First my lord went out   away from his people
over the wave-tumult.   I grieved each dawn
wondered where my lord   my first on earth might be.
Then I went forth   a friendless exile
to seek service   in my sorrow's need.   10
My man's kinsmen   began to plot
by darkened thought   to divide us two
so we most widely   in the world's kingdom
lived wretchedly   and I suffered longing.

My lord commanded me   to move my dwelling here.
I had few loved ones   in this land
or faithful friends.   For this my heart grieves:
that I should find the man   well matched to me
hard of fortune   mournful of mind
hiding his mood   thinking of murder.   20

Blithe was our bearing   often we vowed
that but death alone   would part us two
naught else.   But this is turned round
now . . .   as if it never were
our friendship.   I must far and near
bear the anger   of my beloved.
The man sent me out   to live in the woods
under an oak tree   in this den in the earth.
Ancient this earth hall.   I am all longing.

The valleys are dark   the hills high   30

the yard overgrown   bitter with briars
a joyless dwelling.   Full oft the lack of my lord
seizes me cruelly here.   Friends there are on earth
living beloved   lying in bed
while I at dawn   am walking alone
under the oak tree   through these earth halls.
There I may sit   the summerlong day
there I can weep   over my exile
my many hardships.   Hence I may not rest
from this care of heart   which belongs to me ever   40
nor all this longing   that has caught me in this life.

May that young man   be sad-minded always
hard his heart's thought   while he must wear
a blithe bearing   with care in the breast
a crowd of sorrows.   May on himself depend
all his world's joy.   Be he outlawed far
in a strange folk-land—   that my beloved sits
under a rocky cliff   rimed with frost
a lord dreary in spirit   drenched with water
in a ruined hall.   My lord endures   50
much care of mind.   He remembers too often
a happier dwelling.   Woe be to them
that for a loved one   must wait in longing.

THE FARMER'S CURST WIFE

This anonymous ballad appears in Francis James Child's collection *English and Scottish Popular Ballads.* Robert Burns also wrote a ballad on this same theme. Child summarizes the ballad thus: "The devil comes for a farmer's wife and is made welcome to her by the husband. The woman proves to be no more controllable in hell than she had been at home; she kicks the imps about, and even brains a set of them with her pattens or a maul. For safety's sake, the devil is constrained to take her back to her husband." Similar tales are current in numerous European and Oriental analogs.

1
There was an old farmer in Sussex did dwell,
    (*Chorus of whistlers*)
There was an old farmer in Sussex did dwell,
And he had a bad wife, as many knew well.
    (*Chorus of whistlers*)

2
Then Satan came to the old man at the plough:
'One of your family I must have now.

3
'It is not your eldest son that I crave,
But it is your old wife, and she I will have.'

4
'O welcome, good Satan, with all my heart!
I hope you and she will never more part.'

5
Now Satan has got the old wife on his back,   10
And he lugged her along, like a pedlar's pack.

6
He trudged away till they came to his hall-gate;
Says he, Here, take in an old Sussex chap's mate.

7
O then she did kick the young imps about;
Says one to the other, Let's try turn her out.

8
She spied thirteen imps all dancing in chains,
She up with her pattens and beat out their brains.

9
She knocked the old Satan against the wall:
'Let's turn her out, or she'll murder us all.'

10
Now he's bundled her up on his back amain,   20
And to her old husband he took her again.

11
'I have been a tormentor the whole of my life,
But I neer was tormented so as with your wife.'

THE WEE COOPER OF FIFE

This anonymous Scots ballad is also known as "The Wife Wrapt in Wether's Skin,"
under which title it appears in Francis James Child's *English and Scottish Popular*

Ballads. According to Child, "Robin has married a wife of too high kin to bake or brew, wash or wring. He strips off a wether's skin and lays it on her back, or pins her in it. He dares not beat her, for her proud kind, but he may beat the wether's skin, and does. This makes an ill wife good." The version below is from A. Whitelaw's *Book of Scottish Song* (1855).

1
There was a wee cooper who lived in Fife,
   Nickity, nackity, noo, noo, noo
And he has gotten a gentle wife.
   Hey Willie Wallacky, how John Dougall,
   Alane, quo Rushety, roue, roue, roue

2
She wadna bake, nor she wadna brew,
For the spoiling o her comely hue.

3
She wadna card, nor she wadna spin,
For the shaming o her gentle kin.

4
She wadna wash, nor she wadna wring,
For the spoiling o her gouden ring.

   10

5
The coopers awa to his woo'-pack
And has laid a sheep-skin on his wife's back.

6
"It's I'll no thrash ye, for your proud kin,
But I will thrash my ain sheep-skin."

7
"Oh, I will bake, and I will brew,
And never mair think on my comely hue.

8
"Oh, I will card, and I will spin,
And never mair think on my gentle kin.

9
"Oh, I will wash, and I will wring,
And never mair think on my gouden ring."

   20

10
A' ye who hae gotten a gentle wife
Send ye for the wee cooper o Fife.

THE CLERK'S TALE from THE CANTERBURY TALES

Geoffrey Chaucer   (1340?–1400)

The son of a London vintner, Chaucer entered the service of the Duke of Clarence in 1357, was taken prisoner in France, and was ransomed in 1360. Chaucer married in 1366. His wife, Philippa, died some twenty years later; Chaucer never remarried. His life was spent in public service. As no books were printed in England until 1476, Chaucer's poems had limited circulation in manuscript form.

"The Clerk's Tale" forms part of the so-called marriage debate in *The Canterbury Tales*. The Clerk's point, that a wife has no will but her husband's, is directly opposite to the point the Wife of Bath makes in her tale. The central figure in "The Clerk's Tale" is Griselda, a poor girl who has married a nobleman who has been pressured into marriage by his councillors. One clause in their marriage contract states that she will never question his will or his actions. In the first books of "The Clerk's Tale," the Marquis has pretended to kill their daughter and their son—and Griselda has voiced no objection. Now the Marquis seeks to try Griselda again. This modernized version of Chaucer is by Nevill Coghill.

Meanwhile, according to his cruel bent,
The Marquis sought to test his wife yet more,
And by the uttermost experiment
To prove her spirit to the very core,
Whether she still were steadfast as before;
And so in open audience one day
And in a blustering voice he chose to say:

'It was agreeable enough, forsooth,
To marry you, Griselda, in the flower
Of your obedient love and simple truth,   10
And not for lineage or for worldly dower;
But now I know in very truth that power,
If one reflects, is nothing much to praise;
It is servitude in many ways.

'I may not do as any ploughman may;
My subjects are constraining me to take
Another wife, they clamour day by day.
Even the Pope has thought it fit to slake
Their rancour by consenting, you need make
No doubt of that; indeed I have to say   20
My second wife is now upon her way.

'Strengthen your heart to give her up your place.

As for the dowry that you brought of old,
Take it again, I grant it as a grace;
Go home, rejoin your father in his fold.
No one can count upon his luck to hold,
And I enjoin you to endure the smart
Of fortune's buffets with an even heart.'

She answered patiently without pretence: 30
'My lord, I know as I have always done
That, set against your high magnificence,
My poverty makes no comparison.
It cannot be denied, and I for one
Was never worthy, never in my life,
To be your chambermaid, much less your wife.

'And in this house whose lady you have made me,
As God's my witness whom I love and fear,
And as His power may gladden me and aid me,
I never thought myself the mistress here,   40
Rather a servant, humble and sincere,
To your high honour; so I shall think for ever
Of you, above all creatures whatsoever.

'That you so long of your benignity
Have held me high in honour and display,
Whereas I was not worthy so to be,
I thank my God and you; and now I pray
Revoke it, for there is no more to say.
Gladly I seek my father and will live
My life with him, whatever life may give.

'For I was fostered there when I was small,   50
Only a child, and there I'll live and die
A widow clean in body, heart and all;
I gave my maidenhead to you, and I
Am still your faithful wife, I do not lie.
And God forbid a wife to one so great
Should take another man to be her mate.

'Touching your second wife, may God in grace
Grant you both joy and long prosperity,
For I will gladly yield her up my place
That once was such a happiness to me.   60
But since it pleases you, my lord,' said she,
'In whom was formerly my whole heart's rest,
Then I will go when you shall think it best.

'But as you proffer me what first I brought,
Such dowry as I had, it's in my mind

It was my wretched clothing and worth nought,
And would indeed be hard for me to find.
O blessed God, how noble and how kind
You seemed in speech, in countenance, in carriage,
That day, the day on which we made our marriage!   70

'It's truly said, at least I find it true
For the effect of it is proved in me,
"A love grown old is not the love once new."
And yet whatever the adversity,
Though it were death, my lord, it cannot be
That ever I should repent, though I depart,
For having wholly given you my heart.

'My lord, you know that in my father's place
You stripped me of my rags and in their stead
Gave me rich garments, as an act of grace.   80
I brought you nothing else it may be said
But faith and nakedness and maidenhead.
Here I return your garments and restore
My wedding-ring as well, for evermore.

'And the remainder of the gems you lent
Are in your chamber I can safely say.
Naked out of my father's house I went
And naked I return again to-day;
Gladly I'll do your pleasure, if I may.
But yet I hope you will not make a mock   90
Of me or send me forth without a smock.

'So infamous a thing you could not do
As let the womb in which your children lay
Be seen in nakedness, bare to the view
Of all your people, let me not I pray
Go naked as a worm upon the way.
Bethink yourself, my own dear lord, because
I was your wife, unworthy though I was.

'Therefore in guerdon of my maidenhead
Which, hither brought, returns with me no more,   100
Vouchsafe a payment, give to me instead
Just such a simple smock as once I wore
To hide the womb of one that heretofore
Has been your wife; and here at last I leave you
And bid farewell, dear lord, lest I should grieve you.'

'The smock,' he said, 'you have upon your back
You may retain; remove it to your stall.'
Yet as he spoke his voice began to crack

For pity, and he turned and left the hall.
She stripped her garments in the sight of all
And in her smock, head bare and feet unshod,
Home to her father and his house she trod.

Folk followed weeping when she passed them by,
They railed on fate for all that had occurred.
Her eyes withheld their weeping and were dry
And at this time she did not speak a word.
The news soon reached her father; when he heard
He cursed the day and hour of his birth
That fashioned him a man to live on earth.

He, never doubt it, though so old and poor,
Had ever been suspicious of the match,
Had always thought it never could endure,
In that the marquis, having had the snatch
Of his desires, would feel disgrace attach
To his estate in such a low alliance
And when he could would set it at defiance.

At her approach he hastened forth to meet her
Led by the sound of many a beholder
That wept to see her pass, and he to greet her
Brought her old cloak and cast it on her shoulder
And wept. It fitted not, for it was older
By many a day than was her wedding-dress;
The cloth was coarsely wove, comfortless.

Thus with her father for a certain space
This flower of love and wifely patience stayed.
Never a word or look upon her face
In front of others or alone conveyed
A hint that she had suffered, or betrayed
Any remembrance of her former glory;
Her countenance told nothing of her story.

And that's no wonder; in her high estate
Her spirit had a full humility,
No tender mouth for food, no delicate
Heart's hungering after royal brilliancy
Or show of pomp; benignly, patiently,
She had lived wise in honour, void of pride,
Meek and unchanging at her husband's side.

They speak of Job and his humility,
For clerics when they wish to can endite
Its praises nobly, and especially,
In men—they praise few women when they write;

110

120

130

140

150

Yet none can reach a humbleness as white
As women can, nor can be half so true
As women are, or else it's something new.

Now from Bologna he of whom I spoke,
The earl, arrived. The greater and the less
Got wind of it and all the common folk
Buzzed with the news a second marchioness
Was being brought in all the loftiness
Of pomp and splendour. Such a sight to see   160
Had never been known in all west Lombardy.

The marquis, who had planned and knew it all,
Before the earl had fully reached his place,
Sent down for poor Griselda in her stall;
And she with humble heart and happy face
Came at his bidding, all without a trace
Of swelling thought, and went upon her knees
And greeted him with reverence and at ease.

'Griselda' said he, 'my will is firmly set.
This maiden hither brought to be my bride   170
To-morrow shall as royally be met
As possible, with all I can provide
That's in my house. My servants, side by side
According to their rank, shall wait upon her
As may be best arranged in joy and honour.

'I have no woman of sufficient skill
To decorate the chambers as I hold
They should be decorated. If you will,
I should be glad to see it all controlled
By you who know me and my tastes of old.   180
And though your dress is not a thing of beauty,
I hope at least that you will do your duty.'

'Not only, lord, would I be glad,' said she,
'To do your will; I long and shall endeavour
To serve and please you in my own degree
And not to faint in service, now or ever.
For neither grief or happiness can sever
My love from me. My heart can never rest
Save in the ceaseless will to love you best.'

And she began upon the decorations;   190
There were the boards to set, the beds to make.
All she could do in many occupations
She did, and begged the maids for goodness' sake
To hurry and to sweep and dust and shake,

While she, most serviceable of them all,
Went garnishing the chambers and the hall.

The earl arrived, beginning to alight
With the two children early in the day,
And all the people ran to see the sight
Of so much opulence and rich array.   200
And soon among them there were those to say
That Walter was no fool, and though obsessed
To change his wife, it might be for the best.

'For she is lovelier,' they all agreed,
'And younger than Griselda. Put the case
That fruit will fall to them; a fairer breed
Will issue from such lineage and grace.'
Her brother had so beautiful a face
It caught them with delight, opinion changed
And now applauded what their lord arranged.   210

'O stormy people, frivolous and fickle,
Void of true judgement, turning like a vane,
Whom every novelty and rumour tickle,
How like the moon you are to wax and wane,
Clapping your praises, shouting your disdain,
False judges, dear at a penny as a rule,
Who trusts to your opinion is a fool.'

So said the serious people of the city
Who watched the throng go gazing up and down
Glad merely for the novelty, the pretty   220
New lady that had come to grace the town.
But let me leave the pleasure-seeking clown
And turn to my Griselda, in the press
Of all her labours, in her steadfastness.

Busy in all, she worked, disposed and settled,
Laboured and strove to cater and adorn,
Nor did she seem at all abashed or nettled
Although her clothes were coarse and somewhat torn,
But with a face as cheerful as the morn
Went to the gate with all her retinue   230
To greet the marchioness, and then withdrew.

[In the final section, the Marquis brings back his children and resumes his marriage
with Griselda, who is universally acclaimed as a perfect wife for her patience and
obedience.]

A VALEDICTION: FORBIDDING MOURNING

John Donne   (1573?–1631)

The son of an ironmonger and of the daughter of dramatist John Heywood, Donne
was born in London. He was reared as a Roman Catholic secretly because
Catholicism was under suspicion during Elizabeth's reign. In 1601 Donne was
arrested for his secret marriage to Anne More, niece of the Lord Keeper of the
Great Seal. Gradually Donne gained the sympathy of influential patrons, and in
1614 he was ordained and held several rectorships. Anne More Donne died in 1617,
survived by seven of her fourteen children. In 1621 Donne became dean of St.
Paul's, a position he held until his death. He never remarried.

"A Valediction: Forbidding Mourning" is said to be Donne's gift to his wife before
his departure for France in 1611.

As virtuous men passe mildly away,
   And whisper to their soules, to goe,
Whilst some of their sad friends doe say,
   The breath goes now, and some say, no:

So let us melt, and make no noise,
   No teare-floods, nor sigh-tempests move,
T'were prophanation of our joyes
   To tell the layetie our love.

Moving of th'earth brings harmes and feares,
   Men reckon what it did and meant,   10
But trepidation of the spheares,
   Though greater farre, is innocent.

Dull sublunary lovers love,
   (Whose soule is sense) cannot admit
Absence, because it doth remove
   Those things which elemented it.

But we by a love, so much refin'd,
   That our selves know not what it is,
Inter-assured of the mind,
   Care lesse, eyes, lips, and hands to misse.   20

Our two soules therefore, which are one,
   Though I must goe, endure not yet
A breach, but an expansion,
   Like gold to ayery thinnesse beate.

If they be two, they are two so
  As stiffe twin compasses are two,
Thy soule the fixt foot, makes no show
  To move, but doth, if th'other doe.

And though it in the center sit,
  Yet when the other far doth rome,
It leanes, and hearkens after it,
  And growes erect, as that comes home.

30

Such wilt thou be to mee, who must
  Like th'other foot, obliquely runne;
Thy firmness drawes my circle just,
  And makes me end, where I begunne.

CHORUS from MARIAM

Lady Elizabeth Tanfield Carey   (1585?–1639)

The daughter of the Lord Chief Baron of the Exchequer, Lady Elizabeth was tutored by the poet John Davies of Hereford and became well known for her learning. She married Sir Henry Carey, later Viscount Falkland, and went with him to Ireland when he became lord deputy in 1622. Her conversion to Catholicism in 1625 estranged her from her husband, and she lived the remainder of her life in poverty.

"'Tis not enough for one that is a wife" is a speech of the chorus in Act II of *The Tragedie of Mariam, the Faire Queene of Jewry,* published in 1613 and attributed to "that learned, vertuous and truly noble Ladie E. C."

'Tis not enough for one that is a wife
  To keep her spotless from an act of ill;
But from suspicion she should free her life,
  And bare herself of power as well as will.
'Tis not so glorious for her to be free,
As by her proper self restrained to be.

When she hath spacious ground to walk upon,
  Why on the ridge should she desire to go?
It is no glory to forbear alone
  Those things that may her honour overthrow:
But 'tis thankworthy, if she will not take
All lawful liberties for honour's sake.

10

That wife her hand against her fame doth rear,

That more than to her lord alone will give
A private word to any second ear;
  And though she may with reputation live,
Yet though most chaste, she doth her glory blot,
And wounds her honour, though she kills it not.

When to their husbands they themselves do bind,
  Do they not wholly give themselves away?   20
Or give they but their body, not their mind,
  Reserving that, though best, for others' prey?
No, sure their thoughts no more can be their own,
And therefore should to none but one be known.

Then she usurps upon another's right,
  That seeks to be by public language graced;
And though her thoughts reflect with purest light
  Her mind, if not peculiar, is not chaste.
For in a wife it is no worse to find
A common body, than a common mind.   30

And every mind, though free from thought of ill,
  That out of glory seeks a worth to show,
When any's ears but one therewith thye fill,
  Doth in a sort her pureness overthrow.
Now Mariam had (but that to this she bent)
Been free from fear, as well as innocent.

PARADISE LOST

John Milton   (1608–1674)

Milton's father was a notary who had been disinherited by his Roman Catholic family for joining the Church of England. Milton received his M.A. from Cambridge in 1632. His father's prosperity enabled Milton to devote five years to writing. In 1643 he married Mary Powell, a Royalist half his age; this marriage prompted Milton to write *The Doctrine and Discipline of Divorce.* Mary Powell died after bearing four children. In 1656 Milton married Catherine Woodcocke, who died in childbirth. In 1663 Milton married Elizabeth Minshull. In 1649 Milton had become Cromwell's Latin secretary for foreign affairs, a post he held until the Restoration, though he was completely blind by 1652. Although Milton's books were burned by the public hangman when Charles II gained the throne, Milton himself was spared, probably through the intercession of Andrew Marvell. Milton's three religious works—*Paradise Lost, Paradise Regained,* and *Samson Agonistes*—were written in this last period of his life.

Paradise Lost was completed in 1665 and published in 1667. The following selection is taken from Book 9.

THE ARGUMENT

> Satan *having compast the Earth, with meditated guile returns as a mist by Night into Paradise, enters into the Serpent sleeping.* Adam *and* Eve *in the Morning go forth to their labours, which* Eve *proposes to divide in several places, each labouring apart;* Adam *consents not, alledging the danger, lest that Enemy, of whom they were forewarn'd, should attempt her found alone:* Eve *loath to be thought not circumspect or firm enough, urges her going apart, the rather desirous to make tryal of her strength;* Adam *at last yields: The Serpent finds her alone; his subtle approach, first gazing, then speaking, with much flattery extolling* Eve *above all other Creatures.* Eve *wondring to hear the Serpent speak, asks how he attain'd to human speech and such understanding not till now; the Serpent answers, that by tasting of a certain Tree in the Garden he attain'd both to Speech and Reason, till then void of both:* Eve *requires him to bring her to that Tree, and finds it to be the Tree of Knowledge forbidden: The Serpent now grown bolder, with many wiles and arguments induces her at length to eat; she pleas'd with the taste deliberates a while whether to impart thereof to* Adam *or not, at last brings him of the Fruit, relates what perswaded her to eat thereof:* Adam *at first amaz'd, but perceiving her lost, resolves through vehemence of love to perish with her; and extenuating the trespass, eats also of the Fruit: The Effects thereof in them both; they seek to cover thir nakedness; then fall to variance and accusation of one another. . . .*

. . . .

So saying, her rash hand in evil hour   780
Forth reaching to the Fruit, she pluck'd, she eat:
Earth felt the wound, and Nature from her seat
Sighing through all her Works gave signs of woe,
That all was lost. Back to the Thicket slunk
The guiltie Serpent, and well might, for *Eve*
Intent now wholly on her taste, naught else
Regarded, such delight till then, as seemd,
In Fruit she never tasted, whether true
Or fansied so, through expectation high
Of knowledg, nor was God-head from her thought.   790
Greedily she ingorg'd without restraint,
And knew not eating Death: Satiate at length,
And hight'nd as with Wine, jocond and boon,
Thus to her self she pleasingly began.
O Sovran, vertuous, precious of all Trees
In Paradise, of operation blest
To Sapience, hitherto obscur'd, infam'd,
And thy fair Fruit let hang, as to no end
Created; but henceforth my early care,
Not without Song, each Morning, and due praise   800
Shall tend thee, and the fertil burden ease
Of thy full branches offer'd free to all;

Till dieted by thee I grow mature
In knowledge, as the Gods who all things know;
Though others envie what they cannot give;
For had the gift bin theirs, it had not here
Thus grown. Experience, next to thee I owe,
Best guide; not following thee, I had remain
In ignorance, thou op'nst Wisdoms way,
And giv'st access, though secret she retire.   810
And I perhaps am secret; Heav'n is high,
High and remote to see from thence distinct
Each thing on Earth; and other care perhaps
May have diverted from continual watch
Our great Forbidder, safe with all his Spies
About him. But to *Adam* in what sort
Shall I appeer? shall I to him make known
As yet my change, and give him to partake
Full happiness with mee, or rather not,
But keep the odds of Knowledge in my power   820
Without Copartner? so to add what wants
In Femal Sex, the more to draw his Love,
And render me more equal, and perhaps,
A thing not undesireable, somtime
Superior; for inferior who is free?
This may be well: but what if God have seen,
And Death ensue? then I shall be no more,
And *Adam* wedded to another *Eve,*
Shall live with her enjoying, I extinct;
A death to think. Confirm'd then I resolve,   830
Adam shall share with me in bliss or woe:
So dear I love him, that with him all deaths
I could endure, without him live no life.
. . . .

She gave him of that fair enticing Fruit
With liberal hand: he scrupl'd not to eat
Against his better knowledge, not deceav'd,
But fondly overcome with Femal charm.
Earth trembl'd from her entrails, as again   1000
In pangs, and Nature gave a second groan,
Skie lowr'd and muttering Thunder, som sad drops
Wept at compleating of the mortal Sin
Original; while *Adam* took no thought,
Eating his fill, nor *Eve* to iterate
Her former trespass fear'd, the more to soothe
Him with her lov'd societie, that now
As with new Wine intoxicated both
They swim in mirth, and fansie that they feel
Divinitie within them breeding wings   1010
Wherewith to scorne the Earth: but that false Fruit
Farr other operation first displaid,

Carnal desire enflaming, hee on *Eve*
Began to cast lascivious Eyes, she him
As wantonly repaid; in Lust they burne:
Till *Adam* thus 'gan *Eve* to dalliance move,
. . . .
Her hand he seis'd, and to a shadie bank,
Thick overhead with verdant roof imbowr'd
He led her nothing loath; Flours were the Couch,
Pansies, and Violets, and Asphodel,   1040
And Hyacinth, Earths freshest softest lap.
There they thir fill of Love and Loves disport
Took largely, of thir mutual guilt the Seale,
The solace of thir sin, till dewie sleep
Oppress'd them, wearied with thir amorous play.
Soon as the force of that fallacious Fruit,
That with exhilerating vapour bland
About thir spirits had plaid, and inmost powers
Made erre, was now exhal'd, and grosser sleep
Bred of unkindly fumes, with conscious dreams   1050
Encumberd, now had left them, up they rose
As from unrest, and each the other viewing,
Soon found thir Eyes how op'nd, and thir minds
How dark'nd; innocence, that as a veile
Had shadow'd them from knowing ill, was gon,
Just confidence, and native righteousness
And honour from about them, naked left
To guiltie shame hee cover'd, but his Robe
Uncover'd more, so rose the *Danite* strong
Herculean Samson from the Harlot-lap   1060
Of *Philistean Dalilah,* and wak'd
Shorn of his strength, They destitute and bare
Of all thir vertue: silent, and in face
Confounded long they sate, as struck'n mute,
Till *Adam,* though not less than *Eve* abash't,
At length gave utterance to these words constraind.
   O *Eve,* in evil hour thou didst give eare
To that false Worm, of whomsoever taught
To counterfet Mans voice, true in our Fall,
False in our promis'd Rising; since our Eyes   1070
Op'nd we find indeed, and find we know
Both Good and Evil, Good lost, and Evil got,
Bad Fruit of Knowledge, if this be to know,
Which leaves us naked thus, of Honour void,
Of Innocence, of Faith, of Puritie,
Our wonted Ornaments now soild and staind,
And in our Faces evident the signes
Of foul concupiscence; whence evil store;
Even shame, the last of evils; of the first
Be sure then. How shall I behold the face   1080

Henceforth of God or Angel, earst with joy
And rapture so ofte beheld? those heav'nly shapes
Will dazle now this earthly, with thir blaze
Insufferably bright. O might I here
In solitude live savage, in some glade
Obscur'd, where highest Woods impenetrable
To Starr or Sun-light, spread thir umbrage broad
And brown as Evening: Cover me ye Pines,
Ye Cedars, with innumerable boughs
Hide me, where I may never see them more.   1090
But let us now, as in bad plight, devise
What best may from the present serve to hide
The Parts of each for other, that seem most
To shame obnoxious, and unseemliest seen,
Some Tree whose broad smooth Leaves together sowd,
And girded on our loyns, may cover round
Those middle parts, that this new commer, Shame,
There sit not, and reproach us as unclean.
. . . .
    To whom soon mov'd with touch of blame thus *Eve*.
What words have past thy Lips, *Adam* severe,
Imput'st thou that to my default, or will
Of wandring, as thou call'st it, which who knows
But might as ill have happ'nd thou being by,
Or to thy self perhaps: hadst thou been there,
Or here th' attempt, thou couldst not have discernd
Fraud in the Serpent, speaking as he spake;   1150
No ground of enmitie between us known,
Why hee should mean me ill, or seek to harme.
Was I to have never parted from thy side?
As good have grown there still a liveless Rib.
Being as I am, why didst not thou the Head
Command me absolutely not to go,
Going into such danger as thou saidst?
Too facil then thou didst not much gainsay,
Nay didst permit, approve, and fair dismiss.
Hadst thou bin firm and fixt in thy dissent,   1160
Neither had I transgress'd, nor thou with mee.
    To whom then first incenst *Adam* repli'd,
Is this the Love, is this the recompence
Of mine to thee, ingrateful *Eve*, exprest
Immutable when thou wert lost, not I,
Who might have liv'd and joyd immortal bliss,
Yet willingly chose rather Death with thee:
And am I now upbraided, as the cause
Of thy transgressing? not enough severe,
It seems, in thy restraint: what could I more?   1170
I warn'd thee, I admonish'd thee, foretold
The danger, and the lurking Enemie

That lay in wait; beyond this had bin force,
And force upon free will hath here no place.
But confidence then bore thee on, secure
Either to meet no danger, or to finde
Matter of glorious trial; and perhaps
I also err'd in overmuch admiring
What seemd in thee so perfet, that I thought
No evil durst attempt thee, but I rue   1180
That errour now, which is become my crime,
And thou th' accuser. Thus it shall befall
Him who to worth in Women overtrusting
Lets her will rule; restraint she will not brook,
And left to her self, if evil thence ensue,
Shee first his weak indulgence will accuse.
    Thus they in mutual accusation spent
The fruitless hours, but neither self-condemning,
And of thir vain contest appeer'd no end.

THE END OF THE NINTH BOOK

A LETTER TO HER HUSBAND, ABSENT ON PUBLIC EMPLOYMENT

Anne Dudley Bradstreet   (c. 1612–1672)

Anne Dudley was born in England and married at sixteen. She accompanied her husband and her father, the governor of the Massachusetts Bay Colony, to America, where she raised eight children. In 1650 *The Tenth Muse, Lately Sprung up in America* was published in England; her admiring brother-in-law had taken the manuscript there without her knowledge.

"A Letter to Her Husband" was not intended for publication and did not appear until the posthumous 1678 edition of Bradstreet's poems.

As loving Hind that (Hartless) wants her Deer,
Scuds through the woods and fern with hark'ning ear,
Perplexed, in every bush and nook doth pry,
Her dearest Deer, might answer ear or eye;
So doth my anxious soul, which now doth miss,
A dearer Dear (far dearer Heart) than this,
Still wait with doubts, and hopes, and failing eye,
His voice to hear, or person to descry.
Or as the pensive Dove doth all alone
(On withered bough) most uncouthly bemoan   10

The absence of her Love, and loving Mate,
Whose loss hath made her so unfortunate:
Ev'n thus do I, with many a deep sad groan
Bewail my turtle true, who now is gone,
His presence and his safe return, still woos,
With thousand doleful sighs and mournful coos.
Or as the loving Mullet, that true Fish,
Her fellow lost, nor joy nor life do wish,
But launches on that shore, there for to die,
Where she her captive husband doth espy.   20
Mine being gone, I lead a joyless life,
I have a loving fere, yet seem no wife:
But worst of all, to him can't steer my course,
I here, he there, alas, both kept by force:
Return my Dear, my joy, my only Love,
Unto thy Hind, thy Mullet and thy Dove,
Who neither joys in pasture, house nor streams,
The substance gone, O me, these are but dreams.
Together at one tree, oh let us browse,
And like two Turtles roost within one house,   30
And like the Mullets in one river glide,
Let's still remain but one, till death divide.

    Thy loving Love and Dearest Dear,
    At home, abroad, and every where.

THE UNEQUAL FETTERS

Anne Kingsmill Finch, Countess of Winchilsea   (1661–1720)

Born into the nobility, Anne Kingsmill received her education at home and entered the court as maid of honor to the Duchess of York. In 1684 she married Colonel Heneage Finch; they had no children. In 1690 she retired to her country estate, where she wrote poems on nature, which she circulated among her friends. Pope wrote verses in her honor, and Wordsworth collected an anthology of her poems, partly from unpublished manuscripts.

"The Unequal Fetters," though contained in the folio manuscript of poems (dated around 1702) and probably in circulation among friends, was not published until 1903, when Myra Reynolds brought out *The Poems of Anne Countess of Winchilsea* at the University of Chicago.

Cou'd we stop the time that's flying
  Or recall itt when 'tis past

Put far off the day of Dying
   Or make Youth for ever last
To Love wou'd then be worth our cost.

But since we must loose those Graces
   Which at first your hearts have wonne
And you seek for in new Faces
   When our Spring of Life is done
It wou'd but urdge our ruine on.   10

Free as Nature's first intention
   Was to make us, I'll be found
Nor by subtle Man's invention
   Yeild to be in Fetters bound
By one that walks a freer round.

Mariage does but slightly tye Men
   Whil'st close Pris'ners we remain
They the larger Slaves of Hymen
   Still are begging Love again
At the full length of all their chain.   20

AULD ROBIN GRAY

Lady Anne Lindsay Barnard   (1750–1825)

The daughter of a Scots earl, Lady Anne established a home in London with her widowed sister. There she married Andrew Barnard, with whom she went to South Africa for fourteen years, returning to London at his death. "Auld Robin Gray" was written when Lady Anne was twenty-one. Enchanted by an English-Scotch ballad, but disapproving of the words, which she found improper, she composed a new set of words to accompany the melody. It was only at age seventy-two, in a letter to Sir Walter Scott, that Lady Anne acknowledged having written the verses.

"Auld Robin Gray" was composed in 1771 and published anonymously. In 1824 Sir Walter Scott prepared a thin quarto volume for the Bannatyne Club which included the story of the composition of "Auld Robin Gray," a revised text, and two inferior continuations.

When the sheep are in the fauld, and the kye at hame,
And a' the warld to rest are gane,
The waes o' my heart fa' in showers frae my e'e,
While my gudeman lies sound by me.

Young Jamie lo'ed me weel, and sought me for his bride;
But saving a croun he had naething else beside:
To make the croun a pund, young Jamie gaed to sea;
And the croun and the pund were baith for me.

He hadna been awa' a week but only twa,
When my father brak his arm, and the cow was stown awa';   10
My mother she fell sick,—and my Jamie at the sea—
And auld Robin Gray came a-courtin' me.

My father couldna work, and my mother couldna spin;
I toiled day and night, but their bread I couldna win;
Auld Rob maintain'd them baith, and wi' tears in his e'e
Said, "Jennie, for their sakes, O, marry me!"

My heart it said nay; I look'd for Jamie back;
But the wind it blew high, and the ship it was a wrack;
His ship it was a wrack—Why didna Jamie dee?
Or why do I live to cry, Wae's me!   20

My father urged me sair: my mother didna speak;
But she look'd in my face till my heart was like to break:
They gie'd him my hand, tho' my heart was in the sea;
Sae auld Robin Gray he was gudeman to me.

I hadna been a wife a week but only four,
When mournfu' as I sat on the stane at the door,
I saw my Jamie's wraith,—for I couldna think it he,
Till he said, "I'm come hame to marry thee."

O sair, sair did we greet, and muckle did we say;
We took but ae kiss, and we tore ourselves away: 30
I wish that I were dead, but I'm no like to dee;
And why was I born to say, Wae's me!

I gang like a ghaist, and I carena to spin;
I daurna think on Jamie, for that wad be a sin;
But I'll do my best a guide wife aye to be,
For auld Robin Gray he is kind unto me.

MY LAST DUCHESS

Robert Browning   (1812–1889)

Born into comfortable circumstances, Browning was educated at home. After an attempt at musical composition, he decided at seventeen to become a poet. His first published volume, *Pauline* (1833), was written in response to a visit to St. Petersburg. He also visited Italy. In 1846 he was introduced to Elizabeth Barrett, whose poems he had already read. The marriage, following their elopement, was spent mainly in Italy. After his wife's death in 1861, Browning lived primarily in London. His reputation grew, culminating in the formation of the Browning Society in 1881. Browning died of pneumonia at his son's home in Venice.

"My Last Duchess" was published in 1842.

That's my last Duchess painted on the wall,
Looking as if she were alive. I call
That piece a wonder, now: Frà Pandolf's hands
Worked busily a day, and there she stands.
Will't please you sit and look at her? I said
"Frà Pandolf" by design, for never read
Strangers like you that pictured countenance,
That depth and passion of its earnest glance,
But to myself they turned (since none puts by
The curtain I have drawn for you, but I)   10
And seemed as they would ask me, if they durst,
How such a glance came there; so, not the first
Are you to turn and ask thus. Sir, 'twas not
Her husband's presence only, called that spot
Of joy into the Duchess' cheek: perhaps
Fra Pandolf chanced to say "Her mantle laps
Over my lady's wrist too much," or "Paint
Must never hope to reproduce the faint
Half-flush that dies along her throat:" such stuff
Was courtesy, she thought, and cause enough   20
For calling up that spot of joy. She had
A heart—how shall I say?—too soon made glad,
Too easily impressed; she liked whate'er
She looked on, and her looks went everywhere.
Sir, 'twas all one! My favour at her breast,
The dropping of the daylight in the West,
The bough of cherries some officious fool
Broke in the orchard for her, the white mule
She rode with round the terrace—all and each
Would draw from her alike the approving speech,   30

Or blush, at least. She thanked men,—good! but thanked
Somehow—I know not how—as if she ranked
My gift of a nine-hundred-year-old name
With anybody's gift. Who'd stoop to blame
This sort of trifling? Even had you skill
In speech—(which I have not)—to make your will
Quite clear to such an one, and say, "Just this
Or that in you disgusts me; here you miss,
Or there exceed the mark"—and if she let
Herself be lessoned so, nor plainly set   40
Her wits to yours, forsooth, and made excuse,
—E'en then would be some stooping; and I choose
Never to stoop. Oh sir, she smiled, no doubt,
Whene'er I passed her; but who passed without
Much the same smile? This grew; I gave commands;
Then all smiles stopped together. There she stands
As if alive. Will't please you rise? We'll meet
The company below, then. I repeat,
The Count your master's known munificence
Is ample warrant that no just pretence   50
Of mine for dowry will be disallowed;
Though his fair daughter's self, as I avowed
At starting, is my object. Nay, we'll go
Together down, sir. Notice Neptune, though,
Taming a sea-horse, thought a rarity,
Which Claus of Innsbruck cast in bronze for me!

MODERN LOVE, 1

George Meredith   (1828–1909)

Born the son of a tailor at Portsmouth, Meredith was extremely sensitive to the British prejudice against tailors; it was only after his death that the myth he had created that he was of highborn, illegitimate parentage was dispelled. In 1849 he married the widowed daughter of the novelist Thomas Love Peacock. She deserted him in 1858. From 1862 to 1864 he shared a house with the Rossettis and Charles Swinborne in Chelsea, but left to marry Marie Vulliamy. Known principally for his novels, Meredith published his first of seven volumes of poetry in 1851.

Meredith's sequence *Modern Love,* of which the first poem is printed here, appeared in 1862.

By this he knew she wept with waking eyes:
That, at his hand's light quiver by her head,

The strange low sobs that shook their common bed
Were called into her with a sharp surprise,
And strangled mute, like little gaping snakes,
Dreadfully venomous to him. She lay
Stone-still, and the long darkness flowed away
With muffled pulses. Then, as midnight makes
Her giant heart of Memory and Tears
Drink the pale drug of silence, and so beat
Sleep's heavy measure, they from head to feet
Were moveless, looking through their dead black years,
By vain regret scrawled over the blank wall.
Like sculptured effigies they might be seen
Upon their marriage-tomb, the sword between;
Each wishing for the sword that severs all.

EVE

Christina Georgina Rossetti   (1830–1894)

The youngest child in her family, Rossetti was taught at home by her mother, the sister of Byron's physician. Her first volume of poems was published privately when she was twelve, and a second volume was printed when she was seventeen. Her poems first appeared publicly in the Pre-Raphaelite magazine *The Germ.* A staunch member of the Anglican Church, she broke her engagement to James Collinson, a member of the Pre-Raphaelites, when he reverted to the Catholic Church. She died of cancer after her sixty-fourth birthday.

"Eve" appeared in Rossetti's *The Prince's Progress* in 1866.

"While I sit at the door,
  Sick to gaze within,
  Mine eye weepeth sore
  For sorrow and sin:
  As a tree my sin stands
  To darken all lands;
  Death is the fruit it bore.

"How have Eden bowers grown
  Without Adam to bend them!
  How have Eden flowers blown,
  Squandering their sweet breath,
  Without me to tend them!
  The Tree of Life was ours,
  Tree twelvefold-fruited,

10

Most lofty tree that flower,
Most deeply rooted:
I chose the tree of death.

"Hadst thou but said me nay,
Adam, my brother,
I might have pined away;
I, but none other: 20
God might have let thee stay
Safe in our garden,
By putting me away
Beyond all pardon.

"I, Eve, sad mother
Of all who must live,
I, not another,
Plucked bitterest fruit to give
My friend, husband, lover,—   30
O wanton eyes run over;
Who but I should grieve?—
Cain hath slain his brother:
Of all who must die mother,
Miserable Eve!"

Thus she sat weeping,
Thus Eve, our mother,
Where one lay sleeping
Slain by his brother.
Greatest and least   40
Each piteous beast
To hear her voice
Forgot his joys
And set aside his feast.

The mouse paused in his walk
And dropped his wheaten stalk;
Grave cattle wagged their heads
In rumination;
The eagle gave a cry
From his cloud station;   50
Larks on thyme beds
Forbore to mount or sing;
Bees drooped upon the wing;
The raven perched on high
Forgot his ration;
The conies in their rock,
A feeble nation,
Quaked sympathetical;
The mocking-bird left off to mock;

Huge camels knelt as if   60
In deprecation;
The kind hart's tears were falling;
Chattered the wistful stork;
Dove-voices with a dying fall
Cooed desolation,
Answering grief by grief.
Only the serpent in the dust,
Wriggling and crawling,
Grinned an awful grin, and thrust
His tongue out with its fork.   70

THE STORY OF AN HOUR

Kate O'Flaherty Chopin   (1851–1904)

Kate O'Flaherty was born in St. Louis. Her mother came from an established
French-American family; her father, who died when she was still a child, was Irish.
In 1870 she married Oscar Chopin, of Louisiana, and after a honeymoon in Europe,
they took up residence in New Orleans. They had five sons and a daughter within
twelve years. After her husband died of swamp fever, Chopin returned to St. Louis
at her mother's urging. Chopin's short stories are generally classed with the local-
color movement, but her most impressive work is *The Awakening,* a feminist novel
advocating equal rights and sexual freedom for women. *The Dictionary of American
Biography* states: "It is one of the tragedies of recent American literature that Mrs.
Chopin should have written [*The Awakening,* published in 1899] two decades in
advance of its time, that she should have been so grievously hurt by the attacks of
provincial critics as to lay aside her pen." Chopin died of a brain hemorrhage.

"The Story of an Hour" was written in 1894, following the success of *Bayou Folk,* a
collection of short stories. "The Story of an Hour" was published in Chopin's
collection *A Night in Acadie* (1897).

Knowing that Mrs. Mallard was afflicted with a heart trouble, great care was
taken to break to her as gently as possible the news of her husband's death.
    It was her sister Josephine who told her, in broken sentences; veiled hints
that revealed in half concealing. Her husband's friend Richards was there, too,
near her. It was he who had been in the newspaper office when intelligence of
the railroad disaster was received, with Brently Mallard's name leading the list
of "killed." He had only taken the time to assure himself of its truth by a
second telegram, and had hastened to forestall any less careful, less tender
friend in bearing the sad message.
    She did not hear the story as many women have heard the same, with a

paralyzed inability to accept its significance. She wept at once, with sudden, wild abandonment, in her sister's arms. When the storm of grief had spent itself she went away to her room alone. She would have no one follow her.

There stood, facing the open window, a comfortable, roomy armchair. Into this she sank, pressed down by a physical exhaustion that haunted her body and seemed to reach into her soul.

She could see in the open square before her house the tops of trees that were all aquiver with the new spring life. The delicious breath of rain was in the air. In the street below a peddler was crying his wares. The notes of a distant song which some one was singing reached her faintly, and countless sparrows were twittering in the eaves.

There were patches of blue sky showing here and there through the clouds that had met and piled one above the other in the west facing her window.

She sat with her head thrown back upon the cushion of the chair, quite motionless, except when a sob came up into her throat and shook her, as a child who has cried itself to sleep continues to sob in its dreams.

She was young, with a fair, calm face, whose lines bespoke repression and even a certain strength. But now there was a dull stare in her eyes, whose gaze was fixed away off yonder on one of those patches of blue sky. It was not a glance of reflection, but rather indicated a suspension of intelligent thought.

There was something coming to her and she was waiting for it, fearfully. What was it? She did not know; it was too subtle and elusive to name. But she felt it, creeping out of the sky, reaching toward her through the sounds, the scents, the color that filled the air.

Now her bosom rose and fell tumultuously. She was beginning to recognize this thing that was approaching to possess her, and she was striving to beat it back with her will—as powerless as her two white slender hands would have been.

When she abandoned herself a little whispered word escaped her slightly parted lips. She said it over and over under her breath: "free, free, free!" The vacant stare and the look of terror that had followed it went from her eyes. They stayed keen and bright. Her pulses beat fast, and the coursing blood warmed and relaxed every inch of her body.

She did not stop to ask if it were or were not a monstrous joy that held her. A clear and exalted perception enabled her to dismiss the suggestion as trivial.

She knew that she would weep again when she saw the kind, tender hands folded in death; the face that had never looked save with love upon her, fixed and gray and dead. But she saw beyond that bitter moment a long procession of years to come that would belong to her absolutely. And she opened and spread her arms out to them in welcome.

There would be no one to live for her during those coming years; she would live for herself. There would be no powerful will bending hers in that blind persistence with which men and women believe they have a right to impose a private will upon a fellow-creature. A kind intention or a cruel intention made the act seem no less a crime as she looked upon it in that brief moment of illumination.

And yet she had loved him—sometimes. Often she had not. What did it matter! What could love, the unsolved mystery, count for in face of this possession of self-assertion which she suddenly recognized as the strongest impulse of her being!

"Free! Body and soul free!" she kept whispering.

Josephine was kneeling before the closed door with her lips to the keyhole, imploring for admission. "Louise, open the door! I beg; open the door—you will make yourself ill. What are you doing, Louise? For heaven's sake open the door."

"Go away. I am not making myself ill." No; she was drinking in a very elixir of life through that open window.

Her fancy was running riot along those days ahead of her. Spring days, and summer days, and all sorts of days that would be her own. She breathed a quick prayer that life might be long. It was only yesterday she had thought with a shudder that life might be long.

She arose at length and opened the door to her sister's importunities. There was a feverish triumph in her eyes, and she carried herself unwittingly like a goddess of Victory. She clasped her sister's waist, and together they descended the stairs. Richards stood waiting for them at the bottom.

Some one was opening the front door with a latchkey. It was Brently Mallard who entered, a little travel-stained, composedly carrying his grip-sack and umbrella. He had been far from the scene of accident, and did not even know there had been one. He stood amazed at Josephine's piercing cry; at Richards' quick motion to screen him from the view of his wife.

But Richards was too late.

When the doctors came they said she had died of heart disease—of joy that kills.

MATERNITY

Alice Thompson Meynell   (1847–1922)

Though born in England, Meynell spent most of her childhood in Italy. Her father was a man of means; her mother, a concert pianist; and her older sister, Elizabeth, a painter whose battle scenes had made her famous in girlhood. Meynell's first volume of poems was published in 1875. In 1877 she married the critic and journalist Wilfrid Meynell. Both husband and wife pursued writing careers in order to support themselves and their eight children. After Tennyson's death in 1892, Meynell was seriously considered for poet laureate.

"Maternity" was printed in Meynell's *Later Poems* (1901).

One wept whose only child was dead,
  New-born, ten years ago.
"Weep not; he is in bliss," they said.
  She answered, "Even so,

"Ten years ago was born in pain
  A child, not now forlorn.
But oh, ten years ago, in vain,
  A mother, a mother was born."

THE HILL WIFE

Robert Lee Frost   (1874–1963)

Born in San Francisco, Frost moved to rural New England at the age of ten. He attended Dartmouth and Harvard, but did not take a degree. After a period of miscellaneous jobs, Frost moved to England in 1912; his first book of poetry was published there in 1913. He returned to the States in 1915, settling on a New Hampshire farm. Frost held guest professorships at numerous universities and became famous for his poetry readings. He was asked to read at John F. Kennedy's inauguration in 1962.

"The Hill Wife" was printed in Frost's 1916 collection, *Mountain Interval*.

I. LONELINESS

Her Word

One ought not to have to care
  So much as you and I
Care when the birds come round the house
  To seem to say good-by;

Or care so much when they come back
  With whatever it is they sing;
The truth being we are as much
  Too glad for the one thing

As we are too sad for the other here—
  With birds that fill their breasts

10

But with each other and themselves
And their built or driven nests.

II. HOUSE FEAR

Always—I tell you this they learned—
Always at night when they returned
To the lonely house from far away,
To lamps unlighted and fire gone gray,
They learned to rattle the lock and key
To give whatever might chance to be,
Warning and time to be off in flight:
And preferring the out- to the indoor night,   20
They learned to leave the house door wide
Until they had lit the lamp inside.

III. THE SMILE

Her Word

I didn't like the way he went away.
That smile! It never came of being gay.
Still he smiled—did you see him?—I was sure!
Perhaps because we gave him only bread
And the wretch knew from that that we were poor.
Perhaps because he let us give instead
Of seizing from us as he might have seized.
Perhaps he mocked at us for being wed,   30
Or being very young (and he was pleased
To have a vision of us old and dead).
I wonder how far down the road he's got.
He's watching from the woods as like as not.

IV. THE OFT-REPEATED DREAM

She had no saying dark enough
  For the dark pine that kept
Forever trying the window latch
  Of the room where they slept.

The tireless but ineffectual hands
  That with every futile pass   40
Made the great tree seem as a little bird
  Before the mystery of glass!

It never had been inside the room,
  And only one of the two
Was afraid in an oft-repeated dream
  Of what the tree might do.

V. THE IMPULSE

It was too lonely for her there,
   And too wild,
And since there were but two of them,
   And no child,   50

And work was little in the house,
   She was free,
And followed where he furrowed field,
   Or felled tree.

She rested on a log and tossed
   The fresh chips,
With a song only to herself
   On her lips.

And once she went to break a bough
   Of black alder.   60
She strayed so far she scarcely heard
   When he called her—

And didn't answer—didn't speak—
   Or return.
She stood, and then she ran and hid
   In the fern.

He never found her, though he looked
   Everywhere,
And he asked at her mother's house
   Was she there.   70

Sudden and swift and light as that
   The ties gave,
And he learned of finalities
   Besides the grave.

THE FARMER'S BRIDE

Charlotte Mew   (1869–1928)

Brought up in Bloomsbury, where she spent most of her life, Mew began
contributing to literary periodicals during the 1890s, though her first book of poetry
was not published until 1917. Depressed by the deaths of Thomas Hardy, by whose

influence she had obtained a government pension, and of her sister Anne, who had been her closest companion, Mew committed suicide by swallowing a bottle of disinfectant. A volume of poems, *The Rambling Sailor,* was published posthumously the following year.

"The Farmer's Bride" is the title poem from Mew's 1917 volume, published by The Poetry Workshop.

> Three Summers since I chose a maid,
> Too young maybe—but more's to do
> At harvest-time than bide and woo.
>   When us was wed she turned afraid
> Of love and me and all things human;
> Like the shut of a winter's day.
> Her smile went out, and 'twasn't a woman—
>   More like a little frightened fay.
>   One night, in the Fall, she runned away.
>
> "Out 'mong the sheep, her be," they said,   10
> 'Should properly have been abed;
> But sure enough she wasn't there
> Lying awake with her wide brown stare.
> So over seven-acre field and up-along across the down
> We chased her, flying like a hare
> Before our lanterns. To Church-Town
>   All in a shiver and a scare
> We caught her, fetched her home at last
> And turned the key upon her, fast.
>
> She does the work about the house
> As well as most, but like a mouse: 20
>   Happy enough to chat and play
>   With birds and rabbits and such as they,
>   So long as men-folk keep away.
> "Not near, not near!" her eyes beseech
> When one of us comes within reach.
>   The women say that beasts in stall
>   Look round like children at her call.
>   *I've* hardly heard her speak at all.
>
> Shy as a leveret, swift as he,   30
> Straight and slight as a young larch tree,
> Sweet as the first wild violets, she,
> To her wild self. But what to me?
>
> The short days shorten and the oaks are brown,
>   The blue smoke rises to the low grey sky,
> One leaf in the still air falls slowly down,
>   A magpie's spotted feathers lie

On the black earth spread white with rime,
The berries redden up to Christmas-time.
    What's Christmas-time without there be
    Some other in the house than we!   40

    She sleeps up in the attic there
    Alone, poor maid. 'Tis but a stair
Betwixt us. Oh! my God! the down,
The soft young down of her, the brown,
The brown of her—her eyes, her hair, her hair!

PRIVATE ENTRY IN THE DIARY OF A FEMALE PARENT

Dilys Bennett Laing   (1906–1960)

Dilys Bennett was born in North Wales, where her father was a civil engineer. At two she contracted polio, which left her weak in one leg, and at twelve she underwent surgery for a mastoid infection, which left her nearly deaf in one ear. The family moved to Canada in 1912; in 1926 she went to Europe for two years with her mother to study art and languages. She met Alexander Laing at Gray's Harbor, Washington, in 1928; both had contributed poems to the magazine *Palms*. They were married in Seattle in 1936 and moved to Vermont to live. Laing became an American citizen in 1941. Although she published only three books during her lifetime (1941, 1944, and 1951), her output was extensive, and many of her poems appeared in magazines. She published a single novel (1948) and was, at the time of her death, working on another one, centering on the clash of Spanish and Aztec cultures.

"Private Entry" appeared in *The Quest* magazine and was reprinted by her son in his edition of *Collected Poems* (1967).

He is my own fault. Let me see it straight.
I got him willfully, with joy, and hatched him
a long time intimately, and in him warmed
the flaws and fineness of two ancestries,
before I had my bellyful of him
at last and threw him neck and crop
into the doctor's expert rubber hands.
Since then I've suckled, kissed and smacked him
while he has sucked and wet and beaten me
or all but beaten me, although I rise
out of the ashes at short intervals.
The end will be, perhaps, the end of me,
which will, I humbly guess, be his beginning.

BEDTIME

Denise Levertov   (1923–   )

Born in England, where she was educated privately, Levertov served as a nurse in World War II. Her first book of poems was *Double Image* (1946). She married writer Mitchell Goodman and moved to the United States in 1948. From 1956 to 1958 she lived in Mexico. She served as poetry editor of *The Nation* in 1961 and 1963.

"Bedtime" appeared in Levertov's 1967 collection, *The Sorrow Dance*.

We are a meadow where the bees hum,
mind and body are almost one

as the fire snaps in the stove
and our eyes close,

and mouth to mouth, the covers
pulled over our shoulders,

we drowse as horses drowse afield,
in accord; though the fall cold

surrounds our warm bed, and though
by day we are singular and often lonely.

MUST BE THE SEASON OF THE WITCH

Alurista   (1947–   )

Born in San Diego, Alurista has lived in Mexico and has published two books of poetry. He currently teaches at the University of Texas.

The most important figure in the oral Chicano tradition is *la llorona,* the weeping woman. Called "a central archetype in the memory of La Raza," she was an Indian woman raped by Cortez's soldiers and deserted. She bears a son and, driven insane by grief and a sense of betrayal, kills him—by throwing him down a well, according to some versions of the story. She wanders the countryside searching for her lost child. At night, in the wind, her wailing voice can still be heard. Many claim that *la llorona* is La Malinche, the Indian mistress of Cortez, who eternally laments the betrayal of her people.

"Must be the season of the witch" appeared in *El Grito,* a journal of Mexican-American studies at UCLA, and was published in Alurista's first collection of poems, *Floricanto en Aztlan* (1971).

Must be the season of the witch
    la bruja[1]
    la llorona[2]
she lost her children
    and she cries
en las barrancas of industry[3]
    her children
devoured by computers
    and the gears
Must be the season of the witch
    I hear huesos crack[4]
in pain
    y lloros[5]
la bruja pangs
    sus hijos han olvidado[6]
la magia de Durango[7]
    y la de Moctezuma
    —el Huiclamina

Must be the season of the witch
La bruja llora
sus hijos sufren; sin ella[8]

[1]*la bruja:* the witch.

[2]*la llorona:* the weeping woman.

[3]*en las barrancas:* in the shacks.

[4]*huesos:* bones.

[5]*y lloros:* and weeping.

[6]*sus hijos han olvidado:* her children have forgotten.

[7]*magia:* magic.

[8]*sus hijos sufren; sin ella:* her children suffer, without her.

THE HELPMATE: SUPPLEMENTARY READING

Edward Albee: *The American Dream* and *Who's Afraid of Virginia Woolf?*
Willa Cather: *My Mortal Enemy*
Kate Chopin: *The Storm and Other Stories*
Stephen Crane: "The Bride Comes to Yellow Sky"
Nathaniel Hawthorne: "The Birthmark"
Ernest Hemingway: "Cat in the Rain," "Mr. and Mrs. Eliot," and "The Short and Happy Life of Francis Macomber."
Susan Kaufman: *The Diary of a Mad Housewife*
D. H. Lawrence: *Lady Chatterley's Lover,* "The Rocking Horse Winner," and *Women in Love*
Jack Ludwig: "A Woman of Her Age"
Katherine Mansfield: "Bliss"
Tillie Olsen: *Tell Me a Riddle and Other Stories*
Eugene O'Neill: *Desire under the Elms* and *Long Day's Journey into Night*
Phillip Roth: *Portnoy's Complaint*
William Shakespeare: *Othello* and *The Taming of the Shrew*
George Bernard Shaw: *Candida*
John Steinbeck: *The Grapes of Wrath*
Eudora Welty: "A Curtain of Green"
Edith Wharton: "Roman Fever"
William Wycherly: *The Country Wife*

THE HERO

THE SAGE

Vincent Van Gogh: *L'Arlésienne* (portrait of Mme. Ginoux, Dutch, 1888). [*The Metropolitan Museum of Art. Bequest of Samuel A. Lewisohn, 1951.*]

The sage is an appropriate transitional figure from the section on the heroine to that on the hero. She is defined by her culture as a heroine, but she has wisdom beyond that of the culture, which labels her a virgin, mistress, or helpmate. That wisdom makes her a hero. She understands the world, but she does not engage in heroic action because the world has limited her to passive heroine roles, because she understands the futility of heroic action, or because she is beyond action, as in old age.

The female dress of priests and lawyers in patriarchal cultures indicates the association of women with both spiritual and secular wisdom. Carl Jung explains in psychological terms that men cannot relate to the spiritual world or to the unconscious without the aid of a woman or of the anima (the woman within). Beatrice is therefore essential to Dante's divine vision. In several traditional guises, real women also act as sages. In neighborhood life, women function as informal historians and social critics. Mothers pass on the spiritual, philosophical, and practical knowledge of the culture to their children.

A woman's exploration of the spiritual dimension of life may also result from her experience as a helpmate. Because she ministers to the family's physical needs, she is more keenly aware of transience and death than a man may be. Furthermore, menstruation reminds her every month of the fertility cycle of life and death which governs all living things. In the secular twentieth century, women's interest in the occult may replace their traditional involvement with religion. Martha Quest, in Doris Lessing's *The Four-Gated City,* realizes that the society she lives in makes happiness and fulfillment unlikely for men and virtually impossible for women. In attempting to avoid madness, she begins to experiment with psychic powers and develops extrasensory perception. In the novel these powers are clearly related to the empathic ability necessary to the helpmate in ministering to her family. Martha becomes secretary for Mark Coldridge and ends up managing the family's affairs. Lying in bed at night, she can hear the thoughts of everybody in the house and contemplates what she can do to help them.

Since men control the society, a woman also becomes a sage in the same way all powerless people become wise: she learns to read situations quickly in order to react appropriately and avoid the ill will of those in power. In the traditional role of silent listener, she watches and understands. Freud admitted to Marie Bonaparte that "the great question that has never been answered and which I have not been able to answer, despite my thirty years of research into the feminine soul, is 'What does a woman want?'"[1] Martha Freud never asked the same question about men. Apparently, she knew.

The sage may understand her metaphysical and/or her social reality. She may perceive that social roles limit and negate a woman's identity and preclude personal fulfillment. As Phyllis Chesler explains in *Women and Madness,* this knowledge of limitation may drive women mad, it may force them into accommodation with their society, or it may enable them to act heroically to change the society and their lives. In literature with a male protagonist, the female sage has either innate or previously acquired knowledge. Novels, plays, and long poems with a female protagonist are more likely to describe the process of her psychological development and thus to show the reader how she gains wisdom.

Authors may find that a female protagonist's outer life lacks the dramatic interest required for an interesting plot. Women do not slay dragons, kill whales, or massacre Indians, but they do embark upon journeys of the mind and of the spirit.

Confronted with the possibility of psychological growth, these female characters either transcend the psychological limitations of their roles or are defeated by them. A woman may find psychological development and integration difficult because she is required to play a series of partial roles in response to male needs, because she is taught to deny her passions and her intellect, and because she is encouraged to disguise her true self and submit her will to that of her husband for life. The psychological growth of a woman consequently may be more complex and more interesting than a man's as a subject for literature; for these reasons, novelists have regularly explored this subject over the last two centuries.

One aspect of human development is the psychic integration of reason and passion. The author who endeavors to describe a female protagonist's reconciliation of these Apollonian and Dionysian traits encounters special problems. In Henry Fielding's *Tom Jones,* the young, lusty male hero can "sow wild oats" and learn virtue, prudence, and self-control in the process. As a reward for his growth, he can marry the virtuous Miss Sophia Western and become a respected member of society. If a female protagonist experiences sex before marriage, she is labeled a "fallen woman": Mrs. Gaskell's Ruth, for example, pays for her wild oats with her life.

A woman's confrontation with passion, therefore, must be portrayed less directly than a man's. Ann Radcliffe, in *The Mysteries of Udolpho,* solves this problem by confronting Emily with the "mystery of Udolpho." Her exploration of the castle of Udolpho parallels her journey into her unconscious for the purpose of integrating her "sensibility" with "self-command." In the castle she encounters two portraits. The first is a picture of an unprincipled, lustful woman who was so overcome by sexual passion that she committed murder and then went mad out of grief and despair. The second portrait, the mysterious veiled picture, is a wax image of a decomposing body. In these symbolic and indirect ways, Emily confronts the relationship between sexual passion and death. The narrative of her growing ability to control her terror serves as an objective correlative to her development of sexual and emotional self-control. Her prudence is demonstrated when she refuses to marry the man she loves because he is immoral and poor. Only when Valencourt learns equal self-command (and when they inherit money) can she marry him. More often, psychological integration of passion and reason is denied to women in fiction. In Emily Brontë's *Wuthering Heights,* Catherine denies her passionate nature in prudently marrying Edgar Linton and dies as a result. Only in death can she accept her passions and be united with Heathcliff; their bodies decompose in the same grave, and their ghosts wander the moors together.

The resolution of passion and reason is made difficult or impossible for the female protagonist not only because of the double standard regarding sex but also because of the literary convention that she must choose between the "dark" and "light" man. She can marry the man who represents virtue or the one associated with sexual passion, but not both. Charlotte Brontë's Jane Eyre solves this problem by developing (with the help of certain chance occurrences) the Apollonian other half of her Dionysian suitor, Mr. Rochester. When her passions are awakened by him, Jane maintains self-control and eventually flees to the spiritual and passionless house of the minister, St. John Rivers. The psychological wholeness she achieves culminates in her return and marriage to the tamed and humbled Rochester, who has paid the biblical price for lust by forfeiting a hand and an eye as the result of the burning of Thornfield. A contemporary treatment of a similar dilemma occurs in

Erica Jong's *Fear of Flying,* in which Isadora Wing tries to reconcile her desire for adventure with her need for security. Faced with a choice between the husband who represents security and a lover who represents adventure, she asks why it takes two men to make a whole person. By the end of the novel she realizes that the symbol is not the reality: she cannot achieve psychological completeness through union with any man, and certainly not with a man she sees as representing only half of the whole she desires.

Literary works may also focus on the development by a woman of knowledge about society, as in Jane Austen's *Emma* and other novels of manners. This wisdom makes it possible for a woman to live successfully and effectively in the part of the world open to her. May Bartram in Henry James's "The Beast in the Jungle" combines social knowledge with acute psychological and moral sensitivity. However, other works chronicle a woman's confrontation with the truth of the destructive double-bind situations implicit in the virgin, mistress, and helpmate roles. A woman's understanding of her plight may lead to heroic action, to resignation, or to impotent rage. The recognition of the psychological cost of the helpmate role leads to heroic action in Henrik Ibsen's *A Doll's House,* when Nora leaves Torvald. Other characters become wise too late for such action. Isabel Archer, at the beginning of James's *The Portrait of a Lady,* wants to live fully. After marrying Osmond, she realizes that she has become just another art object in his collection. She does not escape this living death, because she has learned too much. She knows that her alternatives are no better. Gustave Flaubert's Madame Bovary reacts to the boredom of her marriage by experimenting with adultery. She eventually learns that no roles open to her offer fulfillment or happiness, and she commits suicide. In works such as James's *The Wings of the Dove,* we learn that women like Milly Theale, who have superior sensibility and understanding, often are destined to die.

If the sage does not literally die, she may sacrifice her insight and, in part, her self by submitting to conventional wisdom and authority. In Mrs. Gaskell's *Sylvia's Lovers,* Sylvia is a willful, passionate woman. She loves a romantic sailor, but marries a prudent shopkeeper because she and her mother are destitute and because she believes that the sailor is dead. At first she rebels against her plight, but as the novel progresses, she learns to renounce her sexuality and her will. In the closing scene she affirms her love for her dying husband. While this act is "good" in conventional terms, it constitutes a violation of her self. Doris Lessing, in *The Golden Notebook,* describes a similar, but more mundane, example of self-renunciation in women. Awakening at 6 A.M. Anna experiences the "housewife disease":

> The tension in me, so that peace has already gone away from me, is because the current has been switched on: I must-dress-Janet-get-her-breakfast-send-her-off-to-school-get-Michael's-breakfast-don't-forget-I'm-out-of-tea-etc.-etc. With this useless but apparently unavoidable tension resentment is also switched on. Resentment against what? An unfairness. That I should have to spend so much of my time worrying over details. The resentment focuses itself on Michael; although I know with my intelligence it has nothing to do with Michael. And yet I do resent him, because he will spend his day, served by secretaries, nurses, women in all kinds of capacities, who will take this weight off him.

As a sage, she recognizes the injustice of this situation, but she is afraid her lover will leave her if she complains. Furthermore, her knowledge that they both are victims of a dehumanizing system enables her to see the futility of venting her anger on individual men. Her repressed, paralyzing anger is analogous to Sylvia's self-immolation.

The knowledge of the female sage may be revolutionary if she understands what is wrong with the patriarchal system. As in Anne Finch's "The Unequal Fetters," wise women comprehend sexual injustice and ask for equality. In Rachel Speght's "A Dream" and Anne Finch's "Petition for an Absolute Retreat," women explain the need for equality of opportunity in education and for privacy and self-determination.

The fear of woman's knowledge as potentially destructive to patriarchy is evidenced in the recurring persecution of witches and in the ridicule hurled at feminists. When women see no possibility of changing sex role patterns, this potential destruction may manifest itself as self-destruction. In Kate Chopin's *The Awakening,* the woman who understands her relationship to society walks into the sea. Samuel Richardson's Clarissa rejects the societal judgment that she marry Lovelace to save her honor, but her only alternative is to die.

Portraits of sages who are wise before the beginning of the narrative may be either tragic or comic. The tragic sage can be visualized as a sphinx; its stone face represents death or paralysis. The sage knows, but she cannot tell what she knows because she fears either her own destruction or the destruction of another. In Henry James's "The Beast in the Jungle, " May Bartram spends her life understanding and supporting John Marcher. She could teach him to know himself, but chooses to hide from him the knowledge that he has missed life because that knowledge might destroy him ("she had prayed he mightn't know"). Armed with the knowledge that she is stronger than he is, she chooses her own death rather than the possibility of his psychological destruction.

The sage may be unable to communicate her wisdom because that wisdom is alien to her culture or forbidden by it. In parable form, she is Lot's wife, who is transformed into a pillar of salt as punishment for seeing what a patriarchal God had forbidden her to see. Hester Prynne, in Nathaniel Hawthorne's *The Scarlet Letter,* develops into a free thinker, but she cannot reveal her insights because her knowledge is taboo in puritan Salem and because she fears the anarchistic consequences of challenging the values of her culture. She does, however, assure women who come to her "in the continually recurring trials of wounded, wasted, wronged, misplaced, or erring and sinful passion . . . of her firm belief, that, at some brighter period, when the world should have grown ripe for it, in Heaven's own time, a new truth would be revealed, in order to establish the whole relation between man and woman on a surer ground of mutual happiness." As a result, her outer life is defined totally by the puritan values she has learned to question. Because she remains silent, the villagers perceive her inadequately, viewing her only as an allegorical embodiment either of adultery or of charity. Her silence is not without emotional cost, however. At the beginning of the novel her beauty is contrasted to the rigidity of the ironlike puritan magistrates, but as the novel progresses, "her beauty, the warmth and richness of her womanhood, departed, like fading sunshine; and a grey shadow seemed to fall across her."

The knowledge of the sage may threaten the entire framework of the society because it undermines not only society's basic assumptions but also its ways of perceiving and expressing truth. In the twentieth century Mary Ellmann, in

Thinking about Women, points out the difficulty women may have in expressing their wisdom with a patriarchal language which, for example, assumes that "people" is synonymous with "man" or "mankind." The wise woman may require a new language in order to express her knowledge. The sage may also experience paralysis of the will because the heightened consciousness required of the woman who is dependent on a man's whim tends to destroy spontaneity in her action and feelings. She also may be so aware of the complexity of her own motivations and desires that she cannot act. Like Hamlet, the female hero who is aware of multiple truths behind the simplest action or impulse may be arrested by the multiplicity of her knowledge. Many male heroes demonstrate superior ability to act because they lack the debilitating knowledge that women often learn.

Men tend to believe in the myths of their society because, as the people in power, they have the world to confirm their conceptions. Even if they hold no power themselves, they may experience vicariously a sense of power by identifying with the few men actually in control. Women confirm the illusions of men by agreeing with them. Thus men tend to be tragic heroes because the world tells them they can realize their ideals. They are later surprised and destroyed when they fail. The tragic stance is also predominantly male because it involves the willingness to die for one's beliefs out of pride rather than to fit in with the community. Because the female hero's position is not validated by her society, she is less likely to pursue her conviction to its tragic conclusion. Because women sages understand death, meaninglessness, and their place in a patriarchal culture, they often are fatalistic and resigned. The Lady of the Assembly in the anonymous poem included in this section preaches the virtue of perseverance in a world in which women suffer and die because of their relationships with men. The resulting inclination of women to give up their vision and accept their reality makes it likely that the potential sage will be the hero of comedy. Like Shakespeare's Kate in *The Taming of the Shrew,* the female hero's life is more often in the comic mode, which results in accommodation. Had Hamlet been a woman, and therefore taught to distrust his perceptions, he might have said, "How silly of me; all families have problems . . ." instead of killing the King.

In Thomas Hardy's *Jude the Obscure,* the tragic accommodation of Sue Bridewell to Christianity and conventional morality after the death of her children is an ironic commentary on the traditional "happy ending" in which the rebellious woman (for example, Shakespeare's Kate) repents and is rewarded with a happy marriage or heavenly bliss. Even when the female sage is portrayed in a potentially tragic situation, she does not represent the values of the dominant culture, and therefore her fall is not the fall of the society. Portraits of "women's libbers" in contemporary literature and of the "bluestocking" in the eighteenth and nineteenth centuries characterize female insight as deviant and therefore not noble.

The female sage is often portrayed comically instead of tragically because from the unsympathetic point of view she is a fool. Women, like the traditional fool, are often depicted as ignorant or crazy. Their power to apprehend connection and relationship behind apparent division is dismissed as "women's intuition" or "female logic." The sage may actually go mad because her perceptions of the world are not validated. When Carson McCullers, in *Reflections in a Golden Eye,* portrays the growing insanity of a woman forced to doubt her perceptions, she dramatizes in exaggerated form the general situation of the woman in a world defined by men. In the classic film *Gaslight,* the husband uses a variety of methods to make his wife doubt her judgment about reality in order to drive her insane. Psychiatrists encounter this pattern of male behavior in various degrees often enough to have given it the name "gaslighting." Because her husband has the final sanction on whether she is "right" or not, the wife in Charlotte Perkins Gilman's *The Yellow Wall-Paper* comes to doubt her perceptions, even though she understands the world much better than her "sensible," "sane" husband. Like the mythological Cassandra, she cannot communicate what she knows because no one is capable of understanding her.

The female sage is often analogous to Shakespeare's wise fool or to the ancient fool who was believed to possess numinous powers. Like the historical fool, the sage may appear to be mad, simpleminded, or clownish, but she possesses knowledge hidden from the "rational" male. Because they menstruate, give birth to children, and (in our society) wash dishes and change diapers, women are aware of the basic physical realities, which are the basis of comedy. As Walter Kerr explains in *Tragedy and Comedy:* "The basic joke, the one incongruity upon which all other incongruities rest, that a being so entirely free should be so little free is ridiculous. . . . A bishop should not have to go to the bathroom. A weightless astronaut in space should not have to worry about making an appointment with his dentist."[2] Women are therefore the possessors of the comic knowledge of human vulnerability and mortality. As we see in Anne Finch's "Clarinda's Indifference at the Parting with Her Beauty," women are realists about aging and death. This realism enables Yeats's Crazy Jane to reject the church's denigration of the flesh, and Thomas Hardy's "ruined maid" to see past Victorian morality and know that being ruined has its advantages. Lord Raglan explains in *The Hero* that the fool is a descendant of the shaman, who was both priest and fertility figure. According to William Willeford, in *The Fool and His Scepter:* "The babbling fool is one prototype of our relationship to numinous power. . . . The fool stands beside the king, in a sense reflecting him but also suggesting a long-lost element of the king that, we may imagine, had to be sacrificed at the founding of the kingdom, an element without which neither the king nor the kingdom is complete."[3] Yeats's Crazy Jane is a fool in Willeford's sense. She complements the Bishop as the fool traditionally complements the king, and she understands the relationship between spirit and flesh and between sexuality and religious vision.

The sage often feels a oneness with all things, in contrast to the principles of division and categorization, which are the basis of Western patriarchal thinking. As in Edith Sitwell's "An Old Woman," women's wisdom, like the wisdom of the fool, concentrates on unity, even paradox. Sitwell's sage sees all things united and blessed by the sun, including "the clean and the unclean," "young lovers and old lechers," and "beggars" and "misers." "The man-made chasms between man and man / Of creeds and tongues are filled, the guiltless light / Remakes all men and things in holiness." Edna St. Vincent Millay's "What Lips My Lips Have Kissed" shows us that one consequence of this sense of unity is the acceptance of time and process. The sage's knowledge also may be portrayed as the bodily intuitive knowledge of the intellectually deficient. Tennessee Williams writes of Olga, in "The Mattress by the Tomato Patch":

The perishability of the package she comes in has cast on Olga no shadow she can't laugh off. I look at her now, before the return of Tiger from Muscle Beach, and if no thought, no knowledge has yet taken form in the protean jelly-world of brain and nerves, if I am patient enough to wait a few moments longer, this landlady of Picasso may spring up from her mattress and come running into this room with a milky-blue china bowl full of reasons and explanations for all that exists.

Men tend not to marry women who are openly cleverer or wiser than themselves. However, the wife may be a wise fool who masks her wisdom by clowning. The mistress also may play the part of the clown, as in Dorothy Parker's "Big Blonde," to secure the emotional and physical support of a man. Or a wife may play the part of the scatterbrain, as Nora does in Henrik Ibsen's *A Doll's House,* to protect her husband from unpleasant truths. Nora, having illegally obtained money to save her husband's life, pretends incompetence so that he will never suspect she is working to pay the money back. Like the wise fool, who corrects and teaches the king by clowning, the female sage may masquerade as the clownish shrew in order to guide her husband. Where, we might ask, would Socrates have been without Xantippe? The wise fool in these cases plays parts as the artist does, but she lacks the ability to control her life or her environment.

The old woman (for example, Crazy Jane) may speak the truth with impunity because of apparent eccentricity, but it is unlikely she will convince the Bishop of anything. Like Sibyl, who fades away and becomes invisible, the old woman can say anything she pleases because people tend to ignore her. Grandma, in Edward Albee's *The American Dream,* expresses her understanding openly because people do not acknowledge her existence and therefore do not hear what she says.

Portraits of the aging *heroine* emphasize the uselessness and wretchedness of the old woman and reveal the ways in which our society dismisses women as unimportant when they no longer live for a man. Portraits of the old woman in this section, however, show the independent, wise old woman to be admirable, if ineffective. Furthermore, while a younger woman may be prevented from telling what she knows because she is afraid of male rejection, an old woman, who is close to death, paradoxically may be free to reveal her knowledge without fear of the consequences.

Because the literary selections which follow portray the sage sympathetically, they are more likely to be tragic than comic. They celebrate the wise woman, whether heeded or unheeded, because, as Joseph Campbell states in *The Hero with a Thousand Faces,* "the supreme hero . . . is not the one who merely continues the dynamics of the cosmogonic round, but he [she] who reopens the eye—so that through all the comings and goings, delights and agonies of the world panorama, the One Presence will be seen again. This requires a deeper wisdom than the other, and results in a pattern not of action but of significant representation."[4] The complex vision of the sage, then, is a necessary prerequisite to the heroic action which can create a more adequate and human social system for both men and women.

THE SAGE: NOTES

[1]Sigmund Freud, "Femininity," in *New Introductory Lectures on Psychoanalysis* (New York: W. W. Norton & Company, Inc., 1965). Quoted from Susan Lydon, "The

Politics of Orgasm," in *Sisterhood Is Powerful: An Anthology of Writings from the Women's Liberation Movement* (New York: Vintage Books, Random House, Inc., 1970), p. 198.

[2](New York: Simon and Schuster, 1967), p. 145.

[3](Evanston, Ill.: Northwestern University Press, 1969), p. 86.

[4](Princeton, N.J.: Princeton University Press, 1960), p. 345.

THE ASSEMBLY OF LADIES

This anonymous poem was written in the last quarter of the fifteenth century, presumably by a woman, since the persona of the author is feminine. The poem is a dream-allegory in the chivalric tradition and is based on the so-called courts of love held by such ladies as Eleanor of Aquitaine. The poem consists of 108 rhyme royals and was printed in 1532 in a volume entitled *The Workes of Geffray Chaucer newly printed, with dyvers workes which were never in print before.*

THE PALACE OF PLEASANT REGARD

We followed her unto the chamber-door,
"Sisters," quoth she, "come ye in after me."
But wit ye well, there was a paved floor,
The goodliest that any wight might see
And furthermore, about then looked we
On each corner, and upon every wall,
The which was made of beryl and crystal;

Wherein was graven of stories many a one;
First how Phyllis, of womanly pity,
Died piteously, for love of Demophon.   10
Next after was the story of Thisbe,
How she slew herself under a tree.
Yet saw I more, how in right piteous case
For Anthony was slain Cleopatras.

The other side was, how Melusine the sheen
Untruly was deceived in her bain.
There was also Anelida the queen,
Upon Arcite how sore she did complain.
All these stories were graved there, certain;
And many more than I rehearse you here;   20
It were too long to tell you all in-fere.

And because the walles shone so bright,
With fine umple they were all overspread,
To that intent, folk should not hurt their sight;
And thorough [*sic*] it the stories might be read.
Then furthermore I went, as I was led;
And there I saw, withouten any fail,
A chaire set, with full rich apparail.

And five stages it was set from the ground,
Of chalcedony full curiously wrought;   30

With four pommels of gold, and very round,
Set with sapphires, as good as could be thought;
That, wot ye what, if it were thorough sought
As I suppose, from this country to Inde,
Another such it were right far to find!

For, wit ye well, I was right near that,
So as I durst, beholding by and by;
Above there was a rich cloth of estate,
Wrought with the needle full strangely,
Her word thereon; and thus it said truly   40
A endurer, to tell you in wordes few,
With great letters, the better I them knew.

Thus as we stood, a door opened anon;
A gentlewoman, seemly of stature,
Bearing a mace, came out, herself alone;
Soothly, me thought, a goodly creature!
She spoke nothing too loud, I you ensure,
Nor hastily, but with goodly warning:
"Make room," quoth she, "my lady is coming!"

With that anon I saw Perséverance,   50
How she held up the tapet in her hand.
I saw also, in right good ordinance,
This great lady within the tapet stand,
Coming outward, I will ye understand;
And after her a noble company,
I could not tell the number certainly.

THE DREAM

Rachel Speght   (fl. 1617–1621)

Aside from the two books which bear her name, nothing seems to be known about
Rachel Speght. Her first book, a defense of women, was printed in 1617 and was
entitled *A Mouzell for Melastomus, the Cynicall Bayter of, and foule mouthed Barker
against Evahs Sex. Or an Apologeticall Answere to that Irreligious and Illiterate
Pamphlet . . . The Arraignement of Women.*

"The Dream" is a modernized excerpt from Speght's 1621 volume, *Mortalitie's
Memorandum, with a Dream Prefixed, imaginarie in manner, reall in matter.*

Upon a sudden, as I gazing stood,
Thought came to me and asked me of my state,

Inquiring what I was, and what I would,
And why I seemed as one disconsolate.
To whose demand, I thus again replied,
I as a stranger in this place abide.
· ·

—My grief, quoth I, is called Ignorance,
Which makes me differ little from a brute,
For animals are led by nature's lore;
Their seeming silence is but custom's fruit;   10
When they are hurt they have a sense of pain,
But want the sense to cure themselves again.
· ·

—Quoth she, I wish I could prescribe your help;
Your state I pity much and do bewail;
But for my part, though I am much employed,
Yet in my judgment I do often fail.
And therefore I'll commend unto your trial
Experience, of whom take no denial.
· ·

—I sought, I found, she asked me what I would.
Quoth I, your best direction I implore,   20
For I am troubled with an irksome grief,
Which, when I named, quoth she, declare no more,
For I can tell as much as you can say,
And for your cure I'll help you what I may.

The only medicine for your malady,
By which, and nothing else your help is wrought,
Is Knowledge, of the which there is two sorts,
The one is good, the other bad and nought;
The former sort by labour is attained,
The latter may without much toil be gained.   30

But 'tis the good which must effect your cure.
I prayed her then that she would further show
Where I might have it. That I will, quoth she.
In Erudition's garden it doth grow;
And in compassion of your woeful case,
Industry shall conduct you to the place.

Dissuasion hearing her assign my help
(And seeing that consent I did detect)
Did many remores to me propose,
As dullness, and my memory's defect,   40
The difficulty of attaining lore,
My time, and sex, with many others more.

Which when I heard, my mind was much perplexed,
And as a horse new come into the field

Who with a harquebus at first doth start,
So did this shot make me recoil and yield.
But of my fear when some did notice take,
In my behalf, they this reply did make.

First, quoth Desire, Dissuasion, hold thy peace;
These oppositions come not from above.   50
Quoth Truth, they cannot spring from reason's root,
And therefore now thou shalt no victor prove.
No, quoth Industry, be assured this,
Her friends shall make thee of thy purpose miss.

For with my sickle I will cut away
All obstacles that in her way can grow,
And by the issue of her own attempt,
I'll make thee *labor omnia vincet* know.
Quoth Truth, and sith her sex thou dost object,
Thy folly I by reason will detect.   60

Both man and woman of three parts consist,
Which Paul doth body, soul, and spirit call,
And from the soul three faculties arise,
The mind, the will, the power; then wherefore shall
A woman have her intellect in vain,
Or not endeavor Knowledge to attain.

The talent God doth give must be employed,
His own with vantage he must have again;
All parts and faculties were made for use;
The God of Knowledge nothing gave in vain.   70
'Twas Mary's choice our Saviour did approve,
Because that she the better part did love.

. . . .

CLARINDA'S INDIFFERENCE AT PARTING
WITH HER BEAUTY

Anne Finch, Duchess of Winchilsea

See headnote for "The Unequal Fetters," page 124.

"Clarinda's Indifference at Parting with Her Beauty" appears in both the 1698
octavo and the 1702 folio manuscripts of Anne Finch's work. It was first published
by Myra Reynolds in 1903.

Now, age came on, and all the dismal traine
That fright the vitious, and afflicte the vaine.
Departing beauty, now Clarinda spies
Pale in her cheeks, and dying in her eyes;
That youthfull air, that wanders ore the face,
That undescrib'd, that unresisted grace,
Those morning beams, that strongly warm, and shine,
Which men that feel and see, can ne're define,
Now, on the wings of restlesse time, were fled,
And ev'ning shades, began to rise, and spread,   10
When thus resolv'd, and ready soon to part,
Slighting the short repreives of proffer'd art
She spake—
And what, vain beauty, didst thou 'ere atcheive,
When at thy height, that I thy fall shou'd greive,
When, did'st thou e're succesfully persue?
When, did'st thou e're th' appointed foe subdue?
'Tis vain of numbers, or of strength to boast,
In an undisciplin'd, unguided Host,
And love, that did thy mighty hopes deride,   20
Wou'd pay no sacrafice, but to thy pride.
When, did'st thou e're a pleasing rule obtain,
A glorious Empire's but a glorious pain,
Thou, art indeed, but vanity's cheife sourse,
But foyle to witt, to want of witt a curse,
For often, by thy gaudy sign's descry'd
A fool, which unobserv'd, had been untry'd,
And when thou doest such empty things adorn,
'Tis but to make them more the publick scorn.
I know thee well, but weak thy reign wou'd be   30
Did n'one adore, or prize thee more then me.
I see indeed, thy certain ruine neer,
But can't affoard one parting sigh, or tear,
Nor rail at Time, nor quarrell with my glasse,
But unconcern'd, can lett thy glories passe.

TO THE LADIES

Mary Lee, Lady Chudleigh   (1656–1710)

Born into the Devonshire gentry, Mary Lee was privately educated and was later
unhappily married to Sir George Chudleigh. Her outer life was uneventful, though
she published three books during her lifetime: *The Ladies' Defence* (1701), *Poems on
Several Occasions* (1703), and *Essays upon Several Subjects* (1710).

"To the Ladies" is taken from the volume *Poems on Several Occasions.*

Wife and servant are the same,
But only differ in the name,
For when that fatal knot is tied,
Which nothing, nothing can divide,
When she the word *obey* has said,
And man by law supreme has made,
Then all that's kind is laid aside,
And nothing left but state and pride.
Fierce as an eastern prince he grows,
And all his innate rigour shows.   10
Then but to look, to laugh, or speak,
Will the nuptial contract break.
Like mutes, she signs alone must make,
And never any freedom take,
But still be governed by a nod,
And fear her husband as her God;
Him still must serve, him still obey,
And nothing act, and nothing say,
But her haughty Lord thinks fit,
Who with the power, has all the wit.   20
Then shun, oh! shun that wretched state,
And all the fawning flatterers hate;
Value your selves, and men despise,
You must be proud, if you'll be wise.

THE YELLOW WALL-PAPER

Charlotte Perkins Gilman   (1860–1935)

Born in Hartford, Connecticut, Perkins was a teacher "first of drawing and painting, later of general branches and gymnastics," according to the *National Cyclopedia of National Biography.* In 1884 she married Charles Stetson, whom she divorced ten years later, and in 1890 she entered the lecture circuit as a speaker for labor and women's rights. In 1900 she married George Gilman, and from 1909 to 1916 she edited and published *The Forerunner,* a journal of reform. Ill with cancer, she committed suicide in Pasadena, California.

"The Yellow Wall-Paper" was first published, after many difficulties, in *The New England Magazine* for May 1892. It was reprinted in *Great Modern American Stories,* edited by William Dean Howells, in 1920, and by The Feminist Press in 1973.

It is very seldom that mere ordinary people like John and myself secure ancestral halls for the summer.

A colonial mansion, a hereditary estate, I would say a haunted house, and reach the height of romantic felicity—but that would be asking too much of fate!

Still I will proudly declare that there is something queer about it.

Else, why should it be let so cheaply? And why have stood so long untenanted?

John laughs at me, of course, but one expects that in marriage.

John is practical in the extreme. He has no patience with faith, an intense horror of superstition, and he scoffs openly at any talk of things not to be felt and seen and put down in figures.

John is a physician, and *perhaps*—(I would not say it to a living soul, of course, but this is dead paper and a great relief to my mind)—*perhaps* that is one reason I do not get well faster.

You see he does not believe I am sick!

And what can one do?

If a physician of high standing, and one's own husband, assures friends and relatives that there is really nothing the matter with one but temporary nervous depression—a slight hysterical tendency—what is one to do?

My brother is also a physician, and also of high standing, and he says the same thing.

So I take phosphates or phospites—whichever it is, and tonics, and journeys, and air, and exercise, and am absolutely forbidden to "work" until I am well again.

Personally, I disagree with their ideas.

Personally, I believe that congenial work, with excitement and change, would do me good.

But what is one to do?

I did write for a while in spite of them; but it *does* exhaust me a good deal—having to be so sly about it, or else meet with heavy opposition.

I sometimes fancy that in my condition if I had less opposition and more society and stimulus—but John says the very worst thing I can do is to think about my condition, and I confess it always makes me feel bad.

So I will let it alone and talk about the house.

The most beautiful place! It is quite alone, standing well back from the road, quite three miles from the village. It makes me think of English places that you read about, for there are hedges and walls and gates that lock, and lots of separate little houses for the gardeners and people.

There is a *delicious* garden! I never saw such a garden—large and shady, full of box-bordered paths, and lined with long grape-covered arbors with seats under them.

There were greenhouses, too, but they are all broken now.

There was some legal trouble, I believe, something about the heirs and coheirs; anyhow, the place has been empty for years.

That spoils my ghostliness, I am afraid, but I don't care—there is something strange about the house—I can feel it.

I even said so to John one moonlight evening, but he said what I felt was a *draught,* and shut the window.

I get unreasonably angry with John sometimes. I'm sure I never used to be so sensitive. I think it is due to this nervous condition.

But John says if I feel so, I shall neglect proper self-control; so I take pains to control myself—before him, at least, and that makes me very tired.

I don't like our room a bit. I wanted one downstairs that opened on the piazza and had roses all over the window, and such pretty old-fashioned chintz hangings! but John would not hear of it.

He said there was only one window and not room for two beds, and no near room for him if he took another.

He is very careful and loving, and hardly lets me stir without special direction.

I have a schedule prescription for each hour in the day; he takes all care from me, and so I feel basely ungrateful not to value it more.

He said we came here solely on my account, that I was to have perfect rest and all the air I could get. "Your exercise depends on your strength, my dear," said he, "and your food somewhat on your appetite; but air you can absorb all the time." So we took the nursery at the top of the house.

It is a big, airy room, the whole floor nearly, with windows that look all ways, and air and sunshine galore. It was nursery first and then playroom and gymnasium, I should judge; for the windows are barred for little children, and there are rings and things in the walls.

The paint and paper look as if a boys' school had used it. It is stripped off—the paper—in great patches all around the head of my bed, about as far as I can reach, and in a great place on the other side of the room low down. I never saw a worse paper in my life.

One of those sprawling flamboyant patterns committing every artistic sin.

It is dull enough to confuse the eye in following, pronounced enough to constantly irritate and provoke study, and when you follow the lame uncertain curves for a little distance they suddenly commit suicide—plunge off at outrageous angles, destroy themselves in unheard of contradictions.

The color is repellent, almost revolting; a smouldering unclean yellow, strangely faded by the slow-turning sunlight.

It is a dull yet lurid orange in some places, a sickly sulphur tint in others.

No wonder the children hated it! I should hate it myself if I had to live in this room long.

There comes John, and I must put this away,—he hates to have me write a word.

We have been here two weeks, and I haven't felt like writing before, since that first day.

I am sitting by the window now, up in this atrocious nursery, and there is nothing to hinder my writing as much as I please, save lack of strength.

John is away all day, and even some nights when his cases are serious.

I am glad my case is not serious!

But these nervous troubles are dreadfully depressing.

John does not know how much I really suffer. He knows there is no *reason* to suffer, and that satisfies him.

Of course it is only nervousness. It does weigh on me so not to do my duty in any way!

I meant to be such a help to John, such a real rest and comfort, and here I am a comparative burden already!

Nobody would believe what an effort it is to do what little I am able,—to dress and entertain, and order things.

It is fortunate Mary is so good with the baby. Such a dear baby!

And yet I *cannot* be with him, it makes me so nervous.

I suppose John never was nervous in his life. He laughs at me so about this wall-paper!

At first he meant to repaper the room, but afterwards he said that I was letting it get the better of me, and that nothing was worse for a nervous patient than to give way to such fancies.

He said that after the wall-paper was changed it would be the heavy bedstead, and then the barred windows, and then that gate at the head of the stairs, and so on.

"You know the place is doing you good," he said, "and really, dear, I don't care to renovate the house just for a three months' rental."

"Then do let us go downstairs," I said, "there are such pretty rooms there."

Then he took me in his arms and called me a blessed little goose, and said he would go down to the cellar, if I wished, and have it whitewashed into the bargain.

But he is right enough about the beds and windows and things.

It is an airy and comfortable room as any one need wish, and, of course, I would not be so silly as to make him uncomfortable just for a whim.

I'm really getting quite fond of the big room, all but that horrid paper.

Out of one window I can see the garden, those mysterious deepshaded arbors, the riotous old-fashioned flowers, and bushes and gnarly trees.

Out of another I get a lovely view of the bay and a little private wharf belonging to the estate. There is a beautiful shaded lane that runs down there from the house. I always fancy I see people walking in these numerous paths and arbors, but John has cautioned me not to give way to fancy in the least. He says that with my imaginative power and habit of story-making, a nervous weakness like mine is sure to lead to all manner of excited fancies, and that I ought to use my will and good sense to check the tendency. So I try.

I think sometimes that if I were only well enough to write a little it would relieve the press of ideas and rest me.

But I find I get pretty tired when I try.

It is so discouraging not to have any advice and companionship about my work. When I get really well, John says we will ask Cousin Henry and Julia down for a long visit; but he says he would as soon put fireworks in my pillow-case as to let me have those stimulating people about now.

I wish I could get well faster.

But I must not think about that. This paper looks to me as if it *knew* what a vicious influence it had!

There is a recurrent spot where the pattern lolls like a broken neck and two bulbous eyes stare at you upside down.

I get positively angry with the impertinence of it and the everlastingness. Up and down and sideways they crawl, and those absurd, unblinking eyes are everywhere. There is one place where two breaths didn't match, and the eyes go all up and down the line, one a little higher than the other.

I never saw so much expression in an inanimate thing before, and we all know how much expression they have! I used to lie awake as a child and get more entertainment and terror out of blank walls and plain furniture than most children could find in a toy-store.

I remember what a kindly wink the knobs of our big, old bureau used to have, and there was one chair that always seemed like a strong friend.

I used to feel that if any of the other things looked too fierce I could always hop into that chair and be safe.

The furniture in this room is no worse than inharmonious, however, for we had to bring it all from downstairs. I suppose when this was used as a playroom they had to take the nursery things out, and no wonder! I never saw such ravages as the children have made here.

The wall-paper, as I said before, is torn off in spots, and it sticketh closer than a brother—they must have had perseverance as well as hatred.

Then the floor is scratched and gouged and splintered, the plaster itself is dug out here and there, and this great heavy bed which is all we found in the room, looks as if it had been through the wars.

But I don't mind it a bit—only the paper.

There comes John's sister. Such a dear girl as she is, and so careful of me! I must not let her find me writing.

She is a perfect and enthusiastic housekeeper, and hopes for no better profession. I verily believe she thinks it is the writing which made me sick!

But I can write when she is out, and see her a long way off from these windows.

There is one that commands the road, a lovely shaded winding road, and one that just looks off over the country. A lovely country, too, full of great elms and velvet meadows.

This wall-paper has a kind of sub-pattern in a different shade, a particularly irritating one, for you can only see it in certain lights, and not clearly then.

But in the places where it isn't faded and where the sun is just so—I can see a strange, provoking, formless sort of figure, that seems to skulk about behind that silly and conspicuous front design.

There's sister on the stairs!

Well, the Fourth of July is over! The people are all gone and I am tired out. John thought it might do me good to see a little company, so we just had mother and Nellie and the children down for a week.

Of course I didn't do a thing. Jennie sees to everything now.

But it tired me all the same.

John says if I don't pick up faster he shall send me to Weir Mitchell in the fall.

But I don't want to go there at all. I had a friend who was in his hands once, and she says he is just like John and my brother, only more so!

Besides, it is such an undertaking to go so far.

I don't feel as if it was worth while to turn my hand over for anything, and I'm getting dreadfully fretful and querulous.

I cry at nothing, and cry most of the time.

Of course I don't when John is here, or anybody else, but when I am alone.

And I am alone a good deal just now. John is kept in town very often by serious cases, and Jennie is good and lets me alone when I want her to.

So I walk a little in the garden or down that lovely lane, sit on the porch under the roses, and lie down up here a good deal.

I'm getting really fond of the room in spite of the wall-paper. Perhaps *because* of the wall-paper.

It dwells in my mind so!

I lie here on this great immovable bed—it is nailed down, I believe—and follow that pattern about by the hour. It is as good as gymnastics, I assure you. I start, we'll say, at the bottom, down in the corner over there where it has not been touched, and I determine for the thousandth time that I *will* follow that pointless pattern to some sort of a conclusion.

I know a little of the principle of design, and I know this thing was not arranged on any laws of radiation, or alternation, or repetition, or symmetry, or anything else that I ever heard of.

It is repeated, of course, by the breadths, but not otherwise.

Looked at in one way each breadth stands alone, the bloated curves and flourishes—a kind of "debased Romanesque" with *delirium tremens*—go waddling up and down in isolated columns of fatuity.

But, on the other hand, they connect diagonally, and the sprawling outlines run off in great slanting waves of optic horror, like a lot of wallowing seaweeds in full chase.

The whole thing goes horizontally, too, at least it seems so, and I exhaust myself in trying to distinguish the order of its going in that direction.

They have used a horizontal breadth for a frieze, and that adds wonderfully to the confusion.

There is one end of the room where it is almost intact, and there, when the crosslights fade and the low sun shines directly upon it, I can almost fancy radiation after all,—the interminable grotesques seem to form around a common centre and rush off in headlong plunges of equal distraction.

It makes me tired to follow it. I will take a nap I guess.

I don't know why I should write this.
I don't want to.
I don't feel able.
And I know John would think it absurd. But I *must* say what I feel and think in some way—it is such a relief!
But the effort is getting to be greater than the relief.
Half the time now I am awfully lazy, and lie down ever so much.
John says I mustn't lose my strength, and has me take cod liver oil and lots of tonics and things, to say nothing of ale and wine and rare meat.
Dear John! He loves me very dearly, and hates to have me sick. I tried to have a real earnest reasonable talk with him the other day, and tell him how I wish he would let me go and make a visit to Cousin Henry and Julia.
But he said I wasn't able to go, nor able to stand it after I got there; and I did not make out a very good case for myself, for I was crying before I had finished.
It is getting to be a great effort for me to think straight. Just this nervous weakness I suppose.
And dear John gathered me up in his arms, and just carried me upstairs and laid me on the bed, and sat by me and read to me till it tired my head.
He said I was his darling and his comfort and all he had, and that I must take care of myself for his sake, and keep well.
He says no one but myself can help me out of it, that I must use my will and self-control and not let any silly fancies run away with me.
There's one comfort, the baby is well and happy, and does not have to occupy this nursery with the horrid wall-paper.
If we had not used it, that blessed child would have! What a fortunate escape! Why, I wouldn't have a child of mine, an impressionable little thing, live in such a room for worlds.
I never thought of it before, but it is lucky that John kept me here after all, I can stand it so much easier than a baby, you see.
Of course I never mention it to them any more—I am too wise,—but I keep watch of it all the same.
There are things in that paper that nobody knows but me, or ever will.
Behind that outside pattern the dim shapes get clearer every day.
It is always the same shape, only very numerous.
And it is like a woman stooping down and creeping about behind that pattern. I don't like it a bit. I wonder—I begin to think—I wish John would take me away from here!

It is so hard to talk with John about my case, because he is so wise, and because he loves me so.
But I tried it last night.
It was moonlight. The moon shines in all around just as the sun does.

I hate to see it sometimes, it creeps so slowly, and always comes in by one window or another.

John was asleep and I hated to waken him, so I kept still and watched the moonlight on that undulating wall-paper till I felt creepy.

The faint figure behind seemed to shake the pattern, just as if she wanted to get out.

I got up softly and went to feel and see if the paper *did* move, and when I came back John was awake.

"What is it, little girl?" he said. "Don't go walking about like that—you'll get cold."

I thought it was a good time to talk, so I told him that I really was not gaining here, and that I wished he would take me away.

"Why darling!" said he, "our lease will be up in three weeks, and I can't see how to leave before.

"The repairs are not done at home, and I cannot possibly leave town just now. Of course if you were in any danger, I could and would, but you really are better, dear, whether you can see it or not. I am a doctor, dear, and I know. You are gaining flesh and color, your appetite is better, I feel really much easier about you."

"I don't weigh a bit more," said I, "nor as much; and my appetite may be better in the evening when you are here, but it is worse in the morning when you are away!"

"Bless her little heart!" said he with a big hug, "she shall be as sick as she pleases! But now let's improve the shining hours by going to sleep, and talk about it in the morning!"

"And you won't go away?" I asked gloomily.

"Why, how can I, dear? It is only three weeks more and then we will take a nice little trip of a few days while Jennie is getting the house ready. Really dear you are better!"

"Better in body perhaps—" I began, and stopped short, for he sat up straight and looked at me with such a stern, reproachful look that I could not say another word.

"My darling," said he, "I beg of you, for my sake and for our child's sake, as well as for your own, that you will never for one instant let that idea enter your mind! There is nothing so dangerous, so fascinating, to a temperament like yours. It is a false and foolish fancy. Can you not trust me as a physician when I tell you so?"

So of course I said no more on that score, and we went to sleep before long. He thought I was asleep first, but I wasn't, and lay there for hours trying to decide whether that front pattern and the back pattern really did move together or separately.

On a pattern like this, by daylight, there is a lack of sequence, a defiance of law, that is a constant irritant to a normal mind.

The color is hideous enough, and unreliable enough, and infuriating enough, but the pattern is torturing.

You think you have mastered it, but just as you get well underway in following, it turns a back-somersault and there you are. It slaps you in the face, knocks you down, and tramples upon you. It is like a bad dream.

The outside pattern is a florid arabesque, reminding one of a fungus. If you can imagine a toadstool in joints, an interminable string of toadstools, budding and sprouting in endless convolutions—why, that is something like it.

That is, sometimes!

There is one marked peculiarity about this paper, a thing nobody seems to notice but myself, and that is that it changes as the light changes.

When the sun shoots in through the east window—I always watch for that first long, straight ray—it changes so quickly that I never can quite believe it.

That is why I watch it always.

By moonlight—the moon shines in all night when there is a moon—I wouldn't know it was the same paper.

At night in any kind of light, in twilight, candle light, lamplight, and worst of all by moonlight, it becomes bars! The outside pattern I mean, and the woman behind it is as plain as can be.

I didn't realize for a long time what the thing was that showed behind, that dim sub-pattern, but now I am quite sure it is a woman.

By daylight she is subdued, quiet. I fancy it is the pattern that keeps her so still. It is so puzzling. It keeps me quiet by the hour.

I lie down ever so much now. John says it is good for me, and to sleep all I can.

Indeed he started the habit by making me lie down for an hour after each meal.

It is a very bad habit I am convinced, for you see I don't sleep.

And that cultivates deceit, for I don't tell them I'm awake—O no!

The fact is I am getting a little afraid of John.

He seems very queer sometimes, and even Jennie has an inexplicable look.

It strikes me occasionally, just as a scientific hypothesis,—that perhaps it is the paper!

I have watched John when he did not know I was looking, and come into the room suddenly on the most innocent excuses, and I've caught him several times *looking at the paper!* And Jennie too. I caught Jennie with her hand on it once.

She didn't know I was in the room, and when I asked her in a quiet, a very quiet voice, with the most restrained manner possible, what she was doing with the paper—she turned around as if she had been caught stealing, and looked quite angry—asked me why I should frighten her so!

Then she said that the paper stained everything it touched, that she had found yellow smooches on all my clothes and John's, and she wished we would be more careful!

Did not that sound innocent? But I know she was studying that pattern, and I am determined that nobody shall find it out but myself!

Life is very much more exciting now than it used to be. You see I have something more to expect, to look forward to, to watch. I really do eat better, and am more quiet than I was.

John is so pleased to see me improve! He laughed a little the other day, and said I seemed to be flourishing in spite of my wall-paper.

I turned it off with a laugh. I had no intention of telling him it was *because* of the wall-paper—he would make fun of me. He might even want to take me away.

I don't want to leave now until I have found it out. There is a week more, and I think that will be enough.

I'm feeling ever so much better! I don't sleep much at night, for it is so interesting to watch developments; but I sleep a good deal in the daytime.

In the daytime it is tiresome and perplexing.

There are always new shoots on the fungus, and new shades of yellow all over it. I cannot keep count of them, though I have tried conscientiously.

It is the strangest yellow, the wall-paper! It makes me think of all the yellow things I ever saw—not beautiful ones like buttercups, but old foul, bad yellow things.

But there is something else about that paper—the smell! I noticed it the moment we came into the room, but with so much air and sun it was not bad. Now we have had a week of fog and rain, and whether the windows are open or not, the smell is here.

It creeps all over the house.

I find it hovering in the dining-room, skulking in the parlor, hiding in the hall, lying in wait for me on the stairs.

It gets into my hair.

Even when I go to ride, if I turn my head suddenly and surprise it—there is that smell!

Such a peculiar odor, too! I have spent hours in trying to analyze it, to find what it smelled like.

It is not bad—at first, and very gentle, but quite the subtlest, most enduring odor I ever met.

In this damp weather it is awful, I wake up in the night and find it hanging over me.

It used to disturb me at first. I thought seriously of burning the house—to reach the smell.

But now I am used to it. The only thing I can think of that it is like is the *color* of the paper! A yellow smell.

There is a very funny mark on this wall, low down, near the mopboard. A streak that runs round the room. It goes behind every piece of furniture, except the bed, a long, straight, even *smooch,* as if it had been rubbed over and over.

I wonder how it was done and who did it, and what they did it for. Round and round and round—round and round and round—it makes me dizzy!

I really have discovered something at last.

Through watching so much at night, when it changes so, I have finally found out.

The front pattern *does* move—and no wonder! The woman behind shakes it!

Sometimes I think there are a great many women behind, and sometimes only one, and she crawls around fast, and her crawling shakes it all over.

Then in the very bright spots she keeps still, and in the very shady spots she just takes hold of the bars and shakes them hard.

And she is all the time trying to climb through. But nobody could climb through that pattern—it strangles so; I think that is why it has so many heads.

They get through, and then the pattern strangles them off and turns them upside down, and makes their eyes white!

If those heads were covered or taken off it would not be half so bad.

I think that woman gets out in the daytime!

And I'll tell you why—privately—I've seen her!

I can see her out of every one of my windows!

It is the same woman, I know, for she is always creeping, and most women do not creep by daylight.

I see her on that long road under the trees, creeping along, and when a carriage comes she hides under the blackberry vines.

I don't blame her a bit. It must be very humiliating to be caught creeping by daylight!

I always lock the door when I creep by daylight. I can't do it at night, for I know John would suspect something at once.

And John is so queer now, that I don't want to irritate him. I wish he would take another room! Besides, I don't want anybody to get that woman out at night but myself.

I often wonder if I could see her out of all the windows at once.

But, turn as fast as I can, I can only see out of one at one time.

And though I always see her, she *may* be able to creep faster than I can turn!

I have watched her sometimes away off in the open country, creeping as fast as a cloud shadow in a high wind.

If only that top pattern could be gotten off from the under one! I mean to try it, little by little.

I have found out another funny thing, but I shan't tell it this time! It does not do to trust people too much.

There are only two more days to get this paper off, and I believe John is beginning to notice. I don't like the look in his eyes.

And I heard him ask Jennie a lot of professional questions about me. She had a very good report to give.

She said I slept a good deal in the daytime.

John knows I don't sleep very well at night, for all I'm so quiet!

He asked me all sorts of questions, too, and pretended to be very loving and kind.

As if I couldn't see through him!

Still, I don't wonder he acts so, sleeping under this paper for three months.

It only interests me, but I feel sure John and Jennie are secretly affected by it.

Hurrah! This is the last day, but it is enough. John to stay in town over night, and won't be out until this evening.

Jennie wanted to sleep with me—the sly thing! but I told her I should undoubtedly rest better for a night all alone.

That was clever, for really I wasn't alone a bit! As soon as it was moonlight and that poor thing began to crawl and shake the pattern, I got up and ran to help her.

I pulled and she shook, I shook and she pulled, and before morning we had peeled off yards of that paper.

A strip about as high as my head and half around the room.

And then when the sun came and that awful pattern began to laugh at me, I declared I would finish it to-day!

We go away to-morrow, and they are moving all my furniture down again to leave things as they were before.

Jennie looked at the wall in amazement, but I told her merrily that I did it out of pure spite at the vicious thing.

She laughed and said she wouldn't mind doing it herself, but I must not get tired.

How she betrayed herself that time!

But I am here, and no person touches this paper but me,—not *alive!*

She tried to get me out of the room—it was too patent! But I said it was so quiet and empty and clean now that I believed I would lie down again and sleep all I could; and not to wake me even for dinner—I would call when I woke.

So now she is gone, and the servants are gone, and the things are gone, and there is nothing left but that great bedstead nailed down, with the canvas mattress we found on it.

We shall sleep downstairs to-night, and take the boat home to-morrow.

I quite enjoy the room, now it is bare again.

How those children did tear about here!

This bedstead is fairly gnawed!

But I must get to work.

I have locked the door and thrown the key down into the front path.

I don't want to go out, and I don't want to have anybody come in, till John comes.

I want to astonish him.

I've got a rope up here that even Jennie did not find. If that woman does get out, and tries to get away, I can tie her!

But I forgot I could not reach far without anything to stand on!

This bed will *not* move!

I tried to lift and push it until I was lame, and then I got so angry I bit off a little piece at one corner—but it hurt my teeth.

Then I peeled off all the paper I could reach standing on the floor. It sticks horribly and the pattern just enjoys it! All those strangled heads and bulbous eyes and waddling fungus growths just shriek with derision!

I am getting angry enough to do something desperate. To jump out of the window would be admirable exercise, but the bars are too strong even to try.

Besides I wouldn't do it. Of course not. I know well enough that a step like that is improper and might be misconstrued.

I don't like to *look* out of the windows even—there are so many of those creeping women, and they creep so fast.

I wonder if they all come out of that wall-paper as I did?

But I am securely fastened now by my well-hidden rope—you don't get *me* out in the road there!

I suppose I shall have to get back behind the pattern when it comes night, and that is hard!

It is so pleasant to be out in this great room and creep around as I please!

I don't want to go outside. I won't, even if Jennie asks me to.

For outside you have to creep on the ground, and everything is green instead of yellow.

But here I can creep smoothly on the floor, and my shoulder just fits in that long smooch around the wall, so I cannot lose my way.

Why there's John at the door!

It is no use, young man, you can't open it!

How he does call and pound!

Now he's crying for an axe.

It would be a shame to break down that beautiful door!

"John dear!" said I in the gentlest voice, "the key is down by the front steps, under a plantain leaf!"

That silenced him for a few moments.

Then he said—very quietly indeed, "Open the door, my darling!"

"I can't," said I. "The key is down by the front door under a plantain leaf!"

And then I said it again, several times, very gently and slowly, and said it

so often that he had to go and see, and he got it of course, and came in. He
stopped short by the door.

"What is the matter?" he cried. "For God's sake, what are you doing!"

I kept on creeping just the same, but I looked at him over my shoulder.

"I've got out at last," said I, "in spite of you and Jane. And I've pulled off
most of the paper, so you can't put me back!"

Now why should that man have fainted? But he did, and right across my
path by the wall, so that I had to creep over him every time!

THE RUINED MAID

Thomas Hardy   (1840–1928)

The son of a Dorchester stonemason, Hardy began a career in architecture;
however, the success of *Far from the Madding Crowd* in 1874 convinced him that he
should make writing his profession. It also gave him enough money to marry, and
he wed Emma Lavinia Gifford that same year, ending a four-year courtship. After
1896 Hardy wrote no novels, but devoted himself to poetry, which had been his first
literary interest. In 1914, after Emma had died, Hardy married Florence Dugdale, a
writer of children's books.

"The Ruined Maid" appeared in *Poems of the Past and the Present* (1902).

"O 'Melia, my dear, this does everything crown!
Who could have supposed I should meet you in Town?
And whence such fair garments, such prosperi-ty?"—
"O didn't you know I'd been ruined?" said she.

—"You left us in tatters, without shoes or socks,
Tired of digging potatoes, and spudding up docks;
And now you've gay bracelets and bright feathers three!"—
"Yes: that's how we dress when we're ruined," said she.

—"At home in the barton you said 'thee' and 'thou,'
And 'thik oon,' and 'theäs oon,' and 't'other'; but now   10
Your talking quite fits 'ee for high compa-ny!"—
"A polish is gained with one's ruin," said she.

—"Your hands were like paws then, your face blue and bleak,
But now I'm bewitched by your delicate cheek,
And your little gloves fit as on any la-dy!"—
"We never do work when we're ruined," said she.

—"You used to call home-life a hag-ridden dream,
And you'd sigh, and you'd sock; but at present you seem
To know not of megrims or melancho-ly!"—
"True. One's pretty lively when ruined," said she.   20

—"I wish I had feathers, a fine sweeping gown,
And a delicate face, and could strut about Town!"—
"My dear—a raw country girl, such as you be,
Cannot quite expect that. You ain't ruined," said she.

THE BEAST IN THE JUNGLE

Henry James   (1843–1916)

The son of the philosopher Henry James, Sr., and brother of the philosopher and physician William James, Henry was born in New York, where he was privately educated. After 1866 he lived primarily in Europe, becoming a British citizen in 1915 to show his allegiance to the Allied cause in the First World War. He wrote critical articles and reviews and published his first novel in 1871. Thereafter his life was devoted to a series of short stories and novels concerned primarily with the interplay between European and American values. He never married.

"The Beast in the Jungle" was published in *The Better Sort* (1903). It is the story of John Marcher and May Bartram, who first met when they were in their twenties. Meeting again some ten years later, she reminds him: "You said you had from your earliest time, as the deepest thing within you, the sense of being kept for something rare and strange, possibly prodigious and terrible, that was sooner or later to happen to you, that you had in your bones the foreboding and the conviction of, and that would perhaps overwhelm you." She spends the rest of her life waiting for the great event with him. The excerpt which follows contains the closing three sections of James's story.

IV

Then it was that, one afternoon, while the spring of the year was young and new she met all in her own way his frankest betrayal of these alarms. He had gone in late to see her, but evening had n't settled and she was presented to him in that long fresh light of waning April days which affects us often with a sadness sharper than the greyest hours of autumn. The week had been warm, the spring was supposed to have begun early, and May Bartram sat, for the first time in the year, without a fire; a fact that, to Marcher's sense, gave the scene of which she formed part a smooth and ultimate look, an air of knowing, in its immaculate order and cold meaningless cheer, that it would never see a fire again. Her own aspect—he could scarce have said why—intensified this note. Almost as white as wax, with the marks and signs in her face as numerous and as fine as if they had been etched by a needle, with soft white draperies relieved by a faded green scarf on the delicate tone of which the years had further refined, she was the picture of a serene and exquisite but impenetrable sphinx, whose head, or indeed all whose person, might have been powdered with silver. She was a sphinx, yet with her white petals and green fronds she might have been a lily too—only an artificial lily, wonderfully imitated and constantly kept, without dust or stain, though not exempt from a slight droop and a complexity of faint creases, under some clear glass bell. The perfection of household care, of high polish and finish, always reigned in her rooms, but they now looked most as if everything had been wound up, tucked in, put away, so that she might sit with folded hands and with nothing more to do. She was "out of it," to Marcher's vision; her work was over; she communicated with him as across some gulf or from some island of rest that she had already reached, and it made him feel strangely abandoned. Was it—or rather was n't it—that if for so long she had been watching with him the answer to their question must have swum into her ken and taken on its name, so that her occupation was verily gone? He had as much as charged her with this in saying to her, many months before, that she even then knew something she was keeping from him. It was a point he had never since ventured to press, vaguely fearing as he did that it might become a difference, perhaps a disagreement, between them. He had in this later time turned nervous, which was what he in all the other years had never been; and the oddity was that his nervousness should have waited till he had begun to doubt, should have held off so long as he was sure. There was something, it seemed to him, that the wrong word would bring down on his head, something that would so at least ease off his tension. But he wanted not to speak the wrong word; that would make everything ugly. He wanted the knowledge he lacked to drop on him, if drop it could, by its own august weight. If she was to forsake him it was surely for her to take leave. This was why he did n't directly ask her again what she knew; but it was also why, approaching the matter from another side, he said to her in the course of his visit: "What do you regard as the very worst that at this time of day *can* happen to me?"

He had asked her that in the past often enough; they had, with the odd irregular rhythm of their intensities and avoidances, exchanged ideas about it and then had seen the ideas washed away by cool intervals, washed like figures traced in sea-sand. It had ever been the mark of their talk that the oldest allusions in it required but a little dismissal and reaction to come out again, sounding for the hour as new. She could thus at present meet his enquiry quite freshly and patiently. "Oh yes, I've repeatedly thought, only it always seemed to me of old that I could n't quite make up my mind. I thought of dreadful things, between which it was difficult to choose; and so must you have done."

"Rather! I feel now as if I had scarce done anything else. I appear to myself to have spent my life in thinking of nothing *but* dreadful things. A great many of them I've at different times named to you, but there were others I could n't name."

"They were too, too dreadful?"

"Too, too dreadful—some of them."

She looked at him a minute, and there came to him as he met it an inconsequent sense that her eyes, when one got their full clearness, were still as beautiful as they had been in youth, only beautiful with a strange cold light—a light that somehow was a part of the effect, if it was n't rather a part of the cause, of the pale hard sweetness of the season and the hour. "And yet," she said at last, "there are horrors we've mentioned."

It deepened the strangeness to see her, as such a figure in such a picture, talk of "horrors," but she was to do in a few minutes something stranger yet—though even of this he was to take the full measure but afterwards—and the note of it already trembled. It was, for the matter of that, one of the signs that her eyes were having again the high flicker of their prime. He had to admit, however, what she said. "Oh yes, there were times when we did go far." He caught himself in the act of speaking as if it all were over. Well, he wished it were; and the consummation depended for him clearly more and more on his friend.

But she had now a soft smile. "Oh far—!"

It was oddly ironic. "Do you mean you're prepared to go further?"

She was frail and ancient and charming as she continued to look at him, yet it was rather as if she had lost the thread. "Do you consider that we went far?"

"Why I thought it the point you were just making—that we *had* looked most things in the face."

"Including each other?" She still smiled. "But you're quite right. We've had together great imaginations, often great fears; but some of them have been unspoken."

"Then the worst—we have n't faced that. I *could* face it, I believe, if I knew what you think it. I feel," he explained, "as if I had lost my power to conceive such things." And he wondered if he looked as blank as he sounded. "It's spent."

"Then why do you assume," she asked, "that mine is n't?"

"Because you've given me signs to the contrary. It is n't a question for you of conceiving, imagining, comparing. It is n't a question now of choosing." At last he came out with it. "You know something I don't. You've shown me that before."

These last words had affected her, he made out in a moment, exceedingly, and she spoke with firmness. "I've shown you, my dear, nothing."

He shook his head. "You can't hide it."

"Oh, oh!" May Bartram sounded over what she could n't hide. It was almost a smothered groan.

"You admitted it months ago, when I spoke of it to you as of something you were afraid I should find out. Your answer was that I could n't, that I would n't, and I don't pretend I have. But you had something therefore in mind, and I now see how it must have been, how it still is, the possibility that, of all possibilities, has settled itself for you as the worst. This," he went on, "is why I appeal to you. I'm only afraid of ignorance to-day—I'm not afraid of knowledge." And then as for a while she said nothing: "What makes me sure is that I see in your face and feel here, in this air and amid these appearances, that you're out of it. You've done. You've had your experience. You leave me to my fate."

Well, she listened, motionless and white in her chair, as on a decision to be made, so that her manner was fairly an avowal, though still, with a small fine inner stiffness, an imperfect surrender. "It *would* be the worst," she finally let herself say. "I mean the thing I've never said."

It hushed him a moment. "More monstrous than all the monstrosities we've named?"

"More monstrous. Is n't that what you sufficiently express," she asked, "in calling it the worst?"

Marcher thought. "Assuredly—if you mean, as I do, something that includes all the loss and all the shame that are thinkable."

"It would if it *should* happen," said May Bartram. "What we're speaking of, remember, is only my idea."

"It's your belief," Marcher returned. "That's enough for me. I feel your beliefs are right. Therefore if, having this one, you give me no more light on it, you abandon me."

"No, no!" she repeated. "I'm with you—don't you see?—still." And as to make it more vivid to him she rose from her chair—a movement she seldom risked in these days—and showed herself, all draped and all soft, in her fairness and slimness. "I have n't forsaken you."

It was really, in its effort against weakness, a generous assurance, and had the success of the impulse not, happily, been great, it would have touched him to pain more than to pleasure. But the cold charm in her eyes had spread, as she hovered before him, to all the rest of her person, so that it was for the minute almost a recovery of youth. He could n't pity her for that; he could only take her as she showed—as capable even yet of helping him. It was as if, at the same time, her light might at any instant go out; wherefore he must make the most of it. There passed before him with intensity the three or four things he wanted most to know; but the question that came of itself to his lips really covered the others. "Then tell me if I shall consciously suffer."

She promptly shook her head. "Never!"

It confirmed the authority he imputed to her, and it produced on him an extraordinary effect. "Well, what's better than that? Do you call that the worst?"

"You think nothing is better?" she asked.

She seemed to mean something so special that he again sharply wondered, though still with the dawn of a prospect of relief. "Why not, if one does n't *know?*" After which, as their eyes, over his question, met in a silence, the dawn deepened and something to his purpose came prodigiously out of her very face. His own, as he took it in, suddenly flushed to the forehead, and he gasped with the force of a perception to which, on the instant, everything fitted. The sound of his gasp filled the air; then he became articulate. "I see—if I don't suffer!"

In her own look, however, was doubt. "You see what?"

"Why what you mean—what you've always meant."

She again shook her head. "What I mean is n't what I've always meant. It's different."

"It's something new?"

She hung back from it a little. "Something new. It's not what you think. I see what you think."

His divination drew breath then; only her correction might be wrong. "It is n't that I *am* a blockhead?" he asked between faintness and grimness. "It is n't that it's all a mistake?"

"A mistake?" she pityingly echoed. *That* possibility, for her, he saw, would be monstrous; and if she guaranteed him the immunity from pain it would accordingly not be what she had in mind. "Oh no," she declared; "it's nothing of that sort. You've been right."

Yet he could n't help asking himself if she were n't, thus pressed, speaking but to save him. It seemed to him he should be most in a hole if his history should prove all a platitude. "Are you telling me the truth, so that I shan't have been a bigger idiot than I can bear to know? I *have* n't lived with a vain imagination, in the most besotted illusion? I have n't waited but to see the door shut in my face?"

She shook her head again. "However the case stands *that* is n't the truth. Whatever the reality, it *is* a reality. The door is n't shut. The door's open," said May Bartram.

"Then something's to come?"

She waited once again, always with her cold sweet eyes on him. "It's never too late." She had, with her gliding step, diminished the distance between them, and she stood nearer to him, close to him, a minute, as if still charged with the unspoken. Her movement might have been for some finer emphasis of what she was at once hesitating and deciding to say. He had been standing by the chimney-piece, fireless and sparely adorned, a small perfect old French clock and two morsels of rosy Dresden constituting all its furniture; and her hand grasped the shelf while she kept him waiting, grasped it a little as for support and encouragement. She only kept him waiting, however; that is he only waited. It had become suddenly, from her movement and attitude, beautiful and vivid to him that she had something more to give him; her wasted face delicately shone with it—it glittered almost as with the white lustre of silver in her expression. She was right, incontestably, for what he saw in her face was the truth, and strangely, without consequence, while their talk of it as dreadful was still in the air, she appeared to present it as inordinately soft. This, prompting bewilderment, made him but gape the more gratefully for her revelation, so that they continued for some minutes silent, her face shining at him, her contact imponderably pressing, and his stare all kind but all expectant. The end, none the less, was that what he had expected failed to come to him. Something else took place instead, which seemed to consist at first in the mere closing of her eyes. She gave way at the same instant to a slow fine shudder, and though he remained staring—though he stared in fact but the harder—turned off and regained her chair. It was the end of what she had been intending, but it left him thinking only of that.

"Well, you don't say—?"

She had touched in her passage a bell near the chimney and had sunk back strangely pale. "I'm afraid I'm too ill."

"Too ill to tell me?" It sprang up sharp to him, and almost to his lips, the fear she might die without giving him light. He checked himself in time from so expressing his question, but she answered as if she had heard the words.

"Don't you know—now?"

"'Now'—?" She had spoken as if some difference had been made within the moment. But her maid, quickly obedient to her bell, was already with them. "I know nothing." And he was afterwards to say to himself that he must have spoken with odious impatience, such an impatience as to show that, supremely disconcerted, he washed his hands of the whole question.

"Oh!" said May Bartram.

"Are you in pain?" he asked as the woman went to her.

"No," said May Bartram.

Her maid, who had put an arm round her as if to take her to her room, fixed on him eyes that appealingly contradicted her; in spite of which, however, he showed once more his mystification. "What then has happened?"

She was once more, with her companion's help, on her feet, and, feeling withdrawal imposed on him, he had blankly found his hat and gloves and had reached the door. Yet he waited for her answer. "What *was* to," she said.

V

He came back the next day, but she was then unable to see him, and as it was literally the first time this had occurred in the long stretch of their acquaintance he turned away, defeated and sore, almost angry—or feeling at least that such a break in their custom was really the beginning of the end—and wandered alone with his thoughts, especially with the one he was least able to keep down. She was dying and he would lose her; she was dying and his life would end. He stopped in the Park, into which he had passed, and stared before him at his recurrent doubt. Away from her the doubt pressed again; in her presence he had believed her, but as he felt his forlornness he threw himself into the explanation that, nearest at hand, had most of a miserable warmth for him and least of a cold torment. She had deceived him to save him—to put him off with something in which he should be able to rest. What could the thing that was to happen to him be, after all, but just this thing that had begun to happen? Her dying, her death, his consequent solitude—*that* was what he had figured as the Beast in the Jungle, that was what had been in the lap of the gods. He had had her word for it as he left her—what else on earth could she have meant? It was n't a thing of a monstrous order; not a fate rare and distinguished; not a stroke of fortune that overwhelmed and immortalised; it had only the stamp of the common doom. But poor Marcher at this hour judged the common doom sufficient. It would serve his turn, and even as the consummation of infinite waiting he would bend his pride to accept it. He sat down on a bench in the twilight. He had n't been a fool. Something had *been,* as she had said, to come. Before he rose indeed it had quite struck him that the final fact really matched with the long avenue through which he had had to reach it. As sharing his suspense and as giving herself all, giving her life, to bring it to an end, she had come with him every step of the way. He had lived by her aid, and to leave her behind would be cruelly, damnably to miss her. What could be more overwhelming than that?

Well, he was to know within the week, for though she kept him a while at bay, left him restless and wretched during a series of days on each of which he asked about her only again to have to turn away, she ended his trial by receiving him where she had always received him. Yet she had been brought out at some hazard into the presence of so many of the things that were, consciously, vainly, half their past, and there was scant service left in the gentleness of her mere desire, all too visible, to check his obsession and wind up his long trouble. That was clearly what she wanted, the one thing more for her own peace while she could still put out her hand. He was so affected by her state that, once seated by her chair, he was moved to let everything go; it was she herself therefore who brought him back, took up again, before she dismissed him, her last word of the other time. She showed how she wished to leave their business in order. "I'm not sure you understood. You've nothing to wait for more. It *has* come."

Oh how he looked at her! "Really?"

"Really."

"The thing that, as you said, *was* to?"

"The thing that we began in our youth to watch for."

Face to face with her once more he believed her; it was a claim to which he had so abjectly little to oppose. "You mean that it has come as a positive definite occurrence, with a name and a date?"

"Positive. Definite. I don't know about the 'name,' but oh with a date!"

He found himself again too helplessly at sea. "But come in the night—come and passed me by?"

May Bartram had her strange faint smile. "Oh no, it has n't passed you by!"

"But if I have n't been aware of it and it has n't touched me—?"

"Ah your not being aware of it"—and she seemed to hesitate an instant to deal with this—"your not being aware of it is the strangeness *in* the strangeness. It's the wonder *of* the wonder." She spoke as with the softness almost of a sick child, yet now at last, at the end of all, with the perfect straightness of a sibyl. She visibly knew that she knew, and the effect on him was of something co-ordinate, in its high character, with the law that had ruled him. It was the true voice of the law; so on her lips would the law itself have sounded. "It *has* touched you," she went on. "It has done its office. It has made you all its own."

"So utterly without my knowing it?"

"So utterly without your knowing it." His hand, as he leaned to her, was on the arm of her chair, and, dimly smiling always now, she placed her own on it. "It's enough if *I* know it."

"Oh!" he confusedly breathed, as she herself of late so often had done.

"What I long ago said is true. You'll never know now, and I think you ought to be content. You've *had* it," said May Bartram.

"But had what?"

"Why what was to have marked you out. The proof of your law. It has acted. I'm too glad," she then bravely added, "to have been able to see what it's *not*."

He continued to attach his eyes to her, and with the sense that it was all beyond him, and that *she* was too, he would still have sharply challenged her had n't he so felt it an abuse of her weakness to do more than take devoutly what she gave him, take it hushed as to a revelation. If he did speak, it was out of the foreknowledge of his loneliness to come. "If you're glad of what it's 'not' it might then have been worse?"

She turned her eyes away, she looked straight before her; with which after a moment: "Well, you know our fears."

He wondered. "It's something then we never feared?"

On this slowly she turned to him. "Did we ever dream, with all our dreams, that we should sit and talk of it thus?"

He tried for a little to make out that they had; but it was as if their dreams, numberless enough, were in solution in some thick cold mist through which thought lost itself. "It might have been that we could n't talk?"

"Well"—she did her best for him—"not from this side. This, you see," she said, "is the *other* side."

"I think," poor Marcher returned, "that all sides are the same to me." Then, however, as she gently shook her head in correction: "We might n't, as it were, have got across—?"

"To where we are—no. We're *here*"—she made her weak emphasis.

"And much good does it do us!" was her friend's frank comment.

"It does us the good it can. It does us the good that *it* is n't here. It's past. It's behind," said May Bartram. "Before—" but her voice dropped.

He had got up, not to tire her, but it was hard to combat his yearning. She after all told him nothing but that his light had failed—which he knew well enough without her. "Before—?" he blankly echoed.

"Before, you see, it was always to *come.* That kept it present."

"Oh I don't care what comes now! Besides," Marcher added, "it seems to me I liked it better present, as you say, than I can like it absent with *your* absence."

"Oh mine!"—and her pale hands made light of it.

"With the absence of everything." He had a dreadful sense of standing there before her for—so far as anything but this proved, this bottomless drop was concerned—the last time of their life. It rested on him with a weight he felt he could scarce bear, and this weight it apparently was that still pressed out what remained in him of speakable protest. "I believe you; but I can't begin to pretend I understand. *Nothing,* for me, is past; nothing *will* pass till I pass myself, which I pray my stars may be as soon as possible. Say, however," he added, "that I've eaten my cake, as you contend, to the last crumb—how can the thing I've never felt at all be the thing I was marked out to feel?"

She met him perhaps less directly, but she met him unperturbed. "You take your 'feelings' for granted. You were to suffer your fate. That was not necessarily to know it."

"How in the world—when what is such knowledge but suffering?"

She looked up at him a while in silence. "No—you don't understand."

"I suffer," said John Marcher.

"Don't, don't!"

"How can I help at least *that?*"

"*Don't!*" May Bartram repeated.

She spoke it in a tone so special, in spite of her weakness, that he stared an instant—stared as if some light, hitherto hidden, had shimmered across his vision. Darkness again closed over it, but the gleam had already become for him an idea. "Because I have n't the right—?"

"Don't *know*—when you need n't," she mercifully urged. "You need n't—for we should n't."

"Should n't?" If he could but know what she meant!

"No—it's too much."

"Too much?" he still asked but, with a mystification that was the next moment of a sudden to give way. Her words, if they meant something, affected him in this light—the light also of her wasted face—as meaning *all,* and the sense of what knowledge had been for herself came over him with a rush which broke through into a question. "Is it of that then you're dying?"

She but watched him, gravely at first, as to see, with this, where he was, and she might have seen something or feared something that moved her sympathy. "I would live for you still—if I could." Her eyes closed for a little, as if, withdrawn into herself, she were for a last time trying. "But I can't!" she said as she raised them again to take leave of him.

She could n't indeed, as but too promptly and sharply appeared, and he had no vision of her after this that was anything but darkness and doom. They had parted for ever in that strange talk; access to her chamber of pain, rigidly guarded, was almost wholly forbidden him; he was feeling now moreover, in the face of doctors, nurses, the two or three relatives attracted doubtless by the presumption of what she had to "leave," how few were the rights, as they were called in such cases, that he had to put forward, and how odd it might even seem that their intimacy should n't have given him more of them. The stupidest fourth cousin had more, even though she had been nothing in such a person's life. She had been a feature of features in *his,* for what else was it to have been so indispensable? Strange beyond saying were the ways of existence, baffling for him the anomaly of his lack, as he felt it to be, of producible claim. A woman might have been, as it were, everything to him, and it might yet present him in no connexion that any one seemed held to recognise. If this was the case in these closing weeks it was the case more sharply on the occasion of the last offices rendered, in the great grey London cemetery, to what had been mortal, to what had been precious, in his friend. The concourse at her grave was not numerous, but he saw himself treated as scarce more nearly concerned with it than if there had been a thousand others. He was in short from this moment face to face with the fact that he was to profit extraordinarily little by the interest May Bartram had taken in him. He could n't quite have said what he expected, but he had n't surely expected this approach to a double privation. Not only had her interest failed him, but he seemed to feel himself unattended—and for a reason he could n't seize—by the distinction, the dignity, the propriety, if nothing else, of the man markedly bereaved. It was as if in the view of society he had not *been* markedly bereaved, as if there still failed some sign or proof of it, and as if none the less his character could never be affirmed nor the deficiency ever made up. There were moments as the weeks went by when he would have liked, by some almost aggressive act, to take his stand on the intimacy of his loss, in order that it *might* be questioned and his retort, to the relief of his spirit, so recorded; but the moments of an irritation more helpless followed fast on these, the moments during which, turning things over with a good conscience but with a bare horizon, he found himself wondering if he ought n't to have begun, so to speak, further back.

He found himself wondering indeed at many things, and this last speculation had others to keep it company. What could he have done, after all, in her lifetime, without giving them both, as it were, away? He could n't have made known she was watching him, for that would have published the superstition of the Beast. This was what closed his mouth now—now that the Jungle had been threshed to vacancy and that the Beast had stolen away. It sounded too foolish and too flat; the difference for him in this particular, the extinction in his life of the element of suspense, was such as in fact to surprise him. He could scarce have said what the effect resembled; the abrupt cessation, the positive prohibition, of music perhaps, more than anything else, in some place all adjusted and all accustomed to sonority and to attention. If he could at any rate have conceived lifting the veil from his image at some moment of the past (what had he done, after all, if not lift it to *her?*) so to do this to-day, to talk to people at large of the Jungle cleared and confide to them that he now felt it as safe, would have been not only to see them listen as to a goodwife's tale, but really to hear himself tell one. What it presently came to in truth was that poor Marcher waded through his beaten grass, where no life stirred, where no breath sounded, where no evil eye seemed to gleam from a possible lair, very much as if vaguely looking for the Beast, and still more as if acutely missing it. He walked about in an existence that had grown strangely more spacious, and, stopping fitfully in places where the undergrowth of life struck him as closer, asked himself yearningly, wondered secretly and sorely, if it would have lurked here or there. It would have at all events *sprung;* what was at least complete was his belief in the truth itself of the assurance given him. The change from his old sense to his new was absolute and final: what was to happen *had* so absolutely and finally happened that he was as little able to know a fear for his future as to know a hope; so absent in short was any question of anything still to come. He was to live entirely with the other question, that of his unidentified past, that of his having to see his fortune impenetrably muffled and masked.

The torment of this vision became then his occupation; he could n't perhaps have consented to live but for the possibility of guessing. She had told him, his friend, not to guess; she had forbidden him, so far as he might, to know, and she had even in a sort denied the power in him to learn: which were so many things, precisely, to deprive him of rest. It was n't that he wanted, he argued for fairness, that anything past and done should repeat itself; it was only that he should n't, as an anticlimax, have been taken sleeping so sound as not to be able to win back by an effort of thought the lost stuff of consciousness. He declared to himself at moments that he would either win it back or have done with consciousness for ever; he made this idea his one motive in fine, made it so much his passion that none other, to compare with it, seemed ever to have touched him. The lost stuff of consciousness became thus for him as a strayed or stolen child to an unappeasable father; he hunted it up and down very much as if he were knocking at doors and enquiring of the police. This was the spirit in which, inevitably, he set himself to travel; he started on a journey that was to be as long as he could make it; it danced before him that, as the other side of the globe could n't possibly have less to say to him, it might, by a possibility of suggestion, have more. Before he quitted London, however, he made a pilgrimage to May Bartram's grave, took his way to it through the endless avenues of the grim suburban metropolis, sought it out in the wilderness of tombs, and, though he had come but for the renewal of the act of farewell, found himself, when he had at last stood by it, beguiled into long intensities. He stood for an hour, powerless to turn away and yet powerless to penetrate the darkness of death; fixing with his eyes her inscribed name and date, beating his forehead against the fact of the secret they kept, drawing his breath, while he waited, as if some sense would in pity of him rise from the stones. He kneeled on the stones, however, in vain; they kept what they concealed; and if the face of the tomb did become a face for him it was because her two names became a pair of eyes that did n't know him. He gave them a last long look, but no palest light broke.

VI

He stayed away, after this, for a year; he visited the depths of Asia, spending himself on scenes of romantic interest, of superlative sanctity; but what was present to him everywhere was that for a man who had known what *he* had known the world was vulgar and vain. The state of mind in which he had lived for so many years shone out to him, in reflexion, as a light that coloured and refined, a light beside which the glow of the East was garish cheap and thin. The terrible truth was that he had lost—with everything else—a distinction as well; the things he saw could n't help being common when he had become common to look at them. He was simply now one of them himself—he was in the dust, without a peg for the sense of difference; and there were hours when, before the temples of gods and the sepulchres of kings, his spirit turned for nobleness of association to the barely discriminated slab in the London suburb. That had become for him, and more intensely with time and distance, his one witness of a past glory. It was all that was left to him for proof or pride, yet the past glories of Pharaohs were nothing to him as he thought of it. Small wonder then that he came back to it on the morrow of his return. He was drawn there this time as irresistibly as the other, yet with a confidence, almost, that was doubtless the effect of the many months that had elapsed. He had lived, in spite of himself, into his change of feeling, and in wandering over the earth had wandered, as might be said, from the circumference to the centre of his desert. He had settled to his safety and accepted perforce his extinction; figuring to himself, with some colour, in the likeness of certain little old men he remembered to have seen, of whom, all meagre and wizened as they might look, it was related that they had in their time fought twenty duels or been loved by ten princesses. They indeed had been wondrous for others while he was but wondrous for himself; which, however, was exactly the cause of his haste to renew the wonder by getting back, as he might put it, into his own presence. That had quickened his steps and checked his delay. If his visit was prompt it was because he had been separated so long from the part of himself that alone he now valued.

It's accordingly not false to say that he reached his goal with a certain elation and stood there again with a certain assurance. The creature beneath the sod *knew* of his rare experience, so that, strangely now, the place had lost for him its mere blankness of expression. It met him in mildness—not, as before, in mockery; it wore for him the air of conscious greeting that we find, after absence, in things that have closely belonged to us and which seem to confess of themselves to the connexion. The plot of ground, the graven tablet, the tended flowers affected him so as belonging to him that he resembled for the hour a contented landlord reviewing a piece of property. Whatever had happened—well, had happened. He had not come back this time with the vanity of that question, his former worrying "What, *what?*" now practically so spent. Yet he would none the less never again so cut himself off from the spot; he would come back to it every month, for if he did nothing else by its aid he at least held up his head. It thus grew for him, in the oddest way, a positive resource; he carried out his idea of periodical returns, which took their place at last among the most inveterate of his habits. What it all amounted to, oddly enough, was that in his finally so simplified world this garden of death gave him the few square feet of earth on which he could still most live. It was as if, being nothing anywhere else for any one, nothing even for himself, he were just everything here, and if not for a crowd of witnesses or indeed for any witness but John Marcher, then by clear right of the register that he could scan like an open page. The open page was the tomb of his friend, and *there* were the facts of the past, there the truth of his life, there the backward reaches in which he could lose himself. He did this from time to time with such effect that he seemed to wander through the old years with his hand in the arm of a companion who was, in the most extraordinary manner, his other, his younger self; and to wander, which was more extraordinary yet, round and round a third presence—not wandering she, but stationary, still, whose eyes, turning with his revolution, never ceased to follow him, and whose seat was his point, so to speak, of orientation. Thus in short he settled to live—feeding all on the sense that he once *had* lived, and dependent on it not alone for a support but for an identity.

It sufficed him in its way for months and the year elapsed; it would doubtless even have carried him further but for an accident, superficially slight, which moved him, quite in another direction, with a force beyond any of his impressions of Egypt or of India. It was a thing of the merest chance—the turn, as he afterwards felt, of a hair, though he was indeed to live to believe that if light had n't come to him in this particular fashion it would still have come in another. He was to live to believe this, I say, though he was not to live, I may not less definitely mention, to do much else. We allow him at any rate the benefit of the conviction, struggling up for him at the end, that, whatever might have happened or not happened, he would have come round of himself to the light. The incident of an autumn day had put the match to the train laid from of old by his misery. With the light before him he knew that even of late his ache had only been smothered. It was strangely drugged, but it throbbed; at the touch it began to bleed. And the touch, in the event, was the face of a fellow mortal. This face, one grey afternoon when the leaves were thick in the alleys, looked into Marcher's own, at the cemetery, with an expression like the cut of a blade. He felt it, that is, so deep down that he winced at the steady thrust. The person who so mutely assaulted him was a figure he had noticed, on reaching his own goal, absorbed by a grave a short distance away, a grave apparently fresh, so that the emotion of the visitor would probably match it for frankness. This fact alone forbade further attention, though during the time he stayed he remained vaguely conscious of his neighbour, a middle-aged man apparently, in mourning, whose bowed back, among the clustered monuments and mortuary yews, was constantly presented. Marcher's theory that these were elements in contact with which he himself revived, had suffered, on this occasion, it may be granted, a marked, an excessive check. The autumn day was dire for him as none had recently been, and he rested with a heaviness he had not yet known on the low stone table that bore May Bartram's name. He rested without power to move, as if some spring in him, some spell vouchsafed, had suddenly been broken for ever. If he could have done that moment as he wanted he would simply have stretched himself on the slab that was ready to take him, treating it as a place prepared to receive his last sleep. What in all the wide world had he now to keep awake for? He stared before him with the question, and it was then that, as one of the cemetery walks passed near him, he caught the shock of the face.

His neighbour at the other grave had withdrawn, as he himself, with force enough in him, would have done by now, and was advancing along the path on his way to one of the gates. This brought him close, and his pace was slow, so that—and all the more as there was a kind of hunger in his look—the two men were for a minute directly confronted. Marcher knew him at once for one of the deeply stricken—a perception so sharp that nothing else in the picture comparatively lived, neither his dress, his age, nor his presumable character and class; nothing lived but the deep ravage of the features he showed. He *showed* them—that was the point; he was moved, as he passed, by some impulse that was either a signal for sympathy or, more possibly, a challenge to an opposed sorrow. He might already have been aware of our friend, might at some previous hour have noticed in him the smooth habit of the scene, with which the state of his own senses so scantly consorted, and might thereby have been stirred as by an overt discord. What Marcher was at all events conscious of was in the first place that the image of scarred passion presented to him was conscious too—of something that profaned the air; and in the second that, roused, startled, shocked, he was yet the next moment looking after it, as it went, with envy. The most extraordinary thing that had happened to him—though he had given that name to other matters as well—took place, after his immediate vague stare, as a consequence of this impression. The stranger passed, but the raw glare of his grief remained, making our friend wonder in pity what wrong, what wound it expressed, what injury not to be healed. What had the man *had,* to make him by the loss of it so bleed and yet live?

Something—and this reached him with a pang—that *he,* John Marcher, had n't; the proof of which was precisely John Marcher's arid end. No passion had ever touched him, for this was what passion meant; he had survived and maundered and pined, but where had been *his* deep ravage? The extraordinary thing we speak of was the sudden rush of the result of this question. The sight that had just met his eyes named to him, as in letters of quick flame, something he had utterly, insanely missed, and what he had missed made these things a train of fire, made them mark themselves in an anguish of inward throbs. He had seen *outside* of his life, not learned it within, the way a woman was mourned when she had been loved for herself: such was the force of his conviction of the meaning of the stranger's face, which still flared for him as a smoky torch. It had n't come to him, the knowledge, on the wings of experience; it had brushed him, jostled him, upset him, with the disrespect of chance, the insolence of accident. Now that the illumination had begun, however, it blazed to the zenith, and what he presently stood there gazing at was the sounded void of his life. He gazed, he drew breath, in pain; he turned in his dismay, and, turning, he had before him in sharper incision than ever the open page of his story. The name on the table smote him as the passage of his neighbour had done, and what it said to him, full in the face, was that *she* was what he had missed. This was the awful thought, the answer to all the past, the vision at the dread clearness of which he grew as cold as the stone beneath him. Everything fell together, confessed, explained, overwhelmed; leaving him most of all stupefied at the blindness he had cherished. The fate he had been marked for he had met with a vengeance—he had emptied the cup to the lees; he had been the man of his time, *the* man, to whom nothing on earth was to have happened. That was the rare stroke—that was his visitation. So he saw it, as we say, in pale horror, while the pieces fitted and fitted. So *she* had seen it while he did n't, and so she served at this hour to drive the truth home. It was the truth, vivid and monstrous, that all the while he had waited the wait was itself his portion. This the companion of his vigil had at a given moment made out, and she had then offered him the chance to baffle his doom. One's doom, however, was never baffled, and on the day she told him his own had come down she had seen him but stupidly stare at the escape she offered him.

The escape would have been to love her; then, *then* he would have lived. *She* had lived—who could say now with what passion?—since she had loved him for himself; whereas he had never thought of her (ah how it hugely glared at him!) but in the chill of his egotism and the light of her use. Her spoken words came back to him—the chain stretched and stretched. The Beast had lurked indeed, and the Beast, at its hour, had sprung; it had sprung in that twilight of the cold April when, pale, ill, wasted, but all beautiful, and perhaps even then recoverable, she had risen from her chair to stand before him and let him imaginably guess. It had sprung as he did n't guess; it had sprung as she hopelessly turned from him, and the mark, by the time he left her, had fallen where it *was* to fall. He had justified his fear and achieved his fate; he had failed, with the last exactitude, of all he was to fail of; and a moan now rose to his lips as he remembered she had prayed he might n't know. This horror of waking—*this* was knowledge, knowledge under the breath of which the very tears in his eyes seemed to freeze. Through them, none the less, he tried to fix it and hold it; he kept it there before him so that he might feel the pain. That at least, belated and bitter, had something of the taste of life. But the bitterness suddenly sickened him, and it was as if, horribly, he saw, in the truth, in the cruelty of his image, what had been appointed and done. He saw the Jungle of his life and saw the lurking Beast; then, while he looked, perceived it, as by a stir of the air, rise, huge and hideous, for the leap that was to settle him. His eyes darkened—it was close; and, instinctively turning, in his hallucination, to avoid it, he flung himself, face down, on the tomb.

CRAZY JANE TALKS WITH THE BISHOP

William Butler Yeats

See headnote to "Leda and the Swan," page 94.

"Crazy Jane Talks with the Bishop" appeared in 1933 in *The Winding Stair and Other Poems.*

I met the Bishop on the road
And much said he and I.
'Those breasts are flat and fallen now,
Those veins must soon be dry;
Live in a heavenly mansion,
Not in some foul sty.'

'Fair and foul are near of kin,
And fair needs foul,' I cried.
'My friends are gone, but that's a truth
Nor grave nor bed denied,
Learned in bodily lowliness
And in the heart's pride.

'A woman can be proud and stiff
When on love intent;
But Love has pitched his mansion in
The place of excrement;
For nothing can be sole or whole
That has not been rent.'

THE RICHER, THE POORER

Dorothy West   (1910–   )

West was born in Boston and attended Boston University and the Columbia University School of Journalism. She edited *Challenge* and *New Challenge,* black quarterly magazines. Her own writing career began during the Depression, when she was a social worker in Harlem and wrote short stories for newspaper syndication. *The Living Is Easy,* a novel, was published in 1948.

"The Richer, the Poorer" is one of the forty-odd stories West wrote for the New York *Daily News* in the 1940s and 1950s.

Over the years Lottie had urged Bess to prepare for her old age. Over the years Bess had lived each day as if there were no other. Now they were both past sixty, the time for summing up. Lottie had a bank account that had never grown lean. Bess had the clothes on her back, and the rest of her worldly possessions in a battered suitcase.

Lottie had hated being a child, hearing her parents' skimping and scraping. Bess had never seemed to notice. All she ever wanted was to go outside and play. She learned to skate on borrowed skates. She rode a borrowed bicycle. Lottie couldn't wait to grow up and buy herself the best of everything.

As soon as anyone would hire her, Lottie put herself to work. She minded babies, she ran errands for the old.

She never touched a penny of her money, though her child's mouth watered for ice cream and candy. But she could not bear to share with Bess, who never had anything to share with her. When the dimes began to add up to dollars, she lost her taste for sweets.

By the time she was twelve, she was clerking after school in a small variety store. Saturdays she worked as long as she was wanted. She decided to keep her money for clothes. When she entered high school, she would wear a wardrobe that neither she nor anyone else would be able to match.

But her freshman year found her unable to indulge so frivolous a whim, particularly when her admiring instructors advised her to think seriously of college. No one in her family had ever gone to college, and certainly Bess would never get there. She would show them all what she could do, if she put her mind to it.

She began to bank her money, and her bank became her most private and precious possession.

In her third year high she found a job in a small but expanding restaurant, where she cashiered from the busy hour until closing. In her last year high the business increased so rapidly that Lottie was faced with the choice of staying in school or working fulltime.

She made her choice easily. A job in hand was worth two in the future.

Bess had a beau in the school band, who had no other ambition except to play a horn. Lottie expected to be settled with a home and family while Bess was still waiting for Harry to earn enough to buy a marriage license.

That Bess married Harry straight out of high school was not surprising. That Lottie never married at all was not really surprising either. Two or three times she was halfway persuaded, but to give up a job that paid well for a homemaking job that paid nothing was a risk she was incapable of taking.

Bess's married life was nothing for Lottie to envy. She and Harry lived like gypsies, Harry playing in second-rate bands all over the country, even getting himself and Bess stranded in Europe. They were often in rags and never in riches.

Bess grieved because she had no child, not having sense enough to know she was better off without one. Lottie was certainly better off without nieces and nephews to feel sorry for. Very likely Bess would have dumped them on her doorstep.

That Lottie had a doorstep they might have been left on was only because her boss, having bought a second house, offered Lottie his first house at a price so low and terms so reasonable that it would have been like losing money to refuse.

She shut off the rooms she didn't use, letting them go to rack and ruin. Since she ate her meals out, she had no food at home, and did not encourage callers, who always expected a cup of tea.

Her way of life was mean and miserly, but she did not know it. She thought she lived frugally in her middle years so that she could live in comfort and ease when she most needed peace of mind.

The years, after forty, began to race. Suddenly Lottie was sixty, and retired from her job by her boss's son, who had no sentimental feeling about keeping her on until she was ready to quit.

She made several attempts to find other employment, but her dowdy appearance made her look old and inefficient. For the first time in her life Lottie would gladly have worked for nothing, to have some place to go, something to do with her day.

Harry died abroad, in a third-rate hotel, with Bess weeping as hard as if he had left her a fortune. He had left her nothing but his horn. There wasn't even money for her passage home.

Lottie, trapped by the blood tie, knew she would not only have to send for her sister, but take her in when she returned. It didn't seem fair that Bess should reap the harvest of Lottie's lifetime of self-denial.

It took Lottie a week to get a bedroom ready, a week of hard work and hard cash. There was everything to do, everything to replace or paint. When she was through the room looked so fresh and new that Lottie felt she deserved it more than Bess.

She would let Bess have her room, but the mattress was so lumpy, the carpet so worn, the curtains so threadbare that Lottie's conscience pricked her. She supposed she would have to redo that room, too, and went about doing it with an eagerness that she mistook for haste.

When she was through upstairs, she was shocked to see how dismal downstairs looked by comparison. She tried to ignore it, but with nowhere to go to escape it, the contrast grew more intolerable.

She worked her way from kitchen to parlor, persuading herself she was only putting the rooms to right to give herself something to do. At night she slept like a child after a long and happy day of playing house. She was having more fun than she had ever had in her life. She was living each hour for itself.

There was only a day now before Bess would arrive. Passing her gleaming mirrors, at first with vague awareness, then with painful clarity, Lottie saw herself as others saw her, and could not stand the sight.

She went on a spending spree from specialty shops to beauty salon, emerging transformed into a woman who believed in miracles.

She was in the kitchen basting a turkey when Bess rang the bell. Her heart raced, and she wondered if the heat from the oven was responsible.

She went to the door, and Bess stood before her. Stiffly she suffered Bess's embrace, her heart racing harder, her eyes suddenly smarting from the onrush of cold air.

"Oh, Lottie, it's good to see you," Bess said, but saying nothing about Lottie's splendid appearance. Upstairs Bess, putting down her shabby suitcase, said, "I'll sleep like a rock tonight," without a word of praise for her lovely room. At the lavish table, top-heavy with turkey, Bess said, "I'll take light and dark both," with no marveling at the size of the bird, or that there was turkey for two elderly women, one of them too poor to buy her own bread.

With the glow of good food in her stomach, Bess began to spin stories. They were rich with places and people, most of them lowly, all of them magnificent. Her face reflected her telling, the joys and sorrows of her remembering, and above all, the love she lived by that enhanced the poorest place, the humblest person.

Then it was that Lottie knew why Bess had made no mention of her finery, or the shining room, or the twelve-pound turkey. She had not even seen them. Tomorrow she would see the room as it really looked, and Lottie as she really looked, and the warmed-over turkey in its second-day glory. Tonight she saw only what she had come seeking, a place in her sister's home and heart.

She said, "That's enough about me. How have the years used you?"

"It was me who didn't use them," said Lottie wistfully. "I saved for them. I forgot the best of them would go without my ever spending a day or a dollar enjoying them. That's my life story in those few words, a life never lived.

"Now it's too near the end to try."

Bess said, "To know how much there is to know is the beginning of learning to live. Don't count the years that are left us. At our time of life it's the days that count. You've too much catching up to do to waste a minute of a waking hour feeling sorry for yourself."

Lottie grinned, a real wide open grin, "Well, to tell the truth I felt sorry for you. Maybe if I had any sense I'd feel sorry for myself, after all. I know I'm too old to kick up my heels, but I'm going to let you show me how. If I land on my head, I guess it won't matter. I feel giddy already, and I like it."

THE SAGE: SUPPLEMENTARY READING

Edward Albee: *A Delicate Balance*
Anonymous: *Mary Magdalene*
Geoffrey Chaucer: "The Wife of Bath's Tale"
Daniel Defoe: "An Academy for Women," from *An Essay on Projects*
Joan Didion: *Play It as It Lays*
William Faulkner: *The Sound and the Fury,* book IV
Edward Field: "What Grandma Knew"
Elizabeth Gaskell: *Sylvia's Lovers*
Nathaniel Hawthorne: *The Scarlet Letter*
Henry James: *The Portrait of a Lady,* "What Maisie Knew," and *The Wings of the Dove*
Doris Lessing: *The Four-Gated City*
Carson McCullers: *A Member of the Wedding*
Edna St. Vincent Millay: "What Lips My Lips Have Kissed"
Iris Murdock: *A Severed Head*
Flannery O'Connor: "Revelation"
Sylvia Plath: *The Bell Jar*
Katherine Anne Porter: "Old Mortality" and "Pale Horse, Pale Rider"
Theodore Roethke: "Meditations of an Old Woman"
Edith Sitwell: "An Old Woman"
William Butler Yeats: "Words for Music Perhaps," I–VII

THE ARTIST

William Rush: *Comedy* (1808). [*The Edwin Forrest Home.*]

The artist is a hero because she has superior wisdom and initiates action, but she acts secretly or indirectly. Women have always been identified with imagination and creativity; all nine Greek Muses, for example, are women. Women's traditional relationship to the artistic process is an indirect one, however. As Sophia (the goddess of transformation), as anima figure, and as muse, she makes male creativity possible. The goddess Sophia is responsible for physical and spiritual transformation. In ancient cultures women were considered sacred because they magically transformed blood to milk in nursing a child, wheat to bread in baking, and flax to clothing in spinning, weaving, and sewing. Perhaps for this reason women are associated with spiritual transformation as well. Male initiation rituals generally include a symbolic return to the mother-god: the initiate usually enters a labyrinth or cave and thereby experiences symbolically a return to the womb. In Jungian psychology the anima, or female principle, within a man makes it possible for him to integrate the unconscious with the conscious mind. The fairy tale "Beauty and the Beast" is an allegory of the power of a woman's love or of the female principle within the psyche to transform a beast to a man, flesh to spirit, and lust to love. As muse, woman symbolizes the power of the human imagination to unify and give meaning to experience. In Wallace Stevens's "The Idea of Order at Key West," for example, a woman singing by the sea is portrayed as:

> . . . the single artificer of the world
> In which she sang, And when she sang, the sea,
> Whatever self it had, became the self
> That was her song, for she was the maker. Then we,
> As we beheld her striding there alone,
> Knew that there never was a world for her
> Except the one she sang and, singing, made.

A woman may also engage in the artistic process directly. Instead of inspiring men, women may be poets, painters, and musicians themselves, but if they are artists in this direct way, they must then fight the cultural myth that the fine arts belong only to men. In the "Prologue," Anne Bradstreet complains,

> I am obnoxious to each carping tongue
> Who says my hand a needle better fits,
> A poet's pen all scorn I should thus wrong,
> For such despite they cast on female wits:
> If what I do prove well, it won't advance,
> They'll say it's stol'n, or else it was by chance.

Like Bradstreet, a woman may feel the need to apologize for her presumption in writing poetry and to assure male artists that she is not competing with them: "Men can do best, and women know it well. / Preeminence in all and each is yours; / Yet grant some small acknowledgement of ours." Some well-known female authors therefore write secretly. Jane Austen, for example, would cover her work if anyone came in the room. Other women artists, such as Emily Dickinson, do not publish their work. Some of the best-known female writers—for example, Mary Ann Evans (George Eliot) and Charlotte Brontë (Currier Bell)—published under male pseudonyms. Without the male disguise, they might, like Mary Wilkins Freeman's poetess, Betsey Dole, have gone unrecognized. Unlike the male artist, moreover, the female artist faces internal conflicts between the selfless role of the heroine and the self-expressive role of the artist. Virginia Woolf, for example, was encouraged not to have children because a child would interfere with her art.[1] These role conflicts may be one cause of suicides by female authors such as Virginia Woolf, Sylvia Plath, and Anne Sexton.

Some women artists, however, view the creation of literature, music, and visual art objects as a natural extension of women's traditional roles. Women have invented and developed the domestic arts, such as pottery, weaving, quilting, sewing, cooking, and interior decoration. Because these domestic arts are functional and are part of our everyday experience, they have not been recognized by society as aesthetically significant. Women artists also work in the fluid medium of life. The woman who presides over the dinner table or calms the tired or discordant people around her transforms everyday life into beauty. In Virginia Woolf's *To the Lighthouse,* Mr. Ramsay comes to his wife because he knows she has the power to transform his despair into contentment. The creative energy Mrs. Ramsay expends is likened to a fountain, a traditional symbol for the outpouring of the imagination:

> Mrs. Ramsay, who had been sitting loosely, folding her son in her arm, braced herself, and, half turning, seemed to raise herself with an effort, and at once to pour erect into the air a rain of energy, a column of spray, looking at the same time animated and alive as if all her energies were being fused into force, burning and illuminating (quietly though she sat, taking up her stocking again), and into this delicious fecundity, this fountain and spray of life, the fatal sterility of the male plunged itself, like a beak of brass, barren and bare.

The artistic act of making life beautiful for others is often portrayed as a celebration of life. In Virginia Woolf's *Mrs. Dalloway,* Clarissa Dalloway's ex-suitor, Peter Walsh, asks her why she wastes her time giving parties. She explains that they are "an offering for the sake of offering, perhaps . . . [giving parties] is her gift." At the end of one of her social evenings, she has once again succeeded in transforming the raw material of life into beauty. During this evening, Peter comes to understand the value of this gift and therefore pays Clarissa this mental tribute:

> What is this Terror? what is this ecstasy? . . .
> What is it that fills me with extraordinary excitement?
>> It is Clarissa, he said.
>> For there she was.

Clarissa Dalloway and Betsey Dole, in Freeman's "A Poetess," engage in a love affair with life through their art. Similarly, the organist in Thomas Hardy's "The Chapel-Organist" admits, "Lived chaste I have not. Heaven knows it above! . . . / But past all the heavings of passion—it's music has been my life-love!" William Wordsworth's solitary reaper brings joy with her singing not only to herself in her work but also to those who happen to overhear her.

In addition to creating a nurturing and attractive home environment and the magic of a successful party, the traditional woman is an artist when she makes herself beautiful with the use of cosmetics and attractive clothes. William Butler Yeats's "Adam's Curse" likens poetic and political endeavor to the labor of women in the service of personal beauty:

> . . . 'To be born a woman is to know—
> Although they do not talk of it at school—
> That we must labor to be beautiful.'

Anne Finch, in "The Apology," describes the affinity between the woman's physical self-creation and poetic creativity: "Why shou'd it in my Pen be held a fault / Whilst Mira paints her face, to paint a thought."

A woman also may create an emotional and social persona. If a woman openly exhibits those qualities which positively define the male hero—power, strength, aggression, wisdom—she is called a bitch, a castrator, a maladaptive neurotic. She therefore must act the part of the acceptable passive, nurturant, emotional, docile, unintelligent, weak, and exasperating but lovable heroine to be effective in a male-dominated society. In other words, the heroic woman may feel she has to be an actress in order to affect her world. The pressure to play the roles of maiden, mistress, helpmate, and mother makes women into actresses.

The artist's power derives from her secret knowledge of the relationship between appearance and reality. For example, she often understands the truth behind social forms. Rosalind, in Shakespeare's *As You Like It,* dresses up as a man while in the forest of Arden and thus is able to learn the true character and feelings of her suitor, Orlando. The actress in Charles Swinburne's "Stage Love" has lost touch with reality. While Rosalind uses artistic disguises to discover truth, Swinburne's young woman mistakes the romantic parts she plays with actor-lovers for real love. In later years she continues to act out the same romantic role, but the male poet sanctions this role playing because then "the play was played out so for one man's pleasure."

Lily Barth, in Edith Wharton's *The House of Mirth,* plays the part of the passive and trivial heroine, but behind this social self is an artist. Her jewels and furniture, which the world sees as evidences of her triviality, are the tools of her art. Like Alexander Pope's Belinda, in *The Rape of the Lock,* she is an artist-warrior whose weapons are beauty and youth and whose victory is the social and economic security of marriage. Belinda's understanding of the limitations of the eighteenth-century world and her artistic skills in making the most of a limiting situation escape even her creator, who sees her only as a mock hero.

The artist whose medium is life develops a heightened sense of impermanence. John Donne, in "Change," defends female inconstancy by likening women to works of art. If a woman responds to ever-changing events of life, she must constantly be in flux. In the poem Donne also compares women to a stream, and men to its banks:

> Women are like the Arts, forc'd unto none,
> Open to' all searchers, unpriz'd if unknowne,
> . . . .
> —But when they kisse one banke, and leaving this
> Never looke backe, but the next banke doe kisse,
> Then are they purest; Change' is the nursery
> Of musicke, joy, life and eternity.

Because she understands transience and death, the woman artist of life becomes the creator of illusions. Like Scheherezade, the artist may tell stories or transform the world in some other way in order to control her destiny—in Scheherezade's case, to avoid death—by diverting the powerful. She also entertains the individuals without power and thus helps them to escape dull or repressive lives. In Jean Genet's *The Balcony,* Irma manages a brothel of illusions where ordinary men come to play the parts of Judge, Bishop, and General. The "prostitutes" play the counterpart roles of Thief, Sinner, and Horse, and their chief job is to make the men feel important. As illusion maker, Irma ultimately controls the whole country and blinds the populace to the reality of the constant violence and death raging outside her establishment.

The artist rarely can change reality, but she may endeavor to protect others from painful truths. Mrs. Ramsay, in *To the Lighthouse,* shields her children from the frightening skull in their bedroom by draping it with her shawl. Because her son is looking forward to a boat trip to the lighthouse the next morning, she assures him that the weather will be lovely even though she knows a storm is threatening. The traditional role women play in protecting men from insecurity is parodied in Alice Duer Miller's "Love Sonnets of an Anti-Suffragist." The speaker says he loves Mable:

> . . . because with you, as in a dream
> I seem a giant, dominant and strong,
> As in real life I very seldom seem,
> Or only after effort hard and long;
> But you admire everything I do,
> And all I say you greet with, "Oh, how true!"

Because women have taken on this protective function, they often are portrayed in literature as symbols of escape. Faced with harsh adult realities, Sinclair Lewis's Babbitt longs to escape into the ideal world of the female fairy child. Shelley's Jane suggests the alternative of a better world, when she sings "Of some world far from ours, / Where music and moonlight and feeling / Are one."

The artist-actress also is praised as the active creator of illusion and order in a painful, chaotic world. As Robert Graves writes in "She Is No Liar":

> . . . yet she will wash away
> Honey from her lips, blood from her shadowy hand,
> And, dressed at dawn in clean white robes will say,
> ·
> —"Such things no longer are, this is today."

The illusion maker is threatened by several dangers, however. The energy that must be expended to maintain such illusions involves tremendous psychological and physical cost. Dorothy Parker's Big Blonde must be cheerful and a "good sport" so that men will like her and therefore support her. Eventually, she comes to see herself as a workhorse, becomes an alcoholic, and tries to kill herself. The woman who uses cosmetics and fashions to approximate an ideal of physical beauty finds with time and age that these tools become inadequate to maintain the illusion. The poignancy of the plight of the aging beauty is captured in Ivan Albright's painting *Into the World There Came a Soul Called Ida,* in which a scantily dressed, grotesquely ugly old woman grimly surveys herself in the mirror. The female artist who creates a social persona may also have no identity apart from the persona she has created. The protagonist of Kurt Vonnegut's "Who Am I This Time?" does not feel alive except when she is acting. She is unable to relate to people in an honest way because she has no sense of a real self. She meets a similarly identityless man, and they spend the rest of their lives acting out scenes from plays together. The wife and mother in Tillie Olsen's "Tell Me a Riddle," who has given her life for her husband and children, finds at the end that in living entirely for other people, she has lost herself in the role. On her deathbed she expresses bitterness about the loss of her potential self.

The power of the artist-actress derives from her potential completeness. As self-creator, she is androgynous; she is creator and creation, knower and known, will and matter, male and female. If the creator-creation halves of the artist are inadequately integrated, however, she may become schizophrenic, in the sense that she experiences a second self who watches and comments on the actions and feelings of the created self. Because the social actress cannot allow her true feelings to be expressed, she may live in a totally controlled and cerebral world which precludes the spontaneous emotions which are part of sex and love. Her heightened awareness that all ordering of experience falsifies it may make her despair about the possibility of understanding her world. In Doris Lessing's *The Golden Notebook* the protagonist keeps five notebooks. Each is an attempt to separate reality from illusion and give order to experience, thus enabling the protagonist to understand her world. At the end of the novel, she finds herself unable to leave her house; she compulsively arranges and rearranges newspaper clippings, attempting to comprehend and order the events they represent.

The artist of the self may be condemned in literature because of her duplicity. For example, she may be accused of hiding a sinful, sexual inner self with a false virginal surface. As exemplified in the china imagery in William Wycherly's *The Country Wife,* a woman may be portrayed as crude, earthy reality covered by a thin, easily penetrable artistic covering of beauty and purity. This inner-outer dualism associates women with the medieval concept of fruit and chaff, according to which the whole world is a series of deceptive appearances which simultaneously conceal and reveal spiritual truth within.

The artist is often seen as symbolic of the secret destructive evils that underlie the artistic process. As creator of illusions, she is aware of the Dionysian chaos at the base of all life and art. This knowledge gives her the power to destroy. In "Kubla Khan" Coleridge describes the danger of the female to the unsuspecting man:

> As e'er beneath a waning moon was haunted
> By woman wailing for her demon-lover!
> . . . .
>
> It was an Abyssinian maid,
> And on her dulcimer she played,
> Singing of Mount Abora,
> . . . .
>
> —To such a deep delight t'would win me,
> That with music loud and long,
> I would build that dome in air,
> That sunny dome! those caves of ice!
> And all who heard should see them there,
> And all should cry, "Beware! Beware!"

Both the beauty and the danger associated with the woman artist come from this tendency to confuse the appearance with the reality.

The artist who acts out her illusions may be an idealist who finds life in the real world hopelessly inadequate. Like the Lady of Shalott, she sees through the mirror of her mind and imaginatively transforms reality into perfect form. In her affiliation with illusions, the artist may be a tragic hero who creates a subjective reality as an artist creates an ordered design, only to find it shattered at the tragic moment when reality intrudes. Men and women who believe in the ideal of romantic love almost inevitably play roles during courtship; however, the ideal images that the lovers act out may be shattered when they get to know each other after the wedding. Henrik Ibsen's Hedda Gabler wants to live in a romantic world in which actions mean something. Despairing of the ideal, she still longs for the purity of one free and courageous act. When she chooses her former romantic love, Lövborg, to fulfill her dream, the stage directions in her romantic script call for him to die, beautifully and alone. Instead he is shot in the stomach at a brothel. Because she is the only one left to play out the part she has envisioned, Hedda kills herself.

Even if, as in the case of Hedda, the effort to relate art to life is a failure, the act is beautiful and noble, if not necessarily sanctioned, because any assertion of the individual has heroic elements. The protagonist in Faulkner's "A Rose for Emily" transforms her world in an unacceptable way when she kills a man and then sleeps with his corpse, but her act enlivens the monotonous existence of the townspeople when they discover her secret. The female artist is particularly admirable when she attempts to exercise control over her life in a world in which women are given little opportunity for self-determination. When the female artist acts indirectly, she not only avoids tragedy for herself and others but also integrates the passive heroine self with the self-expressive artist: Freeman's poetess will be immortalized because she convinces the young clergyman (whose poems get published) to write a poem about her; Ibsen's Thea Elvstead helps Lövborg and later the widower Tesman to write a great book. The artist who controls the actions of others lives vicariously, but she also successfully merges art with life. The actress's success may be limited, as Hedda's is, however, when she acts by indirection. Others may not want to act out her script because they see themselves as heroes in their own dramas. In William Faulkner's *Absalom, Absalom,* Judith Sutpen explains that human beings are all artists endeavoring to order and create some beauty in their lives. The tragedy is that "the strings are all in one another's way like five or six people all trying to make a rug on the same loom, only each wants to weave his own pattern into the rug." Such is the case of the nameless protagonist of Mary McCarthy's "Cruel and Barbarous Treatment." She creates her own drama of adultery and divorce to the extent that she attempts to engineer a dramatic confrontation between husband and lover, only to find it increasingly difficult to control the script and to direct her own life and the lives of those around her. She is always on stage, directing the play for the purpose of romance and excitement, but in the process she loses both husband and lover and ends by playing the not entirely desirable part of "young divorcée."

The transformation of the ideal world into the real one may be symbolized by the Fates, who spin out human destiny and thereby entrap and immobilize us. Arachne challenges Athena to a spinning contest, and Arachne's skill and artistry are so great that she weaves a more beautiful tapestry than Athena does. Because Arachne threatens and challenges the gods in this way, she is punished. When Athena rips Arachne's creation, Arachne hangs herself and is turned into a spider. The destructive woman who weaves fate may be related in our culture to the woman's major role in molding her children's lives. Because of this powerful influence, she is often portrayed negatively. Psychoanalysts hold the mother to blame for adult neurosis because she is responsible for the social conditioning of the child. In Mary Austin's "The Man Who Was Loved by Women," the woman con artist who acts to ensure her control over her own life and that of her husband is portrayed positively. However, the artist who manipulates others' lives for whatever reason may be condemned or portrayed ambivalently because she tampers with human freedom and will. Mrs. Ramsay, for example, transforms a beautiful dinner into a work of art, but she also encourages Minta Doyle and Paul Rayley to marry unhappily. Finally, the artist who manipulates others may be unfulfilled if she lives vicariously. Her husband's and children's triumphs ultimately belong to them, not to her.

The myth of Icarus and Daedalus demonstrates the sinful pride involved in artistic creation. Daedalus, who makes wings of wax to enable himself and his son to escape from the labyrinth, warns Icarus not to fly too near the sun. Icarus disregards this advice; his wings melt, and he falls into the sea. If the act of painting a picture or composing a symphony is sinful because it approximates God's act of creation, how much more potentially sinful is the artistic process when people are the medium. In "The Artist of the Beautiful," Nathaniel Hawthorne investigates the destructive quality of any artist who attempts to translate the ideal of perfect beauty into life:

> The chase of butterflies was an apt emblem of the ideal pursuit in which he has spent so many golden hours; but would the beautiful idea ever be yielded to his hand like the butterfly that symbolized it? . . .
>
> Alas that the artist, whether in poetry, or whatever other material, may not content himself with the inward enjoyment of the beautiful, but must chase the flitting mystery beyond the verge of his ethereal domain, and crush its frail being in seizing it with a material grasp.

In Hawthorne's "The Birthmark," Aylmer inadvertently murders his wife in the process of making her a perfect art object. Hedda Gabler acts to cause Lövborg's suicide in order to make him the perfect romantic hero. In Joyce Carol Oates's *Do with Me What You Will,* Ardis trains her daughter, Elena, to be a perfect object of beauty, but in so doing she denies Elena her will and her identity.

The artist acts indirectly, as an intermediary between the world of spirit and the world of matter. As a result of the creative act, something appears in the world that was not there before. Reality is changed, added to, new. The following selections celebrate female creativity. They explore the rewards, the contradictions, and the fatal results of the interaction between life and art.

THE ARTIST: NOTE

[1]Quentin Bell, *Virginia Woolf: A Biography* (London: The Hogarth Press, Ltd., 1972), vol. II, p. 8.

WHEN TO HER LUTE CORINNA SINGS

Thomas Campion

See headnote to "Beauty is but a painted hell," page 65.

"When to her lute Corinna sings" is from Campion's *A Book of Airs* (1601).

When to her lute Corinna sings,
Her voice revives the leaden strings,
And doth in highest notes appear,
As any challenged Echo clear;
But when she doth of mourning speak,
E'en with her sighs the strings do break.

And as her lute doth live or die,
Led by her passion, so must I!
For when of pleasure, she doth sing,
My thoughts enjoy a sudden spring;
But if she doth of sorrow speak,
E'en from my heart the strings do break.

TO JANE: THE KEEN STARS WERE TWINKLING

Percy Bysshe Shelley   (1792–1822)

The son of a Sussex squire, Shelley published a volume of poems in collaboration
with his sister Elizabeth before entering Oxford in 1810. He was expelled the
following year for *The Necessity of Atheism*. In London he met Harriet Westbrook,
the daughter of a retired tavern keeper, and they eloped to Edinburgh. In 1812
Shelley went to Dublin, inspired by the cause of Irish freedom, but soon returned to
London, where he met William Godwin. He eloped with Godwin's daughter Mary in
1814. They soon went to Geneva, where they first met Byron. In 1815 Harriet
drowned herself, and Shelley wed Mary. Shelley continued writing poetry until his
own drowning in Italy.

Lines 7 through 24 of the following poem were printed in *The Athenaeum* magazine
in 1832 as "An Ariette for Music, to a Lady Singing to Her Accompaniment on the
Guitar." The poem was not published in its entirety until the second 1839 edition of
Shelley's *Poems*, edited by his widow.

1
The keen stars were twinkling,
And the fair moon was rising among them,
    Dear Jane!
    The guitar was tinkling,
But the notes were not sweet till you sung them
    Again.

2
    As the moon's soft splendor
O'er the faint cold starlight of Heaven
    Is thrown,
    So your voice most tender
To the strings without soul had then given
    Its own.   10

3
    The stars will awaken,
Though the moon sleep a full hour later,
    Tonight;
    No leaf will be shaken
Whilst the dews of your melody scatter
    Delight.

4
    Though the sound overpowers,
Sing again, with your dear voice revealing   20
    A tone
Of some world far from ours,
Where music and moonlight and feeling
    Are one.

THE LADY OF SHALOTT

Alfred, Lord Tennyson   (1809–1892)

Tennyson was the son of a Lincolnshire rector. Among his early works was a book
written with his brothers Frederick and Charles but entitled *Poems of Two Brothers*
(1827). In 1828 Tennyson went to Cambridge, where he met Arthur Hallam, with
whom he later toured the Pyrenees and the Rhine. In 1833 Hallam's death and the
attacks on Tennyson's fourth book of poems plunged him into severe depression. In
1836, at Charles's wedding, Tennyson met Emily Sellwood, Charles's sister-in-law.

They immediately fell in love, but her parents, who considered Tennyson too poor, broke off the courtship in 1840. In 1845 friends obtained for Tennyson a civil list pension on the basis of *Poems* (1842). In 1850 Tennyson published *In Memorium* (for Hallam), married Emily, and became poet laureate following Wordsworth's death. He achieved widespread popularity with *Idylls of the King* in 1859, and he was raised to the peerage by Victoria in 1884. He was buried in the Poets' Corner of Westminster Abbey.

"The Lady of Shalott" was first published in the 1832 edition of *Poems*. It was extensively revised for its publication in the 1842 edition.

PART I

On either side the river lie
Long fields of barley and of rye,
That clothe the world and meet the sky;
And thro' the field the road runs by
      To many-tower'd Camelot;
And up and down the people go,
Gazing where the lilies blow
Round an island there below,
      The island of Shalott.

Willows whiten, aspens quiver,   10
Little breezes dusk and shiver
Thro' the wave that runs for ever
By the island in the river
      Flowing down to Camelot.
Four gray walls, and four gray towers,
Overlook a space of flowers,
And the silent isle imbowers
      The Lady of Shalott.

By the margin, willow-veil'd,
Slide the heavy barges trail'd   20
By slow horses; and unhail'd
The shallop flitteth silken-sail'd
      Skimming down to Camelot:
But who hath seen her wave her hand?
Or at the casement seen her stand?
Or is she known in all the land,
      The Lady of Shalott?

Only reapers, reaping early
In among the bearded barley,
Hear a song that echoes cheerly   30
From the river winding clearly,

      Down to tower'd Camelot:
And by the moon the reaper weary,
Piling sheaves in uplands airy,
Listening, whispers ' 'Tis the fairy
        Lady of Shalott.'

PART II

There she weaves by night and day
A magic web with colours gay.
She has heard a whisper say,
A curse is on her if she stay   40
        To look down to Camelot.
She knows not what the curse may be,
And so she weaveth steadily,
And little other care hath she,
        The Lady of Shalott.

And moving thro' a mirror clear
That hangs before her all the year,
Shadows of the world appear.
There she sees the highway near
        Winding down to Camelot: 50
There the river eddy whirls,
And there the surly village-churls,
And the red cloaks of market girls,
        Pass onward from Shalott.

Sometimes a troop of damsels glad,
An abbot on an ambling pad,
Sometimes a curly shepherd-lad,
Or long-hair'd page in crimson clad,
        Goes by to tower'd Camelot;
And sometimes thro' the mirror blue   60
The knights come riding two and two:
She hath no loyal knight and true,
        The Lady of Shalott.

But in her web she still delights
To weave the mirror's magic sights,
For often thro' the silent nights
A funeral, with plumes and lights
        And music, went to Camelot:
Or when the moon was overhead,
Came two young lovers lately wed;   70
'I am half sick of shadows,' said
        The Lady of Shalott.

PART III

A bow-shot from her bower-eaves,
He rode between the barley-sheaves,
The sun came dazzling thro' the leaves,
And flamed upon the brazen greaves
    Of bold Sir Lancelot.
A red-cross knight for ever kneel'd
To a lady in his shield,
That sparkled on the yellow field,
    Beside remote Shalott.   80

The gemmy bridle glitter'd free,
Like to some branch of stars we see
Hung in the golden Galaxy.
The bridle bells rang merrily
    As he rode down to Camelot:
And from his blazon'd baldric slung
A mighty silver bugle hung,
And as he rode his armour rung,
    Beside remote Shalott.   90

All in the blue unclouded weather
Thick-jewell'd shone the saddle-leather,
The helmet and the helmet-feather
Burn'd like one burning flame together,
    As he rode down to Camelot.
As often thro' the purple night,
Below the starry clusters bright,
Some bearded meteor, trailing light,
    Moves over still Shalott.

His broad clear brow in sunlight glow'd;   100
On burnish'd hooves his war-horse trode;
From underneath his helmet flow'd
His coal-black curls as on he rode,
    As he rode down to Camelot.
From the bank and from the river
He flash'd into the crystal mirror,
'Tirra lirra,' by the river
    Sang Sir Lancelot.

She left the web, she left the loom,
She made three paces thro' the room,   110
She saw the water-lily bloom,
She saw the helmet and the plume,
    She look'd down to Camelot.
Out flew the web and floated wide;

The mirror crack'd from side to side;
'The curse is come upon me,' cried
      The Lady of Shalott.

PART IV

In the stormy east-wind straining,
The pale yellow woods were waning,
The broad stream in his banks complaining,   120
Heavily the low sky raining
      Over tower'd Camelot;
Down she came and found a boat
Beneath a willow left afloat,
And round about the prow she wrote
      The Lady of Shalott.

And down the river's dim expanse
Like some bold seër in a trance,
Seeing all his own mischance—
With a glassy countenance   130
      Did she look to Camelot.
And at the closing of the day
She loosed the chain, and down she lay;
The broad stream bore her far away,
      The Lady of Shalott.

Lying, robed in snowy white
That loosely flew to left and right—
The leaves upon her falling light—
Thro' the noises of the night
      She floated down to Camelot: 140
And as the boat-head wound along
The willowy hills and fields among,
They heard her singing her last song,
      The Lady of Shalott.

Heard a carol, mournful, holy,
Chanted loudly, chanted lowly,
Till her blood was frozen slowly,
And her eyes were darken'd wholly,
      Turn'd to tower'd Camelot.
For ere she reach'd upon the tide   150
The first house by the water-side,
Singing in her song she died,
      The Lady of Shalott.

Under tower and balcony,
By garden-wall and gallery,

A gleaming shape she floated by,
Dead-pale between the houses high,
    Silent into Camelot.
Out upon the wharfs they came;
Knight and burgher, lord and dame,
And round the prow they read her name,   160
    The Lady of Shalott.

Who is this? and what is here?
And in the lighted palace near
Died the sound of royal cheer;
And they cross'd themselves for fear,
    All the knights at Camelot:
But Lancelot mused a little space;
He said, 'She has a lovely face;
God in his mercy lend her grace,   170
    The Lady of Shalott.'

TO GEORGE SAND: A DESIRE

TO GEORGE SAND: A RECOGNITION

Elizabeth Barrett Browning   (1806–1861)

The daughter of a tyrannical and jealous father, she was a semi-invalid, and was largely self-taught. She had already published five volumes of poetry before she met and eloped with Robert Browning in 1846. The couple went first to France and then to Italy. They lived in Florence, where she died of tuberculosis. Her poetry, especially the famous *Sonnets from the Portuguese* (1850), was well received during her lifetime. Robert Browning considered her a better poet than himself.
The two sonnets for French novelist and playwright George Sand (Aurore Dupin, Baroness Dudevant) were published in *Poems* (1844). Earlier, in a letter, Browning had referred to Sand as "the greatest female genius the world ever saw." In 1852, aided by a letter of introduction from Italian patriot leader Guiseppe Mazzini, Browning met Sand in Paris.

TO GEORGE SAND
A Desire

Thou large-brained woman and large-hearted man,
Self-called George Sand! whose soul amid the lions

Of thy tumultuous senses, moans defiance,
And answers roar for roar, as spirits can:
I would some mild miraculous thunder ran
Above the applauded circus, in appliance
Of thine own nobler nature's strength and science,
Drawing two pinions, white as wings of swan,
From thy strong shoulders, to amaze the place
With holier light! That thou to woman's claim,
And man's, might join beside the angel's grace
Of a pure genius sanctified from blame;
Till child and maiden pressed to thine embrace,
To kiss upon thy lips a stainless fame.

TO GEORGE SAND
A Recognition

True genius, but true woman! dost deny
Thy woman's nature with a manly scorn,
And break away the gauds and armlets worn
By weaker women in captivity?
Ah, vain denial! that revolted cry
Is sobbed in by a woman's voice forlorn:—
Thy woman's hair, my sister, all unshorn,
Floats back dishevelled strength in agony,
Disproving thy man's name: and while before
The world thou burnest in a poet-fire,
We see thy woman-heart beat evermore
Through the large flame. Beat purer, heart, and higher,
Till God unsex thee on the heavenly shore,
Where unincarnate spirits purely aspire.

ARACHNE

Rose Terry Cooke   (1827–1892)

Born on a farm near Hartford, Connecticut, Cooke graduated from the Hartford
Female Seminary in 1843; she then taught school in New Jersey and later acted as
governess in a clergyman's family. With the death of her sister, according to the
Dictionary of American Biography, "a call came for her service at home and from
this time her first interest was domestic." Her single collection of verse was
published in 1860, and her short stories found ready acceptance in *Harper's
Magazine* and the *Atlantic Monthly.* In 1873 she married Rollin Cooke, an iron
manufacturer.
"Arachne" was published in 1860 in *Poems.* It is based on the classical myth of

Arachne, whose skill in weaving led her to challenge Athena, goddess of wisdom
and the arts. When Athena met the challenge by destroying the cloth Arachne had
woven, Arachne hanged herself in despair and was metamorphosed into a spider.

I watch her in the corner there,
As, restless, bold, and unafraid,
She slips and floats along the air
Till all her subtile house is made.

Her home, her bed, her daily food
All from that hidden store she draws;
She fashions it and knows it good,
By instinct's strong and sacred laws.

No tenuous threads to weave her nest,
She seeks and gathers there or here;   10
But spins it from her faithful breast,
Renewing still, till leaves are sere.

Then, worn with toil, and tired of life,
In vain her shining traps are set.
Her frost hath hushed the insect strife
And gilded flies her charm forget.

But swinging in the snares she spun.
She sways to every wintry wind:
Her joy, her toil, her errand done,
Her corse the sport of storms unkind.   20

Poor sister of the spinster clan!
I too from out my store within
My daily life and living plan,
My home, my rest, my pleasure spin.

I know thy heart when heartless hands
Sweep all that hard-earned web away:
Destroy its pearled and glittering bands,
And leave thee homeless by the way.

I know thy peace when all is done.
Each anchored thread, each tiny knot,   30
Soft shining in the autumn sun;
A sheltered, silent, tranquil lot.

I know what thou hast never known,
—Sad presage to a soul allowed;—
That not for life I spin, alone.
But day by day I spin my shroud.

STAGE LOVE

Algernon Charles Swinburne   (1837–1909)

Born of aristocratic stock, Swinburne attended Oxford, where he made his acquaintance with the Pre-Raphaelite poets and painters. In 1860 he left Oxford for London and embarked upon a literary career. With the publication of *Atalanta in Calydon* (1865), Swinburne became famous overnight. However, the publication of *Poems and Ballads* the following year provoked a storm of denunciation of the work's obscenity and decadence. Swinburne's nervousness and bellicose qualities were aggravated by an increasing drinking problem. In 1879 the solicitor Walter Theodore Watts, with the permission of Swinburne's mother, installed him at his villa at Putney, where he lived a tamed existence until his death thirty years later from pneumonia.

"Stage Love" is one of the poems from *Poems and Ballads* (1866).

When the game began between them for a jest,
He played king and she played queen to match the best;
Laughter soft as tears, and tears that turned to laughter,
These were things she sought for years and sorrowed after.

Pleasure with dry lips, and pain that walks by night;
All the sting and all the stain of long delight;
These were things she knew not of, that knew not of her,
When she played at half a love with half a lover.

Time was chorus, gave them cues to laugh or cry;
They would kill, befool, amuse him, let him die;
Set him webs to weave to-day and break to-morrow,
Till he died for good in play, and rose in sorrow.

What the years mean; how time dies and is not slain;
How love grows and laughs and cries and wanes again;
These were things she came to know, and take their measure,
When the play was played out so for one man's pleasure.

A POETESS

Mary Eleanor Wilkins Freeman   (1852–1930)

Born in Randolph, Massachusetts, Freeman spent the first part of her life in various Massachusetts villages. The *Dictionary of American Biography* states: "Her first stories were not the work of a girl, as was then generally supposed, but the work of a woman over thirty, who had time as well as the natural ability for observation." Her short stories are considered masterpieces, and she was a leading local colorist of New England rural life. At the age of fifty she married Dr. Charles Freeman and moved to New Jersey, where she lived until her death. The later years of her marriage were unhappy.

"A Poetess" was collected in *A New England Nun and Other Stories* (1891).

The garden-patch at the right of the house was all a gay spangle with sweet-peas and red-flowering beans, and flanked with feathery asparagus. A woman in blue was moving about there. Another woman, in a black bonnet, stood at the front door of the house. She knocked and waited. She could not see from where she stood the blue-clad woman in the garden. The house was very close to the road, from which a tall evergreen hedge separated it, and the view to the side was in a measure cut off.

The front door was open; the woman had to reach to knock on it, as it swung into the entry. She was a small woman and quite young, with a bright alertness about her which had almost the effect of prettiness. It was to her what greenness and crispness are to a plant. She poked her little face forward, and her sharp pretty eyes took in the entry and a room at the left, of which the door stood open. The entry was small and square and unfurnished, except for a well-rubbed old card-table against the back wall. The room was full of green light from the tall hedge, and bristling with grasses and flowers and asparagus stalks.

"Betsey, you there?" called the woman. When she spoke, a yellow canary, whose cage hung beside the front door, began to chirp and twitter.

"Betsey, you there?" the woman called again. The bird's chirps came in a quick volley; then he began to trill and sing.

"She ain't there," said the woman. She turned and went out of the yard through the gap in the hedge; then she looked around. She caught sight of the blue figure in the garden. "There she is," said she.

She went around the house to the garden. She wore a gay cashmere-patterned calico dress with her mourning bonnet, and she held it carefully away from the dewy grass and vines.

The other woman did not notice her until she was close to her and said, "Good-mornin', Betsey." Then she started and turned around.

"Why, Mis' Caxton! That you?" said she.

"Yes. I've been standin' at your door for the last half-hour. I was jest goin' away when I caught sight of you out here."

In spite of her brisk speech her manner was subdued. She drew down the corners of her mouth sadly.

"I declare I'm dreadful sorry you had to stan' there so long!" said the other woman.

She set a pan partly filled with beans on the ground, wiped her hands, which were damp and green from the wet vines, on her apron, then extended her right one with a solemn and sympathetic air.

"It don't make much odds, Betsey," replied Mrs. Caxton. "I ain't got much to take up my time nowadays." She sighed heavily as she shook hands, and the other echoed her.

"We'll go right in now. I'm dreadful sorry you stood there so long," said Betsey.

"You'd better finish pickin' your beans."

"No; I wa'n't goin' to pick any more. I was jest goin' in."

"I declare, Betsey Dole, I shouldn't think you'd got enough for a cat!" said Mrs. Caxton, eying the pan.

"I've got pretty near all there is. I guess I've got more flowerin' beans than eatin' ones, anyway."

"I should think you had," said Mrs. Caxton, surveying the row of bean-poles topped with swarms of delicate red flowers. "I should think they were pretty near all flowerin' ones. Had any peas?"

"I didn't have more'n three or four messes. I guess I planted sweet-peas mostly. I don't know hardly how I happened to."

"Had any summer squash?"

"Two or three. There's some more set, if they ever get ripe. I planted some gourds. I think they look real pretty on the kitchen shelf in the winter."

"I should think you'd got a sage bed big enough for the whole town."

"Well, I have got a pretty good-sized one. I always liked them blue sage-blows. You'd better hold up your dress real careful goin' through here, Mis' Caxton, or you'll get it wet."

The two women picked their way through the dewy grass, around a corner of the hedge, and Betsey ushered her visitor into the house.

"Set right down in the rockin-chair," said she. "I'll jest carry these beans out into the kitchen."

"I should think you'd better get another pan and string 'em, or you won't get 'em done for dinner."

"Well, mebbe I will, if you'll excuse it, Mis' Caxton. The beans had ought to boil quite a while; they're pretty old."

Betsey went into the kitchen and returned with a pan and an old knife. She seated herself opposite Mrs. Caxton, and began to string and cut the beans.

"If I was in your place I shouldn't feel as if I'd got enough to boil a kettle for," said Mrs. Caxton, eying the beans. "I should 'most have thought when you didn't have any more room for a garden than you've got that you'd planted more real beans and peas instead of so many flowerin' ones. I'd rather have a good mess of green peas boiled with a piece of salt pork than all the sweet-peas you could give me. I like flowers well enough, but I never set up for a butterfly, an' I want something else to live on." She looked at Betsey with pensive superiority.

Betsey was near-sighted; she had to bend low over the beans in order to string them. She was fifty years old, but she wore her streaky light hair in curls like a young girl. The curls hung over her faded cheeks and almost concealed them. Once in a while she flung them back with a childish gesture which sat strangely upon her.

"I dare say you're in the right of it," she said, meekly.

"I know I am. You folks that write poetry wouldn't have a single thing to eat growin' if they were left alone. And that brings to mind what I come for. I've been thinkin' about it ever since—our—little Willie—left us." Mrs. Caxton's manner was suddenly full of shamefaced dramatic fervor, her eyes reddened with tears.

Betsey looked up inquiringly, throwing back her curls. Her face took on unconsciously lines of grief so like the other woman's that she looked like her for the minute.

"I thought maybe," Mrs. Caxton went on, tremulously, "you'd be willin' to—write a few lines."

"Of course I will, Mis' Caxton. I'll be glad to, if I can do 'em to suit you," Betsey said, tearfully.

"I thought jest a few—lines. You could mention how—handsome he was, and good, and I never had to punish him but once in his life, and how pleased he was with his little new suit, and what a sufferer he was, and—how we hope he is at rest—in a better land."

I'll try, Mis' Caxton, I'll try," sobbed Betsey. The two women wept together for a few minutes.

"It seems as if—I couldn't have it so sometimes," Mrs. Caxton said, brokenly. "I keep thinkin' he's in the other—room. Every time I go back home when I've been away it's like—losin' him again. Oh, it don't seem as if I could go home and not find him there—it don't, it don't! Oh, you don't know anything about it, Betsey. You never had any children!"

"I don't s'pose I do, Mis' Caxton; I don't s'pose I do."

Presently Mrs. Caxton wiped her eyes. "I've been thinkin'," said she, keeping her mouth steady with an effort, "that it would be real pretty to have—some lines printed on some sheets of white paper with a neat black border. I'd like to send some to my folks, and one to the Perkinses in Brigham, and there's a good many others I thought would value 'em."

"I'll do jest the best I can, Mis' Caxton, an' be glad to. It's little enough anybody can do at such times."

Mrs. Caxton broke out weeping again. "Oh, it's true, it's true, Betsey!"

she sobbed. "Nobody can do anything, and nothin' amounts to anything—poetry or anything else—when he's *gone*. Nothin' can bring him back. Oh, what shall I do, what shall I do?"

Mrs. Caxton dried her tears again, and arose to take leave. "Well, I must be goin', or Wilson won't have any dinner," she said, with an effort at self-control.

"Well, I'll do jest the best I can with the poetry," said Betsey. "I'll write it this afternoon." She had set down her pan of beans and was standing beside Mrs. Caxton. She reached up and straightened her black bonnet, which had slipped backward.

"I've got to get a pin," said Mrs. Caxton, tearfully. "I can't keep it anywheres. It drags right off my head, the veil is so heavy."

Betsey went to the door with her visitor. "It's dreadful dusty, ain't it?" she remarked, in that sad, contemptuous tone with which one speaks of discomforts in the presence of affliction.

"Terrible," replied Mrs. Caxton. "I wouldn't wear my black dress in it nohow; a black bonnet is bad enough. This dress is 'most too good. It's enough to spoil everything. Well, I'm much obliged to you, Betsey, for bein' willin' to do that."

"I'll do jest the best I can, Mis' Caxton."

After Betsey had watched her visitor out of the yard she returned to the sitting-room and took up the pan of beans. She looked doubtfully at the handful of beans all nicely strung and cut up. "I declare I don't know what to do," said she. "Seems as if I should kind of relish these, but it's goin' to take some time to cook 'em, tendin' the fire an' everything, an' I'd ought to go to work on that poetry. Then, there's another thing, if I have 'em to-day, I can't to-morrow. Mebbe I shall take more comfort thinkin' about 'em. I guess I'll leave 'em over till to-morrow."

Betsey carried the pan of beans out into the kitchen and set them away in the pantry. She stood scrutinizing the shelves like a veritable Mother Hubbard. There was a plate containing three or four potatoes and a slice of cold boiled pork, and a spoonful of red jelly in a tumbler; that was all the food in sight. Betsey stooped and lifted the lid from an earthen jar on the floor. She took out two slices of bread. "There!" said she. "I'll have this bread and that jelly this noon, an' to-night I'll have a kind of dinner-supper with them potatoes warmed up with the pork. An' then I can sit right down an' go to work on that poetry."

It was scarcely eleven o'clock, and not time for dinner. Betsey returned to the sitting-room, got an old black portfolio and pen and ink out of the chimney cupboard, and seated herself to work. She meditated, and wrote one line, then another. Now and then she read aloud what she had written with a solemn intonation. She sat there thinking and writing, and the time went on. The twelve-o'clock bell rang, but she never noticed it; she had quite forgotten the bread and jelly. The long curls drooped over her cheeks; her thin yellow hand, cramped around the pen, moved slowly and fitfully over the paper. The light in the room was dim and green, like the light in an arbor, from the tall hedge before the windows. Great plumy bunches of asparagus waved over the tops of the looking-glass; a framed sampler, a steel engraving of a female head taken from some old magazine, and sheaves of dried grasses hung on or were fastened to the walls; vases and tumblers of flowers stood on the shelf and table. The air was heavy and sweet.

Betsey in this room, bending over her portfolio, looked like the very genius of gentle, old-fashioned, sentimental poetry. It seemed as if one, given the premises of herself and the room, could easily deduce what she would write, and read without seeing those lines wherein flowers rhymed sweetly with vernal bowers, home with beyond the tomb, and heaven with even.

The summer afternoon wore on. It grew warmer and closer; the air was full of the rasping babble of insects, with the cicadas shrilling over them; now and then a team passed, and a dust cloud floated over the top of the hedge; the canary at the door chirped and trilled, and Betsey wrote poor little Willie Caxton's obituary poetry.

Tears stood in her pale blue eyes; occasionally they rolled down her cheeks, and she wiped them away. She kept her handkerchief in her lap with her portfolio. When she looked away from the paper she seemed to see two childish forms in the room—one purely human, a boy clad in his little girl petticoats, with a fair chubby face; the other in a little straight white night-gown, with long, shining wings, and the same face. Betsey had not enough imagination to change the face. Little Willie Caxton's angel was still himself to her, although decked in the paraphernalia of the resurrection.

"I s'pose I can't feel about it nor write about it anything the way I could if I'd had any children of my own an' lost 'em. I s'pose it *would* have come home to me different," Betsey murmured once, sniffing. A soft color flamed up under her curls at the thought. For a second the room seemed all aslant with white wings, and smiling with the faces of children that had never been. Betsey straightened herself as if she were trying to be dignified to her inner consciousness. "That's one trouble I've been clear of, anyhow," said she; "an' I guess I can enter into her feelin's considerable."

She glanced at a great pink shell on the shelf, and remembered how she had often given it to the dead child to play with when he had been in with his mother, and how he had put it to his ear to hear the sea.

"Dear little fellow!" she sobbed, and sat awhile with her handkerchief at her face.

Betsey wrote her poem upon backs of old letters and odd scraps of paper. She found it difficult to procure enough paper for fair copies of her poems when composed; she was forced to be very economical with the first draft. Her portfolio was piled with a loose litter of written papers when she at length arose and stretched her stiff limbs. It was near sunset; men with dinner-pails were tramping past the gate, going home from their work.

Betsey laid the portfolio on the table. "There! I've wrote sixteen verses," said she, "an' I guess I've got everything in. I guess she'll think that's enough. I can copy it off nice to-morrow. I can't see to-night to do it, anyhow."

There were red spots on Betsey's cheeks; her knees were unsteady when she walked. She went into the kitchen and made a fire, and set on the tea-kettle. "I guess I won't warm up them potatoes to-night," said she; "I'll have the bread an' jelly, an' save 'em for breakfast. Somehow I don't seem to feel so much like 'em as I did, an' fried potatoes is apt to lay heavy at night."

When the kettle boiled, Betsey drank her cup of tea and soaked her slice of bread in it; then she put away her cup and saucer and plate, and went out to water her garden. The weather was so dry and hot it had to be watered every night. Betsey had to carry the water from a neighbor's well; her own was dry. Back and forth she went in the deepening twilight, her slender body strained to one side with the heavy water-pail, until the garden-mould looked dark and wet. Then she took in the canary-bird, locked up her house, and soon her light went out. Often on these summer nights Betsey went to bed without lighting a lamp at all. There was no moon, but it was a beautiful starlight night. She lay awake nearly all night, thinking of her poem. She altered several lines in her mind.

She arose early, made herself a cup of tea, and warmed over the potatoes, then sat down to copy the poem. She wrote it out on both sides of note-paper, in a neat, cramped hand. It was the middle of the afternoon before it was finished. She had been obliged to stop work and cook the beans for dinner, although she begrudged the time. When the poem was fairly copied, she rolled it neatly and tied it with a bit of black ribbon; then she made herself ready to carry it to Mrs. Caxton's.

It was a hot afternoon. Betsey went down the street in her thinnest dress—an old delaine, with delicate bunches of faded flowers on a faded green ground. There was a narrow green belt ribbon around her long waist. She wore a green barège bonnet, stiffened with rattans, scooping over her face, with her curls pushed forward over her thin cheeks in two bunches, and she carried a small green parasol with a jointed handle. Her costume was obsolete, even in the little country village where she lived. She had worn it every summer for the last twenty years. She made no more change in her attire than the old perennials in her garden. She had no money with which to buy new clothes, and the old satisfied her. She had come to regard them as being as unalterably a part of herself as her body.

Betsey went on, setting her slim, cloth-gaitered feet daintily in the hot sand of the road. She carried her roll of poetry in a black-mitted hand. She walked rather slowly. She was not very strong; there was a limp feeling in her knees; her face, under the green shade of her bonnet, was pale and moist with the heat.

She was glad to reach Mrs. Caxton's and sit down in her parlor, damp and cool and dark as twilight, for the blinds and curtains had been drawn all day. Not a breath of the fervid out-door air had penetrated it.

"Come right in this way; it's cooler than the sittin'-room," Mrs. Caxton said; and Betsey sank into the hair-cloth rocker and waved a palm-leaf fan.

Mrs. Caxton sat close to the window in the dim light, and read the poem. She took out her handkerchief and wiped her eyes as she read. "It's beautiful, beautiful," she said, tearfully, when she had finished. "It's jest as comfortin' as it can be, and you worked that in about his new suit so nice. I feel real obliged to you, Betsey, and you shall have one of the printed ones when they're done. I'm goin' to see to it right off."

Betsey flushed and smiled. It was to her as if her poem had been approved and accepted by one of the great magazines. She had the pride and self-wonderment of recognized genius. She went home buoyantly, under the wilting sun, after her call was done. When she reached home there was no one to whom she could tell her triumph, but the hot spicy breath of the evergreen hedge and the fervent sweetness of the sweet-peas seemed to greet her like the voices of friends.

She could scarcely wait for the printed poem. Mrs. Caxton brought it, and she inspected it, neatly printed in its black border. She was quite overcome with innocent pride.

"Well, I don't know but it does read pretty well," said she.

"It's beautiful," said Mrs. Caxton, fervently. "Mr. White said he never read anything any more touchin', when I carried it to him to print. I think folks are goin' to think a good deal of havin' it. I've had two dozen printed."

It was to Betsey like a large edition of a book. She had written obituary poems before, but never one had been printed in this sumptuous fashion. "I declare I think it would look pretty framed!" said she.

"Well, I don't know but it would," said Mrs. Caxton. "Anybody might have a neat little black frame, and it would look real appropriate."

"I wonder how much it would cost?" said Betsey.

After Mrs. Caxton had gone, she sat long, staring admiringly at the poem, and speculating as to the cost of a frame. "There ain't no use; I can't have it nohow, not if it don't cost more'n a quarter of a dollar," said she.

Then she put the poem away and got her supper. Nobody knew how frugal Betsey Dole's suppers and breakfasts and dinners were. Nearly all her food in the summer came from the scanty vegetables which flourished between the flowers in her garden. She ate scarcely more than her canary-bird, and sang as assiduously. Her income was almost infinitesimal: the interest at a low per cent. of a tiny sum in the village savings-bank, the remnant of her father's little hoard after his funeral expenses had been paid. Betsey had lived upon it for twenty years, and considered herself well-to-do. She had never received a cent for her poems; she had not thought of such a thing as possible. The appearance of this last in such shape was worth more to her than its words represented in as many dollars.

Betsey kept the poem pinned on the wall under the looking-glass; if any one came in, she tried with delicate hints to call attention to it. It was two weeks after she received it that the downfall of her innocent pride came.

One afternoon Mrs. Caxton called. It was raining hard. Betsey could scarcely believe it was she when she went to the door and found her standing there.

"Why, Mis' Caxton!" said she. "Ain't you wet to your skin?"

"Yes, I guess I be, pretty near. I s'pose I hadn't ought to come 'way down here in such a soak; but I went into Sarah Rogers's a minute after dinner, and something she said made me so mad, I made up my mind I'd come down here and tell you about it if I got drowned." Mrs. Caxton was out of breath; rain-drops trickled from her hair over her face; she stood in the door and shut her umbrella with a vicious shake to scatter the water from it. "I don't know what you're goin' to do with this," said she; "it's drippin'."

"I'll take it out an' put it in the kitchen sink."

"Well, I'll take off my shawl here too, and you can hang it out in the kitchen. I spread this shawl out. I thought it would keep the rain off me some. I know one thing, I'm goin' to have a waterproof if I live."

When the two women were seated in the sitting-room, Mrs. Caxton was quiet for a moment. There was a hesitating look on her face, fresh with the moist wind, with strands of wet hair clinging to the temples.

"I don't know as I had ought to tell you," she said, doubtfully.

"Why hadn't you ought to?"

"Well, I don't care; I'm goin' to, anyhow, I think you'd ought to know, an' it ain't so bad for you as it is for me. It don't begin to be. I put considerable money into 'em. I think Mr. White was pretty high, myself."

Betsey looked scared. "What is it?" she asked, in a weak voice.

"*Sarah Rogers says that the minister told her Ida that that poetry you wrote was jest as poor as it could be, an' it was in dreadful bad taste to have it printed an' sent round that way.* What do you think of that?"

Betsey did not reply. She sat looking at Mrs. Caxton as a victim whom the first blow had not killed might look at her executioner. Her face was like a pale wedge of ice between her curls.

Mrs. Caxton went on. "Yes, she said that right to my face, word for word. An' there was something else. She said the minister said that you had never wrote anything that could be called poetry, an' it was a dreadful waste of time. I don't s'pose he thought 'twas comin' back to you. You know he goes with Ida Rogers, an' I s'pose he said it to her kind of confidential when she showed him the poetry. There! I gave Sarah Rogers one of them nice printed ones, an' she acted glad enough to have it. Bad taste! H'm! If anybody wants to say anything against that beautiful poetry, printed with that nice black border, they can. I don't care if it's the minister, or who it is. I don't care if he does write poetry himself, an' has had some printed in a magazine. Maybe his ain't quite so fine as he thinks 'tis. Maybe them magazine folks jest took his for lack of something better. I'd like to have you send that poetry there. Bad taste! I jest got right up. 'Sarah Rogers,' says I, 'I hope you won't never do anything yourself in any worse taste.' I trembled so I could hardly speak, and I made up my mind I'd come right straight over here."

Mrs. Caxton went on and on. Betsey sat listening, and saying nothing.

She looked ghastly. Just before Mrs. Caxton went home she noticed it. "Why, Betsey Dole," she cried, "you look as white as a sheet. You ain't takin' it to heart as much as all that comes to, I hope. Goodness, I wish I hadn't told you!"

"I'd a good deal ruther you told me," replied Betsey, with a certain dignity. She looked at Mrs. Caxton. Her back was as stiff as if she were bound to a stake.

"Well, I thought you would," said Mrs. Caxton, uneasily; "and you're dreadful silly if you take it to heart, Betsey, that's all I've got to say. Goodness, I guess I don't, and it's full as hard on me as 'tis on you!"

Mrs. Caxton arose to go. Betsey brought her shawl and umbrella from the kitchen, and helped her off. Mrs. Caxton turned on the door-step and looked back at Betsey's white face. "Now don't go to thinkin' about it any more," said she. "I ain't goin' to. It ain't worth mindin'. Everybody knows what Sarah Rogers is. Good-by."

"Good-by, Mis' Caxton," said Betsey. She went back into the sitting-room. It was a cold rain, and the room was gloomy and chilly. She stood looking out of the window, watching the rain pelt on the hedge. The bird-cage hung at the other window. The bird watched her with his head on one side; then he began to chirp.

Suddenly Betsey faced about and began talking. It was not as if she were talking to herself; it seemed as if she recognized some other presence in the room. "I'd like to know if it's fair," said she. "I'd like to know if you think it's fair. Had I ought to have been born with the wantin' to write poetry if I couldn't write it—had I? Had I ought to have been let to write all my life, an' not know before there wa'n't any use in it? Would it be fair if that canary-bird there, that ain't never done anything but sing, should turn out not to be singin'? Would it, I'd like to know? S'pose them sweet-peas shouldn't be smellin' the right way? I ain't been dealt with as fair as they have, I'd like to know if I have."

The bird trilled and trilled. It was as if the golden down on his throat bubbled. Betsey went across the room to a cupboard beside the chimney. On the shelves were neatly stacked newspapers and little white rolls of writing-paper. Betsey began clearing the shelves. She took out the newspapers first, got the scissors, and cut a poem neatly out of the corner of each. Then she took up the clipped poems and the white rolls in her apron, and carried them into the kitchen. She cleaned out the stove carefully, removing every trace of ashes; then she put in the papers, and set them on fire. She stood watching them as their edges curled and blackened, then leaped into flame. Her face twisted as if the fire were curling over it also. Other women might have burned their lovers' letters in agony of heart. Betsey had never had any lover, but she was burning all the love-letters that had passed between her and life. When the flames died out she got a blue china sugar-bowl from the pantry and dipped the ashes into it with one of her thin silver teaspoons; then she put on the cover and set it away in the sitting-room cupboard.

The bird, who had been silent while she was out, began chirping again. Betsey went back to the pantry and got a lump of sugar, which she stuck between the cage wires. She looked at the clock on the kitchen shelf as she went by. It was after six. "I guess I don't want any supper to-night," she muttered.

She sat down by the window again. The bird pecked at his sugar. Betsey shivered and coughed. She had coughed more or less for years. People said she had the old-fashioned consumption. She sat at the window until it was quite dark; then she went to bed in her little bedroom out of the sitting-room. She shivered so she could not hold herself upright crossing the room. She coughed a great deal in the night.

Betsey was always an early riser. She was up at five the next morning. The sun shone, but it was very cold for the season. The leaves showed white in a north wind, and the flowers looked brighter than usual, though they were bent with the rain of the day before. Betsey went out in the garden to straighten her sweet-peas.

Coming back, a neighbor passing in the street eyed her curiously. "Why, Betsey, you sick?" said she.

"No, I'm kinder chilly, that's all," replied Betsey.

But the woman went home and reported that Betsey Dole looked dreadfully, and she didn't believe she'd ever see another summer.

It was now late August. Before October it was quite generally recognized that Betsey Dole's life was nearly over. She had no relatives, and hired nurses were rare in this little village. Mrs. Caxton came voluntarily and took care of her, only going home to prepare her husband's meals. Betsey's bed was moved into the sitting-room, and the neighbors came every day to see her, and brought little delicacies. Betsey had talked very little all her life; she talked less now, and there was a reticence about her which somewhat intimidated the other women. They would look pityingly and solemnly at her, and whisper in the entry when they went out.

Betsey never complained; but she kept asking if the minister had got home. He had been called away by his mother's illness, and returned only a week before Betsey died.

He came over at once to see her. Mrs. Caxton ushered him in one afternoon.

"Here's Mr. Lang come to see you, Betsey," said she, in the tone she would have used towards a little child. She placed the rocking-chair for the minister, and was about to seat herself, when Betsey spoke:

"Would you mind goin' out in the kitchen jest a few minutes, Mis' Caxton?" said she.

Mrs. Caxton arose, and went out with an embarrassed trot. Then there was silence. The minister was a young man—a country boy who had worked his way through a country college. He was gaunt and awkward, but sturdy in his loose clothes. He had a homely, impetuous face, with a good forehead.

He looked at Betsey's gentle, wasted face, sunken in the pillow, framed by its clusters of curls; finally he began to speak in the stilted fashion, yet with a certain force by reason of his unpolished honesty, about her spiritual welfare. Betsey listened quietly; now and then she assented. She had been a church member for years. It seemed now to the young man that this elderly maiden, drawing near the end of her simple, innocent life, had indeed her lamp, which no strong winds of temptation had ever met, well trimmed and burning.

When he paused, Betsey spoke. "Will you go to the cupboard side of the chimney and bring me the blue sugar-bowl on the top shelf?" said she, feebly.

The young man stared at her a minute; then he went to the cupboard, and brought the sugar-bowl to her. He held it, and Betsey took off the lid with her weak hand. "Do you see what's in there?" said she.

"It looks like ashes."

"It's—the ashes of all—the poetry I—ever wrote."

"Why, what made you burn it, Miss Dole?"

"I found out it wa'n't worth nothin'."

The minister looked at her in a bewildered way. He began to question if she were not wandering in her mind. He did not once suspect his own connection with the matter.

Betsey fastened her eager, sunken eyes upon his face. "What I want to know is—if you'll 'tend to—havin' this—buried with me."

The minister recoiled. He thought to himself that she certainly was wandering.

"No, I ain't out of my head," said Betsey. "I know what I'm sayin'. Maybe it's queer soundin', but it's a notion I've took. If you'll—'tend to it, I shall be—much obliged. I don't know anybody else I can ask."

"Well, I'll attend to it, if you wish me to, Miss Dole," said the minister, in a serious, perplexed manner. She replaced the lid on the sugar-bowl, and left it in his hands.

"Well, I shall be much obliged if you will 'tend to it; an' now there's something else," said she.

"What is it, Miss Dole?"

She hesitated a moment. "You write poetry, don't you?"

The minister colored. "Why, yes; a little sometimes."

"It's good poetry, ain't it? They printed some in a magazine."

The minister laughed confusedly. "Well, Miss Dole. I don't know how good poetry it may be, but they did print some in a magazine."

Betsey lay looking at him. "I never wrote none that was—good," she whispered, presently; "but I've been thinkin'—if you would jest write a few—lines about me—afterward— I've been thinkin' that—mebbe my—dyin' was goin' to make me—a good subject for—poetry, if I never wrote none. If you would jest write a few lines."

The minister stood holding the sugar-bowl; he was quite pale with bewilderment and sympathy. "I'll—do the best I can, Miss Dole," he stammered.

"I'll be much obliged," said Betsey, as if the sense of grateful obligation was immortal like herself. She smiled, and the sweetness of the smile was as evident through the drawn lines of her mouth as the old red in the leaves of a withered rose. The sun was setting; a red beam flashed softly over the top of the hedge and lay along the opposite wall; then the bird in his cage began to chirp. He chirped faster and faster until he trilled into a triumphant song.

TO THE LIGHTHOUSE

Virginia Stephen Woolf   (1882–1941)

The daughter of a famous English scholar and the goddaughter of James Russell Lowell, Woolf was educated at home. In 1912 she married Leonard Woolf, later a leader of the British Labour party. Her first novel, *The Voyage Out,* was published in 1915. In 1917 she and her husband hand-set a volume containing one story by each of them, thus giving birth to the Hogarth Press, which became one of the most influential presses of its day because of its publication of new authors. The Woolfs were members of the Bloomsbury Group, and she was one of Freud's earliest exponents in England. Fearing the recurrence of a mental breakdown such as she had suffered some twenty-five years before, she drowned herself.

To the Lighthouse was first published in 1927. The excerpt which follows is section 17 of the novel.

But what have I done with my life? thought Mrs. Ramsay, taking her place at the head of the table, and looking at all the plates making white circles on it. "William, sit by me," she said. "Lily," she said, wearily, "over there." They had that—Paul Rayley and Minta Doyle—she, only this—an infinitely long table and plates and knives. At the far end, was her husband, sitting down, all in a heap, frowning. What at? She did not know. She did not mind. She could not understand how she had ever felt any emotion or affection for him. She had a sense of being past everything, through everything, out of everything, as she helped the soup, as if there was an eddy—there—and one could be in it, or one could be out of it, and she was out of it. It's all come to an end, she thought, while they came in one after another. Charles Tansley—"Sit there, please," she said—Augustus Carmichael—and sat down. And meanwhile she waited, passively, for some one to answer her, for something to happen. But this is not a thing, she thought, ladling out soup, that one says.

Raising her eyebrows at the discrepancy—that was what she was thinking, this was what she was doing—ladling out soup—she felt, more and more strongly, outside that eddy; or as if a shade had fallen, and, robbed of colour, she saw things truly. The room (she looked round it) was very shabby. There was no beauty anywhere. She forebore to look at Mr. Tansley. Nothing seemed to have merged. They all sat separate. And the whole of the effort of merging and flowing and creating rested on her. Again she felt, as a fact without hostility, the sterility of men, for if she did not do it nobody would do it, and so, giving herself the little shake that one gives a watch that has stopped, the old familiar pulse began beating, as the watch begins ticking— one, two, three, one, two, three. And so on and so on, she repeated, listening to it, sheltering and fostering the still feeble pulse as one might guard a weak flame with a newspaper. And so then, she concluded, addressing herself by bending silently in his direction to William Bankes—poor man! who had no wife, and no children and dined alone in lodgings except for tonight; and in pity for him, life being now strong enough to bear her on again, she began all this business, as a sailor not without weariness sees the wind fill his sail and yet hardly wants to be off again and thinks how, had the ship sunk, he would have whirled round and round and found rest on the floor of the sea.

"Did you find your letters? I told them to put them in the hall for you," she said to William Bankes.

Lily Briscoe watched her drifting into that strange no-man's land where to follow people is impossible and yet their going inflicts such a chill on those who watch them that they always try at least to follow them with their eyes as one follows a fading ship until the sails have sunk beneath the horizon.

How old she looks, how worn she looks, Lily thought, and how remote. Then when she turned to William Bankes, smiling, it was as if the ship had turned and the sun had struck its sails again, and Lily thought with some amusement because she was relieved, Why does she pity him? For that was the impression she gave, when she told him that his letters were in the hall. Poor William Bankes, she seemed to be saying, as if her own weariness had been partly pitying people, and the life in her, her resolve to live again, had been stirred by pity. And it was not true, Lily thought; it was one of those misjudgments of hers that seemed to be instinctive and to arise from some need of her own rather than of other people's. He is not in the least pitiable. He has his work, Lily said to herself. She remembered, all of a sudden as if she had found a treasure, that she had her work. In a flash she saw her picture, and thought, Yes, I shall put the tree further in the middle; then I shall avoid that awkward space. That's what I shall do. That's what has been puzzling me. She took up the salt cellar and put it down again on a flower in pattern in the table-cloth, so as to remind herself to move the tree.

"It's odd that one scarcely gets anything worth having by post, yet one always wants one's letters," said Mr. Bankes.

What damned rot they talk, thought Charles Tansley, laying down his spoon precisely in the middle of his plate, which he had swept clean, as if, Lily thought (he sat opposite to her with his back to the window precisely in the middle of view), he were determined to make sure of his meals. Everything about him had that meagre fixity, that bare unloveliness. But nevertheless, the fact remained, it was almost impossible to dislike any one if one looked at them. She liked his eyes; they were blue, deep set, frightening.

"Do you write many letters, Mr. Tansley?" asked Mrs. Ramsay, pitying him too, Lily supposed; for that was true of Mrs. Ramsay—she pitied men always as if they lacked something—women never, as if they had something. He wrote to his mother; otherwise he did not suppose he wrote one letter a month, said Mr. Tansley, shortly.

For he was not going to talk the sort of rot these people wanted him to talk. He was not going to be condescended to by these silly women. He had been reading in his room, and now he came down and it all seemed to him silly, superficial, flimsy. Why did they dress? He had come down in his ordinary clothes. He had not got any dress clothes. "One never gets anything worth having by post"—that was the sort of thing they were always saying. They made men say that sort of thing. Yes, it was pretty well true, he thought. They never got anything worth having from one year's end to another. They did nothing but talk, talk, talk, eat, eat, eat. It was the women's fault. Women made civilisation impossible with all their "charm," all their silliness.

"No going to the Lighthouse tomorrow, Mrs. Ramsay," he said, asserting himself. He liked her; he admired her; he still thought of the man in the drain-pipe looking up at her; but he felt it necessary to assert himself.

He was really, Lily Briscoe thought, in spite of his eyes, but then look at his nose, look at his hands, the most uncharming human being she had ever met. Then why did she mind what he said? Women can't write, women can't paint—what did that matter coming from him, since clearly it was not true to him but for some reason helpful to him, and that was why he said it? Why did her whole being bow, like corn under a wind, and erect itself again from this abasement only with a great and rather painful effort? She must make it once more. There's the sprig on the table-cloth; there's my painting; I must move the tree to the middle; that matters—nothing else. Could she not hold fast to that, she asked herself, and not lose her temper, and not argue; and if she wanted revenge take it by laughing at him?

"Oh, Mr. Tansley," she said, "do take me to the Lighthouse with you. I should so love it."

She was telling lies he could see. She was saying what she did not mean to annoy him, for some reason. She was laughing at him. He was in his old flannel trousers. He had no others. He felt very rough and isolated and lonely. He knew that she was trying to tease him for some reason; she didn't want to go to the Lighthouse with him; she despised him: so did Prue Ramsay; so did they all. But he was not going to be made a fool of by women, so he turned deliberately in his chair and looked out of the window and said, all in a jerk, very rudely, it would be too rough for her tomorrow. She would be sick.

It annoyed him that she should have made him speak like that, with Mrs. Ramsay listening. If only he could be alone in his room working, he thought, among his books. That was where he felt at his ease. And he had never run a penny into debt; he had never cost his father a penny since he was fifteen; he had helped them at home out of his savings; he was educating his sister. Still, he wished he had known how to answer Miss Briscoe properly; he wished it had not come out all in a jerk like that. "You'd be sick." He wished he could think of something to say to Mrs. Ramsay, something which would show her that he was not just a dry prig. That was what they all thought him. He turned to her. But Mrs. Ramsay was talking about people he had never heard of to William Bankes.

"Yes, take it away," she said briefly, interrupting what she was saying to Mr. Bankes to speak to the maid. "It must have been fifteen—no, twenty years ago—that I last saw her," she was saying, turning back to him again as if she could not lose a moment of their talk, for she was absorbed by what they were saying. So he had actually heard from her this evening! And was Carrie still living at Marlow, and was everything still the same? Oh, she could remember as if it were yesterday—going on the river, feeling very cold. But if the Mannings made a plan they stuck to it. Never should she forget Herbert killing a wasp with a teaspoon on the bank! And it was still going on, Mrs. Ramsay mused, gliding like a ghost among the chairs and tables of that drawing-room on the banks of the Thames where she had been so very, very cold twenty years ago; but now she went among them like a ghost; and it fascinated her, as if, while she had changed, that particular day, now become very still and beautiful, had remained there, all these years. Had Carrie written to him herself? she asked.

"Yes. She says they're building a new billiard room," he said. No! No! That was out of the question! Building a billiard room! It seemed to her impossible.

Mr. Bankes could not see that there was anything very odd about it. They were very well off now. Should he give her love to Carrie?

"Oh," said Mrs. Ramsay with a little start, "No," she added, reflecting that she did not know this Carrie who built a new billiard room. But how strange, she repeated, to Mr. Bankes's amusement, that they should be going on there still. For it was extraordinary to think that they had been capable of going on living all these years when she had not thought of them more than once all that time. How eventful her own life had been, during those same years. Yet perhaps Carrie Manning had not thought about her either. The thought was strange and distasteful.

"People soon drift apart," said Mr. Bankes, feeling, however, some satisfaction when he thought that after all he knew both the Mannings and the Ramsays. He had not drifted apart he thought, laying down his spoon and wiping his clean-shaven lips punctiliously. But perhaps he was rather unusual, he thought, in this; he never let himself get into a groove. He had friends in all circles. . . . Mrs. Ramsay had to break off here to tell the maid something about keeping food hot. That was why he preferred dining alone. All those interruptions annoyed him. Well, thought William Bankes, preserving a demeanour of exquisite courtesy and merely spreading the fingers of his left hand on the table-cloth as a mechanic examines a tool beautifully polished and ready for use in an interval of leisure, such are the sacrifices one's friends ask of one. It would have hurt her if he had refused to come. But it was not worth it for him. Looking at his hand he thought that if he had been alone dinner would have been almost over now; he would have been free to work. Yes, he thought, it is a terrible waste of time. The children were dropping in still. "I wish one of you would run up to Roger's room," Mrs. Ramsay was saying. How trifling it all is, how boring it all is, he thought, compared with the other thing—work. Here he sat drumming his fingers on the table-cloth when he might have been—he took a flashing bird's-eye view of his work. What a waste of time it all was to be sure! Yet, he thought, she is one of my oldest friends. I am by way of being devoted to her. Yet now, at this moment her presence meant absolutely nothing to him: her beauty meant nothing to him; her sitting with her little boy at the window—nothing, nothing. He wished only to be alone and to take up that book. He felt uncomfortable; he felt treacherous, that he could sit by her side and feel nothing for her. The truth was that he did not enjoy family life. It was in this sort of state that one asked oneself, What does one live for? Why, one asked oneself, does one take all these pains for the human race to go on? Is it so very desirable? Are we attractive as a species? Not so very, he thought, looking at those rather untidy boys. His favourite, Cam, was in bed, he supposed. Foolish questions, vain questions, questions one never asked if one was occupied. Is human life this? Is human life that? One never had time to think about it. But here he was asking himself that sort of question, because Mrs. Ramsay was giving orders to servants, and also because it had struck him, thinking how surprised Mrs. Ramsay was that Carrie Manning should still exist, that friendships, even the best of them, are frail things. One drifts apart. He reproached himself again. He was sitting beside Mrs. Ramsay and he had nothing in the world to say to her.

"I'm so sorry," said Mrs. Ramsay, turning to him at last. He felt rigid and barren, like a pair of boots that have been soaked and gone dry so that you can hardly force your feet into them. Yet he must force his feet into them. He must make himself talk. Unless he were very careful, she would find out this treachery of his; that he did not care a straw for her, and that would not be at all pleasant, he thought. So he bent his head courteously in her direction.

"How you must detest dining in this bear garden," she said, making use, as she did when she was distracted, of her social manner. So, when there is a strife of tongues, at some meeting, the chairman, to obtain unity, suggests that every one shall speak in French. Perhaps it is bad French; French may not contain the words that express the speaker's thoughts; nevertheless speaking French imposes some order, some uniformity. Replying to her in the same language, Mr. Bankes said, "No, not at all," and Mr. Tansley, who had no knowledge of this language, even spoke thus in words of one syllable, at once suspected its insincerity. They did talk nonsense, he thought, the Ramsays; and he pounced on this fresh instance with joy, making a note which, one of these days, he would read aloud, to one or two friends. There, in a society where one could say what one liked he would sarcastically describe "staying with the Ramsays" and what nonsense they talked. It was worth while doing it once, he would say; but not again. The women bored one so, he would say. Of course Ramsay had dished himself by marrying a beautiful woman and having eight children. It would shape itself something like that, but now, at this moment, sitting stuck there with an empty seat beside him, nothing had shaped itself at all. It was all in scraps and fragments. He felt extremely, even physically, uncomfortable. He wanted somebody to give him a chance of asserting himself. He wanted it so urgently that he fidgeted in his chair, looked at this person, then at that person, tried to break into their talk, opened his mouth and shut it again. They were talking about the fishing industry. Why did no one ask him his opinion? What did they know about the fishing industry?

Lily Briscoe knew all that. Sitting opposite him, could she not see, as in an X-ray photograph, the ribs and thigh bones of the young man's desire to impress himself, lying dark in the mist of his flesh—that thin mist which convention had laid over his burning desire to break into the conversation? But, she thought, screwing up her Chinese eyes, and remembering how he sneered at women, "can't paint, can't write," why should I help him to relieve himself?

There is a code of behaviour, she knew, whose seventh article (it may be) says that on occasions of this sort it behoves the woman, whatever her own occupation may be, to go to the help of the young man opposite so that he may expose and relieve the thigh bones, the ribs, of his vanity, of his urgent desire to assert himself; as indeed it is their duty, she reflected, in her old maidenly fairness, to help us, suppose the Tube were to burst into flames. Then, she thought, I should certainly expect Mr. Tansley to get me out. But how would it be, she thought, if neither of us did either of these things? So she sat there smiling.

"You're not planning to go to the Lighthouse, are you, Lily," said Mrs. Ramsay. "Remember poor Mr. Langley; he had been round the world dozens of times, but he told me he never suffered as he did when my husband took him there. Are you a good sailor, Mr. Tansley?" she asked.

Mr. Tansley raised a hammer: swung it high in air; but realising, as it descended, that he could not smite that butterfly with such an instrument as this, said only that he had never been sick in his life. But in that one sentence lay compact, like gunpowder, that his grandfather was a fisherman; his father a chemist; that he had worked his way up entirely himself; that he was proud of it; that he was Charles Tansley—a fact that nobody there seemed to realise; but one of these days every single person would know it. He scowled ahead of him. He could almost pity these mild cultivated people, who would be blown sky high, like bales of wool and barrels of apples, one of these days by the gunpowder that was in him.

"Will you take me, Mr. Tansley?" said Lily, quickly, kindly, for, of course, if Mrs. Ramsay said to her, as in effect she did, "I am drowning, my dear, in seas of fire. Unless you apply some balm to the anguish of this hour and say something nice to that young man there, life will run upon the rocks—indeed I hear the grating and the growling at this minute. My nerves are taut as fiddle strings. Another touch and they will snap"—when Mrs. Ramsay said all this, as the glance in her eyes said it, of course for the hundred and fiftieth time Lily Briscoe had to renounce the experiment—what happens if one is not nice to that young man there—and be nice.

Judging the turn in her mood correctly—that she was friendly to him now—he was relieved of his egotism, and told her how he had been thrown out of a boat when he was a baby; how his father used to fish him out with a boat-hook; that was how he had learnt to swim. One of his uncles kept the light on some rock or other off the Scottish coast, he said. He had been there with him in a storm. This was said loudly in a pause. They had to listen to him when he said that he had been with his uncle in a lighthouse in a storm. Ah, thought Lily Briscoe, as the conversation took this auspicious turn, and she felt Mrs. Ramsay's gratitude (for Mrs. Ramsay was free now to talk for a moment herself), ah, she thought, but what haven't I paid to get it for you? She had not been sincere.

She had done the usual trick—been nice. She would never know him. He would never know her. Human relations were all like that, she thought, and the worst (if it had not been for Mr. Bankes) were between men and women. Inevitably these were extremely insincere she thought. Then her eye caught the salt cellar, which she had placed there to remind her, and she remembered that next morning she would move the tree further towards the middle, and her spirits rose so high at the thought of painting tomorrow that she laughed out loud at what Mr. Tansley was saying. Let him talk all night if he liked it.

"But how long do they leave men on a Lighthouse?" she asked. He told her. He was amazingly well informed. And as he was grateful, and as he liked her, and as he was beginning to enjoy himself, so now, Mrs. Ramsay thought, she could return to that dream land, that unreal but fascinating place, the Mannings' drawing-room at Marlow twenty years ago; where one moved about without haste or anxiety, for there was no future to worry about. She knew what had happened to them, what to her. It was like reading a good book again, for she knew the end of that story, since it had happened twenty years ago, and life, which shot down even from this dining-room table in cascades, heaven knows where, was sealed up there, and lay, like a lake, placidly between its banks. He said they had built a billiard room—was it possible? Would William go on talking about the Mannings? She wanted him to. But, no—for some reason he was no longer in the mood. She tried. He did not respond. She could not force him. She was disappointed.

"The children are disgraceful," she said, sighing. He said something about punctuality being one of the minor virtues which we do not acquire until later in life.

"If at all," said Mrs. Ramsay merely to fill up space, thinking what an old maid William was becoming. Conscious of his treachery, conscious of her wish to talk about something more intimate, yet out of mood for it at present, he felt come over him the disagreeableness of life, sitting there, waiting.

Perhaps the others were saying something interesting? What were they saying?

That the fishing season was bad; that the men were emigrating. They were talking about wages and unemployment. The young man was abusing the government. William Bankes, thinking what a relief it was to catch on to something of this sort when private life was disagreeable, heard him say something about "one of the most scandalous acts of the present government." Lily was listening; Mrs. Ramsay was listening; they were all listening. But already bored, Lily felt that something was lacking; Mr. Bankes felt that something was lacking. Pulling her shawl round her Mrs. Ramsay felt that something was lacking. All of them bending themselves to listen thought, "Pray heaven that the inside of my mind may not be exposed," for each thought, "The others are feeling this. They are outraged and indignant with the government about the fishermen. Whereas, I feel nothing at all." But perhaps, thought Mr. Bankes, as he looked at Mr. Tansley, here is the man. One was always waiting for the man. There was always a chance. At any moment the leader might arise; the man of genius, in politics as in anything else. Probably he will be extremely disagreeable to us old fogies, thought Mr. Bankes, doing his best to make allowances, for he knew by some curious physical sensation, as of nerves erect in his spine, that he was jealous, for himself partly, partly more probably for his work, for his point of view, for his science; and therefore he was not entirely open-minded or altogether fair, for Mr. Tansley seemed to be saying, You have wasted your lives. You are all of you wrong. Poor old fogies, you're hopelessly behind the times. He seemed to be rather cocksure, this young man; and his manners were bad. But Mr. Bankes bade himself observe, he had courage; he had ability; he was extremely well up in the facts. Probably, Mr. Bankes thought, as Tansley abused the government, there is a good deal in what he says.

"Tell me now . . ." he said. So they argued about politics, and Lily looked at the leaf on the table-cloth; and Mrs. Ramsay, leaving the argument entirely in the hands of the two men, wondered why she was so bored by this talk, and wished, looking at her husband at the other end of the table, that he would say something. One word, she said to herself. For if he said a thing, it would make all the difference. He went to the heart of things. He cared about fishermen and their wages. He could not sleep for thinking of them. It was altogether different when he spoke; one did not feel then, pray heaven you don't see how little I care, because one did care. Then, realising that it was because she admired him so much that she was waiting for him to speak, she felt as if somebody had been praising her husband to her and their marriage, and she glowed all over without realising that it was she herself who had praised him. She looked at him thinking to find this in his face; he would be looking magnificent. . . . But not in the least! He was screwing his face up, he was scowling and frowning, and flushing with anger. What on earth was it about? she wondered. What could be the matter? Only that poor old Augustus had asked for another plate of soup—that was all. It was unthinkable, it was detestable (so he signalled to her across the table) that Augustus should be beginning his soup over again. He loathed people eating when he had finished. She saw his anger fly like a pack of hounds into his eyes, his brow, and she knew that in a moment something violent would explode, and then—thank goodness! she saw him clutch himself and clap a brake on the wheel, and the whole of his body seemed to emit sparks but not words. He sat there scowling. He had said nothing, he would have her observe. Let her give him the credit for that! But why after all should poor Augustus not ask for another plate of soup? He had merely touched Ellen's arm and said:

"Ellen, please, another plate of soup," and then Mr. Ramsay scowled like that.

And why not? Mrs. Ramsay demanded. Surely they could let Augustus have his soup if he wanted it. He hated people wallowing in food, Mr. Ramsay frowned at her. He hated everything dragging on for hours like this. But he had controlled himself, Mr. Ramsay would have her observe, disgusting though the sight was. But why show it so plainly, Mrs. Ramsay demanded (they looked at each other down the long table sending these questions and answers across, each knowing exactly what the other felt). Everybody could see, Mrs. Ramsay thought. There was Rose gazing at her father, there was Roger gazing at his father; both would be off in spasms of laughter in another second, she knew, and so she said promptly (indeed it was time):

"Light the candles," and they jumped up instantly and went and fumbled at the sideboard.

Why could he never conceal his feelings? Mrs. Ramsay wondered, and she wondered if Augustus Carmichael had noticed. Perhaps he had; perhaps he had not. She could not help respecting the composure with which he sat there, drinking his soup. If he wanted soup, he asked for soup. Whether people laughed at him or were angry with him he was the same. He did not like her, she knew that; but partly for that very reason she respected him, and looking at him, drinking soup, very large and calm in the failing light, and monumental, and contemplative, she wondered what he did feel then, and why he was always content and dignified; and she thought how devoted he was to Andrew, and would call him into his room, and Andrew said, "show him things." And there he would lie all day long on the lawn brooding presumably over his poetry, till he reminded one of a cat watching birds, and then he clapped his paws together when he had found the word, and her husband said, "Poor old Augustus—he's a true poet," which was high praise from her husband.

Now eight candles were stood down the table, and after the first stoop the flames stood upright and drew with them into visibility the long table entire, and in the middle a yellow and purple dish of fruit. What had she done with it, Mrs. Ramsay wondered, for Rose's arrangement of the grapes and pears, of the horny pink-lined shell, of the bananas, made her think of a trophy fetched from the bottom of the sea, of Neptune's banquet, of the bunch that hangs with vine leaves over the shoulder of Bacchus (in some picture), among the leopard skins and the torches lolloping red and gold. . . . Thus brought up suddenly into the light it seemed possessed of great size and depth, was like a world in which one could take one's staff and climb hills, she thought, and go down into valleys, and to her pleasure (for it brought them into sympathy momentarily) she saw that Augustus too feasted his eyes on the same plate of fruit, plunged in, broke off a bloom there, a tassel here, and returned, after feasting, to his hive. That was his way of looking, different from hers. But looking together united them.

Now all the candles were lit up, and the faces on both sides of the table were brought nearer by the candle light, and composed, as they had not been in the twilight, into a party round a table, for the night was now shut off by panes of glass, which, far from giving any accurate view of the outside world, rippled it so strangely that here, inside the room, seemed to be order and dry land; there, outside, a reflection in which things wavered and vanished, waterily.

Some change at once went through them all, as if this had really happened, and they were all conscious of making a party together in a hollow, on an island; had their common cause against that fluidity out there. Mrs. Ramsay, who had been uneasy, waiting for Paul and Minta to come in, and unable, she felt, to settle to things, now felt her uneasiness changed to expectation. For now they must come, and Lily Briscoe, trying to analyse the cause of the sudden exhilaration, compared it with that moment on the tennis lawn, when solidity suddenly vanished, and such vast spaces lay between them; and now the same effect was got by the many candles in the sparely furnished room, and the uncurtained windows, and the bright mask-like look of faces seen by candlelight. Some weight was taken off them; anything might happen, she felt. They must come now, Mrs. Ramsay thought, looking at the door, and at that instant, Minta Doyle, Paul Rayley, and a maid carrying a great dish in her hands came in together. They were awfully late; they were horribly late, Minta said, as they found their way to different ends of the table.

"I lost my brooch—my grandmother's brooch," said Minta with a sound of lamentation in her voice, and a suffusion in her large brown eyes, looking down, looking up, as she sat by Mr. Ramsay, which roused his chivalry so that he bantered her.

How could she be such a goose, he asked, as to scramble about the rocks in jewels?

She was by way of being terrified of him—he was so fearfully clever, and the first night when she had sat by him, and he talked about George Eliot, she had been really frightened, for she had left the third volume of *Middlemarch* in the train and she never knew what happened in the end; but afterwards she got on perfectly, and made herself out even more ignorant than she was, because he liked telling her she was a fool. And so tonight, directly he laughed at her, she was not frightened. Besides, she knew, directly she came into the room that the miracle had happened; she wore her golden haze. Sometimes she had it; sometimes not. She never knew why it came or why it went, or if she had it until she came into the room and then she knew instantly by the way some man looked at her. Yes, tonight she had it, tremendously; she knew that by the way Mr. Ramsay told her not to be a fool. She sat beside him, smiling.

It must have happened then, thought Mrs. Ramsay; they are engaged. And for a moment she felt what she had never expected to feel again—jealousy. For he, her husband, felt it too—Minta's glow; he liked these girls, these golden-reddish girls, with something flying, something a little wild and harum-scarum about them, who didn't "scrape their hair off," weren't, as he said about poor Lily Briscoe, ". . . skimpy." There was some quality which she herself had not, some lustre, some richness, which attracted him, amused him, led him to make favourites of girls like Minta. They might cut his hair from him, plait him watch-chains, or interrupt him at his work, hailing him (she heard them), "Come along, Mr. Ramsay; it's our turn to beat them now," and out he came to play tennis.

But indeed she was not jealous, only, now and then, when she made herself look in her glass a little resentful that she had grown old, perhaps, by her own fault. (The bill for the greenhouse and all the rest of it.) She was grateful to them for laughing at him. ("How many pipes have you smoked today, Mr. Ramsay?" and so on), till he seemed a young man; a man very attractive to women, not burdened, not weighed down with the greatness of his labours and the sorrows of the world and his fame or his failure, but again as she had first known him, gaunt but gallant; helping her out of a boat, she remembered; with delightful ways, like that (she looked at him, and he looked astonishingly young, teasing Minta). For herself—"Put it down there," she said, helping the Swiss girl to place gently before her the huge brown pot in which was the Boeuf en Daube—for her own part she liked her boobies. Paul must sit by her. She had kept a place for him. Really, she sometimes thought she liked the boobies best. They did not bother one with their dissertations. How much they missed, after all, these very clever men! How dried up they did become, to be sure. There was something, she thought as he sat down, very charming about Paul. His manners were delightful to her, and his sharp-cut nose and his bright blue eyes. He was so considerate. Would he tell her—now that they were all talking again—what had happened?

"We went back to look for Minta's brooch," he said, sitting down by her. "We"—that was enough. She knew from the effort, the rise in his voice to surmount a difficult word that it was the first time he had said "we." "We did this, we did that." They'll say that all their lives, she thought, and an exquisite scent of olives and oil and juice rose from the great brown dish as Marthe, with a little flourish, took the cover off. The cook had spent three days over that dish. And she must take great care, Mrs. Ramsay thought, diving into the soft mass, to choose a specially tender piece for William Bankes. And she peered into the dish, with its shiny walls and its confusion of savoury brown and yellow meats and its bay leaves and its wine, and thought. This will celebrate the occasion—a curious sense rising in her, at once freakish and tender, of celebrating a festival, as if two emotions were called up in her, one profound—for what could be more serious than the love of man for woman, what more commanding, more impressive, bearing in its bosom the seeds of death; at the same time these lovers, these people entering into illusion glittering eyed, must be danced round with mockery, decorated with garlands.

"It is a triumph," said Mr. Bankes, laying his knife down for a moment. He had eaten attentively. It was rich; it was tender. It was perfectly cooked. How did she manage these things in the depths of the country? he asked her. She was a wonderful woman. All his love, all his reverence, had returned; and she knew it.

"It is a French receipe of my grandmother's," said Mrs. Ramsay, speaking with a ring of great pleasure in her voice. Of course it was French. What passes for cookery in England is an abomination (they agreed). It is putting cabbages in water. It is roasting meat till it is like leather. It is cutting off the delicious skins of vegetables. "In which," said Mr. Bankes, "all the virtue of the vegetable is contained." And the waste, said Mrs. Ramsay. A whole French family could live on what an English cook throws away. Spurred on by her sense that William's affection had come back to her, and that everything was all right again, and that her suspense was over, and that now she was free both to triumph and to mock, she laughed, she gesticulated, till Lily thought, How childlike, how absurd she was, sitting up there with all her beauty opened again in her, talking about the skins of vegetables. There was something frightening about her. She was irresistible. Always she got her own way in the end, Lily thought. Now she had brought this off—Paul and Minta, one might suppose, were engaged. Mr. Bankes was dining here. She put a spell on them all, by wishing, so simply, so directly, and Lily contrasted that abundance with her own poverty of spirit, and supposed that it was partly that belief (for her face was all lit up—without looking young, she looked radiant) in this strange, this terrifying thing, which made Paul Rayley, sitting at her side, all of a tremor, yet abstract, absorbed, silent. Mrs. Ramsay, Lily felt, as she talked about the skins of vegetables, exalted that, worshipped that; held her hands over it to warm them, to protect it, and yet, having brought it all about, somehow laughed, led her victims, Lily felt, to the altar. It came over her too now—the emotion, the vibration, of love. How inconspicuous she felt herself by Paul's side! He, glowing, burning; she, aloof, satirical; he, bound for adventure; she, moored to the shore; he, launched, incautious; she, solitary, left out—and, ready to implore a share, if it were disaster, in his disaster, she said shyly:

"When did Minta lose her brooch?"

He smiled the most exquisite smile, veiled by memory, tinged by dreams. He shook his head. "On the beach," he said.

"I'm going to find it," he said, "I'm getting up early." This being kept secret from Minta, he lowered his voice, and turned his eyes to where she sat, laughing, beside Mr. Ramsay.

Lily wanted to protest violently and outrageously her desire to help him, envisaging how in the dawn on the beach she would be the one to pounce on the brooch half-hidden by some stone, and thus herself be included among the sailors and adventurers. But what did he reply to her offer? She actually said with an emotion that she seldom let appear, "Let me come with you," and he laughed. He meant yes or no—either perhaps. But it was not his meaning—it was the odd chuckle he gave, as if he had said, Throw yourself over the cliff if you like, I don't care. He turned on her cheek the heat of love, its horror, its cruelty, its unscrupulosity. It scorched her, and Lily, looking at Minta, being charming to Mr. Ramsay at the other end of the table, flinched for her exposed to these fangs, and was thankful. For at any rate, she said to herself, catching sight of the salt cellar on the pattern, she need not marry, thank Heaven: she need not undergo that degradation. She was saved from that dilution. She would move the tree rather more to the middle.

Such was the complexity of things. For what happened to her, especially staying with the Ramsays, was to be made to feel violently two opposite things at the same time; that's what you feel, was one; that's what I feel, was the other, and then they fought together in her mind, as now. It is so beautiful, so exciting, this love, that I tremble on the verge of it, and offer, quite out of my own habit, to look for a brooch on a beach; also it is the stupidest, the most barbaric of human passions, and turns a nice young man with a profile like a gem's (Paul's was exquisite) into a bully with a crowbar (he was swaggering, he was insolent) in the Mile End Road. Yet, she said to herself, from the dawn of time odes have been sung to love; wreaths heaped and roses; and if you asked nine people out of ten they would say they wanted nothing but this—love; while the women, judging from her own experience, would all the time be feeling, This is not what we want; there is nothing more tedious, puerile, and inhumane than this; yet it is also beautiful and necessary. Well then, well then? she asked, somehow expecting the others to go on with the argument, as if in an argument like this one threw one's own little bolt which fell short obviously and left the others to carry it on. So she listened again to what they were saying in case they should throw any light upon the question of love.

"Then," said Mr. Bankes, "there is that liquid the English call coffee."

"Oh, coffee!" said Mrs. Ramsay. But it was much rather a question (she was thoroughly roused, Lily could see, and talked very emphatically) of real butter and clean milk. Speaking with warmth and eloquence, she described the iniquity of the English dairy system, and in what state milk was delivered at the door, and was about to prove her charges, for she had gone into the matter, when all round the table, beginning with Andrew in the middle, like a fire leaping from tuft to tuft of furze, her children laughed; her husband laughed; she was laughed at, fire-encircled, and forced to veil her crest, dismount her batteries, and only retaliate by displaying the raillery and ridicule of the table to Mr. Bankes as an example of what one suffered if one attacked the prejudices of the British Public.

Purposely, however, for she had it on her mind that Lily, who had helped her with Mr. Tansley, was out of things, she exempted her from the rest; said "Lily anyhow agrees with me," and so drew her in, a little fluttered, a little startled. (For she was thinking about love.) They were both out of things, Mrs. Ramsay had been thinking, both Lily and Charles Tansley. Both suffered from the glow of the other two. He, it was clear, felt himself utterly in the cold; no woman would look at him with Paul Rayley in the room. Poor fellow! Still, he had his dissertation, the influence of somebody upon something: he could take care of himself. With Lily it was different. She faded, under Minta's glow; became more inconspicuous than ever, in her little grey dress with her little puckered face and her little Chinese eyes. Everything about her was so small. Yet, thought Mrs. Ramsay, comparing her with Minta, as she claimed her help (for Lily should bear her out she talked no more about her dairies than her husband did about his boots—he would talk by the hour about his boots) of the two, Lily at forty will be the better. There was in Lily a thread of something; a flare of something; something of her own which Mrs. Ramsay liked very much indeed, but no man would, she feared. Obviously, not, unless it were a much older man, like William Bankes. But then he cared, well, Mrs. Ramsay sometimes thought that he cared, since his wife's death, perhaps for her. He was not "in love" of course; it was one of those unclassified affections of which there are so many. Oh, but nonsense, she thought; William must marry Lily. They have so many things in common. Lily is so fond of flowers. They are both cold and aloof and rather self-sufficing. She must arrange for them to take a long walk together.

Foolishly, she had set them opposite each other. That could be remedied tomorrow. If it were fine, they should go for a picnic. Everything seemed possible. Everything seemed right. Just now (but this cannot last, she thought, dissociating herself from the moment while they were all talking about boots) just now she had reached security; she hovered like a hawk suspended; like a flag floated in an element of joy which filled every nerve of her body fully and sweetly, not noisily, solemnly rather, for it arose, she thought, looking at them all eating there, from husband and children and friends; all of which rising in this profound stillness (she was helping William Bankes to one very small piece more, and peered into the depths of the earthenware pot) seemed now for no special reason to stay there like a smoke, like a fume rising upwards, holding them safe together. Nothing need be said; nothing could be said. There it was, all round them. It partook, she felt, carefully helping Mr. Bankes to a specially tender piece, of eternity; as she had already felt about something different once before that afternoon; there is a coherence in things, a stability; something, she meant, is immune from change, and shines out (she glanced at the window with its ripple of reflected lights) in the face of the flowing, the fleeting, the spectral, like a ruby; so that again tonight she had the feeling she had had once today, already, of peace, of rest. Of such moments, she thought, the thing is made that endures.

"Yes," she assured William Bankes, "there is plenty for everybody."

"Andrew," she said, "hold your plate lower, or I shall spill it." (The Boeuf en Daube was a perfect triumph.) Here, she felt, putting the spoon down, was the still space that lies about the heart of things, where one could move or rest; could wait now (they were all helped) listening; could then, like a hawk which lapses suddenly from its high station, flaunt and sink on laughter easily, resting her whole weight upon what at the other end of the table her husband was saying about the square root of one thousand two hundred and fifty-three. That was the number, it seemed, on his watch.

What did it all mean? To this day she had no notion. A square root? What was that? Her sons knew. She leant on them; on cubes and square roots; that was what they were talking about now; on Voltaire and Madame de Staël; on the character of Napoleon; on the French system of land tenure; on Lord Rosebery; on Creevey's Memoirs: she let it uphold her and sustain her, this admirable fabric of the masculine intelligence, which ran up and down, crossed this way and that, like iron girders spanning the swaying fabric, upholding the world, so that she could trust herself to it utterly, even shut her eyes, or flicker them for a moment, as a child staring up from its pillow winks at the myriad layers of the leaves of a tree. Then she woke up. It was still being fabricated. William Bankes was praising the Waverley novels.

He read one of them every six months, he said. And why should that make Charles Tansley angry? He rushed in (all, thought Mrs. Ramsay, because Prue will not be nice to him) and denounced the Waverley novels when he knew nothing about it, nothing about it whatsoever, Mrs. Ramsay thought, observing him rather than listening to what he said. She could see how it was from his manner—he wanted to assert himself, and so it would always be with him till he got his Professorship or married his wife, and so need not be always saying, "I—I—I." For that was what his criticism of poor Sir Walter, or perhaps it was Jane Austen, amounted to. "I—I—I." He was thinking of himself and the impression he was making, as she could tell by the sound of his voice, and his emphasis and his uneasiness. Success would be good for him. At any rate they were off again. Now she need not listen. It could not last, she knew, but at the moment her eyes were so clear that they seemed to go round the table unveiling each of these people, and their thoughts and their feelings, without effort like a light stealing under water so that its ripples and the reeds in it and the minnows balancing themselves, and the sudden silent trout are all lit up hanging, trembling. So she saw them; she heard them; but whatever they said had also this quality, as if what they said was like the movement of a trout when, at the same time, one can see the ripple and the gravel, something to the right, something to the left; and the whole is held together; for whereas in active life she would be netting and separating one thing from another; she would be saying she liked the Waverley novels or had not read them; she would be urging herself forward; now she said nothing. For the moment, she hung suspended.

"Ah, but how long do you think it'll last?" said somebody. It was as if she had antennae trembling out from her, which, intercepting certain sentences, forced them upon her attention. This was one of them. She scented danger for her husband. A question like that would lead, almost certainly, to something being said which reminded him of his own failure. How long would he be read—he would think at once. William Bankes (who was entirely free from all such vanity) laughed, and said he attached no importance to changes in fashion. Who could tell what was going to last—in literature or indeed in anything else?

"Let us enjoy what we do enjoy," he said. His integrity seemed to Mrs. Ramsay quite admirable. He never seemed for a moment to think, But how does this affect me? But then if you had the other temperament, which must have praise, which must have encouragement, naturally you began (and she knew that Mr. Ramsay was beginning) to be uneasy; to want somebody to say, Oh, but your work will last, Mr. Ramsay, or something like that. He showed his uneasiness quite clearly now by saying, with some irritation, that, anyhow, Scott (or was it Shakespeare?) would last him his lifetime. He said it irritably. Everybody, she thought, felt a little uncomfortable, without knowing why. Then Minta Doyle, whose instinct was fine, said bluffly, absurdly, that she did not believe that any one really enjoyed reading Shakespeare. Mr. Ramsay said grimly (but his mind was turned away again) that very few people liked it as much as they said they did. But, he added, there is considerable merit in some of the plays nevertheless, and Mrs. Ramsay saw that it would be all right for the moment anyhow; he would laugh at Minta, and she, Mrs. Ramsay saw, realising his extreme anxiety about himself, would, in her own way, see that he was taken care of, and praise him, somehow or other. But she wished it was not necessary: perhaps it was her fault that it was necessary. Anyhow, she was free now to listen to what Paul Rayley was trying to say about books one had read as a boy. They lasted, he said. He had read some of Tolstoi at school. There was one he always remembered, but he had forgotten the name. Russian names were impossible, said Mrs. Ramsay. "Vronsky," said Paul. He remembered that because he always thought it such a good name for a villain. "Vronsky," said Mrs. Ramsay; "Oh, *Anna Karenina*," but that did not take them very far; books were not in their line. No, Charles Tansley would put them both right in a second about books, but it was all so mixed up with, Am I saying the right thing? Am I making a good impression? that, after all, one knew more about him than about Tolstoi, whereas, what Paul said was about the thing, simply, not himself, nothing else. Like all stupid people, he had a kind of modesty too, a consideration for what you were feeling, which, once in a way at least, she found attractive. Now he was thinking, not about himself or about Tolstoi, but whether she was cold, whether she felt a draught, whether she would like a pear.

No, she said, she did not want a pear. Indeed she had been keeping guard over the dish of fruit (without realising it) jealously, hoping that nobody would touch it. Her eyes had been going in and out among the curves and shadows of the fruit, among the rich purples of the lowland grapes, then over the horny ridge of the shell, putting a yellow against a purple, a curved shape against a round shape, without knowing why she did it, or why, every time she did it, she felt more and more serene; until, oh, what a pity that they should do it—a hand reached out, took a pear, and spoilt the whole thing. In sympathy she looked at Rose. She looked at Rose sitting between Jasper and Prue. How odd that one's child should do that!

How odd to see them sitting there, in a row, her children, Jasper, Rose, Prue, Andrew, almost silent, but with some joke of their own going on, she guessed, from the twitching at their lips. It was something quite apart from everything else, something they were hoarding up to laugh over in their own room. It was not about their father, she hoped. No, she thought not. What was it, she wondered, sadly rather, for it seemed to her that they would laugh when she was not there. There was all that hoarded behind those rather set, still, mask-like faces, for they did not join in easily; they were like watchers, surveyors, a little raised or set apart from the grown-up people. But when she looked at Prue tonight, she saw that this was not now quite true of her. She was just beginning, just moving, just descending. The faintest light was on her face, as if the glow of Minta opposite, some excitement, some anticipation of happiness was reflected in her, as if the sun of the love of men and women rose over the rim of the table-cloth, and without knowing what it was she bent towards it and greeted it. She kept looking at Minta, shyly, yet curiously, so that Mrs. Ramsay looked from one to the other and said, speaking to Prue in her own mind, You will be as happy as she is one of these days. You will be much happier, she added, because you are my daughter, she meant; her own daughter must be happier than other people's daughters. But dinner was over. It was time to go. They were only playing with things on their plates. She would wait until they had done laughing at some story her husband was telling. He was having a joke with Minta about a bet. Then she would get up.

She liked Charles Tansley, she thought, suddenly; she liked his laugh. She liked him for being so angry with Paul and Minta. She liked his awkwardness. There was a lot in that young man after all. And Lily, she thought, putting her napkin beside her plate, she always has some joke of her own. One need never bother about Lily. She waited. She tucked her napkin under the edge of her plate. Well, were they done now? No. That story had led to another story. Her husband was in great spirits tonight, and wishing, she supposed, to make it all right with old Augustus after that scene about the soup, had drawn him in—they were telling stories about some one they had both known at college. She looked at the window in which the candle flames burnt brighter now that the panes were black, and looking at that outside the voices came to her very strangely, as if they were voices at a service in a cathedral, for she did not listen to the words. The sudden bursts of laughter and then one voice (Minta's) speaking alone, reminded her of men and boys crying out the Latin words of a service in some Roman Catholic cathedral. She waited. Her husband spoke. He was repeating something, and she knew it was poetry from the rhythm and the ring of exultation, and melancholy in his voice:

Come out and climb the garden path,
    Luriana, Lurilee.
The China rose is all abloom and buzzing with the yellow bee.

The words (she was looking at the window) sounded as if they were floating like flowers on water out there, cut off from them all, as if no one had said them, but they had come into existence of themselves.

"And all the lives we ever lived and all the lives to be are full of trees and changing leaves." She did not know what they meant, but, like music, the words seemed to be spoken by her own voice, outside her self, saying quite easily and naturally what had been in her mind the whole evening while she said different things. She knew, without looking round, that every one at the table was listening to the voice saying:

I wonder if it seems to you,
    Luriana, Lurilee

with the same sort of relief and pleasure that she had, as if this were, at last, the natural thing to say this were their own voice speaking.

But the voice stopped. She looked round. She made herself get up. Augustus Carmichael had risen and, holding his table napkin so that it looked like a long white robe he stood chanting:

To see the Kings go riding by
Over lawn and daisy lea
With their palm leaves and cedar sheaves,
    Luriana, Lurilee,

and as she passed him, he turned slightly towards her repeating the last words:

Luriana, Lurilee

And bowed to her as if he did her homage. Without knowing why, she felt that he liked her better than he had ever done before; and with a feeling of relief and gratitude she returned his bow and passed through the door which he held open for her.

It was necessary now to carry everything a step further. With her foot on the threshold she waited a moment longer in a scene which was vanishing even as she looked, and then, as she moved and took Minta's arm and left the room, it changed, it shaped itself differently; it had become, she knew, giving one last look at it over her shoulder, already the past.

WOMAN LOOKING AT A VASE OF FLOWERS

Wallace Stevens   (1879–1955)

Born in Reading, Pennsylvania, Stevens attended Harvard and the New York Law School, receiving his degree in 1903. From 1916 until his death, Stevens was associated with the Hartford Accident and Indemnity Company, of which he became vice president in 1934. He first gained recognition for his writing in 1914, when he won a prize from *Poetry Magazine.* His first book of poems, *Harmonium,* was published in 1923. The last six years of his life saw Stevens receive the Bollinger Prize in poetry, two National Book Awards, and a Pulitzer Prize.

"Woman Looking at a Vase of Flowers" appeared in *Parts of a World* (1942).

It was as if thunder took form upon
The piano, that time: the time when the crude
And jealous grandeurs of sun and sky
Scattered themselves in the garden, like
The wind dissolving into birds,
The clouds becoming braided girls.
It was like the sea poured out again
In east wind beating the shutters at night.

Hoot, little owl within her, how
High blue became particular   10
In the leaf and bud and how the red,
Flicked into pieces, points of air,
Became—how the central, essential red
Escaped its large abstraction, became,
First, summer, then a lesser time,
Then the sides of peaches, of dusky pears.

Hoot how the inhuman colors fell
Into place beside her, where she was,
Like human conciliations, more like
A profounder reconciling, an act,   20
An affirmation free from doubt.
The crude and jealous formlessness
Became the form and the fragrance of things
Without clairvoyance, close to her.

SONG TO ISHTAR

Denise Levertov

See headnote to "Bedtime," page 139.

"Song to Ishtar" appeared in Levertov's collection *O Taste and See* (1964).

The moon is a sow
and grunts in my throat
Her great shining shines through me
so the mud of my hollow gleams
and breaks in silver bubbles

She is a sow
and I a pig and a poet

When she opens her white
lips to devour me I bite back
and laughter rocks the moon

In the black of desire
we rock and grunt, grunt and
shine

THE ARTIST: SUPPLEMENTARY READING

Jane Austen: *Emma*
Robert Frost: "Provide, Provide"
Nathaniel Hawthorne: "The Artist of the Beautiful"
Henrik Ibsen: *Hedda Gabler*
Henry James: *The Golden Bowl*
Ben Jonson: *Epicoene, or the Silent Woman*
Doris Lessing: *The Golden Notebook*
Robert Lowell: "The Banker's Daughter"
W. Somerset Maugham: "The Colonel's Lady"
Mary McCarthy: "Cruel and Barbarous Treatment" and *The Group*
Arthur Miller: *After the Fall*
Dorothy Parker: "Big Blonde"
Alexander Pope: *The Rape of the Lock*
William Shakespeare: *As You Like It* and *The Winter's Tale*
Muriel Spark: *The Prime of Miss Jean Brodie*
Wallace Stevens: "Sunday Morning"
John Updike: "The Bulgarian Poetess"
Kurt Vonnegut, Jr.: "Who Am I This Time?"
Edith Wharton: *The House of Mirth*
Virginia Woolf: *Mrs. Dalloway*

THE WARRIOR

Edouard Manet: *Mademoiselle Victorine in the Costume of an Espada* (French, 1862). [*The Metropolitan Museum of Art, the H. O. Havemeyer Collection. Bequest of Mrs. H. O. Havemeyer, 1929.*]

The warrior initiates action that affects the world. She is the hero as defined by Joseph Campbell: "the champion not of things become but of things becoming; the dragon to be slain by him [her] is precisely the monster of the status quo: Holdfast, the keeper of the past."[1] She is a revolutionary who moves beyond her culture's female role definitions and refuses to be dependent on a man; she therefore ventures alone onto the road of trials, obstacles, and temptations. Symbolically, she descends into the underworld of unknown, uncategorized experience, and she returns wise, whole, and free. In order to become a warrior, she must confront the voices within and without that condemn her independence. She risks destruction at the hands of a patriarchal society which sees her "unfeminine" action as psychologically unhealthy and in need of remedy or as socially and theologically evil and deserving of punishment. Neither Joan of Arc nor Sylvia Plath's Esther, in *The Bell Jar*, can or will adjust to the traditional heroine role: Joan is burned at the stake; Esther is given shock treatments.

Literary portraits of the female warrior include those of traditional women who transcend the limitations of their heroine roles and those of revolutionaries who reject those roles. The heroine, when seen from a different point of view, may be a warrior. From her own perspective, every woman is the hero of her own story. Paul Roche, in "What Makes Her Special?" recognizes that even the shabby, innocuous-looking woman in the crowded cafeteria "walks with what she's chosen to some shore." The static temptress or selfless helpmate may actually be an active person who makes life decisions and affects her world. After all, even Cinderella works all day while she waits for the Prince to come. Whether a female character is seen as heroic depends on the author's point of view. Women are portrayed as heroes when they are protagonists and when we see the world through their eyes. Thus the traditional woman in her role as lover, mother, worker, or friend may be presented as a warrior.

Most novels with a female central character focus on the hero as lover. The narrative pattern of these works represents a reversal of the traditional romance, in which the man does brave deeds in order to win the maiden. The story of a woman's search for a mate may be a version of the quest myth, with the discovery of the Holy Grail or sacred fish replaced by the attainment of love, wealth, and social prestige. In the myth of Cupid and Psyche, Psyche performs labors analogous to those of Hercules in order to win Cupid, and their marriage produces a child, called Pleasure. Richardson's Pamela resists the temptations of immorality and slays the dragon of Squire B——'s lust in order to win the prize, which is the same attractive and wealthy Squire B——. In this sense, the love story may be the female equivalent of the Horatio Alger stories. For a woman, however, virtue rather than hard work makes her worthy of the wealth and happiness which she earns by making a successful marriage.

The mythic prototype of the heroic mother is Demeter (Ceres). In contrast to the wicked stepmother of the Rapunzel and Cinderella stories, Demeter is the good, protective mother whose daughter Persephone (Proserpine) is abducted by Pluto and carried off to the underworld. The terms of this myth are matriarchal because the standard of value is female. Demeter searches for Persephone everywhere and threatens to withdraw fertility from the world and thereby destroy humanity if her daughter is not found. Zeus promises that if Persephone will not eat anything while in Hades, she will be returned to her mother. But because Persephone eats some pomegranate seeds, she is allowed to spend only six months of the year with

Demeter. Demeter's grief during Persephone's six-months absence is said to be responsible for autumn and winter.

The heroism of mothers tends to be tragic because mothers must witness the unhappiness, pain, and/or death of their children (as in Eudora Welty's "A Worn Path") or because the children grow up and leave home. Margaret Drabble, in *Thank You All Very Much*, provides us with the portrait of a woman contemplating her love for her child: "A bad investment, I knew, this affection, and one that would leave me in the dark and the cold in years to come." Whether tragic or not, motherhood in literature often transforms heroines into heroes. Marguerite Johnson, in Maya Angelou's *I Know Why the Caged Bird Sings*, becomes heroic in bearing an illegitimate child because she is forced to assume responsibility for her life and that of her son. As she explains: "I had a baby. He was beautiful and mine. Totally mine. No one had bought him for me. No one had helped me endure the sickly gray months. I had had help in the child's conception, but no one could deny that I had had an immaculate pregnancy." Drabble's Rosamund Stacey credits motherhood with bringing her heroic knowledge:

> There was one thing in the world that I knew about, and that one thing was Octavia. I had lost the taste for half-knowledge. George, I could see, knew nothing with such certainty. I neither envied nor pitied his indifference, for he was myself, the self that but for accident, but for fact, but for chance, but for womanhood, I would still have been.

The qualitites required for motherhood are the same as those required for political leadership. Dilsey, in William Faulkner's *The Sound and the Fury*; Molly Beauchamp, in Faulkner's "The Fire and the Hearth"; and Ma, in John Steinbeck's *The Grapes of Wrath,* are celebrated as nurturing, benevolent monarchs of the home. Queen Elizabeth I and Queen Victoria of England, Catherine the Great of Russia, and Golda Meir of Israel are among many admired and accomplished political leaders and sovereigns.

Traditional women also are heroic as workers. In spite of the cultural myth that women do not work, women constitute 31.5 percent of the full-time and 53.6 percent of the part-time work force in the United States, according to 1973 Department of Labor statistics, and almost all women do unpaid labor in the home. During the struggle for women's suffrage, Alice Duer Miller wrote:

> We hope that the 900,000 sewing machine operatives, the 40,000 saleswomen, the 32,000 laundry operatives, the 20,000 knitting and silk mill girls, the 17,000 women janitors and cleaners, the 12,000 cigar-makers, to say nothing of the 700,000 other women and girls in industry in New York State, will remember when they have drawn off their long gloves and tasted their oysters to tell their dinner partners that they are opposed to woman suffrage because they fear it might take women out of the home.[2]

Thomas Hood's "The Song of the Shirt," Rose Cooke's "Arachne," and Agnes Smedley's *Daughter of Earth* explore the life of women who work in factories and in the home. The nineteenth-century feminist Sojourner Truth reminds us that very few women have been allowed the luxury of idleness:

> That man over there says that women need to be helped into carriages, and lifted over ditches, and to have the best place everywhere. Nobody ever helps me into

carriages, or over mud-puddles, or gives me any best place! And ain't I a woman? Look at me! Look at my arm! I have ploughed and planted, and gathered into barns, and no man could head me! And ain't I a woman? I could work as much and eat as much as a man—when I could get it—and bear the lash as well! And ain't I a woman? I have borne thirteen children, and seen them most all sold off to slavery, and when I cried out with my mother's grief, none but Jesus heard me! And ain't I a woman?

Eldridge Cleaver, in *Soul on Ice*, describes the situation of the strong black woman who is despised for not fulfilling the white middle-class ideal of the "light," delicate woman of luxury. This double-bind situation affects all working-class women and, to some extent, all women who work in or out of the home. The myth of female fragility has served to keep women economically dependent. It also has resulted in sexual and emotional insecurity for the woman who does not fulfill the role of the beautiful and fragile ornament. The woman who succeeds as an ornament may envy the strong, productive woman; the working woman may envy the fragile, dependent woman because she has succeeded in fulfilling the ideal.

In spite of the forces which divide women, they often become warriors to help each other. In the myth of Philomela and Procne, for example, women cooperate to escape male domination. Tereus forcibly seduces Philomela. When he discovers that his wife, Procne, has learned of his crime, he cuts out her tongue and banishes her to the slave quarters. In retribution, Philomela and Procne kill his children and serve them to him for dinner. In Susan Glaspell's "A Jury of Her Peers," neighbor women realize that a woman has murdered her heartless husband, and they conspire to protect her from prosecution.

The prospect of female friendship and cooperation replacing competition is threatening to the patriarchal system. The women's movement, therefore, is often interpreted as a threat to men. Collective resistance to patriarchy begins with the Furies, who are remnants of a matriarchal society. They pursue Orestes for the murder of his mother and, hence, fight for women. The Furies are replaced in later literature by the witch. While in Hades, Persephone preferred the company of Hecate, goddess of the witches, to that of Pluto. The widespread belief that witchcraft (as well as astrology, Tarot cards, and the I Ching) is a matriarchal holdover suggests the revolutionary nature of the witch. The destructive witch appears in William Shakespeare's *Macbeth* and in Thomas Gray's "The Fatal Sisters." The power and the fearsomeness of witches come from their supernatural knowledge and their cooperation with one another in covens. The wise old woman, especially if she was ugly and eccentric, historically was in danger of persecution as a witch.

In twentieth-century literature by feminists, however, the negative image of the forceful, wise woman as witch is replaced by a positive one. Jean Tepperman, in "Witch"; Susan Suttheim, in "For Witches"; and Sylvia Plath, in "Lady Lazarus" and "Strings," embrace the image of the destructive female witch as a positive revolutionary force in the war to free women from patriarchy. By identifying with the formerly negative image in a positive way, such artists dispel the power of the stereotype, which has served to enforce socially acceptable, docile female behavior. In works such as Robin Morgan's "Lesbian Poem," the assertion of lesbianism works in the same way to free women from fear of social condemnation. In "Monster," Morgan embraces the "unfeminine" image of the violent woman, saying, "I want a woman's revolution like a lover. / I lust for it. . . . / I will say, however, that you, men, will have to be freed, / as well, though we women may have to kick and kill you / into freedom."

The warrior, therefore, may be a virgin, mistress, or wife, but she is not controlled by her culture's definitions of that role. The virgin and the spinster may be portrayed as warriors when they refuse to be defined by cultural myths. In Mary Wilkins Freeman's "A New England Nun," the concept of the "old maid" is redefined when the protagonist refuses to marry because she prefers the freedom and beauty of the single life. Similarly, the heroism of Mrs. Warren, in George Bernard Shaw's *Mrs. Warren's Profession*, and of Bertoldt Brecht's Mother Courage renders the terms "prostitute" and "camp follower" ridiculous by their inadequacy to describe these women. Even though Richardson's Clarissa accepts the cultural assumption of the value of chastity, she asserts her independence of the ideal of female subservience and the worthlessness of the "fallen" woman by refusing to marry her rapist, on the grounds that he is morally unworthy of her. Similarly, William Congreve's Millamant and Geoffrey Chaucer's Wife of Bath are warriors because they demand equality in marriage.

The female hero may also be a warrior in the literal sense. According to Greek and Roman mythology, the Amazons fought on equal terms with the toughest male heroes. The descendant of the Amazon in American popular culture is Wonder Woman, who habitually saves women from evil men and makes feminist speeches on the ability of women to save themselves from oppression. The women who battled heroically for the rights of women and against slavery in nineteenth-century America were warriors, but they are seldom portrayed sympathetically in established literature. Female warriors are positively portrayed when they fight for more socially accepted causes. The Anglo-Saxon poems "Judith" and "Elene" and Mark Twain's "Saint Joan of Arc" recount the physical bravery and ability of great female military leaders. William Shakespeare's *Antony and Cleopatra* focuses on the nobility of a great woman monarch.

Cultural forces entrap the virgin, mistress, helpmate, sage, and artist in double-bind situations which preclude direct heroic action. Although these forces also act upon the warrior, she is able to act independently, in some cases, because her actions are validated by a higher authority. Joan of Arc, for example, hears voices from God. Wonder Woman is able to act because she has truly exceptional powers. In other situations, the warrior can act because she lacks the sage's knowledge of the futility of action, because she does not understand all the implications of her situation, or because she does not question or analyze her motives. Henry James, in *The Bostonians*, reveals to the reader that Olive Chancellor's philanthropy is at least partially the result of latent lesbianism and of the desire of a rich woman to know "poor people"; but Chancellor is able to participate in the feminist movement because she has no awareness of divided or suspect motives. Similarly, Brecht's Mother Courage is not paralyzed by guilt because she profits from the war while attempting to protect her sons from conscription.

The wisdom of the female active hero, however, may exceed that of her male counterpart. The male hero often is blinded by the power of his position in the patriarchal society. He needs the fool to teach him to be wise. The female hero who has the acquired knowledge of the powerless may act with clearer vision. While Sophocles's Oedipus blindly ignores the evidence that he has killed his father and married his mother, Sophocles's Antigone understands both her motives for burying her brother in defiance of the law and the consequences of her action.

The female hero's wisdom is often a prerequisite for heroic action—especially for heroism which is in opposition to women's prescribed roles. In Henrik Ibsen's *A Doll's House* and in Erica Jong's *Fear of Flying*, what the protagonist learns makes it impossible for her to continue to be a dependent helpmate. The speaker in Elizabeth Barrett Browning's *Aurora Leigh* refuses marriage because she understands the inherent destructiveness of the supporting role. Charlotte Brontë's Jane Eyre argues for the female right of independent action:

> It is in vain to say human beings ought to be satisfied with tranquility: they must have action; and they will make it if they cannot find it. Millions are condemned to a stiller doom than mine, and millions are in silent revolt against their lot. Nobody knows how many rebellions besides political rebellions ferment in the masses of life which people earth. Women are supposed to be very calm generally: but women feel just as men feel; they need exercise for their faculties, and a field for their efforts as much as their brothers do; they suffer from too rigid a constraint, too absolute a stagnation, precisely as men would suffer; and it is narrow-minded in their more privileged fellow-creatures to say that they ought to confine themselves to making puddings and knitting stockings, to playing on the piano and embroidering bags. It is thoughtless to condemn them, or laugh at them, if they seek to do more or learn more than custom has pronounced necessary for their sex.

If this desire for action causes a woman to refuse the heroine role, her refusal is a revolutionary act.

In works which trace the evolution of a heroine to a hero, the stages of the protagonist's journey are essentially the same for the revolutionary female warrior as for the traditional male hero. According to Joseph Campbell, the active hero's adventure occurs in three stages: (1) the departure, which includes the call to adventure, the initial refusal of the call, supernatural aid, the crossing of the first threshold, and the entering of the belly of the whale; (2) the initiation, which includes the road of trials, the meeting with the god of the opposite sex, the meeting with the figure of temptation of the opposite sex, atonement with the parent of the same sex, and the ultimate boon; and (3) the return, which includes the refusal of the return, the magic flight, rescue from without, the crossing of the return threshold, mastery of the two worlds, and freedom to live.[3] Literary works about the female warrior tend to focus on the departure. Because a woman is not expected to engage in a heroic quest, embarking on the quest at all is a revolutionary and heroic refusal to conform. The preheroic woman often experiences the heroine's situation in exaggerated form. The grotesque extreme of the traditional situation opens her eyes and enables her to see the limitations of her role, forcing her to assume the burdens of active heroism. Medea, for example, is not constitutionally designed to be a selfless helpmate to the insensitive Jason, but when she is asked to play the part of the docile, wronged woman in response to Jason's desertion of her and his marriage to a younger woman, she is inflamed by anger sufficiently to kill their two sons and Jason's new bride.

The female warrior *often* initially refuses the call to adventure. Her final decision depends on a chance incident or an encounter which parallels the supernatural aid given the mythological hero. The title character of Louis Auchincloss's "The 'True Story' of Lavinia Todd" is unhappily married to a prominent lawyer. She loses control at Ada Tilney's dinner party and begins to cry. The hostess's daughter, Fran, leads her upstairs, listens to the story of her life, and tells her that she should write it down for publication. The recognition she receives as an author gives her the strength and clarity of vision to accept a divorce and to begin her own life. Nora's slamming of the door at the end of Ibsen's play is perhaps the best-known example of the crossing of the first threshold. It is only the *first* threshold for women such as Nora because, in the working world, a woman still finds herself dealing with the patriarchal system. The crossing of the first threshold, however, is an important act of refusal. In contemporary history, Rosa Parks, a maid in Montgomery, Alabama, refused to give her seat to a white man on a bus, and thus began the boycott which ended segregation on buses in the South. As Albert Camus writes in *The Rebel*:

> What is a rebel? A man who says no, but whose refusal does not imply a renunciation. . . . The very moment the slave refuses to obey the humiliating orders of his master, he simultaneously rejects the condition of slavery. The act of rebellion carries him far beyond the point he had reached by simply refusing. . . . As a last resort, he is willing to accept the final defeat, which is death, rather than be deprived of the personal sacrament that he would call, for example, freedom.[4]

In the first stage of the hero's adventure, she is transformed from object to subject, from passive observer to active participant, from pursued to pursuer, and from known to knower. Instead of being formed by her culture, she becomes her own active creator because she must invent the self she wishes to be. The androgynous role of the warrior hero is virginal in that she is one-in-herself. Antigone does not need to depend on a man in either the decision to bury her brother or the act. In fact, Creon fears that if he allows her to bury Polyneices without punishment, he will become a woman, and she a man. While Antigone acts, Electra remains inactive, in a state of impotent rage because she looks to father and brother for support. Her brother tells her to see herself as whole and therefore capable of action without male help; specifically, he tells her to accept the warrior in herself.

The female hero does not need a man to complete her because she confronts and internalizes the animus, or the man within. However, as the male hero is often aided by the goddess, the female warrior receives strength from the helpful god or the "light" male. As Bonamy Dobrée writes of Millamant, in William Congreve's *The Way of the World*:

> For Millamant is a woman; she has the inestimable power of giving, but she is rightly jealous of herself, and is not to be undervalued. She is alive and breathing, hiding a real personality behind the only too necessary artifices of her sex. Once assured of Mirabell's love, she divests herself of her armour, and shows a perfect frankness. . . .[5]

In H. Rider Haggard's science-fiction novel *She*, the virgin goddess Ayesha reveals the secret of her immortality to the beloved Leo. When she stands naked before him in the cave, her 2000-year-old self immediately enters the world of time and death, and she disintegrates. The details of this moment are reminiscent of the change from virgin to sexual woman discussed in the introduction to the section on the mistress, but Haggard also provides us with another interpretation:

> Ayesha locked up in her living tomb, waiting from age to age for the coming of her lover, worked but a small change in the order of the world. But Ayesha, strong and happy in her love, clothed with immortal youth, godlike beauty and power, and the wisdom of the centuries, would have revolutionized society, and even perchance have changed the destinies of Mankind. Thus, she opposed herself to the eternal law, and, strong though she was, by it was swept back into nothingness—swept back with shame and hideous mockery!

The love of a man transforms a passive, waiting woman into a potential revolutionary. A current example of this phenomenon in life is the growing number of women who marry so that they will have a man to encourage and aid them in their careers.[6] They assume that men and women (or women and women) can serve as helpmates to each other, without the career of either being sacrificed.

As male heroes meet temptresses and "dark" women, female heroes meet male tempters and "dark" men, who are associated with sexuality and Dionysian energy. Most novels about female protagonists describe the encounter with the rake. The woman is "ruined" if she gives in to him; if she rejects him, she grows spiritually. The sexual encounter with the dark man or god is portrayed positively in works such as Muriel Rukeyser's "Mortal Girl," in which the coming of the god suggests a spiritual or psychological experience. In many works, the tempter is death, who comes in the guise of a lover, as in Emily Dickinson's "Because I could not stop for Death." Similarly, male vampires combine a grotesque eroticism with the threat of death. Such tempters are analogous to the female erotic destroyers found in John Keats's "La Belle Dame sans Merci" and in Nathaniel Hawthorne's "Rappaccini's Daughter."

The meeting with the older guide of the same sex is problematical in works about women. In a few twentieth-century works, such as Virginia Woolf's *To the Lighthouse* and Doris Lessing's *The Four-Gated City*, the warrior is able to recognize the power of the female mentor who has strength and wisdom not acknowledged by her culture. However, because of the denigration of the female principle in Western society and the resulting definition of women as nonmales, the female hero frequently is unable to find the wise female guide, or she may share the prejudices of her culture and be unable to believe in a female mentor. In myth, in fairy tale, and in literature, the good mother and female role model is either dead or ineffectual. Considering the classic "search for the father" theme in literature, Kurt Vonnegut, Jr., writes in *Breakfast of Champions*: "It seems to me that really truthful American novels would have the heroes and heroines alike looking for *mothers* instead [of fathers]. This needn't be embarrassing. It's simply true. A mother is much more useful. I wouldn't feel particularly good if I found another father."

After the stages of encounter and initiation, the hero traditionally returns from the quest: Ibsen's Nora, when she is truly "master of the two worlds" and free to live fully in the family, may choose to live with a man and children again. Generally, however, the female warrior is unlikely to return from her quest. After all, the male hero can expect admiration and encouragement as rewards for his adventurousness. The classic male hero, moreover, is integrally connected with his kingdom. In the fisher king myths (see Jessie Weston's *From Ritual to Romance*) his physical or mental wound causes sterility in the kingdom. When he finds the Holy Grail or the sacred fish and returns from his journey, fertility is restored. Unlike the male hero, the adventurous woman is a deviant. Like all antiheroes, she is unlikely to change the society. The wisdom she brings back from her quest is at odds with the values of the male society, and she may be unable to articulate her new wisdom in the established patriarchal vocabulary and patterns of thought. As discussed in the introduction to the section on the sage, she may be seen only as a fool or a lunatic. The wisdom of Joan of Arc, for example, is incomprehensible to the patriarchal figures who preside over her trial. Even her admiring historians stress her ignorance, in spite of the fact that she demonstrates not only military and political genius but also a psychological understanding of Charles and the other male characters which prompts them to confide in her. Because it cannot be expressed in the male vocabulary and syntax of our society, the wisdom of women, as was explained in relation to the sage, may be trapped within them.

In modern literature and life, both female and male heroes elect not to return to the family and or to the larger social unit. In classical American works such as Herman Melville's *Moby Dick*, Mark Twain's *Huckleberry Finn*, and James Fenimore Cooper's *Leather-stocking Tales,* as well as in the popular western in which the hero rides off alone into the sunset at the end, men avoid women because their presence imposes dehumanizing sex roles. (See Leslie Fiedler's *Love and Death in the American Novel*.) If a man marries, he must settle down and keep a job. Similarly, women are finding it necessary to avoid men in order to achieve psychological integration and freedom and to avoid pressure to conform to female sex role stereotypes. Many modern novels, including Doris Lessing's *The Four-Gated City*, Kurt Vonnegut, Jr.'s, *Cat's Cradle,* Thomas Pynchon's *Gravity's Rainbow*, and Joyce Carol Oates's *Wonderland*, are apocalyptic in that they suggest the total destruction of the past, of the social order, and of human life as we know it. The destruction of society is the logical outgrowth of the hero's inability to return. There is no longer a goal at the end of the road, and so the warrior makes a value of being "on the road," "on the bus," or "moving on."

Bill Haywood, at the 1905 founding convention of the Industrial Workers of the World, suggested a possible model for the return. Historically, the heroic quest for Americans has taken the form of the journey westward, but this journey rests on the premise that American heroes do not return. Haywood explained:

> We fellows out west were once east; . . . if we don't know what we are up against, our fathers probably did. My great-grandfather lived in Boston. My grandfather lived in Iowa. My father carried mail in Colorado before there was a railroad. I have been still farther west, until they told me it was only a few miles to the rolling billows of the Pacific, and I concluded that the Haywood family had better turn back, that we had been driven to the frontiers until there were no more frontiers. So I have come back to Chicago; that is, on the frontier of this industrial union movement, which I hope to see grow throughout this country until it takes in a great majority of the working people, and that these working people will rise in revolt against the capitalist system.[7]

We have yet to see the great literary work about a woman who returns from the heroic quest to fight inequality between the sexes and among the races and classes.

The selections that follow, however, indicate that women who escape entrapment by limiting sex role definitions and who can act directly in the world have a greater chance for fulfillment and social effectiveness than women in any other category included in this anthology. This insistence upon a free and active life distinguishes the warrior from the sage and the artist. The sage is entrapped by her wisdom; the artist is restricted by the need to act indirectly. The warrior may be punished for her violation of the strictures—sexual, religious, or economic—of her society, but inside she is free and whole, having created and acted upon her own inner voices and having openly confronted the world. This anthology, therefore, ends as it begins, with the woman who is one-in-herself and hence can affect her own destiny and influence the world around her.

THE WARRIOR: NOTES

[1]Joseph Campbell, *The Hero with a Thousand Faces* (Princeton, N.J.: Princeton University Press, 1960), p. 337.

[2]"To the Great Dining out Majority," reprinted in Martha Bensley Bruère and Mary Ritter Beard, *Laughing Their Way: Women's Humor in America* (New York: The Macmillan Company, 1934), p. 222.

[3]Campbell, op. cit., passim.

[4](New York: Vintage Books, Random House, Inc., 1956), p. 15.

[5]Bonamy Dobrée, "Congreve," in John Loftis (ed.), *Restoration Drama: Modern Essays in Criticism* (New York: Oxford University Press, 1966), p. 118.

[6]Louise Bickman, "Personality Constructs Distinguishing Women Planning to Marry from Those Planning to Live Independently Immediately after Graduation," dissertation in progress, University of Pennsylvania, 1975.

[7]As reported in "Eloquent Orators on Industrial Unionism," *Miner's Magazine*, Aug. 10, 1905, p. 13.

JUDITH

"Judith" is an anonymous Anglo-Saxon fragment preserved in the British Museum. It is contained in the Cotton Vitellius A XV manuscript, which also contains *Beowulf*. Apparently, "Judith" was at one time transcribed in a separate book, of which the opening pages are now lost; thus the poem begins *in medias res*. Although the true origins of the poem are hidden, scholarship has placed the date for its composition about A.D. 930. As it stands in manuscript, the poem is in the late West Saxon dialect, but scholars have hypothesized that it might have been translated from a Northumbrian or Anglian source. The poem essentially follows the story of Judith as it appears in the Vulgate Bible, and it falls into that category of the religious epic depicting the deeds of a heroic saint.

. . . She did not lose faith in his gifts on this far-spreading earth; then truly she found protection there in the famous Prince when she most needed the favour of the highest Judge, that He, the Lord of creation, should guard her against the greatest danger. The glorious Father in heaven bestowed that boon on her because she never failed in firm faith in the Almighty. Then Holofernes, as I heard, eagerly sent forth a bidding to wine, and dressed up dainties wondrously sumptuous. The prince of men bade all the eldest thanes come; the shield-bearing warriors attended in great haste; the chiefs of the people came to the mighty leader. It was on the fourth day that Judith, wise in thought, a woman of fairy beauty, first sought him.

X

Then they went to sit down at the banquet, exulting to carousal, all his companions in evil, bold corslet warriors. Often down the benches there deep bowls were borne, brimming beakers, too, and goblets for the guests. Daring shield-warriors, doomed to death, laid hold on them, though the leader, the dread master of men, had no thought of his fate. Then Holofernes, gold-friend of men, grew merry with the pouring out of wine; he laughed and called aloud, clamoured and made outcries, so that the children of men could hear from afar how he of stern mood stormed and shouted; proud and fevered by mead, he often urged the guests on the benches to bear themselves bravely. Thus the wicked one, the stern giver of treasure, drenched his officers all day in wine, till they lay swooning; he vanquished all his veterans with drink as if they were stricken by death, void of all virtue. Thus did the prince of men order the guests to be plied until the dark night drew near the children of men.

Then, steeped in malice, he ordered the blessed maid to be brought with speed, laden with rings, adorned with circlets, to his bed. Quickly, the retainers did as their prince, the chief of corslet warriors, bade. Straightway they stepped to the guest-house where they found wise Judith; and then the shield-warriors promptly led the noble maid to the lofty pavilion, where the mighty man was ever wont to rest at night, Holofernes abhorred by the Saviour. There was a fair curtain, all golden, hung round the leader's couch, so that the evil man, the prince of warriors, could look through on each of the sons of men who entered there, and no man on him, unless the proud man bade one of his mighty warriors draw nearer him to hold council. Quickly then they brought the wise woman to the couch; then, troubled in mind, the men went to proclaim to their lord that the holy virgin had been led to his pavilion.

Then the renowned ruler of cities grew jubilant in his heart; he thought to stain the radiant woman with pollution and foulness. The glorious Judge, the Prince of majesty, was not minded to let that come to pass, but He, the Lord, the Master of warriors, kept him from that thing. Then the fiendish wanton with evil intent went to seek his bed with a band of followers, where forthwith in one night he was to lose his life. Then the unsparing sovereign of men had reached on earth his violent death, such a one as he had deserved while he dwelt in this world under the canopy of the clouds. Thus, fuddled with wine, the chieftain fell in the midst of his couch, as if he had no wits in his mind; the warriors passed out of the chamber with utmost haste, men sated with wine, who had brought the traitor, the hateful tyrant, to his bed for the last time.

Then did the Saviour's glorious servant ponder deeply how she might most easily spoil the monster of life, before he awoke with foul lust. Then the Creator's handmaiden, with curling tresses, grasped a sharp sword hardened in the storms of battle, and with her right hand drew it from the scabbard. Then she began to call upon the name of the Lord of heaven, the Saviour of all who dwell upon the earth, and she spoke these words:

'I pray to Thee, God of creation, Spirit of comfort, Son all powerful, Glory of the Trinity, for Thy mercy in my need. Now is my heart greatly kindled and mournful my mood, sorely stirred with sorrows; give me, O Lord of heaven, victory and true faith, that with this sword I may cut down this dealer of sudden death; grant me my salvation, O stern Prince of men; never had I greater need of Thy mercy. Avenge now, O Lord of might, noble Giver of glory, what angers my mind, kindles my heart.'

Then the highest Judge straightway inspired her with courage, as He does all men here who seek His aid in a right mind and true faith. Then her heart grew large; hope was renewed in the holy maid. Then she grasped the unbeliever hard by his hair; with her hands she drew him towards her to his shame, and with cunning laid the malicious one down, the hateful man, as she best could contrive to do with the caitiff. Then the maiden with curling tresses struck the hostile foe with gleaming sword, so that she cut his neck half through; and, drunken and stricken, he lay in a swoon. He was not yet dead, wholly lifeless; the undaunted woman once again fiercely smote the heathen hound, so that his head rolled forth on the floor. The foul carcass lay dead behind; the spirit departed elsewhere under the deep cliff, and there it was humbled, bound for ever in torment, surrounded with serpents, fettered with agonies, held fast in hell-fire after death. Nor need he hope, engulfed in gloom, that he may leave that hall of serpents, but there he must dwell for ever without end in that dark home, empty of joy.

XI

Judith then had won illustrious fame in fight, as God granted unto her, the Prince of heaven, who gave her victory. Then the wise maiden swiftly brought the warrior's head all bloody in the bag in which her servant, a fair-cheeked woman of excellent virtue, had fetched thither the food for them both, and Judith gave it then all gory into her hand, to her attendant, the prudent woman, to bear home. Forwards they fared thence, the two valorous women, until, bold-hearted, they passed clear of the host, the triumphant maidens, so that they could clearly behold Bethulia, the walls of the fair city shining. Then, ring-adorned, they sped their steps, till, glad of heart, they had reached the rampart gate. Warriors were sitting; watchmen were keeping guard in the stronghold, as Judith, the maiden of wisdom, the woman of valour, had bidden the sorrowing people before, when she went on her venture. Then had the loved one come again to her people, and then the wise woman quickly commanded one of the men to come to her from the far-spreading fortress and admit her with speed through the rampart gate, and she spoke these words to the victorious people:

'I am able to tell you a thing of note, that no longer you need sorrow in soul. God, the glorious King, is gracious unto you. That has been made manifest far throughout the world, that glorious success is coming to you in splendour, and that exaltation has been granted after the afflictions you long have endured.'

Then the citizens were glad when they heard how the holy maiden spoke over the high rampart. The people rejoiced, the host hastened to the fortress gate, men and women together, old and young, in troops and throngs, in swarms and crowds; surged and ran in thousands towards the maiden of the Lord. The hearts of all men in the mead city were made glad when they learned that Judith was come again to her home, and then in haste they let her in with reverence. Then the wise maiden, decked with gold, bade her heedful handmaid uncover the warrior's head and show it all bleeding for a sign to the citizens of how she had sped in battle. Then the noble woman spoke to all the host:

'Victorious heroes, chiefs of the people, here you can clearly behold the head of the most hateful heathen warrior, of Holofernes now dead, who most among men dealt us out death, bitter sorrows, and was minded to do yet more; but God did not grant him longer life to lay afflictions upon us. With God's help I reft him of life. Now I wish to pray all of you citizens and shield-bearing warriors to fit yourselves forthwith for fight. When God the Creator, the merciful King, shall send from the east the shining light, bear forth the shields, the bucklers before your breasts and the corslets, the gleaming helms, into the thick of the foe; lay low the leaders, the fated chiefs, with bloody blades. Your enemies are doomed to death, and you shall gain glory, fame in the fight, as the mighty Lord has shown you by my hand.'

Then the band of bold men was quickly made ready, men brave in battle; the valiant men and warriors marched out, bore banners of victory; they set straight forward to the fight, heroes beneath their helmets, from the sacred stronghold at break of dawn; the shields rang, resounded loudly. The lean wolf in the wood rejoiced at that, and the dark raven, the bird greedy for slaughter; both knew that the warriors purposed to provide them with a feast of fated men; and behind them flew the dewy-feathered eagle, hungry for food; dark-coated, horny-beaked, it sang a song of war. The men of battle marched on, warriors to the strife, protected by shields, hollow linden targes—they who erstwhile had borne the flaunting of foreigners, the taunt of the heathen. All the Assyrians were rigorously requited for that at the spear-play when the Hebrews under their banners had come upon the camp. Then keenly they shot forth showers of arrows, adders of war, from their bows of horn, strong shafts; the raging warriors loudly stormed, cast spears into the press of brave men; wroth were the heroes, the dwellers in the land, against the hateful race; sternly they stepped forward; stout of heart, they harshly aroused their ancient foes overcome by mead. The men with their hands drew from the sheaths the brightly adorned blades with trusty edges; fiercely they smote the Assyrian warriors, contrivers of evil; they spared no living man of the host, mean or mighty, whom they could overcome.

XII

So all morning the clansmen pursued the foreign people, until those who were angered, the chief guardians of the host, perceived that the Hebrews had violently shown them the stroke of the sword. They went to declare that in words before the eldest thanes, roused up the warriors and in terror announced to them sudden tidings, a morning alarm to men overcome by mead, dread play of swords. Then forthwith, as I heard, heroes doomed to perish shook off sleep, and sad men pressed in crowds towards the pavilion of the evil one, Holofernes. They meant straightway to make known the battle to their lord, before the terror, the might of the Hebrews, came down upon him. All supposed that the prince of men and the fair maid were together in the beautiful tent, Judith the noble and the lecher, terrible and fierce. Yet there was not one of the earls who dared awaken the warrior, or seek to find out how the soldier had fared with the sacred maiden, the virgin of the Lord. The troop drew near, the host of the Hebrews; they fought hard with keen swords; fiercely with blood-stained brands they made requital for ancient quarrels, for old grudges. The glory of the Assyrians was destroyed in that day's work, their haughtiness made humble. The men stood round their prince's pavilion, exceeding bold but gloomy in mind. Then all together they, without God to believe in, began to shout, to call loudly and to gnash their teeth, grinding their teeth in sorrow. Then their glory was past, their success and deeds of prowess. The earls wished to waken their friendly lord; they did not succeed. Then tardily and late one of the warriors grew so bold as to venture undaunted into the tent, so strongly need drove him. Then he found his bestower of gold lying pale on the bed, reft of his spirit, despoiled of life. Then forthwith he fell cold on the ground; fierce in heart, he began to tear his hair and his robe also, and spoke these words to the warriors who in sadness remained there without:

'Here is our ruin revealed and shown to be at hand, that now in tribulation the time has come upon us when we must perish together, fall in fight. Here lies our ruler, headless, hewn by the sword.'

Then, sad of soul, they cast their weapons down; despairing, they hastened to flee. At their back fought a powerful host, until the greatest part of the army were stretched on the field of victory, laid low by war, hewn by swords, a delight to the wolves and also a joy to birds greedy for slaughter. Those who lived fled from the shields of their foes. Behind them went the army of the Hebrews, honoured with victory, made glorious with fame; the Lord God, the Almighty Prince, gave them fair help. Then the valiant heroes hastily wrought a passage with their blood-stained blades through the press of foemen; they hacked the targes, cleft the roof of shields. The fighters were enraged in the conflict, the Hebrew men; the warriors lusted exceedingly at that time after battle. There fell to earth the greater part of Assyrian nobility, the hateful race; few came alive to their native land. Valiant men turned back, warriors in retreat, amid carnage, reeking corpses. The dwellers in the land had a chance to spoil the most hateful ones, their ancient foes now lifeless, of bloody booty, beautiful ornaments, shields and broad swords, brown helmets, precious treasures. The guardians of their country had gloriously conquered their foes on the field of battle, put their old enemies to sleep with swords; those who were most hateful to them of living nations lay on the field.

Then all the tribe, most famous of peoples, proud, curly-haired, bore and brought to the fair city of Bethulia for the space of a month helmets and hip-swords, grey corslets, war-trappings of men decked with gold, treasures more splendid than any man among the sages can tell. The warriors won all that by courage, bold in battle under the banners by the wise counsel of Judith, the valorous virgin. The warlike earls brought to her from the pursuit the sword and blood-stained helmet of Holofernes as a guerdon, likewise wide corslets decked with red gold and all the wealth and private property that the stern prince of warriors possessed, rings and bright treasures; they gave that to the fair woman of wisdom. Judith ascribed the glory of all that to the Lord of hosts who endued her with honour, fame in the realm of the world and likewise reward in heaven, the meed of victory in the splendour of the sky, because she ever held true faith in the Almighty. At the end she doubted not at all of the reward which long while she had yearned for. Therefore glory for ever be to the dear Lord who in His own mercy created the wind and the airs, the skies and spacious realms, and likewise the fierce streams and the joys of heaven.

THE WAY OF THE WORLD

William Congreve   (1670–1729)

The son of an army officer, Congreve attended college briefly in Dublin and began reading for the law in London. He was catapulted to fame at the age of twenty-three by his first comedy, *The Old Bachelor*. Thereafter he wrote for the stage, including the libretto for Handel's opera *Semele*, until his masterpiece, *The Way of the World*, was coolly received. He devoted himself to society; he never married.

This debate on marriage comes from the fourth act of *The Way of the World*, produced in 1700.

MILLAMANT. Ay, ay, ha, ha, ha,
Like Phoebus *sung the no less am'rous Boy.*

Enter Mirabell.

MIRABELL. ————*Like* Daphne *she as lovely and as Coy.* Do you lock your self up from me, to make my search more Curious? Or is this pretty Artifice Contriv'd, to Signifie that here the Chase must end, and my pursuit be Crown'd, for you can fly no further.—

MILLAMANT. Vanity! No————I'll fly and be follow'd to the last moment, tho' I am upon the very Verge of Matrimony, I expect you shou'd solicite me as much as if I were wavering at the grate of a Monastery, with one foot over the threshold. I'll be solicited to the very last, nay and afterwards.

MIRABELL. What, after the last?

MILLAMANT. O, I should think I was poor and had nothing to bestow, if I were reduc'd to an Inglorious ease; and free'd from the Agreeable fatigues of sollicitation.

MIRABELL. But do not you know, that when favours are conferr'd upon Instant and tedious Sollicitation, that they diminish in their value, and that both the giver loses the grace, and the receiver lessens his Pleasure?

MILLAMANT. It may be in things of common Application; but never sure in Love. O, I hate a Lover, that can dare to think, he draws a moments air, Independent on the Bounty of his Mistress. There is not so Impudent a thing in Nature, as the sawcy look of an assured man, Confident of Success. The Pedantick arrogance of a very Husband, has not so Pragmatical an Air. Ah! I'll never marry, unless I am first made sure of my will and pleasure.

MIRABELL. Wou'd you have 'em both before Marriage? Or will you be contented with the first now, and stay for the other till after grace?

MILLAMANT. Ah don't be Impertinent————My dear Liberty, shall I leave thee? My faithful Solitude, my darling Contemplation, must I bid you then Adieu? ay-h adieu.—my morning thoughts, agreeable wakings, indolent slumbers, all ye *douceurs*, ye *Someils du Matin*, adieu—I can't do't, 'tis more than Impossible—positively *Mirabell*, I'll lie a Bed in a morning as long as I please.

MIRABELL. Then I'll get up in a morning as early as I please.

MILLAMANT. Ah! Idle Creature, get up when you will———and dee hear, I won't be call'd names after I'm Married; positively I won't be call'd Names.

MIRABELL. Names!

MILLAMANT. Ay as Wife, Spouse, My dear, Joy, Jewel, Love, Sweet heart and the rest of that Nauseous Cant, in which Men and their Wives are so fulsomely familiar,———I shall never bear that,———Good *Mirabell* don't let us be familiar or fond, nor kiss before folks, like my Lady *Fadler* and Sr. *Francis*: Nor goe to *Hide-Park* together the first *Sunday* in a New Chariot, to provoke Eyes and Whispers; And then never to be seen there together again; as if we were proud of one another the first Week, and asham'd of one another for ever After. Let us never Visit together, nor go to a Play together, But let us be very strange and well bred: let us be as strange as if we had been married a great while; and as well bred as if we were not marri'd at all.

MIRABELL. Have you any more Conditions to offer? Hitherto your demands are pretty reasonable.

MILLAMANT. Trifles,———As liberty to pay and receive visits to and from whom I please, to write and receive Letters, without Interrogatories or wry Faces on your part. To wear what I please; and choose Conversation with regard only to my own taste; to have no obligation upon me to converse with Wits that I don't like, because they are your acquaintance; or to be intimate with Fools, because they may be your Relations. Come to Dinner when I please, dine in my dressing room when I'm out of humour without giving a reason. To have my Closet Inviolate; to be sole Empress of my Tea-table, which you must never presume to approach without first asking leave. And lastly, where ever I am, you shall always knock at the door before you come in. These Articles subscrib'd, If I continue to endure you a little longer, I may by degrees dwindle into a Wife.

MIRABELL. Your bill of fare is something advanc'd in this latter account. Well, have I Liberty to offer Conditions—that when you are dwindl'd into a Wife, I may not be beyond Measure enlarg'd into a Husband?

MILLAMANT. You have free leave; propose your utmost, speak and spare not.

MIRABELL. I thank you. *Inprimis* then, I Covenant that your acquaintance be General; that you admit no sworn Confident, or Intimate of your own Sex; No she friend to skreen her affairs under your Countenance and tempt you to make tryal of a Mutual Secresie. No Decoy-Duck to wheadle you a *fop*———*scrambling* to the Play in a Mask———then bring you home in a pretended fright, when you think you shall be found out. ———And rail at me for missing the Play, and disappointing the Frolick which you had to pick me up and prove my Constancy.

MILLAMANT. Detestable *Inprimis*! I go to the Play in a Mask!

MIRABELL. *Item*, I Article, that you continue to like your own Face, as long as I shall. And while it passes Current with me, that you endeavour not to new Coin it. To which end, together with all Vizards for the day, I prohibit all Masks for the Night, made of oil'd skins and I know not what———Hog's-bones, Hare's-gall, Pig-water, and the marrow of a roasted Cat. In short, I forbid all Commerce with the Gentlewoman in *what-de-call-it*-Court. *Item*, I shut my doors against all Bauds with Baskets, and penny-worths of *Muslin, China, Fans, Atlases*, &c.—*Item* when you shall be Breeding—

MILLAMANT. Ah! Name it not.

MIRABELL. Which may be presum'd, with a blessing on our endeavours—

MILLAMANT. Odious endeavours!

MIRABELL. I denounce against all strait-Laceing, Squeezing for a Shape, till you mold my boy's head like a Sugar-loaf; and instead of a Man-child, make me the Father to a Crooked-billet. Lastly to the Dominion of the *Tea-Table*, I submit.—But with *proviso*, that you exceed not in your province; but restrain your self to Native and Simple *Tea-Table* drinks, as *Tea, Chocolate* and *Coffee*. As likewise to Genuine and, Authoriz'd *Tea-table* talk,———such as mending of Fashions, spoiling Reputations, railing at absent Friends, and so forth—but that on no account you encroach upon the mens prerogative, and presume to drink healths, or toste fellows; for prevention of which; I banish all *Foreign Forces*, all Auxiliaries to the *Tea-Table*, as *Orange-Brandy*, all *Anniseed, Cinamon, Citron* and *Barbado's-Waters*, together with *Ratifia* and the most noble Spirit of *Clary*,———but for *Couslip-Wine, Poppy-Water* and all *Dormitives*, those I allow,———these *proviso's* admitted, in other things I may prove a tractable and complying Husband.

MILLAMANT. O horrid *proviso's*! filthy strong Waters! I toste fellows, Odious Men! I hate your Odious *proviso's*.

MIRABELL. Then wee're agreed. Shall I kiss your hand upon the Contract? and here comes one to be a witness to the Sealing of the Deed.

THE SCHOOLMISTRESS

William Shenstone   (1714–1763)

The son of a churchwarden, Shenstone entered Oxford in 1732, and although he remained there for ten years, he did not take a degree. In 1745 he bought the estate of Leasowes at Halesowen, where he had been born, and devoted his energy and finances to its beautification, which gained him fame as one of the pioneers of English landscape gardening. Shenstone never married, and although he wrote verse throughout his life, adverse criticism led him never to publish beyond the two volumes brought out during his years at Oxford.

"The Schoolmistress," a portrait of Shenstone's own teacher, Sarah Lloyd, was published in 1742.

IN IMITATION OF SPENSER.

Auditae voces, vagitus et ingens,
Infantumque animae flentes in limine primo.   VIRG.

ADVERTISEMENT.

What particulars in Spenser were imagined most proper for the author's imitation on this occasion, are his language, his simplicity, his manner of description, and a peculiar tenderness of sentiment remarkable throughout his works.

1

    Ah me! full sorely is my heart forlorn,
    To think how modest worth neglected lies,
    While partial Fame doth with her blasts adorn
    Such deeds alone, as pride and pomp disguise;
    Deeds of ill sort, and mischievous emprize:
    Lend me thy clarion, Goddess! let me try
    To sound the praise of Merit, ere it dies;
    Such as I oft have chaunced to espy
Lost in the dreary shades of dull obscurity.

2

    In every village mark'd with little spire,   10
    Embower'd in trees, and hardly known to fame,
    There dwells, in lowly shed and mean attire,
    A matron old, whom we schoolmistress name,
    Who boasts unruly brats with birch to tame;
    They grieven sore, in piteous durance pent,
    Awed by the power of this relentless dame,
    And ofttimes, on vagaries idly bent,
For unkempt hair, or task unconn'd, are sorely shent.

3

    And all in sight doth rise a birchen tree,
    Which Learning near her little dome did stow,   20
    Whilom a twig of small regard to see,
    Though now so wide its waving branches flow,
    And work the simple vassals mickle woe;
    For not a wind might curl the leaves that blew,
    But their limbs shudder'd, and their pulse beat low,
    And as they look'd they found their horror grew,
And shaped it into rods, and tingled at the view.

4

    So have I seen (who has not, may conceive),
    A lifeless phantom near a garden placed,
    So doth it wanton birds of peace bereave,   30

Of sport, of song, of pleasure, of repast;
They start, they stare, they wheel, they look aghast;
Sad servitude! such comfortless annoy
May no bold Briton's riper age e'er taste!
Ne superstition clog his dance of joy,
Ne vision empty, vain, his native bliss destroy.

5

Near to this dome is found a patch so green,
On which the tribe their gambols do display.
And at the door imprisoning board is seen,
Lest weakly wights of smaller size should stray,　　　　　　40
Eager, perdie, to bask in sunny day!
The noises intermix'd, which thence resound,
Do Learning's little tenement betray;
Where sits the dame, disguised in look profound,
And eyes her fairy throng, and turns her wheel around.

6

Her cap, far whiter than the driven snow,
Emblem right meet of decency does yield;
Her apron, dyed in grain, as blue, I trow,
As in the harebell that adorns the field;
And in her hand, for scepter, she does wield　　　　　　50
Tway birchen sprays; with anxious fear entwined,
With dark distrust, and sad repentance fill'd,
And stedfast hate, and sharp affliction join'd,
And fury uncontroll'd, and chastisement unkind.

7

Few but have kenn'd, in semblance meet portray'd,
The childish faces, of old Æol's train,
Libs, Notus, Auster: these in frowns array'd,
How then would fare on earth, or sky, or main,
Were the stern god to give his slaves the rein?
And were not she rebellious breasts to quell,　　　　　　60
And were not she her statutes to maintain,
The cot no more, I ween, were deem'd the cell
Where comely Peace of Mind, and decent Order dwell.

8

A russet stole was o'er her shoulders thrown,
A russet kirtle fenced the nipping air;
'Twas simple russet, but it was her own;
'Twas her own country bred the flock so fair;
'Twas her own labour did the fleece prepare;
And sooth to say, her pupils, ranged around,
Through pious awe, did term it passing rare;　　　　　　70

For they in gaping wonderment abound,
And think, no doubt, she been the greatest wight on ground.

9

   Albeit ne flattery did corrupt her truth,
Ne pompous title did debauch her ear;
Goody, good-woman, gossip, n'aunt, forsooth,
Or dame, the sole additions she did hear;
Yet these she challenged, these she held right dear;
Ne would esteem him act as mought behove,
Who should not honour'd eld with these revere;
For never title yet so mean could prove,   80
But there was eke a mind which did that title love.

10

   One ancient hen she took delight to feed,
The plodding pattern of the busy dame,
Which ever and anon, impell'd by need,
Into her school, begirt with chickens, came,
Such favour did her past deportment claim;
And, if neglect had lavish'd on the ground
Fragment of bread, she would collect the same;
For well she knew, and quaintly could expound,   90
What sin it were to waste the smallest crumb she found.

11

   Herbs too, she knew, and well of each could speak,
That in her garden sipp'd the silvery dew,
Where no vain flower disclosed a gaudy streak,
But herbs for use, and physick, not a few,
Of grey renown, within those borders grew;
The tufted basil, pun-provoking thyme,
Fresh baum, and marygold of chearful hue,
The lowly gill, that never dares to climb,
And more I fain would sing, disdaining here to rhyme.

12

   Yet euphrasy may not be left unsung,   100
That gives dim eyes to wander leagues around;
And pungent radish, biting infant's tongue;
And plantain ribb'd, that heals the reaper's wound;
And marjoram sweet, in shepherd's posie found;
And lavender, whose pikes of azure bloom
Shall be, erewhile, in arid bundles bound,
To lurk amidst the labours of her loom,
And crown her kerchiefs clean with mickle rare perfume.

13

   And here trim rosemarine, that whilom crown'd
The daintiest garden of the proudest peer;   110
Ere, driven from its envied site, it found

A sacred shelter for its branches here;
Where edged with gold its glittering skirts appear.
O wassel days! O customs meet and well!
Ere this was banish'd from its lofty sphere;
Simplicity then sought this humble cell,
Nor ever would she more with thane and lordling dwell.

14

Here oft the dame, on Sabbath's decent eve,
Hymned such psalms as Sternhold forth did mete;
If winter 'twere, she to her hearth did cleave,   120
But in her garden found a summer-seat:
Sweet melody! to hear her then repeat
How Israel's sons, beneath a foreign king,
While taunting foemen did a song entreat,
All for the nonce untuning every string,
Uphung their useless lyres—small heart had they to sing.

15

For she was just, and friend to virtuous lore,
And pass'd much time in truly virtuous deed;
And, in those elfins' ears, would oft deplore,
The times when Truth by Popish rage did bleed,   130
And tortious death was true Devotion's meed;
And simple Faith in iron chains did mourn,
That nould on wooden image place her creed;
And lawny saints in smouldering flames did burn:
Ah! dearest Lord! forfend thilk days should e'er return.

16

In elbow-chair, like that of Scottish stem
By the sharp tooth of cankering Eld defaced,
In which, when he receives his diadem,
Our sovereign prince and liefest liege is placed,
The matron sate; and some with rank she graced,   140
(The source of children's and of courtiers' pride!)
Redress'd affronts, for vile affronts there pass'd,
And warn'd them not the fretful to deride,
But love each other dear, whatever them betide.

17

Right well she knew each temper to descry,
To thwart the proud, and the submiss to raise;
Some with vile copper prize exalt on high,
And some entice with pittance small of praise;
And other some with baleful sprig she 'frays:
Even absent, she the reins of power doth hold,   150
While with quaint arts the giddy crowd she sways;
Forewarn'd, if little bird their pranks behold,
'Twill whisper in her ear, and all the scene unfold.
. . . .

THE SPEECH OF MISS POLLY BAKER

Benjamin Franklin   (1706–1790)

Born in Boston, the fifteenth child of a soap and candle maker, Franklin rose to eminence in America and Europe as a scientist, inventor, printer, author, tradesman, statesman, patriot, and diplomat. His role in the American Revolution and in the adoption of the Constitution can scarcely be exaggerated.

"The Speech of Miss Polly Baker" first appeared in the *General Advertiser* in London on April 15, 1747, and was reprinted fifteen times in Britain and four times in America that same year. It was reprinted in Sweden and France, where it was used to support deism and the French Revolution.

The speech of Miss Polly Baker before a Court of Judicature, at Connecticut near Boston in New England; where she was prosecuted the fifth time for having a bastard child: Which influenced the court to dispense with her punishment, and which induced one of her judges to marry her the next day—by whom she had fifteen children.

"May it please the honorable bench to indulge me in a few words: I am a poor, unhappy woman, who have no money to fee lawyers to plead for me, being hard put to it to get a living. I shall not trouble your honors with long speeches; for I have not the presumption to expect that you may, by any means, be prevailed on to deviate in your sentence from the law, in my favor. All I humbly hope is that your honors would charitably move the governor's goodness on my behalf, that my fine may be remitted. This is the fifth time, gentlemen, that I have been dragged before your court on the same account; twice I have paid heavy fines, and twice have been brought to public punishment, for want of money to pay those fines. This may have been agreeable to the laws, and I don't dispute it; but since laws are sometimes unreasonable in themselves, and therefore repealed; and others bear too hard on the subject in particular circumstances, and therefore there is left a power somewhere to dispense with the execution of them; I take the liberty to say that I think this law, by which I am punished, both unreasonable in itself, and particularly severe with regard to me, who have always lived an inoffensive life in the neighborhood where I was born, and defy my enemies (if I have any) to say I ever wronged any man, woman, or child. Abstracted from the law, I cannot conceive (may it please your honors) what the nature of my offense is. I have brought five fine children into the world, at the risk of my life; I have maintained them well by my own industry, without burdening the township, and would have done it better if it had not been for the heavy charges and fines I have paid. Can it be a crime (in the nature of things, I mean) to add to the king's subjects, in a new country, that really wants people? I own it, I should think it rather a praiseworthy than a punishable action. I have debauched no other woman's husband, nor enticed any other youth; these things I never was charged with; nor has anyone the least cause of complaint against me, unless, perhaps, the minister of justice, because I have had children without being married, by which they have missed a wedding fee. But can this be a fault of mine? I appeal to your honors. You are pleased to allow I don't want sense; but I must be stupefied to the last degree, not to prefer the honorable state of wedlock to the condition I have lived in. I always was, and still am, willing to enter into it; and doubt not by behaving well in it, having all the industry, frugality, fertility, and skill in economy appertaining to a good wife's character. I defy anyone to say I ever refused an offer of the sort: on the contrary, I readily consented to the only proposal of marriage that ever was made me, which was when I was a virgin, but too easily confiding in the person's sincerity that made it, I unhappily lost my honor by trusting to his; for he got me with child, and then forsook me.

"That very person, you all know, he is now become a magistrate of this country; and I had hopes he would have appeared this day on the bench, and have endeavored to moderate the court in my favor; then I should have scorned to have mentioned it; but I must now complain of it, as unjust and unequal, that my betrayer and undoer, the first cause of all my faults and miscarriages (if they must be deemed such), should be advanced to honor and power in this government that punishes my misfortunes with stripes and infamy. I should be told, 'tis like, that were there no act of assembly in the case, the precepts of religion are violated by my transgressions. If mine is a religious offense, leave it to religious punishments. You have already excluded me from the comforts of your church communion. Is not that sufficient? You believe I have offended heaven, and must suffer eternal fire: Will not that be sufficient? What need is there then of your additional fines and whipping? I own I do not think as you do, for, if I thought what you call a sin was really such, I could not presumptuously commit it. But, how can it be believed that heaven is angry at my having children, when to the little done by me toward it, God has been pleased to add his divine skill and admirable workmanship in the formation of their bodies, and crowned the whole by furnishing them with rational and immortal souls?

"Forgive me, gentlemen, if I talk a little extravagantly on these matters; I am no divine, but if you, gentlemen, must be making laws, do not turn natural and useful actions into crimes by your prohibitions. But take into your wise consideration the great and growing number of bachelors in the country, many of whom, from the mean fear of the expenses of a family, have never sincerely and honorably courted a woman in their lives; and by their manner of living leave unproduced (which is little better than murder) hundreds of their posterity to the thousandth generation. Is not this a greater offense against the public good than mine? Compel them, then, by law, either to marriage, or to pay double the fine of fornication every year. What must poor young women do, whom customs and nature forbid to solicit the men, and who cannot force themselves upon husbands, when the laws take no care to provide them any, and yet severely punish them if they do their duty without them; the duty of the first and great command of nature and nature's God, *increase and multiply*; a duty, from the steady performance of which nothing has been able to deter me, but for its sake I have hazarded the loss of the public esteem, and have frequently endured public disgrace and punishment; and therefore ought, in my humble opinion, instead of a whipping, to have a statue erected to my memory."

THE FATAL SISTERS

Thomas Gray   (1716–1771)

Born in London, where his father was an exchange broker, Gray lived with his mother, Dorothy Antrobus, after his parents' separation. Gray was educated by his uncles at Eton and Cambridge, and he visited the Continent in 1739, returning to England in 1741. In 1744 he received his law degree, though he never practiced; he spent the remainder of his life in scholarship at Cambridge. He never married.

A manuscript copy of "The Fatal Sisters," dated 1761, shows that it was first titled "The Song of the Valkyries." It was given its present title and first published in the 1768 edition of *Poems by Mr. Gray*.

PREFACE

> *In the Eleventh Century* Sigurd, *Earl of the Orkney-Islands, went with a fleet of ships and a considerable body of troops into Ireland, to the assistance of* Sictryg *with the silken beard, who was then making war on his father-in-law* Brian, *King of Dublin: the Earl and all his forces were cut to pieces, and* Sictryg *was in danger of a total defeat; but the enemy had a greater loss by the death of* Brian, *their King, who fell in the action. On Christmas-day, (the day of the battle,) a Native of* Caithness *in Scotland saw at a distance a number of persons on horseback riding full speed towards a hill, and seeming to enter into it. Curiosity led him to follow them, till looking through an opening in the rocks he saw twelve gigantic figures resembling women: they were all employed about a loom; and as they wove, they sung the following dreadful Song; which when they had finished, they tore the web into twelve pieces, and (each taking her portion) galloped Six to the North and as many to the South.*

Now the storm begins to lower,
(Haste, the loom of Hell prepare,)
Iron-sleet of arrowy shower
Hurtles in the darken'd air.

Glitt'ring lances are the loom,
Where the dusky warp we strain,

Weaving many a Soldier's doom,
Orkney's woe, and *Randver's* bane.

See the griesly texture grow,
('Tis of human entrails made,)
And the weights, that play below,   10
Each a gasping Warriour's head.

Shafts for shuttles, dipt in gore,
Shoot the trembling cords along.
Sword, that once a Monarch bore,
Keep the tissue close and strong.

Mista black, terrific Maid,
Sangrida, and *Hilda* see,
Join the wayward work to aid:
'Tis the woof of victory.   20

Ere the ruddy sun be set,
Pikes must shiver, javelins sing,
Blade with clattering buckler meet,
Hauberk crash, and helmet ring.

(Weave the crimson web of war)
Let us go, and let us fly,
Where our Friends the conflict share,
Where they triumph, where they die.

As the paths of fate we tread,
Wading thro' th' ensanguin'd field:
Gondula, and *Geira*, spread   30
O'er the youthful King your shield.

We the reins to slaughter give,
Ours to kill, and ours to spare:
Spite of danger he shall live.
(Weave the crimson web of war.)

They, whom once the desart-beach
Pent within its bleak domain,
Soon their ample sway shall stretch
O'er the plenty of the plain.   40

Low the dauntless Earl is laid,

Note: The *Valkyriur* were female Divinities, Servants of *Odin* (or *Woden*) in the Gothic
mythology. Their name signifies *Chusers of the slain*. They were mounted on swift horses, with
drawn swords in their hands; and in the throng of battle selected such as were destined to
slaughter, and conducted them to *Valhalla*, the hall of *Odin*, or paradise of the Brave; where they
attended the banquet, and served the departed Heroes with horns of mead and ale.

Gor'd with many a gaping wound:
Fate demands a nobler head;
Soon a King shall bite the ground.

Long his loss shall Eirin weep,
Ne'er again his likeness see;
Long her strains in sorrow steep,
Strains of Immortality!

Horror covers all the heath,
Clouds of carnage blot the sun. 50
Sisters, weave the web of death;
Sisters, cease, the work is done.

Hail the task, and hail the hands!
Songs of joy and triumph sing!
Joy to the victorious bands;
Triumph to the younger King.

Mortal, thou that hear'st the tale,
Learn the tenour of our song.
Scotland, thro' each winding vale
Far and wide the notes prolong. 60

Sisters, hence with spurs of speed:
Each her thundering faulchion wield;
Each bestride her sable steed.
Hurry, hurry, to the field.

RICHES I HOLD IN LIGHT ESTEEM

Emily Jane Brontë   (1818–1848)

With Charlotte Brontë and two older sisters, Emily Brontë was sent in 1824 to a
cheap boarding school for poor clergymen's daughters, where Maria and Elizabeth
Brontë died of malnutrition and the lack of sanitation. At Charlotte Brontë's
insistence, Emily and Anne Brontë allowed their poems to be published in the
volume *Poems of Currer, Ellis and Acton Bell* (1846). *Wuthering Heights* was
published the following year, again under Brontë's masculine pseudonym. She
caught cold at her brother Branwell's funeral and died of an inflammation of the
lungs.

"Riches I hold in light esteem" is dated March 1, 1841.

Riches I hold in light esteem
And Love I laugh to scorn

And lust of Fame was but a dream
That vanished with the morn—

And if I pray, the only prayer
That moves my lips for me
Is—"Leave the heart that now I bear
And give me liberty."

Yes, as my swift days near their goal
'Tis all that I implore—
Through life and death, a chainless soul
With courage to endure!

THE SONG OF THE SHIRT

Thomas Hood   (1799–1845)

Hood was born in London, where he was educated privately. He first worked as an illustrator and would have made a career of engraving except that his health would not allow it. In 1821 he became the editor of the *London Magazine*, and in 1824 he married. After holding other editorial positions, he went to Germany to live in 1835. In 1840 he returned to England and reentered the magazine world. His health totally broken by the strain of founding *Hood's Magazine*, he died a year later.

"The Song of the Shirt" was first published in *Punch* for December 16, 1843, and was collected in Hood's *Poems* in 1846.

With fingers weary and worn,
    With eyelids heavy and red,
A Woman sat, in unwomanly rags,
    Plying her needle and thread—
        Stitch! stitch! stitch!
In poverty, hunger, and dirt,
    And still with a voice of dolorous pitch
She sang the "Song of the Shirt!"

    "Work! work! work!
While the cock is crowing aloof!
    And work—work—work,
Till the stars shine through the roof!
It's O! to be a slave
    Along with the barbarous Turk,
Where woman has never a soul to save,
    If this is Christian work!

    "Work—work—work
Till the brain begins to swim;

10

Work—work—work   20
Till the eyes are heavy and dim!
Seam, and gusset, and band,
    Band, and gusset, and seam,
        Till over the buttons I fall asleep,
    And sew them on in a dream!

"O! Men, with Sisters dear!
    O! Men! with Mothers and Wives!
It is not linen you're wearing out,
    But human creatures' lives!
        Stitch—stitch—stitch,
    In poverty, hunger, and dirt,   30
Sewing at once, with a double thread,
    A Shroud as well as a Shirt.

"But why do I talk of Death?
    That Phantom of grisly bone,
I hardly fear his terrible shape,
    It seems so like my own—
    It seems so like my own,
    Because of the fasts I keep,
Oh! God! that bread should be so dear,
    And flesh and blood so cheap!   40

    "Work—work—work!
    My labour never flags;
And what are its wages? A bed of straw,
    A crust of bread—and rags.
That shatter'd roof—and this naked floor—
    A table—a broken chair—
And a wall so blank, my shadow I thank
    For sometimes falling there!

    "Work—work—work!
From weary chime to chime,   50
    Work—work—work—
As prisoners work for crime!
    Band, and gusset, and seam,
    Seam, and gusset, and band,
Till the heart is sick, and the brain benumb'd,
    As well as the weary hand.

    "Work—work—work,
In the dull December light,
    And work—work—work,
When the weather is warm and bright—   60
While underneath the eaves
    The brooding swallows cling

As if to show me their sunny backs
  And twit me with the spring.

"Oh! but to breathe the breath
Of the cowslip and primrose sweet—
  With the sky above my head,
And the grass beneath my feet,
For only one short hour
  To feel as I used to feel,
Before I knew the woes of want
  And the walk that costs a meal!

70

"Oh but for one short hour!
  A respite however brief!
No blessed leisure for Love or Hope,
  But only time for Grief!
A little weeping would ease my heart,
  But in their briny bed
My tears must stop, for every drop
  Hinders needle and thread!"

80

With fingers weary and worn,
  With eyelids heavy and red,
A woman sat in unwomanly rags,
  Plying her needle and thread—
    Stitch! stitch! stitch!
In poverty, hunger, and dirt,
And still with a voice of dolorous pitch,
Would that its tone could reach the Rich!
  She sang this "Song of the Shirt!"

PROSERPINE

Mary Wollstonecraft Godwin Shelley   (1797–1851)

Mary Shelley was the daughter of radical philosopher William Godwin and feminist
Mary Wollstonecraft, who wrote *A Vindication of the Rights of Women* and who
died at her birth. She ran away with the already-married Percy Bysshe Shelley in
1814. They married in 1816 and lived in Italy in the company of Byron; it was here
that she wrote *Frankenstein* (1822). She was depressed during this time because her
father refused to associate with her; two of her three children also died during this
period. William, a child in *Frankenstein* who is murdered by the Frankenstein
monster, bears a striking resemblance to her third child, also named William.
Shelley died in Italy, and she rejected later suitors, saying, "I want to be Mary
Shelley on my tombstone." She returned to England, where she edited her

husband's literary remains and attempted his biography. Although she wrote four novels, she never equaled the power of her first work.

Proserpine is one of two mythological dramas left unfinished at Mary Shelley's death. The excerpt that follows is the second act.

ACT II

Scene
The Plain of Enna as before.

Enter Ino & Eunoe.

EUNOE. How weary am I! and the hot sun flushes
    My cheeks that else were white with fear and grief[.]
    E'er since that fatal day, dear sister nymph,
    On which we lost our lovely Proserpine,
    I have but wept and watched the livelong night
    And all the day have wandered through the woods[.]
INO. How all is changed since that unhappy eve!
    Ceres forever weeps, seeking her child,
    And in her rage has struck the land with blight;
    Trinacria mourns with her;—its fertile fields   10
    Are dry and barren, and all little brooks
    Struggling scarce creep within their altered banks;
    The flowers that erst were wont with bended heads,
    To gaze within the clear and glassy wave,
    Have died, unwatered by the failing stream.—
    And yet their hue but mocks the deeper grief
    Which is the fountain of these bitter tears.
    But who is this, that with such eager looks
    Hastens this way?—
EUNOE.   'Tis fairest Arethuse,   20
    A stranger naiad, yet you know her well.
INO. My eyes were blind with tears.

Enter Arethusa

                    Dear Arethuse,
    Methinks I read glad tidings in your eyes,
    Your smiles are the swift messengers that bear
    A tale of coming joy, which we alas!
    Can answer but with tears, unless you bring
    To our grief solace, Hope to our Despair.
    Have you found Proserpine? or know you where
    The loved nymph wanders, hidden from our search?   30
ARETHUSA. Where is the corn-crowned Ceres? I have hastened
    To ease her anxious heart.
EUNOE.   Oh! dearest Naiad,
    Herald of joy! Now will great Ceres bless
    Thy welcome coming & more welcome tale.

INO. Since that unhappy day when Ceres lost
  Her much-loved child, she wanders through the isle;
  Dark blight is showered from her looks of sorrow;—
  And where tall corn and all seed-bearing grass
  Rose from beneath her step, they wither now   40
  Fading under the frown of her bent brows:
  The springs decrease;—the fields whose delicate green
  Was late her chief delight, now please alone,
  Because they, withered, seem to share her grief.
ARETHUSA. Unhappy Goddess! how I pity thee!
INO. At night upon high Etna's topmost peak
  She lights two flames, that shining through the isle
  Leave dark no wood, or cave, or mountain path,
  Their sunlike splendour makes the moon-beams dim,
  And the bright stars are lost within their day.   50
  She's in yon field,—she comes towards this plain,
  Her loosened hair has fallen on her neck,
  Uncircled by the coronal of grain:—
  Her cheeks are wan,—her step is faint & slow.

Enter Ceres.

CERES. I faint with weariness: a dreadful thirst
  Possesses me! Must I give up the search?
  Oh! never, dearest Proserpine, until
  I once more clasp thee in my vacant arms!
  Help me, dear Arethuse! fill some deep shell
  With the clear waters of thine ice-cold spring,   60
  And bring it me;—I faint with heat and thirst.
ARETHUSA. My words are better than my freshest waves[:]
  I saw your Proserpine—
CERES.   Arethusa, where?
  Tell me! my heart beats quick, & hope and fear
  Cause my weak limbs to fail me.—
ARETHUSA.   Sit, Goddess,
  Upon this mossy bank, beneath the shade
  Of this tall rock, and I will tell my tale.
  The day you lost your child, I left my source.   70
  With my Alpheus I had wandered down
  The sloping shore into the sunbright sea;
  And at the coast we paused, watching the waves
  Of our mixed waters dance into the main:—
  When suddenly I heard the thundering tread
  Of iron hoofed steeds trampling the ground,
  And a faint shriek that made my blood run cold.
  I saw the King of Hell in his black car,
  And in his arms he bore your fairest child,
  Fair as the moon encircled by the night,—   80
  But that she strove, and cast her arms aloft,
  And cried, "My Mother!"—When she saw me near

She would have sprung from his detested arms,
And with a tone of deepest grief, she cried,
"Oh, Arethuse!" I hastened at her call—
But Pluto when he saw that aid was nigh,
Struck furiously the green earth with his spear,
Which yawned,—and down the deep Tartarian gulph
His black car rolled—the green earth closed above.

CERES. (*starting up*) Is this thy doom, great Jove? & shall Hell's king   90
    Quitting dark Tartarus, spread grief and tears
    Among the dwellers of your bright abodes?
    Then let him seize the earth itself, the stars,—
    And all your wide dominion be his prey!—
    Your sister calls upon your love, great King!
    As you are God I do demand your help!—
    Restore my child, or let all heaven sink,
    And the fair world be chaos once again!

INO. Look[!] in the East that loveliest bow is formed[:]   100
    Heaven's single-arched bridge, it touches now
    The Earth, and 'mid the pathless wastes of heaven
    It paves a way for Jove's fair Messenger;—
    Iris descends, and towards this field she comes.

ARETHUSA. Sovereign of Harvests, 'tis the Messenger
    That will bring joy to thee. Thine eyes light up
    With sparkling hope, thy cheeks are pale with dread.

Enter Iris.

CERES. Speak, heavenly Iris! let thy words be poured
    Into my drooping soul, like dews of eve
    On a too long parched field.—Where is my Proserpine?

IRIS. Sister of Heaven, as by Joves throne I stood   110
    The voice of thy deep prayer arose,—it filled
    The heavenly courts with sorrow and dismay:
    The Thunderer frowned, & heaven shook with dread.
    I bear his will to thee, 'tis fixed by fate,
    Nor prayer nor murmur e'er can alter it.
    If Proserpine while she has lived in hell
    Has not polluted by Tartarian food
    Her heavenly essence, then she may return,
    And wander without fear on Enna's plain,
    Or take her seat among the Gods above.   120
    If she has touched the fruits of Erebus,
    She never may return to upper air,
    But doomed to dwell amidst the shades of death,
    The wife of Pluto and the Queen of Hell.

CERES. Joy treads upon the sluggish heels of care!
    The child of heaven disdains Tartarian food.
    Pluto[,] give up thy prey! restore my child!

IRIS. Soon she will see again the sun of Heaven,
    By gloomy shapes, inhabitants of Hell,

Attended, and again behold the field 130
Of Enna, the fair flowers & the streams,
Her late delight,—& more than all, her Mother.
INO. Our much-loved, long-lost Mistress, do you come?
And shall once more your nymphs attend your steps?
Will you again irradiate this isle—
That drooped when you were lost? & once again
Trinacria smile beneath your Mother's eye?

(Ceres and her companions are ranged on one side in eager expectation; from the cave on the other, enter Proserpine, attended by various dark & gloomy shapes bearing torches; among which Ascalaphus. Ceres & Proserpine embrace;—her nymphs surround her.)

CERES. Welcome, dear Proserpine! Welcome to light,
To this green earth and to your Mother's arms.
You are too beautiful for Pluto's Queen; 140
In the dark Stygian air your blooming cheeks
Have lost their roseate tint, and your bright form
Has faded in that night unfit for thee.
PROSERPINE. Then I again behold thee, Mother dear:—
Again I tread the flowery plain of Enna,
And clasp thee, Arethuse, & you, my nymphs;
I have escaped from hateful Tartarus,
The abode of furies and all loathed shapes
That thronged around me, making hell more black.
Oh! I could worship thee, light giving Sun, 150
Who spreadest warmth and radiance o'er the world.
Look at the branches of those chesnut trees,
That wave to the soft breezes, while their stems
Are tinged with red by the sun's slanting rays.
And the soft clouds that float 'twixt earth and sky.
How sweet are all these sights! There all is night!
No God like that (*pointing to the sun*) smiles on the Elysian plains,
The air [is] windless, and all shapes are still.
IRIS. And must I interpose in this deep joy,
And sternly cloud your hopes? Oh! answer me, 160
Art thou still, Proserpine, a child of light?
Or hast thou dimmed thy attributes of Heaven
By such Tartarian food as must for ever
Condemn thee to be Queen of Hell & Night?
PROSERPINE. No, Iris, no,—I still am pure as thee:
Offspring of light and air, I have no stain
Of Hell. I am for ever thine, oh, Mother!
CERES. (*to the shades from Hell*) Begone, foul visitants to upper air!
Back to your dens! nor stain the sunny earth
By shadows thrown from forms so foul—Crouch in! 170
Proserpine, child of light, is not your Queen!
(*to the nymphs*)
Quick bring my car,—we will ascend to heaven,

Deserting Earth, till by decree of Jove,
Eternal laws shall bind the King of Hell
To leave in peace the offspring of the sky.
ASCALAPHUS. Stay, Ceres! By the dread decree of Jove
    Your child is doomed to be eternal Queen
    Of Tartarus,—nor may she dare ascend
    The sunbright regions of Olympian Jove,
    Or tread the green Earth 'mid attendant nymphs.   180
    Proserpine, call to mind your walk last eve,
    When as you wandered in Elysian groves,
    Through bowers for ever green, and mossy walks,
    Where flowers never die, nor wind disturbs
    The sacred calm, whose silence soothes the dead,
    Nor interposing clouds, with dun wings, dim
    Its mild and silver light, you plucked its fruit,
    You ate of a pomegranate's seeds—
CERES.   Be silent,
    Prophet of evil, hateful to the Gods!   190
    Sweet Proserpine, my child, look upon me.
    You shrink; your trembling form & pallid cheeks
    Would make his words seem true which are most false[.]
    Thou didst not taste the food of Erebus;—
    Offspring of Gods art thou,—nor Hell, nor Jove
    Shall tear thee from thy Mother's clasping arms.
PROSERPINE. If fate decrees, can we resist? farewel!
    Oh! Mother, dearer to your child than light,
    Than all the forms of this sweet earth & sky,
    Though dear are these, and dear are my poor nymphs,   200
    Whom I must leave;—oh! can immortals weep?
    And can a Goddess die as mortals do,
    Or live & reign where it is death to be?
    Ino, dear Arethuse, again you lose
    Your hapless Proserpine, lost to herself
    When she quits you for gloomy Tartarus.
CERES. Is there no help, great Jove? If she depart
    I will descend with her—the Earth shall lose
    Its proud fertility, and Erebus
    Shall bear my gifts throughout th' unchanging year.   210
    Valued till now by thee, tyrant of Gods!
    My harvests ripening by Tartarian fires
    Shall feed the dead with Heaven's ambrosial food.
    Wilt thou not then repent, brother unkind,
    Viewing the barren earth with vain regret,
    Tho didst not shew more mercy to my child?
INO. We will all leave the light and go with thee,
    In Hell thou shalt be girt by Heaven-born nymphs,
    Elysium shall be Enna,—thou'lt not mourn
    Thy natal plain, which will have lost its worth   220
    Having lost thee, its nursling and its Queen.

ARETHUSA. I will sink down with thee;—my lily crown
    Shall bloom in Erebus, portentous loss
    To Earth, which by degrees will fade & fall
    In envy of our happier lot in Hell;—
    And the bright sun and the fresh winds of heaven
    Shall light its depths and fan its stagnant air.

(They cling round Proserpine; the Shades of Hell seperate and stand between them.)

ASCALAPHUS. Depart! She is our Queen! Ye may not come!
    Hark to Jove's thunder! shrink away in fear
    From unknown forms, whose tyranny ye'll feel   230
    In groans and tears if ye insult their power.
IRIS. Behold Jove's balance hung in upper sky;
    There are ye weighed,—to that ye must submit.
CERES. Oh! Jove, have mercy on a Mother's prayer!
    Shall it be nought to be akin to thee?
    And shall thy sister, Queen of fertile Earth,
    Derided be by these foul shapes of Hell?
    Look at the scales, they're poized with equal weights!
    What can this mean? Leave me not[,] Proserpine[,]
    Cling to thy Mother's side! He shall not dare   240
    Divide the sucker from the parent stem.
                         (embraces her)
ASCALAPHUS. He is almighty! who shall set the bounds
    To his high will? let him decide our plea!
    Fate is with us, & Proserpine is ours!

(He endeavours to part Ceres & Proserpine, the nymphs prevent him.)

CERES. Peace, ominous bird of Hell & Night! Depart!
    Nor with thy skriech disturb a Mother's grief.
    Avaunt! It is to Jove we pray, not thee.
IRIS. Thy fate, sweet Proserpine, is sealed by Jove.
    When Enna is starred by flowers, and the sun
    Shoots his hot rays strait on the gladsome land,   250
    When Summer reigns, then thou shalt live on Earth,
    And tread these plains, or sporting with your nymphs,
    Or at your Mother's side, in peaceful joy.
    But when hard frost congeals the bare, black ground,
    The trees have lost their leaves, & painted birds
    Wailing for food sail through the piercing air;
    Then you descend to deepest night and reign
    Great Queen of Tartarus, 'mid shadows dire,
    Offspring of Hell,—or in the silent groves
    Of fair Elysium through which Lethe runs,   260
    The sleepy river; where the windless air
    Is never struck by flight or song of bird,—
    But all is calm and clear, bestowing rest,
    After the toil of life, to wretched men,

Whom thus the Gods reward for sufferings
Gods cannot know; a throng of empty shades!
The endless circle of the year will bring
Joy in its turn, and seperation sad;
Six months to light and Earth,—six months to Hell.

PROSERPINE. Dear Mother, let me kiss that tear which steals   270
Down your pale cheek altered by care and grief.
This is not misery; 'tis but a slight change
From our late happy lot. Six months with thee,
Each moment freighted with an age of love:
And the six short months in saddest Tartarus
Shall pass in dreams of swift returning joy.
Six months together we shall dwell on earth,
Six months in dreams we shall companions be,
Jove's doom is void; we are forever joined.

CERES. Oh, fairest child! sweet summer visitor!   280
Thy looks cheer me, so shall they cheer this land
Which I will fly, thou gone. Nor seed of grass,
Or corn shall grow, thou absent from the earth;
But all shall lie beneath in hateful night
Until at thy return, the fresh green springs,
The fields are covered o'er with summer plants.
And when thou goest the heavy grain will droop
And die under my frown, scattering the seeds,
That will not reappear till your return.
Farewel, sweet child, Queen of the nether world,   290
There shine as chaste Diana's silver car
Islanded in the deep circumfluous night.
Giver of fruits! for such thou shalt be styled,
Sweet Prophetess of Summer, coming forth
From the slant shadow of the wintry earth,
In thy car drawn by snowy-breasted swallows!
Another kiss, & then again farewel!
Winter in losing thee has lost its all,
And will be doubly bare, & hoar, & drear,
Its bleak winds whistling o'er the cold pinched ground   300
Which neither flower or grass will decorate.
And as my tears fall first, so shall the trees
Shed their changed leaves upon your six months tomb:
The clouded air will hide from Phoebus' eye
The dreadful change your absence operates.
Thus has black Pluto changed the reign of Jove,
He seizes half the Earth when he takes thee.

A WOMAN WAITS FOR ME

Walt Whitman   (1819–1892)

Born on Long Island and educated in Brooklyn, Whitman was active in printing and journalism from an early age, writing a large number of conventional short stories for newspaper publication. In 1855 he published the first edition of *Leaves of Grass*, which he continued to revise and enlarge until his death. In 1862 Whitman became involved in hospital work. He served briefly as a clerk in the Indian Bureau in Washington, where he lived until 1873. He spent his last nineteen years at Camden, New Jersey, cultivating his image as "the good gray poet."

"A woman waits for me" first appeared in the 1856 edition of *Leaves of Grass*, under the title "Poem of Procreation." It was given its present title in the 1867 edition. This text is Whitman's final version.

A woman waits for me, she contains all, nothing is lacking,
Yet all were lacking if sex were lacking, or if the moisture of the right man
　　were lacking.

Sex contains all, bodies, souls,
Meanings, proofs, purities, delicacies, results, promulgations,
Songs, commands, health, pride, the maternal mystery, the seminal milk,
All hopes, benefactions, bestowals, all the passions, loves, beauties, delights
　　of the earth,
All the governments, judges, gods, follow'd persons of the earth,
These are contain'd in sex as parts of itself and justifications of itself.

Without shame the man I like knows and avows the deliciousness of his
　　sex,
Without shame the woman I like knows and avows hers.　　　　　　　　10

Now I will dismiss myself from impassive women,
I will go stay with her who waits for me, and with those women that are
　　warm-blooded and sufficient for me,
I see that they understand me and do not deny me,
I see that they are worthy of me, I will be the robust husband of those
　　women.

They are not one jot less than I am,
They are tann'd in the face by shining suns and blowing winds,
Their flesh has the old divine suppleness and strength,
They know how to swim, row, ride, wrestle, shoot, run, strike, retreat,
　　advance, resist, defend themselves,
They are ultimate in their own right—they are calm, clear, well-possess'd of
　　themselves.

I draw you close to me, you women,   20
I cannot let you go, I would do you good,
I am for you, and you are for me, not only for our own sake, but for others'
     sakes,
Envelop'd in you sleep greater heroes and bards,
They refuse to awake at the touch of any man but me.

It is I, you women, I make my way,
I am stern, acrid, large, undissuadable, but I love you,
I do not hurt you any more than is necessary for you,
I pour the stuff to start sons and daughters fit for these States, I press with
     slow rude muscle,
I brace myself effectually, I listen to no entreaties,
I dare not withdraw till I deposit what has so long accumulated   30
     within me.

Through you I drain the pent-up rivers of myself,
In you I wrap a thousand onward years,
On you I graft the grafts of the best-beloved of me and America,
The drops I distil upon you shall grow fierce and athletic girls, new artists,
     musicians, and singers,
The babes I beget upon you are to beget babes in their turn,
I shall demand perfect men and women out of my love-spendings,
I shall expect them to interpenetrate with others, as I and you interpenetrate
     now,
I shall count on the fruits of the gushing showers of them, as I count on the
     fruits of the gushing showers I give now,
I shall look for loving crops from the birth, life, death, immortality, I plant so
     lovingly now.

THE COMING WOMAN

Mary Weston Fordham   (fl. 1897)

Virtually nothing is known regarding Fordham. She was apparently a student at
Tuskegee Institute, for her volume of poems, *Magnolia Leaves*, was published at
Tuskegee in 1897 and carries an "Introductory" by Booker T. Washington, who
closes by saying: "The readers I trust will find as much to praise and admire as I
have done." In her "Preface," Fordham states: "I hope that [this volume] will be
kindly received as simply the harbinger of what may be expected from generations
to come; and shall consider its mission as being fulfilled if it should be the means of
arousing and stimulating some of our youth to higher and greater efforts along this
line."

"The Coming Woman" appears in *Magnolia Leaves*.

Just look, 'tis a quarter past six, love—
　And not even the fires are caught;
Well, you know I must be at the office—
　But, as usual, the breakfast 'll be late.

Now hurry and wake up the children;
　And dress them as fast as you can;
"Poor dearies," I know they'll be tardy,
　Dear me, "what a slow, poky man!"

Have the tenderloin broiled nice and juicy—　　　　　10
　Have the toast browned and buttered all right;
And be sure you settle the coffee:
　Be sure that the silver is bright.

When ready, just run up and call me—
　At eight, to the office I go,
Lest poverty, grim, should o'ertake us—
　"'Tis bread and butter," you know.

The bottom from stocks may fall out,
　My bonds may get below par;
Then surely, I seldom could spare you　　　　　20
　A nickel, to buy a cigar.

All ready? Now, while I am eating,
　Just bring up my wheel to the door;
Then wash up the dishes; and, mind now,
　Have dinner promptly at four;

For to-night is our Woman's Convention,
　And I am to speak first, you know—
The men veto us in private,
　But in public they shout, "That's so."

So "by-by"—In case of a rap, love,　　　　　30
　Before opening the door, you must look;
O! how could a civilized woman
　Exist, without a man cook.

SAINT JOAN OF ARC

Mark Twain   (Samuel Langhorne Clemens: 1835–1910)

Born in Florida, Missouri, Clemens spent his boyhood in Hannibal. At thirteen he was apprenticed to a printer, and at twenty-two to a steamboat pilot. He moved to Virginia City, Nevada Territory, in 1861; it was there that he first used the pseudonym "Mark Twain" (February 3, 1863). In 1864 Twain went to San Francisco, where he published "The Celebrated Jumping Frog of Calaveras County," his first work to gain him national attention. In 1870 he married Olivia, and they set up house in Hartford, Connecticut, where they had three daughters. In 1884 Clemens established his own publishing firm, which brought out *The Adventures of Huckleberry Finn* (1885). In financial difficulties, he moved his family to Europe in 1891; by 1894 his publishing firm had failed, and having overinvested in a typesetting machine that proved impractical, Clemens was bankrupt. His affairs were taken over by Standard Oil magnate Henry Huttleston Rogers, through whose management Clemens again became solvent. In 1895 his eldest daughter died; his wife died in 1903, in Florence, Italy. Oxford awarded Clemens an honorary degree in 1907, and in 1908 he built a home in Redding, Connecticut, where he spent his last years.

Clemens had been fascinated with the story of Joan of Arc since his first encounter with it, at the age of thirteen. His first treatment of the story is *The Personal Recollections of Joan of Arc*, published in *Harper's Magazine* from April 1895 to April 1896 as the translation of a work "by the Sieur Louis de Conte (her Page and Secretary)." Clemens published the work under a pseudonym because he felt his own reputation as a humorist would color people's reactions to what he considered a serious and important study. His authorship was acknowledged when the *Recollections* was published in book form in 1896. His second treatment of the story, "Saint Joan of Arc," originally appeared in *Harper's Magazine* for December 1904 and was collected in *The $30,000 Bequest and Other Stories* in 1906.

NOTE

> *The Official Record of the Trials and Rehabilitation of Joan of Arc is the most remarkable history that exists in any language; yet there are few people in the world who can say they have read it: in England and America it has hardly been heard of.*
> *Three hundred years ago Shakespeare did not know the true story of Joan of Arc; in his day it was unknown even in France. For four hundred years it existed rather as a vaguely defined romance than as definite and authentic history. The true story remained buried in the official archives of France from the Rehabilitation of 1456 until Quicherat dug it out and gave it to the world two generations ago, in lucid and understandable modern French. It is a deeply fascinating story. But only in the Official Trials and Rehabilitation can it be found in its entirety.—M. T.*

Chapter I

The evidence furnished at the Trials and Rehabilitation sets forth Joan of Arc's strange and beautiful history in clear and minute detail. Among all the multitude of biographies that freight the shelves of the world's libraries, *this is the only one whose validity is confirmed to us by oath.* It gives us a vivid picture of a career and a personality of so extraordinary a character that we are helped to accept them as actualities by the very fact that both are beyond the inventive reach of fiction. The public part of the career occupied only a mere breath of time—it covered but two years; but what a career it was! The personality which made it possible is one to be reverently studied, loved, and marveled at, but not to be wholly understood and accounted for by even the most searching analysis.

In Joan of Arc at the age of sixteen there was no promise of a romance. She lived in a dull little village on the frontiers of civilization; she had been nowhere and had seen nothing; she knew none but simple shepherd folk; she had never seen a person of note; she hardly knew what a soldier looked like; she had never ridden a horse, nor had a warlike weapon in her hand; she could neither read nor write: she could spin and sew; she knew her catechism and her prayers and the fabulous histories of the saints, and this was all her learning. That was Joan at sixteen. What did she know of law? of evidence? of courts? of the attorney's trade? of legal procedure? Nothing. Less than nothing. Thus exhaustively equipped with ignorance, she went before the court at Toul to contest a false charge of breach of promise of marriage; she conducted her cause herself, without any one's help or advice or any one's friendly sympathy, and won it. She called no witnesses of her own, but vanquished the prosecution by using with deadly effectiveness its own testimony. The astonished judge threw the case out of court, and spoke of her as "this marvelous child."

She went to the veteran Commandant of Vaucouleurs and demanded an escort of soldiers, saying she must march to the help of the King of France, since she was commissioned of God to win back his lost kingdom for him and set the crown upon his head. The Commandant said, "What, you? You are only a child." And he advised that she be taken back to her village and have her ears boxed. But she said she must obey God, and would come again, and again, and yet again, and finally she would get the soldiers. She said truly. In time he yielded, after months of delay and refusal, and gave her the soldiers; and took off his sword and gave her that, and said, "Go—and let come what may." She made her long and perilous journey through the enemy's country, and spoke with the King, and convinced him. Then she was summoned before the University of Poitiers to prove that she *was* commissioned of God and not of Satan, and daily during three weeks she sat before that learned congress unafraid, and capably answered their deep questions out of her ignorant but able head and her simple and honest heart; and again she won her case, and with it the wondering admiration of all that august company.

And now, aged seventeen, she was made Commander-in-Chief, with a prince of the royal house and the veteran generals of France for subordinates; and at the head of the first army she had ever seen, she marched to Orleans, carried the commanding fortresses of the enemy by storm in three desperate assaults, and in ten days raised a siege which had defied the might of France for seven months.

After a tedious and insane delay caused by the King's instability of character and the treacherous counsels of his ministers, she got permission to take the field again. She took Jargeau by storm; then Meung; she forced Beaugency to surrencer; then—in the open field—she won the memorable victory of Patay against Talbot, "the English lion," and broke the back of the Hundred Years' War. It was a campaign which cost but seven weeks of time; yet the political results would have been cheap if the time expended had been fifty years. Patay, the unsung and now long-forgotten battle, was the Moscow of the English power in France; from the blow struck that day it was destined never to recover. It was the beginning of the end of an alien dominion which had ridden France intermittently for three hundred years.

Then followed the great campaign of the Loire, the capture of Troyes by assault, and the triumphal march past surrendering towns and fortresses to Rheims, where Joan put the crown upon her King's head in the Cathedral, amid wild public rejoicings, and with her old peasant father there to see these things and believe his eyes if he could. She had restored the crown and the lost sovereignty; the King was grateful for once in his shabby poor life, and asked her to name her reward and have it. She asked for nothing for herself, but begged that the taxes of her native village might be remitted forever. The prayer was granted, and the promise kept for three hundred and sixty years. Then it was broken, and remains broken to-day. France was very poor then, she is very rich now; but she has been collecting those taxes for more than a hundred years.

Joan asked one other favor: that now that her mission was fulfilled she might be allowed to go back to her village and take up her humble life again with her mother and the friends of her childhood; for she had no pleasure in the cruelties of war, and the sight of blood and suffering wrung her heart. Sometimes in battle she did not draw her sword, lest in the splendid madness of the onset she might forget herself and take an enemy's life with it. In the Rouen Trials, one of her quaintest speeches—coming from the gentle and girlish source it did—was her naïve remark that she had "never killed any one." Her prayer for leave to go back to the rest and peace of her village home was not granted.

Then she wanted to march at once upon Paris, take it, and drive the English out of France. She was hampered in all the ways that treachery and the King's vacillation could devise, but she forced her way to Paris at last, and fell badly wounded in a successful assault upon one of the gates. Of course her men lost heart at once—she was the only heart they had. They fell back. She begged to be allowed to remain at the front, saying victory was sure. "I will take Paris now or die!" she said. But she was removed from the field by force;

the King ordered a retreat, and actually disbanded his army. In accordance with a beautiful old military custom Joan devoted her silver armor and hung it up in the Cathedral of St. Denis. Its great days were over.

Then, by command, she followed the King and his frivolous court and endured a gilded captivity for a time, as well as her free spirit could; and whenever inaction became unbearable she gathered some men together and rode away and assaulted a stronghold and captured it.

At last in a sortie against the enemy, from Compiègne, on the 24th of May (when she was turned eighteen), she was herself captured, after a gallant fight. It was her last battle. She was to follow the drums no more.

Thus ended the briefest epoch-making military career known to history. It lasted only a year and a month, but it found France an English province, and furnishes the reason that France is France to-day and not an English province still. Thirteen months! It was, indeed, a short career; but in the centuries that have since elapsed five hundred millions of Frenchmen have lived and died blest by the benefactions it conferred; and so long as France shall endure, the mighty debt must grow. And France is grateful; we often hear her say it. Also thrifty: she collects the Domremy taxes.

Chapter II

Joan was fated to spend the rest of her life behind bolts and bars. She was a prisoner of war, not a criminal, therefore hers was recognized as an honorable captivity. By the rules of war she must be held to ransom, and a fair price could not be refused if offered. John of Luxembourg paid her the just compliment of requiring a prince's ransom for her. In that day that phrase represented a definite sum—61,125 francs. It was, of course, supposable that either the King or grateful France, or both, would fly with the money and set their fair young benefactor free. But this did not happen. In five and a half months neither King nor country stirred a hand nor offered a penny. Twice Joan tried to escape. Once by a trick she succeeded for a moment, and locked her jailer in behind her, but she was discovered and caught; in the other case she let herself down from a tower sixty feet high, but her rope was too short, and she got a fall that disabled her and she could not get away.

Finally, Cauchon, Bishop of Beauvais, paid the money and bought Joan—ostensibly for the Church, to be tried for wearing male attire and for other impieties, but really for the English, the enemy into whose hands the poor girl was so piteously anxious not to fall. She was now shut up in the dungeons of the Castle of Rouen and kept in an iron cage, with her hands and feet and neck chained to a pillar; and from that time forth during all the months of her imprisonment, till the end, several rough English soldiers stood guard over her night and day—and not outside her room, but in it. It was a dreary and hideous captivity, but it did not conquer her: nothing could break that invincible spirit. From first to last she was a prisoner a year; and she spent the last three months of it on trial for her life before a formidable array of ecclesiastical judges, and disputing the ground with them foot by foot and inch by inch with brilliant generalship and dauntless pluck. The spectacle of that solitary girl, forlorn and friendless, without advocate or adviser, and without the help and guidance of any copy of the charges brought against her or rescript of the complex and voluminous daily proceedings of the court to modify the crushing strain upon her astonishing memory, fighting that long battle serene and undismayed against these colossal odds, stands alone in its pathos and its sublimity; it has nowhere its mate, either in the annals of fact or in the inventions of fiction.

And how fine and great were the things she daily said, how fresh and crisp—and she so worn in body, so starved, and tired, and harried! They run through the whole gamut of feeling and expression—from scorn and defiance, uttered with soldierly fire and frankness, all down the scale to wounded dignity clothed in words of noble pathos; as, when her patience was exhausted by the pestering delvings and gropings and searchings of her persecutors to find out what kind of devil's witchcraft she had employed to rouse the war spirit in her timid soldiers, she burst out with, "What I said was, '*Ride these English down*'—and I did it myself!" and as, when insultingly asked why it was that *her* standard had place at the crowning of the King in the Cathedral of Rheims rather than the standards of the other captains, she uttered that touching speech, "*It had borne the burden, it had earned the honor*"—a phrase which fell from lips without premeditation, yet whose moving beauty and simple grace it would bankrupt the arts of language to surpass.

Although she was on trial for her life, she was the only witness called on either side; the only witness summoned to testify before a packed jury commissioned with a definite task: to find her guilty, whether she was guilty or not. She must be convicted out of her own mouth, there being no other way to accomplish it. Every advantage that learning has over ignorance, age over youth, experience over inexperience, chicane over artlessness, every trick and trap and gin devisable by malice and the cunning of sharp intellects practised in setting snares for the unwary—all these were employed against her without shame; and when these arts were one by one defeated by the marvelous intuitions of her alert and penetrating mind, Bishop Cauchon stooped to a final baseness which it degrades human speech to describe: a priest who pretended to come from the region of her own home and to be a pitying friend and anxious to help her in her sore need was smuggled into her cell, and he misused his sacred office to steal her confidence; she confided to him the things sealed from revealment by her Voices, and which her prosecutors had tried so long in vain to trick her into betraying. A concealed confederate set it all down and delivered it to Cauchon, who used Joan's secrets, thus obtained, for her ruin.

Throughout the Trials, whatever the foredoomed witness said was twisted from its true meaning when possible, and made to tell against her; and whenever an answer of hers was beyond the reach of twisting it was not allowed to go upon the record. It was upon one of these latter occasions that she uttered that pathetic reproach—to Cauchon: "Ah, you set down everything that is against me, but you will not set down what is for me."

That this untrained young creature's genius for war was wonderful, and her generalship worthy to rank with the ripe products of a tried and trained military experience, we have the sworn testimony of two of her veteran subordinates—one, the Duc d'Alençon, the other the greatest of the French generals of the time, Dunois, Bastard of Orleans; that her genius was as great—possibly even greater—in the subtle warfare of the forum we have for witness the records of the Rouen Trials, that protracted exhibition of intellectual fence maintained with credit against the master-minds of France; that her moral greatness was peer to her intellect we call the Rouen Trials again to witness, with their testimony to a fortitude which patiently and steadfastly endured during twelve weeks the wasting forces of captivity, chains, loneliness, sickness, darkness, hunger, thirst, cold, shame, insult, abuse, broken sleep, treachery, ingratitude, exhausting sieges of cross-examination, the threat of torture, with the rack before her and the executioner standing ready: yet never surrendering, never asking quarter, the frail wreck of her as unconquerable the last day as was her invincible spirit the first.

Great as she was in so many ways, she was perhaps even greatest of all in the lofty things just named—her patient endurance, her steadfastness, her granite fortitude. We may not hope to easily find her mate and twin in these majestic qualities; where we lift our eyes highest we find only a strange and curious contrast—there in the captive eagle beating his broken wings on the Rock of St. Helena.

Chapter III

The Trials ended with her condemnation. But as she had conceded nothing, confessed nothing, this was victory for her, defeat for Cauchon. But his evil resources were not yet exhausted. She was persuaded to agree to sign a paper of slight import, then by treachery a paper was substituted which contained a recantation and a detailed confession of everything which had been charged against her during the Trials and denied and repudiated by her persistently during the three months; and this false paper she ignorantly signed. This was a victory for Cauchon. He followed it eagerly and pitilessly up by at once setting a trap for her which she could not escape. When she realized this she gave up the long struggle, denounced the treason which had been practised against her, repudiated the false confession, reasserted the truth of the testimony which she had given in the Trials, and went to her martyrdom with the peace of God in her tired heart, and on her lips endearing words and loving prayers for the cur she had crowned and the nation of ingrates she had saved.

When the fires rose about her and she begged for a cross for her dying lips to kiss, it was not a friend but an enemy, not a Frenchman but an alien, not a comrade in arms but an English soldier, that answered that pathetic prayer. He broke a stick across his knee, bound the pieces together in the form of the symbol she so loved, and gave it her; and his gentle deed is not forgotten, nor will be. . . .

A WORN PATH

Eudora Welty   (1909–   )

Welty was born in Jackson, Mississippi, where her father was head of an insurance company. She attended the Mississippi State College for Women from 1925 to 1927 and went on to receive her B.A. from the University of Wisconsin in 1929. After a brief stay at Columbia University, where she studied advertising, she returned to Jackson; she has pursued a writing career there ever since, winning the Pulitzer Prize in 1973 for her novel *The Optimist's Daughter*.

"A Worn Path" is from the collection *A Curtain of Green and Other Stories* (1941).

It was December—a bright frozen day in the early morning. Far out in the country there was an old Negro woman with her head tied in a red rag, coming along a path through the pinewoods. Her name was Phoenix Jackson. She was very old and small and she walked slowly in the dark pine shadows, moving a little from side to side in her steps, with the balanced heaviness and lightness of a pendulum in a grandfather clock. She carried a thin, small cane made from an umbrella, and with this she kept tapping the frozen earth in front of her. This made a grave and persistent noise in the still air, that seemed meditative like the chirping of a solitary little bird.

She wore a dark striped dress reaching down to her shoe tops, and an equally long apron of bleached sugar sacks, with a full pocket: all neat and tidy, but every time she took a step she might have fallen over her shoelaces, which dragged from her unlaced shoes. She looked straight ahead. Her eyes were blue with age. Her skin had a pattern all its own of numberless branching wrinkles and as though a whole little tree stood in the middle of her forehead, but a golden color ran underneath, and the two knobs of her cheeks were illumined by a yellow burning under the dark. Under the red rag her hair came down on her neck in the frailest of ringlets, still black, and with an odor like copper.

Now and then there was a quivering in the thicket. Old Phoenix said, "Out of my way, all you foxes, owls, beetles, jack rabbits, coons and wild animals! . . . Keep out from under these feet, little bob-whites. . . . Keep the big wild hogs out of my path. Don't let none of those come running my direction. I got a long way." Under her small black-freckled hand her cane, limber as a buggy whip, would switch at the brush as if to rouse up any hiding things.

On she went. The woods were deep and still. The sun made the pine needles almost too bright to look at, up where the wind rocked. The cones dropped as light as feathers. Down in the hollow was the mourning dove—it was not too late for him.

The path ran up a hill. "Seem like there is chains about my feet, time I get this far," she said, in the voice of argument old people keep to use with themselves. "Something always take a hold of me on this hill—pleads I should stay."

After she got to the top she turned and gave a full, severe look behind her where she had come. "Up through pines," she said at length. "Now down through oaks."

Her eyes opened their widest, and she started down gently. But before she got to the bottom of the hill a bush caught her dress.

Her fingers were busy and intent, but her skirts were full and long, so that before she could pull them free in one place they were caught in another. It was not possible to allow the dress to tear. "I in the thorny bush," she said. "Thorns, you doing your appointed work. Never want to let folks pass, no sir. Old eyes thought you was a pretty little *green* bush."

Finally, trembling all over, she stood free, and after a moment dared to stoop for her cane.

"Sun so high!" she cried, leaning back and looking, while the thick tears went over her eyes. "The time getting all gone here."

At the foot of this hill was a place where a log was laid across the creek.

"Now comes the trial," said Phoenix.

Putting her right foot out, she mounted the log and shut her eyes. Lifting her skirt, leveling her cane fiercely before her, like a festival figure in some parade, she began to march across. Then she opened her eyes and she was safe on the other side.

"I wasn't as old as I thought," she said.

But she sat down to rest. She spread her skirts on the bank around her and folded her hands over her knees. Up above her was a tree in a pearly cloud of mistletoe. She did not dare to close her eyes, and when a little boy brought her a plate with a slice of marble-cake on it she spoke to him. "That would be acceptable," she said. But when she went to take it there was just her own hand in the air.

So she left that tree, and had to go through a barbed-wire fence. There she had to creep and crawl, spreading her knees and stretching her fingers like a baby trying to climb the steps. But she talked loudly to herself: she could not let her dress be torn now, so late in the day, and she could not pay for having her arm or her leg sawed off if she got caught fast where she was.

At last she was safe through the fence and risen up out in the clearing. Big dead trees, like black men with one arm, were standing in the purple stalks of the withered cotton field. There sat a buzzard.

"Who you watching?"

In the furrow she made her way along.

"Glad this not the season for bulls," she said, looking sideways, "and the good Lord made his snakes to curl up and sleep in the winter. A pleasure I don't see no two-headed snake coming around that tree, where it come once. It took a while to get by him, back in the summer."

She passed through the old cotton and went into a field of dead corn. It whispered and shook and was taller than her head. "Through the maze now," she said, for there was no path.

Then there was something tall, black, and skinny there, moving before her.

At first she took it for a man. It could have been a man dancing in the field. But she stood still and listened, and it did not make a sound. It was as silent as a ghost.

"Ghost," she said sharply, "who be you the ghost of? For I have heard of nary death close by."

But there was no answer—only the ragged dancing in the wind.

She shut her eyes, reached out her hand, and touched a sleeve. She found a coat and inside that an emptiness, cold as ice.

"You scarecrow," she said. Her face lighted. "I ought to be shut up for good," she said with laughter. "My senses is gone. I too old. I the oldest people I ever know. Dance, old scarecrow," she said, "while I dancing with you."

She kicked her foot over the furrow, and with mouth drawn down, shook her head once or twice in a little strutting way. Some husks blew down and whirled in streamers about her skirts.

Then she went on, parting her way from side to side with the cane, through the whispering field. At last she came to the end, to a wagon track where the silver grass blew between the red ruts. The quail were walking around like pullets, seeming all dainty and unseen.

"Walk pretty," she said. "This the easy place. This the easy going."

She followed the track, swaying through the quiet bare fields, through the little strings of trees silver in their dead leaves, past cabins silver from weather, with the doors and windows boarded shut, all like old women under a spell sitting there. "I walking in their sleep," she said, nodding her head vigorously.

In a ravine she went where a spring was silently flowing through a hollow log. Old Phoenix bent and drank. "Sweet-gum makes the water sweet," she said, and drank more. "Nobody know who made this well, for it was here when I was born."

The track crossed a swampy part where the moss hung as white as lace from every limb. "Sleep on, alligators, and blow your bubbles." Then the track went into the road.

Deep, deep the road went down between the high green-colored banks. Overhead the live-oaks met, and it was as dark as a cave.

A black dog with a lolling tongue came up out of the weeds by the ditch. She was meditating, and not ready, and when he came at her she only hit him a little with her cane. Over she went in the ditch, like a little puff of milkweed.

Down there, her senses drifted away. A dream visited her, and she reached her hand up, but nothing reached down and gave her a pull. So she lay there and presently went to talking. "Old woman," she said to herself, "that black dog come up out of the weeds to stall you off, and now there he sitting on his fine tail, smiling at you."

A white man finally came along and found her—a hunter, a young man, with his dog on a chain.

"Well, Granny!" he laughed, "What are you doing there?"

"Lying on my back like a June-bug waiting to be turned over, mister," she said, reaching up her hand.

He lifted her up, gave her a swing in the air, and set her down. "Anything broken, Granny?"

"No sir, them old dead weeds is springy enough," said Phoenix, when she had got her breath. "I thank you for your trouble."

"Where do you live, Granny?" he asked, while the two dogs were growling at each other.

"Away back yonder, sir, behind the ridge. You can't even see it from here."

"On your way home?"

"No sir, I going to town."

"Why, that's too far! That's as far as I walk when I come out myself, and I get something for my trouble." He patted the stuffed bag he carried, and there hung down a little closed claw. It was one of the bob-whites, with its beak hooked bitterly to show it was dead. "Now you go on home, Granny!"

"I bound to go to town, mister," said Phoenix. "The time come around."

He gave another laugh, filling the whole landscape. "I know you old colored people! Wouldn't miss going to town to see Santa Claus!"

But something held old Phoenix very still. The deep lines in her face went into a fierce and different radiation. Without warning, she had seen with her own eyes a flashing nickel fall out of the man's pocket onto the ground.

"How old are you, Granny?" he was saying.

"There is no telling, mister," she said, "no telling."

Then she gave a little cry and clapped her hands and said, "Git on away from here, dog! Look! Look at that dog!" She laughed as if in admiration. "He ain't scared of nobody. He a big black dog." She whispered, "Sic him!"

"Watch me get rid of that cur," said the man. "Sic him, Pete! Sic him!"

Phoenix heard the dogs fighting, and heard the man running and throwing sticks. She even heard a gunshot. But she was slowly bending forward by that time, further and further forward, the lids stretched down over her eyes, as if she were doing this in her sleep. Her chin was lowered almost to her knees. The yellow palm of her hand came out from the fold of her apron. Her fingers slid down and along the ground under the piece of money with the grace and care they would have in lifting an egg from under a setting hen. Then she slowly straightened up, she stood erect, and the nickel was in her apron pocket. A bird flew by. Her lips moved. "God watching me the whole time. I come to stealing."

The man came back, and his own dog panted about them. "Well, I scared him off that time," he said, and then he laughed and lifted his gun and pointed it at Phoenix.

She stood straight and faced him.

"Doesn't the gun scare you?" he said, still pointing it.

"No, sir, I seen plenty go off closer by, in my day, and for less than what I done," she said, holding utterly still.

He smiled, and shouldered the gun. "Well, Granny," he said, "you must be a hundred years old, and scared of nothing. I'd give you a dime if I had any money with me. But you take my advice and stay home, and nothing will happen to you."

"I bound to go on my way, mister," said Phoenix. She inclined her head in the red rag. Then they went in different directions, but she could hear the gun shooting again and again over the hill.

She walked on. The shadows hung from the oak trees to the road like curtains. Then she smelled wood-smoke, and smelled the river, and she saw a steeple and the cabins on their steep steps. Dozens of little black children whirled around her. There ahead was Natchez shining. Bells were ringing. She walked on.

In the paved city it was Christmas time. There were red and green electric lights strung and crisscrossed everywhere, and all turned on in the daytime. Old Phoenix would have been lost if she had not distrusted her eyesight and depended on her feet to know where to take her.

She paused quietly on the sidewalk where people were passing by. A lady came along in the crowd, carrying an armful of red-, green- and silver-wrapped presents; she gave off perfume like the red roses in hot summer, and Phoenix stopped her.

"Please, missy, will you lace up my shoe?" She held up her foot.

"What do you want, Grandma?"

"See my shoe," said Phoenix. "Do all right for out in the country, but wouldn't look right to go in a big building."

"Stand still then, Grandma," said the lady. She put her packages down on the sidewalk beside her and laced and tied both shoes tightly.

"Can't lace 'em with a cane," said Phoenix. "Thank you, missy. I doesn't mind asking a nice lady to tie up my shoe, when I gets out on the street."

Moving slowly and from side to side, she went into the big building, and into a tower of steps, where she walked up and around and around until her feet knew to stop.

She entered a door, and there she saw nailed up on the wall the document that had been stamped with the gold seal and framed in the gold frame, which matched the dream that was hung up in her head.

"Here I be," she said. There was a fixed and ceremonial stiffness over her body.

"A charity case, I suppose," said an attendant who sat at the desk before her.

But Phoenix only looked above her head. There was sweat on her face, the wrinkles in her skin shone like a bright net.

"Speak up, Grandma," the woman said. "What's your name? We must have your history, you know. Have you been here before? What seems to be the trouble with you?"

Old Phoenix only gave a twitch to her face as if a fly were bothering her.

"Are you deaf?" cried the attendant.

But just then the nurse came in.

"Oh, that's just old Aunt Phoenix," she said. "She doesn't come for herself—she has a little grandson. She makes these trips just as regular as clockwork. She lives away back off the Old Natchez Trace." She bent down. "Well, Aunt Phoenix, why don't you just take a seat? We won't keep you standing after your long trip." She pointed.

The old woman sat down, bolt upright in the chair.

"Now, how is the boy?" asked the nurse.

Old Phoenix did not speak.

"I said, how is the boy?"

But Phoenix only waited and stared straight ahead, her face very solemn and withdrawn into rigidity.

"Is his throat any better?" asked the nurse. "Aunt Phoenix, don't you hear me? Is your grandson's throat any better since the last time you came for the medicine?"

With her hands on her knees, the old woman waited, silent, erect and motionless, just as if she were in armor.

"You mustn't take up our time this way, Aunt Phoenix," the nurse said. "Tell us quickly about your grandson, and get it over. He isn't dead, is he?"

At last there came a flicker and then a flame of comprehension across her face, and she spoke.

"My grandson. It was my memory had left me. There I sat and forgot why I made my long trip."

"Forgot?" The nurse frowned. "After you came so far?"

Then Phoenix was like an old woman begging a dignified forgiveness for waking up frightened in the night. "I never did go to school, I was too old at the Surrender," she said in a soft voice. "I'm an old woman without an education. It was my memory fail me. My little grandson, he is just the same, and I forgot it in the coming."

"Throat never heals, does it?" said the nurse, speaking in a loud, sure voice to old Pheonix. By now she had a card with something written on it, a little list. "Yes. Swallowed lye. When was it?—January—two-three years ago—"

Phoenix spoke unasked now. "No, missy, he not dead, he just the same. Every little while his throat begin to close up again, and he not able to swallow. He not get his breath. He not able to help himself. So the time come around, and I go on another trip for the soothing medicine."

"All right. The doctor said as long as you came to get it, you could have it," said the nurse. "But it's an obstinate case."

"My little grandson, he sit up there in the house all wrapped up, waiting by himself," Phoenix went on. "We is the only two left in the world. He suffer and it don't seem to put him back at all. He got a sweet look. He going to last. He wear a little patch quilt and peep out holding his mouth open like a little bird. I remembers so plain now. I not going to forget him again, no, the whole enduring time. I could tell him from all the others in creation."

"All right." The nurse was trying to hush her now. She brought her a bottle of medicine. "Charity," she said, making a check mark in a book.

Old Phoenix held the bottle close to her eyes, and then carefully put it into her pocket.

"I thank you," she said.

"It's Christmas time, Grandma," said the attendant. "Could I give you a few pennies out of my purse?"

"Five pennies is a nickel," said Phoenix stiffly.

"Here's a nickel," said the attendant.

Phoenix rose carefully and held out her hand. She received the nickel and then fished the other nickel out of her pocket and laid it beside the new one. She stared at her palm closely, with her head on one side.

Then she gave a tap with her cane on the floor.

"This is what come to me to do," she said. "I going to the store and buy my child a little windmill they sells, made out of paper. He going to find it hard to believe there such a thing in the world. I'll march myself back where he waiting, holding it straight up in this hand."

She lifted her free hand, gave a little nod, turned around, and walked out of the doctor's office. Then her slow step began on the stairs, going down.

LINEAGE

Margaret Walker   (1915–   )

Born in Birmingham, Alabama, the daughter of a minister, Walker attended Gilbert Academy in New Orleans and Northwestern University. During the Depression she worked on the WPA Writers' Project, compiling information on the growing black ghetto of Chicago's North Side. She attended the Writer's Workshop at the University of Iowa and has taught at Livingston and Jackson State Colleges.

"Lineage" is taken from *For My People*, which won the Yale Younger Poets Prize in 1942.

My grandmothers were strong.
They followed plows and bent to toil.

They moved through fields sowing seed.
They touched earth and grain grew.
They were full of sturdiness and singing.
My grandmothers were strong.

My grandmothers are full of memories
Smelling of soap and onions and wet clay
With veins rolling roughly over quick hands
They have many clean words to say.
My grandmothers were strong.
Why am I not as they?

WHAT MAKES HER SPECIAL?

Paul Roche   (1928–   )

Born in India, Roche received his degree from the Gregorian University in Rome.
He has lived in the West Indies, Mexico, and the United States, where he has
taught and lectured. His translations of the Greek classics are famous. He presently
lives in Berkshire, England, with his wife and four children.

"What Makes Her Special?" appeared in *To Tell the Truth* (1967).

Do not despise her
With her faded face and fashionless dress,
Sham pearls, greenish blouse,
Forty-five or so, in the crowded cafeteria.
Do not despise her as she says:
"A pot of tea and the baked haddock please."
The voice is between
Genteel bovine and the alertly saccharine.
Mediocre? Nothing special?
Somewhere in each soul a seismoscopic flicker   10
Breaks on the infinite a persona.
Do not then say "mediocre."
Somewhere in those neutral eyes a murder lies
Or could; oh do not be surprised—she is special.

Somewhere in each pupil
Sits a murderer or could, or someone crucified.
The light that lightens every man
Comes hidden in a voice;
She speaks her own peculiar sheen alone
Where choice is tragedy and tragedy is choice.   20

Watch her go. No matter what her name
Somewhere she explodes the realms of fame.
She walks with what she's chosen to some shore
Where instant recognition is of right:
Already famous in oblivion, she is known
(Could *not* be more)
And even here shall rise
In sham pearls and greenish blouse
To shout with individual light.

WITCH

Jean Tepperman   (1945–   )

Tepperman was active in the student movement at college and later worked in an
SDS community-organizing project in Chicago. She was a staff member of *The Old
Mole*, an underground newspaper in Cambridge, as well as a member of Bread and
Roses, a socialist women's liberation group in Boston. Her poems have appeared in
Lion Rampant, Motive, The Old Mole, The Red Pencil, and the anthologies
Sisterhood Is Powerful and *No More Masks*.

They told me
I smile prettier with my mouth closed.
They said—
better cut your hair—
long, it's all frizzy,
looks Jewish.
They hushed me in restaurants
looking around them
while the mirrors above the table
jeered infinite reflections   10
of a raw, square face.
They questioned me
when I sang in the street.
They stood taller at tea
smoothly explaining
my eyes on the saucers,
trying to hide the hand grenade
in my pants pocket,
or crouched behind the piano.
They mocked me with magazines   20
full of breasts and lace,
published their triumph
when the doctor's oldest son

married a nice sweet girl.
They told me tweed-suit stories
of various careers of ladies.
I woke up at night
afraid of dying.
They built screens and room dividers
to hide unsightly desire
sixteen years old   30
raw and hopeless
they buttoned me into dresses
covered with pink flowers.
They waited for me to finish
then continued the conversation.
I have been invisible,
weird and supernatural.
I want my black dress.
I want my hair
curling wild around me.   40
I want my broomstick
from the closet where I hid it.
Tonight I meet my sisters
in the graveyard.
Around midnight
if you stop at a red light
in the wet city traffic,
watch for us against the moon.
We are screaming,
we are flying,   50
laughing, and won't stop.

THE WARRIOR: SUPPLEMENTARY READING

Maya Angelou: *I Know Why the Caged Bird Sings*
Jane Austen: *Pride and Prejudice* and *Sense and Sensibility*
Charlotte Brontë: *Jane Eyre*
Emily Brontë: *Wuthering Heights*
Dorothy Canfield: "Through Pity and Terror . . ."
Lewis Carroll: *Alice's Adventures in Wonderland* and *Through the Looking Glass*
Willa Cather: *My Ántonia*
Kate Chopin: *The Awakening*
Daniel Defoe: *Moll Flanders*
Thomas Deloney: *The Gentle Craft*
Margaret Drabble: *Thank You All Very Much*
Theodore Dreiser: *Sister Carrie*
William Faulkner: "The Fire and the Hearth" and *Light in August*
Nikki Giovanni: *Gemini*
Susan Glaspell: "A Jury of Her Peers"

Radclyffe Hall: *The Well of Loneliness*
Henrik Ibsen: *A Doll's House*
Shirley Jackson: *Life among the Savages*
Henry James: *The Bostonians*
Sarah Orne Jewett: "The Flight of Betsey Lane"
Erica Jong: *Fear of Flying*
D. H. Lawrence: *The Rainbow*
Doris Lessing: *The Summer before the Dark*
John Logan: "Cycle for Mother Cabrini"
Carson McCullers: "The Ballad of the Sad Café"
George Meredith: *The Egoist*
Joyce Carol Oates: *Do With Me What You Will*
Flannery O'Connor: "Greenleaf"
William Shakespeare: *Antony and Cleopatra*
George Bernard Shaw: *Major Barbara, Mrs. Warren's Profession,* and *Saint Joan*
Agnes Smedley: *Daughter of Earth*

BIBLIOGRAPHY

Arals, Heather: "Venus and Adonis: The Education of a Goddess," *Studies in English Literature,* **3**:31–51.

Arethusa, **6** ("Women in Antiquity" issue).

Bald, Marjory: *Women Writers of the Nineteenth Century* (London: Cambridge University Press, 1923).

Beauvoir, Simone de: *The Second Sex,* translated and edited by H. M. Parshley (New York: Alfred A. Knopf, Inc., 1971).

Benson, Mary Sumner: *Women in Eighteenth-Century America* (New York: Columbia University Press, 1935).

Bergeron, David M.: "*The Wife of Bath* and Shakespeare's *The Taming of the Shrew,*" *University Review,* **35**:279–286.

Bird, Caroline: *Born Female: The High Cost of Keeping Women Down* (New York: Pocket Books, Inc., 1971).

Boyd, Beverly (ed.): *The Middle English Miracles of the Virgin* (San Marino, Calif.: Huntington Library, 1964).

Bradford, Gamaliel: *Elizabethan Women* (Boston: Houghton Mifflin Company, 1936).

Brien, Delores: "William Faulkner and the Myth of Woman," *Research Studies,* **35**:132–140.

Bristol, Frank Milton: *Heroines of History: Typical Heroines of Mythology, of Shakespeare, of the Bible* (New York: The Abingdon Press, 1914).

Brown, Hallie Quinn: *Homespun Heroines and Other Women of Distinction* (New York: Books for Libraries Press, 1971).

Bruère, Martha Bensley, and Mary Ritter Beard: *Laughing Their Way: Women's Humor in America* (New York: The Macmillan Company, 1934).

Brustein, Robert: "The Monstrous Regiment of Women: Sources for the Satiric View of the Court Lady in English Drama," *Renaissance and Modern Essays,* **48**:35–50.

Chayes, Irene H.: "Little Girls Lost: Problems of a Romantic Archetype," *Bulletin of the New York Public Library,* **67**:579–592.

Chesler, Phyllis: *Women and Madness* (Garden City, N.Y.: Doubleday & Company, Inc., 1972).

Conway, Jill: "Stereotypes of Femininity in a Theory of Sexual Evolution," *Victorian Studies,* **14**:47–62.

Cornillon, Susan Koppelman (ed.): *Images of Women in Fiction: Feminist Perspectives* (Bowling Green, Ohio: Bowling Green University Press, 1972).

Crow, Duncan: *The Victorian Woman* (London: George Allen & Unwin, Ltd., 1971).

Cunningham, A. P.: "The 'New Woman Fiction' of the 1890's," *Victorian Studies,* **17**:177–186.

Davis, Elizabeth Gould: *The First Sex* (Baltimore: Penguin Books, Inc., 1972).

Deegan, Dorothy Yost: *The Stereotype of the Single Woman in American Novels* (New York: Kings Crown Press, 1951).

Donaldson, E. Talbot: "The Myth of Courtly Love," *Ventures,* **5**:16–23.

Ellmann, Mary: *Thinking about Women* (New York: Harcourt, Brace & World, Inc., 1968).

Emslie, Macdonald: "Codes of Love and Class Distinctions," *Essays in Criticism,* **5**:1–17.

Enscoe, Gerald E.: *Eros and the Romantics: Sexual Love as a Theme in Coleridge, Shelley, and Keats* (The Hague: Mouton, 1967).

Epton, Vina: *Love and the English* (London: Cassell & Co., Ltd., 1960).

Fiedler, Leslie: *Love and Death in the American Novel* (New York: Stein and Day Incorporated, 1966).

Fletcher, Jefferson Butler: *The Religion of Beauty in Women, and Other Essays on Platonic Love in Poetry and Society* (New York: The Macmillan Company, 1911).

Fletcher, Marie: "The Southern Woman in the Fiction of Kate Chopin," *Louisiana History,* **7**:117–132.

Forrey, Carolyn: "The New Woman Revisited," *Women's Studies,* **2**:37–56.

Friedan, Betty: *The Feminine Mystique* (New York: W. W. Norton & Company, Inc., 1963).

Friend, Beverly: "Virgin Territory: Woman and Sex in Science Fiction," *Extrapolation,* **14**:49–58.

Furness, Clifton Joseph (ed.): *The Genteel Female: An Anthology* (New York: Alfred A. Knopf, Inc., 1931).

Gagen, Jean Elisabeth: *The New Woman: Her Emergence in English Drama, 1600–1730* (New York: Twayne Publishers, Inc., 1954).

Gillie, Christopher: "Women by Chaucer: The Wife of Bath, Criseyde," *Character in English Literature* (New York: Barnes & Noble, Inc., 1965), pp. 41–55.

Goldfarb, Russell M.: *Sexual Repression and Victorian Literature* (Lewisburg, Pa.: Bucknell University Press, 1970).

Gorsky, Susan R.: "Old Maids and New Women: Alternatives to Marriage in Englishwomen's Novels, 1847–1915," *Journal of Popular Culture,* **7**:68–85.

Haining, Peter (ed.): *The Gentlewomen of Evil: An Anthology of Rare Supernatural Stories from the Pens of Victorian Ladies* (New York: Taplinger Publishing Co., Inc., 1967).

Hardwick, Elizabeth: *Seduction and Betrayal: Women in Literature* (New York: Random House, Inc., 1974).

Hays, Hoffman Reynolds: *The Dangerous Sex: The Myth of Feminine Evil* (New York: G. P. Putnam's Sons, 1964).

Heilbrun, Carolyn: *Toward a Recognition of Androgyny* (New York: Alfred A. Knopf, Inc., 1973).

Hook, Lucyle (ed.): *The Female Wits* (Los Angeles: University of California, Clark Memorial Library, 1967).

Howells, William Dean: *Heroines of Fiction*, with illustrations by H. C. Christy and others (New York: Harper & Brothers, 1901).

Janeway, Elizabeth: *Man's World, Woman's Place* (New York: Dell Publishing Co., Inc., 1971).

Jarmuth, Sylvia L.: *Dickens' Use of Women in His Novels* (New York: Excelsior, 1967).

Jayal, Shakambari: *The Status of Women in the Epics* (Delhi: Motilal Banarsidass, 1966).

Jessup, Josephine Lurie: *The Faith of Our Feminists: A Study in the Novels of Edith Wharton, Ellen Glasgow, Willa Cather* (New York: Richard R. Smith, Publisher, Inc., 1958).

Kolodny, Annette: "The Land-as-Woman: Literary Convention and Latent Psychological Content," *Women's Studies*, **1**:167–182.

Loss, Archie K.: "The Pre-Raphaelite Women, the Symbolist Femme-Enfant, and the Girl with the Long Flowing Hair in the Earlier Work of Joyce," *Journal of Modern Literature*, **3**:3–23.

McCormic, Jane: "Witchcraft in Literature," *Psychic*, **4**:50–54.

Martin, Hazel T.: *Petticoat Rebels: A Study of the Novels of Social Protest of George Eliot, Elizabeth Gaskell, and Charlotte Bronte* (New York: Helios, 1968).

Matossian, Mary Kilborne: "In the Beginning, God Was a Woman," *Journal of Social History*, **6**:325–343.

Mayne, Ethel C.: *Browning's Heroines* (London: Chatto & Windus, Ltd., 1913).

Meldrum, Ronald M.: "Three of Henry James's Dark Ladies," *Research Studies*, **37**:54–60.

Mews, Hazel: *Frail Vessels: Women's Role in Women's Novels from Fanny Burney to George Eliot* (London: Athlone Press, 1969).

Millett, Kate: *Sexual Politics* (Garden City, N.Y.: Doubleday & Company, Inc., 1970).

Moers, Ellen: "Willa Cather and Colette: Mothers of Us All," *World*, **2**:51–53.

————: "Women and Monsters," *New York Review of Books*, Part I, **21**:24–29; Part II, **21**:35–39.

Moore, Katharine: *Cordial Relations: The Maiden Aunt in Fact and Fiction* (London: William Heinemann, Ltd., 1966).

Murtaugh, Daniel M.: "Women and Geoffrey Chaucer," *Journal of English Literary History*, **38**:473–492.

Newman, F. X.: *The Meaning of Courtly Love* (Albany: State University of New York Press, 1968).

Oliver, Peter: *A Galaxy of Disagreeable Women from Mrs. Gaskell, J. B. Priestley, Charles Dickens, Jane Austen, William Thackeray, Lewis Carroll, Anthony Trollope* (New York: P. and K. Oliver, 1937).

Osmond, Rosalie E.: "Body, Soul, and Marriage Relationship: The History of an Analogy," *Journal of the History of Ideas*, **34**:283ff.

Overbeck, Pat T.: "Chaucer's Good Woman," *Chaucer Review*, **2**:75–94.

Papshvila, Helen (Waite): *All the Happy Endings: A Study of the Domestic Novel in America, the Women Who Wrote It, the Women Who Read It, in the 19th Century* (New York: Harper & Brothers, 1956).

Patai, Daphne: "Utopia for Whom?" *Aphra*, **5**:2–16.

Pattee, Fred Lewis: *The Feminine Fifties* (Port Washington, N.Y.: Kennikat Press, 1940).

Pearson, Lu Emily: *Elizabethan Love Conventions* (New York: Barnes & Noble, Inc., 1966).

Phillips, Margaret, and A. S. Tomkinson: *English Women in Life and Letters* (New York: Oxford University Press, 1927).

Pratt, Annis: "Women and Nature in Modern Fiction," *Contemporary Literature*, **13**:476–490.

Reuben, Elaine: "Feminist Criticism in the Classroom, or 'What Do You Mean We, White Man?'" *Women's Studies*, **1**:315–325.

Rogers, Katharine M.: "The Pressure of Convention on Thackeray's Women," *Modern Language Review*, **67**:257–263.

————: *The Troublesome Helpmate: A History of Misogyny in Literature* (Seattle: University of Washington Press, 1966).

Roszak, Betty, and Theodore Roszak (eds.): *Masculine/Feminine: Readings in Sexual Mythology and the Liberation of Women* (New York: Harper & Row, Publishers, Incorporated, 1969).

Rougemont, Denis de: *Love in the Western World*, translated by Montgomery Belgion (New York: Pantheon Books, a division of Random House, Inc., 1956).

Rubenius, Aina: *The Woman Question in Mrs. Gaskell's Life Works* (Cambridge, Mass.: Harvard University Press, 1950).

Russ, Joanna: "Somebody's Trying to Kill Me and I Think It's My Husband: The Modern Gothic," *Journal of Popular Culture*, **6**:666–691.

Schafer, Edward H.: "Dragon Ladies, Water Fairies, Fish Maidens, Rain Mothers, and Other Hybrid Creatures," *Horizon*, **25**:104–109.

Schecter, Harold: "Kali on Main Street: The Rise of the Terrible Mother in America," *Journal of Popular Culture*, **7**:251–263.

Sharma, P. P.: "Charlotte Brontë: Champion of Woman's Economic Independence," *Brontë Society Transactions*, **14**:38–40.

Shaw, Sharon: "Hemingway's (Mis)treatment of Women Characters," *Moving Out*, **4**:42–43.

Showalter, Elaine: *Women's Liberation and Literature* (New York: Harcourt Brace Jovanovich, 1971).

Sonstroem, David: *Rossetti and the Fair Lady* (Middletown, Conn.: Wesleyan University Press, 1970).

Spacks, Patricia: "Free Women," *The Hudson Review*, **24**:559–573.

Stone, Donald D.: "Victorian Feminism and the Nineteenth Century Novel," *Women's Studies*, **1**:65–91.

Stowe, Harriett Elizabeth (Beecher): *Woman in Sacred History: A Series of Sketches Drawn from Scriptural, Historical, and Legendary Sources* (New York: Fords, Howard and Hulbeit, 1873).

Thomson, Patricia: *The Victorian Heroine: A Changing Ideal, 1837–1873* (London: Oxford University Press, 1956).

Toback, Phyllis Brooks: "Herrick's 'Corinna's Going A-Maying' and the Epithalamic Tradition," *Seventeenth-Century News*, **24**, item 15.

Trilling, Diana: "The Image of Women in Contemporary Literature," in Robert Jay Lifton (ed.), *The Woman in America* (Boston: Houghton Mifflin Company, 1965), pp. 52–71.

Turco, Lewis: "The Matriarchy of American Poetry," *College English*, **34**:1067–1074.

Utley, Francis Lee: *The Crooked Rib: An Analytical Index to the Argument about Women in English and Scots Literature to the End of the Year 1568* (Columbus: Ohio State University Press, 1944).

Utter, Robert Palfrey, and Gwendolyn Bridges Needham: *Pamela's Daughters* (New York: The Macmillan Company, 1936).

Wasserstrom, William: *Heiress of All the Ages: Sex and Sentiment in the Genteel Tradition* (Minneapolis: The University of Minnesota Press, 1959).

Weathers, Winston: "Christina Rossetti: The Sisterhood of Self," *Victorian Poetry*, **3**:81–89.

Wells, Nancy: "Women in American Literature," *English Journal*, **62**:1159–1161.

Woolf, Virginia: *A Room of One's Own* (New York: Harcourt, Brace & World, Inc., 1957).

Wright, F. A.: *Feminism in Greek Literature, from Homer to Aristotle* (Port Washington, N.Y.: Kennikat Press, 1969).

Zahler, Leah: "Matriarchy and Myth," *Aphra*, **4**:25–32.

Zlotnick, Joan: "A Woman's Will: Kate Chopin on Selfhood, Wifehood, and Motherhood," *Markham Review*, **3**:[1]–[5].

For further bibliographical items, see the quarterly journal entitled *Women Studies Abstracts*, P.O. Box 6, Rush, New York 14543.

ACKNOWLEDGMENTS

Alurista. "Must be the season of the witch." Reprinted by permission of the author.

Geoffrey Chaucer. "The Clerk's Tale" from THE CANTERBURY TALES, translated by Nevill Coghill (Penguin Classics). Copyright © Nevill Coghill, 1951, 1958, 1960. Reprinted by permission of Penguin Books Ltd.

Emily Dickinson. "I started Early—Took my Dog." Reprinted by permission of the publishers and the Trustees of Amherst College from Thomas H. Johnson, Editor, THE POEMS OF EMILY DICKINSON, Cambridge, Mass.: The Belknap Press of Harvard University Press. Copyright 1951, 1955, by The President and Fellows of Harvard College.

T. S. Eliot. "The Waste Land" in COLLECTED POEMS 1909–1962 by T. S. Eliot, copyright 1936, by Harcourt Brace Jovanovich, Inc.; copyright 1963, 1964, by T. S. Eliot. Reprinted by permission of the publishers.

William Faulkner. "A Rose for Emily." Copyright 1930 and renewed 1958 by William Faulkner. Reprinted from COLLECTED STORIES OF WILLIAM FAULKNER by permission of Random House, Inc.

Robert Frost. "The Hill Wife" from THE POETRY OF ROBERT FROST, edited by Edward Connery Lathem. Copyright 1916, © 1969 by Holt, Rinehart and Winston, Inc. Copyright 1944 by Robert Frost. Reprinted by permission of Holt, Rinehart and Winston, Inc.

Charlotte Perkins Gilman. "The Yellow Wall-Paper." Reissued by The Feminist Press, 1972; reprinted by permission.

Thomas Hardy. "The Ruined Maid," reprinted by permission of Macmillan Publishing Company, Inc., from COLLECTED POEMS by Thomas Hardy. Copyright 1925 by Macmillan Publishing Co., Inc.

JUDITH from ANGLO-SAXON POETRY, translated by R. K. Gordon. Everyman's Library Edition. Reprinted by permission of the publishers, E. P. Dutton & Co., Inc.

Dilys Laing. "Private Entry in the Diary of a Female Parent." Reprinted by permission of David Laing.

Denise Levertov. "Bedtime." From THE SORROW DANCE. Copyright © 1966 by Denise Levertov Goodman. Reprinted by permission of New Directions Publishing Corporation.

Denise Levertov. "Song to Ishtar." From O TASTE AND SEE. Copyright © 1962 by Denise Levertov Goodman. Reprinted by permission of New Directions Publishing Corporation.

Charlotte Mew. "The Farmer's Bride." Reprinted by permission of Gerald Duckworth & Co. Ltd., London.

Edna St. Vincent Millay. "And you as well must die, beloved dust." From COLLECTED POEMS, Harper & Row. Copyright 1921, 1948, by Edna St. Vincent Millay.

Paul Roche. "What Makes Her Special?" Reprinted by permission of Gerald Duckworth & Co. Ltd, London.

Muriel Rukeyser. "Mortal Girl." Reprinted by permission of Monica McCall, International Creative Management. Copyright © 1951 by Muriel Rukeyser.

Wallace Stevens. "Woman Looking at a Vase of Flowers." Copyright 1942 and renewed 1970 by Holly Stevens. Reprinted from THE COLLECTED POEMS OF WALLACE STEVENS by permission of Alfred A. Knopf, Inc.

Jean Tepperman. "Witch." Reprinted from NO MORE MASKS: AN ANTHOLOGY OF POEMS BY WOMEN, edited by Florence Howe and Ellen Bass, Doubleday Anchor Books, Garden City, N.Y., 1973.

Jean Toomer. "Fern." From CANE by Jean Toomer. Copyright 1923 by Boni & Liveright, Inc. Copyright © 1951 by Jean Toomer. Reprinted by permission of Liveright, Publishers, New York.

Margaret Walker. "Lineage." Reprinted from FOR MY PEOPLE by permission of the author.

Eudora Welty. "A Worn Path." Copyright 1941, 1969, by Eudora Welty. Reprinted from her volume A CURTAIN OF GREEN AND OTHER STORIES, by permission of Harcourt Brace Jovanovich, Inc.

Dorothy West. "The Richer, the Poorer." Reprinted by permission of the Bertha Klausner International Literary Agency, Inc.

Phillis Wheatley. "On the Death of a Young Lady of Five Years of Age." From THE POEMS OF PHILLIS WHEATLEY, edited by Julian D. Mason, Jr. Reprinted by permission of The University of North Carolina Press.

"The Wife's Lament" from WOMEN POETS IN ENGLISH, edited and translated by Ann Stanford. Copyright © 1972 by Ann Stanford. Used with permission of McGraw-Hill Book Company.

Virginia Woolf. TO THE LIGHTHOUSE, copyright 1927, by Harcourt Brace Jovanovich, Inc.; renewed, 1955, by Leonard Woolf. Reprinted by permission of the publishers.

William Butler Yeats. "Crazy Jane Talks with the Bishop." Reprinted by permission of Macmillan Publishing Co., Inc., from COLLECTED POEMS by William Butler Yeats. Copyright 1933 by Macmillan Publishing Co., Inc., renewed 1961 by Bertha Georgie Yeats.

William Butler Yeats. "Leda and the Swan." Reprinted by permission of Macmillan Publishing Co., Inc., from COLLECTED POEMS by William Butler Yeats. Copyright 1928 by Macmillan Publishing Co., Inc., renewed 1956 by Bertha Georgie Yeats.

Pearson,

WHO AM I

McGraw-Hi

305 pages